MW00445877

SAILING THE BIG FLUSH

Here's to You
Joan!
Thanks for all your Love
through the Years
Fair winds,
Love from Your Sister
Eileen

SAILING THE

BIG FLUSH

Eileen Beaver

SEABOARD PRESS

JAMES A. ROCK & COMPANY, PUBLISHERS

Sailing The Big Flush by Eileen Beaver

SEABOARD PRESS

is an imprint of JAMES A. ROCK & CO., PUBLISHERS

Sailing The Big Flush copyright ©2009 by Eileen Beaver

Front Cover Photo, "Stuck in the Shubenacadie"
copyright ©2009 by Eileen M. Beaver *(Day 13, page 173)*

Maps on pages xxvi and xxvii copyright ©2009 by Doug Beaver

Special contents of this edition copyright ©2009 by Seaboard Press

Address comments and inquiries to:
SEABOARD PRESS
900 South Irby, #508
Florence, SC 29501

E-mail:
jrock@rockpublishing.com   lrock@rockpublishing.com
Internet URL: www.rockpublishing.com

Trade Paperback ISBN: 978-1-59663-785-6

Library of Congress Control Number: 2007923151

Printed in the United States of America

First Edition: 2009

Music Soundtrack and Audio Book
available from
www.sailingthebigflush.com

For Brooke

You always care

Where I am

Where I've been

Where I'm going

And about all the
good parts in between

ACKNOWLEDGMENTS

A very big special thanks—one of those I-couldn't-have-done-it-without-you-thanks—to *Bill and Jean Beaver and Nanny Winner*. Through your concerted efforts you have managed to help and encourage me in ways too numerous to mention.

CONTENTS

Introduction xi

About Daniel MacNaughton xxiii

The Route xxiv

Area Maps and The Bay of Fundy .... xxv-xxvii

A Few Words About Tides xxix

Prologue 1

Day 1 5

Day 2 30

Day 3 39

Day 4 45

Day 5 59

Day 6 65

Day 7 83

Day 8 96

Day 9 111

Day 10 120

Day 11 131

Day 12 142

Day 13 164

Day 14 183

Day 15 195

Day 16 221

Day 17 230

Day 18 248

Day 19 257

Day 20 266

Day 21 286

Day 22 301

Day 23 320

Day 24 339

Day 25 350

Day 26 371

Day 27 383

Day 28 388

Day 29 396

Day 30 407

Epilogue 430

Epilogue II 434

The *Guillemot* 443

Guillemot Schematic 444

Glossary 449

PHOTOGRAPHS

Dan MacNaughton .... *xxiii*

Eastport, Maine *12*

Dipper Harbour *38*

Black River *42*

Black River *42*

St Martins *54*

Isle Haute *69*

Cape Chinecto *69*

Advocate Harbour *81*

Advocate Harbour *82*

Minas Basin *87*

Parrsboro *103*

Parrsboro *107*

Parrsboro *114*

Sailing To Five Islands *117*

The Five Islands "Islands" *121*

Mouth of The Shubenacadie *139*

Stuck in The Stewiacke *161*

Stuck in the Middle of The Shube *173*

Lake Guillemot *173*

Shubenacadie *185*

Cobequid Bay *186*

Maitland *207*

Private Beach Shack next to Five Islands Campground *232*

Next to Five Islands Campground *250*

Sailing into Parrsboro *255*

Dipper Harbour *390*

Sailing to Beaver Harbour *394*

Avonturr *Sailing by Eastport, en route to Bocabec River* *409*

The Avonturr, *after weathering a hurricane off of Cape Hatteras* ... *409*

Eastport *422*

McMasters Island *439*

The Guillemot *at rest on its legs* *441*

Detail of the Guillemot *leg* *442*

Sailing, sailing, all me life is sailing *446*

A journey is different than a trip. On a trip, more often than not, you know where you're going and how you're going to get there. On a journey, however, it's not so much about arriving at your destination as it is about what you discover, and the events along the way.

Introduction

During a lifetime organized more by the needs of boats than by anything else, God knows, I've read a lot of stories about cruises. The feel of the stories, like the cruises, range from the day to day, through the terrifying, to the sublime, and this story combines all three.

The cruise described in this book is one of the great small boat adventures of our time, an epic voyage in exotic and rarely-traveled waters that happen to be in the very back yard of some of the northeast's most well-known cruising grounds. It's a story I would be delighted to read regardless of who wrote it, but I'm particularly pleased in this case because Eileen Beaver and her husband Doug are my friends, and due to the fortuitous interaction of our personalities, values, and circumstances that friendship helped to bring the cruise to pass.

It so happens that a number of years ago when I was working part time as a boat broker, I brought Doug Beaver together with *Guillemot* (we pronounce this Gill-a-mot), the boat that is one of the primary players in this adventure. During that process Doug and I realized that, whatever our dissimilarities as individuals, we agreed about virtually everything to do with life, people, music, boats, the land, and the sea. It's as though we started one great, fascinating conversation way back then which, with only occasional pauses, has continued ever since.

The cruise described in this book grew out of Doug's most treasured values: taking the path less traveled, finding the adventure in every day, bringing out the best in other people, taking only positive actions, talking about only positive things, and finding fundamental truths in nature.

Eileen Beaver, who tells the story, accompanied her husband on this cruise, but as you will see, she was on a somewhat different voyage, making discoveries about herself and her mate even as she became a full partner in the execution of a unique cruise in challenging waters.

Doug and Eileen came back from this cruise changed people, deeper, more serene, and closer together. They did a great thing together, and it made them better.

Eastport, Maine, population something just under 2,000, is the Easternmost City in the U.S.A., on the Canadian border as far Down East as you can get. I moved there with my extended family in 1989, to run the only boat yard for miles in any direction—a story worth telling another time.

I first met Doug Beaver at the Eastport breakwater, on a hazy late-summer day when I was varnishing the brightwork on my old William Atkin-designed ketch *Eric*. I had just returned from a long and eventful cruise to the west along the Maine coast and back, and was thoroughly enjoying one of those little high-water marks one experiences over the years. I was in the perfect mood to meet one of the great friends of my life.

Doug is one of the easiest people in the world to meet, because his goal is always to figure out what it is that's cool about each person he meets. While he's devoid of shyness, he's never trying to impress anyone. Taken together with his gift for words and an ever-present sense of humor, it means he is liked by everyone on contact.

So anyway, up he walks, full of enthusiasm and with a million questions about sailing, wooden boats, cruising, and living aboard, and it turned out, a tremendous inclination to just plain listen. If you're me, you've got to love a guy like that. By the time I'd taken an hour or so to show him the boat, stepping around the wet varnish, we were friends.

It was a couple of months later that he showed up again, pulling into our very sleepy little boat yard in his ancient, camouflage-painted, half-home-built Toyota Land Cruiser. After the initial pleasantries he announced that he wanted to buy a sailboat, a wooden sailboat, and he wanted to be able to live aboard it and cruise around. He didn't want to race, he wanted to relax and have fun. He wanted to be able to take some friends with him, and the primary point of having it was to get out into nature and savor it. He had done virtually no sailing. When I asked, he said that yes, he had done some backpacking and motorcycle camping, and loved it. I called that a good sign. In one of the soundest moves of my life I literally reached under the counter, pulled out the listing for *Guillemot* and said, "I think you should buy this boat."

I showed him at least a dozen other listings, but only to explain the virtues of *Guillemot* by comparison. There's an appendix in the back of this book that will explain them to the interested reader, but the basic point is that *Guillemot* is uniquely well-suited both to Doug and Eileen's highly social day-sailing around Passamaquoddy Bay, and the sort of "expeditionary" cruising that Doug likes to do.

We soon went to inspect the boat, which belonged to my close friends Lucia and Bob Knight (Lucia and I are co-authors of *The Encyclopedia of Yacht Designers*). Bob, Doug and I took *Guillemot* out on a very windy November day for a demonstration sail. It was Doug's first time sailing anything larger than a Sunfish. Bob and I got us out of the harbor and then gave Doug a quick rundown on how the sails worked and how to take the boat to windward, which he then proceeded to do, calmly, perfectly efficiently, and even with a certain style. Bob and I were somewhat aghast, as we were presented with a prodigy. He simply shouldn't have been able to do what he did, with that little experience. Doug occasionally says I taught him to sail, but all I can take credit for is exposing him to it—Doug and sailing seem to have known each other before.

By early spring *Guillemot* was in our boat yard with Doug living aboard and performing spring maintenance and upgrades. My brother Tom and I were impressed by his willingness to listen and just simply try what we suggested, a rare and, I must say, truly *pleasant* quality in a human being. He endured the realization of exactly what "wooden boat maintenance" really meant, adjusted his timetable, put the boat in the water a bit later than he'd intended but in fine order, spent the summer knocking around Passamaquoddy Bay, and then proceeded to sail the boat to New Jersey. Tom and I were at first very doubtful, but then we said, "If anyone can do it with that little experience, Doug can." And he did, with only a few minor mishaps on the way.

Soon he had bought a house in Eastport, and was working at the boat yard, and became a welcome daily presence in our lives. Doug is a natural host, and his house became a lot of people's favorite place in town, so that *we* all became a daily presence in *his* life. While at Doug's house we always find ways to amuse ourselves, but really it's all about conversation. It's a place where everyone has their turn, and people who seldom speak are drawn out, and nearly every conversation arrives at consensus, with laughter. And somehow it's Doug doing it, whether he's got something to say or is just putting in a word now and then.

You can't know Doug for more than a few hours before he'll pull out his guitar and proceed to blow your mind with the sheer quality of his music. It's not only a matter of skill—he's a skilled vocalist and guitar player—but he has that thing that only a few people have—the ability to bring a diverse crowd of people together in a powerful, positive shared experience. His gift for performance is exceeded only by his gift for songwriting, and taken together they are essentially his fundamental gift for conversation elevated into art.

After a couple of eventful years, Doug met Eileen and quickly brought her into his life and therefore into the center of a great many other people's lives. Eileen was older than Doug, and up until about fifteen minutes ago had been part of what we all thought of as a high-society elite, a crowd with whom we seldom mixed by more or less mutual agreement. At the time ours was a rather hard-drinking and rough-talking, decidedly working-class crowd. Eileen was the owner of an actual pillbox hat, and had never drunk beer directly from a bottle or pumped her own gas. I gave it two months, or maybe until February, the month the modern Passamaquoddies call, Divorce Moon.

I think it was the shared love of vodka that really sealed the relationship. Eileen had been a very, very good girl for a very, very long time and was now suddenly ready to do "something completely different." Doug had acquired a certain appreciation for women with what he would describe as, "a good attitude." Their courtship quickly became the stuff of legend.

And where Doug is a musician, Eileen is a cook. I'm not just saying she's a good cook. HEAR ME. This woman is a God-damn *cook*. Few who were there will forget the evening early on, when a mixed crowd of aesthetes, boozers, petty criminals and general reprobates were slouching around Doug's kitchen table drinking whatever was available and probably heading for empty-stomach ugliness of one sort or another, when a giant pizza descended onto the table, bubbling hot and smelling exactly like a million dollars. Someone says, "What's this?" and Eileen brightly sings, "Quattro formaggio!" We made it one of her names. I guess she's the only little red-headed woman in America who's called "Quattro."

Eileen makes cooking look easy. She strolls around the kitchen and carries on a conversation while she cuts a few things up. There are occasional bursts of flame and steam, and then this magnificent meal appears, often feeding six or eight people. Doug and Eileen are vegetarians, but this is not the vegetarian food I've had before. It is of another order entirely, pungent, satisfying, profound. Meat seems wholly unnecessary. I urge the reader to pay attention to what Eileen has to say about food in this book. In this story she's producing superb meals, not just adequate ones, in a galley the size of a shower stall, and she's not even suffering (or at least, not all the time).

As sometimes happens when people are a great match, Doug and Eileen have brought out the best in each other. Doug's partying is now a bit more mellow. Eileen can now pump her own gas, and wears a rope for a belt (she still owns the pillbox hat). The kitchen table is a little better lit. The house has décor. Florence, the big white enamel oil range that we always say is a no-nonsense down east girl in appliance form, cranks out the heat and browns the tortillas. I have my spot on the bench by the window, and Doug beats out the best damned blues you ever heard, while Eileen serves up another masterpiece and the room is full of smiles.

We sum it all up as, *The Kitchen Table*, that whole experience of music, laughter, food, drink, and conversation that has taken place lo, these many years. It's a place where everybody's welcome as long as they keep it positive and behave themselves. It's a place where the lion lies down with the lamb. It's about 50 square feet of floor space where a whole bunch of people have had some of the best times of their lives.

The Kitchen Table is only the nucleus (for us) of the greater organism that is Eastport, a tiny city on an island. The uniqueness of America's Easternmost City can be conjured by the places it is compared to. With the feeling of an isolated frontier town, it strongly resembles Sicily, Alaska, home of the TV Show *Northern Exposure.* With its long smuggling heritage and tolerance of eccentricity, it is sometimes called "The Key West of the North." With an economy that followed the collapse of the local fishing industry and struggles back upward with a mix of artists and tourists, it is compared to Provincetown. With a labor pool that is laid back to the point that it drives some visitors insane, it is, sometimes, the northernmost island of the Bahamas. Some, in the mid-winter produce aisle of the local market, have compared it to Czechoslovakia.

The reason it is so fine has a lot to do with the fact that there aren't very many people here, or anywhere near here, and there's not a lot of prepared entertainment. You can't be part of a faction and have enough friends, so there's a strong emphasis on getting along. The unusual diversity of Eastport's past makes it unusually accepting of diversity today. Sometimes you might go to the local bar for a drink, but more often you bring a six-pack and sit around someone's kitchen table, maybe Doug and Eileen's. There's poverty and vice and occasional violence in town, but those with a negative attitude are a dying breed here, as more and more people move in who simply love it reinforcing those who feel that way and are already here.

Eastport and its kitchen tables is one of the worlds we share, and the Passamaquoddy Bay region is another, larger world that provides the context. A great system of tidal estuaries and small, protected bays, it is one of the best cruising grounds in the world, especially for small boats. Protected by its remoteness and by its reputation for tide and fog, it is largely undeveloped, increasingly preserved by public land trusts, and almost empty, even of sailboats—the perfect way to get around. *Guillemot* and *Eric* have done a lot of day sailing and cruising throughout the area, often loaded to capacity with friends, and sailing under what I might dare call MacNaughton's Rules: No Schedule, No Itinerary, No Problem.

The region is all about cold water, fog, eagles, whales, seals, sea birds, fir trees, and black volcanic rock. But mostly it is about tide, (approx. 22 ft) provided courtesy of the Bay of Fundy, the door-keeper (maybe the bouncer) that guards the gates of Passamaquoddy.

The powerful and rhythmic tides of the Bay of Fundy are the background music over which Eileen Beaver tells her story in this book. In most parts of the world and even elsewhere on the coast of Maine (Penobscot Bay is approx. 9 ft) the tide does not define the cruising sailor's day to the extent it does in Fundy, but in this tale the tide (more than 50 ft) is a major character, a fundamental part of the plot.

The tide is an elemental force in the sailor's world along with wind, waves, fog, the sun and the moon. They blend and combine and influence each other to form the ever changing seascape upon which a yacht sails

Yachtsmen from areas having little tide are apt to view large tides as a major inconvenience, barring travel, as they sometimes do, in certain directions at certain times of the day. Many are actually alarmed and disoriented by strong currents, which can make it seem as though the whole world is sliding sideways, or like some invisible force is pulling one's vessel toward a hazard, or like one's vessel is not performing in a predictable fashion. Some get over it, and some don't.

A steady diet of cruising in the bays surrounding Eastport convinces some of us, like myself and Doug Beaver, that the tide adds more to sailing than it takes away.

For one thing it is a gigantic force that can be harnessed to desirable effect. It can propel your boat toward its destination with little or no expenditure of fuel or effort. It can help to move your boat against the wind. It can make it possible to lift large weights off the bottom. It can make it cheap and easy to work on the bottom of one's boat while it is grounded out. It can make it possible to place one's boat securely on a friendly shore while bad weather passes by.

Whatever direction one wishes to travel in, the tidal currents run that way twice a day, so if one is willing to be flexible in one's schedule, one can always travel when the tide is fair and thus operate with unusual speed and efficiency at all times. Those who have not experienced areas of strong tidal currents are apt to assume that one will need to use a motor much of the time. Doug and I and others have found that in fact one almost never uses the engine, and then for very short periods.

I have often said that sailing is good for us partly because it constitutes an act of submission to forces larger than ourselves, something that was part of life for our ancestors but is rare in the ready-made and standardized world in which most of us live today. Large tides just add to sailing one more force to which we must submit in order to achieve an acceptable percentage of our goals.

Sailing is like a chess game, and sailing in current is like 3-D chess. Far from being just a hindrance to sailing, current constitutes a whole other moving fluid that can be exploited to advantage by the fluid-flow machines we call sailboats, and can add to the pleasure we find in simply operating such a machine.

Playing the current to best advantage is all about local knowledge, and the years we have spent learning the ever-changing but predictable patterns of current in the bay has proven to be one of the greatest pleasures we all have found, sailing in our local waters. Where there is current there is often a countercurrent near the shore, running in the opposite direction. If the shore is irregular in shape, those countercurrents may be wide and strong, and can be used to move one's boat against the current. In between the two currents is a line of eddies. Doug was the first person I've known to point out that a sailboat seems to pick up speed through the water when one is sailing right along that line, which I find to be at once true, and difficult to explain. The ever-changing menu of options, the constant computation of the relative advantages of various courses of action, the well rehearsed dance of maneuvering a familiar sailboat and the seascape in which one does it, combine to create an intensely rewarding experience, if you like that sort of thing.

The enormous forces generated by current can make it a harsh teacher, as harsh as wind and wave themselves. It can frustrate our efforts to oppose it. When the changing tide opposes a strong wind it can change smooth water to rough very quickly. It can make it difficult to avoid obstructions down-current from one's boat. Good seamanship combined with a bit of experience allows one to make sound predictions, however.

The slow and steady beat of the tide is part of the music of cruising in the remarkable estuaries in and around the Bay of Fundy, and with familiarity one comes to perceive and perhaps to love the vastness of its power and beauty, the deep tones of its melody, and the delicacy and grace of its smallest ripples and eddies. This book is all about that kind of love, as well as others more human.

In making this cruise, Doug realized a dream and fulfilled the promise of the *Guillemot*. Eileen got her feet under her and got to know and like herself and her husband. In writing this book she found her voice. In reading it I think and hope you may be inspired toward love, adventure, friendship and the feeling only nature in her majesty can instill.

This first book won't be the last to spring from the Kitchen Table and the Fundy tides—be sure to keep a weather eye peeled, for the next.

Daniel MacNaughton
Eastport and Searsmont, Maine
February, 2007

About Daniel MacNaughton

Dan MacNaughton grew up in a sailing family, and disgusting as it may sound, his first word really was "boat." He's owned eight of them, of varying descriptions. He is currently sailing an Amphibiette named *Spar Hawk*, which is a smaller cousin of *Guillemot*, one of this book's major characters. A longtime resident of Eastport, Maine, where he helped to run a family boat yard, he is now manager of Rockport Marine, a prominent wooden boat building and maintenance yard on Penobscot Bay. With Lucia Del Sol Knight he is co-author of *The Encyclopedia of Yacht Designers*, and when much younger was the first Associate Editor of *WoodenBoat Magazine*. In his writing he has come to advocate strength and simplicity in boats, honesty and a positive attitude in people, and a strong connection to nature and the lessons it has to teach.

This is Dan MacNaughton enjoying one of many happy days sailing the Passamaquoddy Bay region on Guillemot, *with Doug and Eileen and a host of other mutual friends. He always says he never needs to have any better days than these.*

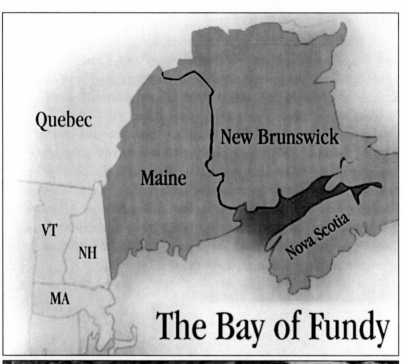

The Bay of Fundy

The Route

Eastport, Maine to Dipper Harbour, New Brunswick

Dipper Harbour to Black's River

Black's River to St Martens

St. Martins to Isle Haute, Nova Scotia

Isle Haute to Advocate Harbour

Advocate Harbour to Parrsboro (on Farrell's River)

Parrsboro to Five Islands

Five Islands to mouth of the Shubenacadie River

Mouth of Shube to *Stuck up by Stewiacke*

Stewiacke to *Stuck in middle of Shube*

Middle of Shube to Maitland

Maitland to Five Islands

Five Islands to Parrsboro

Parrsboro to Outside of Spencer's Island

Spencer's to Margaretsville

Margaretsville to Parker's Cove

Parker's Cove to Dipper Harbour, New Brunswick

Dipper to Beaver Harbour

Beaver Harbour to Bocabec River, New Brunswick
(in the Passamaquoddy Bay)

Bocabec to Eastport, Maine

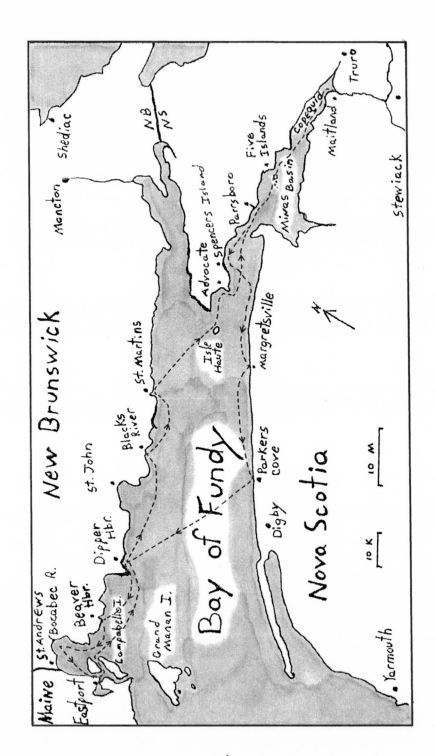

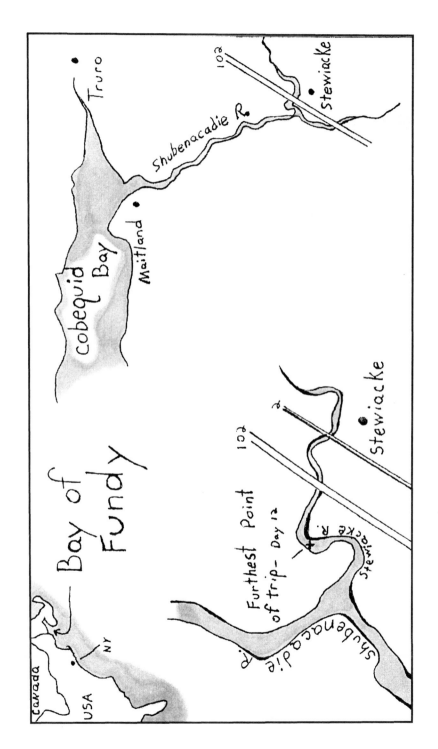

A Few Words About Tides

The tide is a result of cosmic forces, specifically the gravitational force of the moon. The moon's gravity pulls some of the water that covers the better part of our planet, into a bulge we call high tide. This bulge of water is always present on the surface of the ocean where it is closest to the moon, and as the moon orbits the earth, high tide occurs around the world, moving in step with it.

The gravity of the orbiting moon also causes the earth to wobble a bit in its own orbit, always pulling the planet slightly away from the path it would follow if the moon were not there. In doing so, it pulls the planet away from the water that is on the side of the earth *farthest* from the moon and causes a high tide there, as well. Low tide forms a belt, all around the world, midway between the two high-tide bulges.

Thus, due to the pull of the moon upon the water and upon the planet beneath the water, there are always two high tides at any given time, on opposite sides of the earth. With the moon completing an orbit in a bit less than 24 hours, this means there are two high tides and two low tides every day.

If there were no land, the tide would be a simpler phenomenon than it is, but the continents restrict the water's ability to form these perfect tidal bulges. The water in the oceans does the best it can to respond to the call of the moon, but the land only allows certain currents to flow.

The shape of the land and of the ocean floor determine the direction and, to some extent, the speed of the tidal currents. The Bay of Fundy is long and deep. The the tides run in and out, somewhat like water sloshing in a bathtub, with the momentum of the water carrying it farther in and farther out than it does in most other areas, even those quite nearby.

In Penobscot Bay, near the mouth of the Bay of Fundy, about halfway along the Maine coast, the range between high and low tide is approximately nine feet.

In Eastport, farther up in the Bay of Fundy and at the extreme eastern end of the Maine coast, the tidal range is approximately 22 feet.

At the head of Fundy, where *Guillemot* and her people travel in this story, the tidal range is over 50 feet.

The gravitational pull of the sun and the planets also influence the tides, introducing daily variations in the tidal range that the average person can only predict through the use of tide tables. To keep it interesting, the wind and the changing pressure of the air also influence the tides in a manner, and to an extent only partially predictable by meteorologists, just before the fact.

—*Dan MacNaughton*

The Birdies Know

The birdies know that the best time to sing is in the morning
When the sun lights the top of the trees.

Turn your face to the sky,
Turn your voice way up high,
And sing into the morning breeze.

You've got to sing out yesterday's frustrations,
Make it a new day.
As hard as it may be,
Don't let those bastards get you down.
Kick 'em in the Ass, send 'em to another town.
Say, "Bother someone else don't bother me."

You can chase your money to the end,
And that's where you'll get, my friend.
Wonderin' what happened to the beginning,

And the good parts in between.

When it's time to go,
It's time to go, hey there ain't no second show,
And no money back no matter how you scream.

Ya gotta wonder why, in your mind,
You're so sad all the time.
Don't squander your existence.
You don't see like others see.
Turn your fat face to the sky.
Turn your lousy voice up high
And sing it with the birdies in the trees.
The birdies know that the best time to sing is in the morning!

—*Doug Beaver, song, 1987*

Prologue

Wednesday, 6 September 1991, 10 a.m.
Visalia, California

I sit, quite poised at my dining table, viewing through my window our glistening swimming pool and the third green of the Visalia Country Club. Soft classical music "plays in the background. I have completed my step aerobics and my weight workout in the gym at our tennis club. My schedule for the rest of the day is neatly printed in my day planner:

Morning	
8:30–10:00	Exercise
10:00–11:30	Work on Cocktail Party
Afternoon	
12:00–1:15	Lunch with Joan & JoJo
1:30–3:00	Nail Appointment while Jag is being washed
3:15	Pick kids up at school
4:00	Take Brooke to dance lessons
	Kyle walks to golf league
4:45 7:00	Social Club Board meeting at the Country Club

I can feel the breeze wafting through the French doors leading to the back deck, and I hear the leaves of the Magnolia and Pepper trees fluttering, just outside. I'm enjoying the quiet serenity of be-

1

ing here in the house all alone. On Monday the housekeeper was here all day and Tuesdays I lead a Bible study group so on that day the house is full of chattering women.

In these tranquil minutes, I'm going over the menu for my next cocktail party and the guest list of 200. I picture my upstairs closet and try to visualize what I might wear for the party and then I think of how the bar and the food might be arranged.

I'm feeling pretty good about life. I'm 40 years old and I've been married for 20 years. I wear matching underwear and marble surrounds my Jacuzzi bathtub. My gardens are filled with roses, azaleas, gardenias, and camellias. The large urns near the pool are filled with ferns and sago palms. Baskets overflow with flowers on my various decks; the entry courtyard is enveloped by lush greenery and filled with the serene tinkling sound of a little fountain. My automatic sprinkling systems are strategically placed and timed to water each section with precision.

I glance with approval into the mirror of my antique French china hutch. Hair, pearls and silk scarf ...

Then the deep and booming voice of God speaks to me from out of the clouds.

"Eileen"

Now, who is calling me from the back deck?

"Eileen!"

Could that be the answering machine?

"E I L E E E E N !"

"Where are you?"

"Eileen. It's the Lord"

I grab the phone and dial 9, 1...

"Eileen! I want you to go live on a 25 ft Amphibi-con..."

I hang up the phone.

"OK, Lord, I'm listening. What is an Amphibi-con?"

"It's a very small 46-year-old wooden sailboat. You will cook, eat and sleep on board."

"I will?"

"You will poop in a Reliance and pee in a Lady John."

"Please, Lord, what's a Reliance? And what's a Lady John?"

"A Reliance is a sort of glorified bucket and a Lady John is like a jug with an adaptor to fit your private parts."

"Oooookaaaaay, "

"You will sail this boat on a journey to the to the Minas Basin where there is fifty-four feet of tide and the harbours go dry. When the water goes away your boat will rest on its keel, balanced by wooden legs. You will wear Baffins, a Tilley's and stretch jeans. You will become more familiar with mud than with many of my other creations.

"What's a minus basin? What's a Baffin? What the hell, excuse me, is a Tilley?"

"You'll find out. Thirty days and thirty nights you will store your food in the bilge of the boat. You will sail 300 miles, round trip, from your home in Eastport, Maine and, while the boat in which you are sailing has a maximum speed of about 6 knots, you will, in fact, travel at speeds approaching 15 knots."

"Right. What you said. Where will I sleep? What about showers?"

"You will sleep in a V-berth in a sleeping bag and about the shower thing .... I'm still working on that one."

"Please, Lord, why will I do these things?"

"You are to try and find your center."

"If you say so. Not to question your judgment, Lord, but wouldn't it make more sense to pick some young camper type who would think this sounds adventuresome and fun? Someone who doesn't expect turn-down service and a mint on her pillow? Someone who can *sail,* perhaps?"

"Eileen"

"I've spent my whole life looking for the perfect garlic mincer. Nobody told me I was supposed to be searching for my center. Frankly this is not what I expected when I prayed for guidance."

"EILEEN!"

"Yes, Lord?"

"Do you remember Noah?"

"Well, yeah, I've gone to Sunday school all my life. But what will people think? I can't just leave for 30 days. Look at my day planner— I'm booked every weekend!!!!"

"Eileen, Noah was on the ark for over two years and......"

"Lord, I don't think I'm tough enough to do such a thing."

"Eileen, Noah had worse problems than you will have. At times the seas were so rough, the hippos were pooping straight up. There were elephants with allergies... ."

"Lord, remember that time I went to Portmeirion, Wales? The tide emptied out of that bay, couldn't I have found my center there?"

"Noah had pregnant giraffes... ."

"Lord, I really don't do life-changing adventures. I'm better at gardening, dinner parties, or how about shopping? Maybe my center is at the South Coast Plaza!"

"Noah had to feed all of them!"

"Okay, so when is this supposed to happen? Next week Kyle has a dentist appointment, Brooke wants to have a sleepover Friday night ...

"Eileen, this will occur in September 2001."

"2001! I'll be 50 years old!!!! I just can't believe this. I already have bad knees!"

"Eileen."

"If I've lived that long without my center, do you really think finding one is all that necessary? Besides, there has to be someone else out there with more of a deficiency in character than me!"

"EILEEN! LET'S TALK ABOUT MOSES!"

"Right! Yes. Let's talk about Moses. *He* had all those *miracles* going for *Him,* burning bushes, his staff changed to snakes, manna from Heaven and that whole bit."

"Eileen—*he* was on foot in the desert. *He* journeyed 300 miles and it took him *40* years!"

"Oh, OKEY DOKEY. If you say so. I'll just mark it down on my calendar. You promise just 30 days? You say, September 2001? I guess I'm with you, Lord. I just hope you're gonna be with me. But what about my home, my family, and my friends?"

"Your life will not be the same, Eileen!"

"You mean the hen dung is going to hit the fan?"

"Really Eileen. Only Baptists call it HEN DUNG!"

Day 1

Friday, August 31, 2001

Dipper Harbour, New Brunswick, is splashed with colorful working boats and here and there a few lonely sailboats. We start to anchor in what looks to be a good spot until we observe nearby a sailboat so tattered that the owner must have the same opinion we do—that it isn't safe to step aboard, let alone go sailing. This boat seems condemned to lie at her mooring until the threads of her Chinese-made shackle pins rot away. We figure that one day, with a puff of wind and a tug from the tidal current, she will suddenly behave like a rhino escaping from a zoo. My Captain doesn't want to be there when she does, so we turn away from the inviting-looking space. I affirm this wise decision by stating what every experienced sea wife should know—about the only bit of cruising knowledge I have confidence to utter, "Besides the owner didn't tie off the halyards."

Avoiding the *pang, pang, pang* of halyards against metal masts was one of the first things my husband/Captain taught me.

We cruise around for a while looking for our perfect-for-one-evening anchorage. Doug is considering all the variables involved, while I scan the shoreline and the rest of the neighboring boats. Here, in Dipper, the houses match the boats in a charming mix of bright blues, greens, aquas and yellows, along with the beiges and deep reds more typical of the New England we have left behind. The Captain turns a deaf ear to my unsolicited opinions of the color palette, but one of the sailboats is so "loud" that it goes beyond charming and simply hurts my eyes. The light aqua green hull was passable—but the four different shades of green on the trim, sail cover and canvas top are just too much!

The bow of a fishing boat with *Black Diamond*, Yarmouth, Nova Scotia painted on its stern, is calmly nodding next to *The Wife and I*. They both look large and heavy compared to a skiff that is bouncing wildly, showing off its cream hull and turquoise insides. The big show on the dance floor of the harbour tonight is the *The Choir Boys* and *Miss D* doing the Cha Cha, with *The Misty Green* (painted appropriately) keeping the beat right alongside.

When anchoring in an unfamiliar harbour there are a few rather important details to consider. Besides other boats (our distance from them and the noises they produce), the direction of the wind, the contents of the harbour floor and the nature of the holding ground, here in the Bay of Fundy there are the tides to consider. In this harbour, we figure the tide fluctuates about 20-23 feet from low to high. The current swishes, dips and swirls the *Guillemot* around like we are in the arms of a Latin American dancer trying to teach us the tango.

All tucked in now, I take a few minutes to lounge in the cockpit to write in my journal. I'm finding it difficult to keep my pen steady. The wind this evening is merely a cool breeze, but we are doing the jerk, hesitate, swing, bop, jump, and the mashed potato around the hopefully set anchor.

Doug has lit our little wood stove and the heat travels out through the wide hatchway to warm me. I can hear my stomach growl over the sounds of the *Guillemot's* dance steps, so I guess it's show time. I rhumba to the galley where my rice has been soaking in water with dried Indian red peppers. I'm using all the vegetables from the fridge back at our house in Eastport first, so I clean and chop fresh green beans and carrots, add a little dill seed and coriander seed, and cook them all together for a one-pot meal. Just before I serve it, *alfresco* in the cockpit, I top our servings with diced green bell peppers, feta cheese, and the most delicious tomatoes I have ever had in my life, from our friend Ruttley's garden. He and his wife Lynne are bee-keepers and from the results from their garden the bees are doing their jobs, their life-sustaining job of pollinating.

For all those out there who are wondering what type of refrig-eration we have on board—I can tell you the brand name: Sub-Zero! The Zero stands for NONE and Sub stands for below the water line. We are sailing without any ice or refrigeration. Don't imagine cans of Dinty Moore Beef Stew and sauerkraut. The only canned foods on board are albacore tuna and tomatoes. For the last several years we have removed meat and poultry from our diets. This makes storing our food, cooking, and cleanup much easier, since we don't have to worry nearly as much about what bacteria may be lurking in dark corners to do us harm. The bilge is the lower part of the boat and is kept cold by the frigid water of the Bay of Fundy. The water temperature is around 50 degrees, and in the dry spots under the quarter berths, the galley, and the cockpit sole it keeps our perishables from perishing for quite some time.

This is the first cruise we'd made with the complete abandon-ment of ice and Doug is elated. Several times I've heard the Captain exclaim in joyous tones, "Yahoo! No more wet packages and soggy food in the bottom of the icebox!"

Last week our friends, Pat and Carl, were visiting from Mary-land and diligently helped us load the *Guillemot* with all our provi-sions. Being some of the most thoughtful people we know, they provided us with the essentials—Skye Vodka and Jamison Whiskey. Through the whole long loading and stowing process the Captain's manner implied that I had over-packed and over-provisioned. I wanted to point out that 30 rolls of his precious Charmin® Plus With Aloe toilet paper for 30 days seemed on the excessive side to the rest of us! But no, I just calmly advised the Captain, without a murmur of annoyance, "I will use it—I will use it! If not, the veggies can go overboard." I gave Pat a conspiratorial smile and then double-checked to be sure the vodka and whiskey had been securely stowed.

As I clean up from dinner, I glance at the clock propped up next to the stove. It says 7 p.m. but, since on our first night out we have entered the Atlantic Provinces of Canada, it is officially 8 p.m. Earlier, while in the cockpit, somewhere deep inside me I felt a rush of enthusiasm. I could smell the fire and the drifting aroma of the cooking dinner. I felt happy to be experiencing this way of life and travel and happy to breathe deeply of the rich sea air and to wait expectantly for the sunset. I even felt comfortable and content and not at all disappointed when the temperature fell and I realized the overcast skies would not provide much of a display. Truthfully my memory banks are still overflowing from all the sunsets at Eastport's Deep Cove where, in late summer and fall evenings, we make it our ritual to pop down to the pier for the big show—where the sky is full of luscious pastels like the makeup counter at Macy's.

I keep an anxious eye on the depth sounder. It shows 9.5 feet and when we arrived at 4:30 p.m. it was 5 feet. Since the tide is flooding, we will let scope out as the water deepens. The amount of the scope should be the ratio of the anchor rode to depth of water or 7:1. That means if we are in 10 ft of water we should pay out 70 feet of rode.

The Captain just called from down below requesting that I tighten the main sheet so the main boom will not move around so much. We put the sail cover on for the evening, just in case a spark would fly up from the wood stove. We also have a long, extended pipe we put in place when the stove is in use. Another request from the Captain, as he lies in the V-berth resting from a long, hard day, "Eileen, will you loosen the jib sheet so the stove pipe doesn't burn it?"

The temperature is dropping so we may only have another hour to leave the canvas door to the companionway open.

At 8:40 it is definitely time to shut the canvas door. It's not just that it lets in the cold but that it lets out the coziness. My last looks before dark make me wonder two things: a cormorant just dipped down and brought up a small sculpin for his dinner—so I wonder if that's why they call it Dipper Harbour? And I wonder, as I scan the shoreline, if the boats are painted to match the houses or vice versa?

The wind has died now and the Captain and I are writing in our logs, but he's so tired he can hardly concentrate. As we dry our backpacks and boat bags (mementos of today's sail) near the fire, we smile and welcome the now quiet rocking of the boat. We listen to the low hum of whatever is going on at the pier. Before a yawning fit sets in and I lose ink in my pen for the third time tonight, I must tell you of our first day's sail. "Doug, do you remember where I put my extra pack of ink pens?" The Captain takes on a thoughtful but doubtful expression but utters no helpful advice. I'm almost too tired to look but I realize the odds are I will need them. I turn around to the shelf behind me and, in my exhausted state, say, "If that's not where it is, I'm not going to look any further." The Captain opens his mouth to release a large yawn and nods his head slowly with perfect understanding.

This Morning, 10 a.m.

We are taking the top of the tide out of Eastport. Our friend, Dana, is perched high on the dock of Federal Marine when he looks up to see us make our departure. "Good luck, have fun!" he calls giving us a big wave. He turned before I had the binoculars focused. I wanted to see if he had a look of envy or relief on his face. Doug, of course, says envy. I put my money on the 'better you than me' expression!

Dana's wife, Patty, works at the IGA supermarket here in town. The gossip in the produce section was that we were planning a big cruise up the St John River and we got all our information off the computer. I set the record straight with Patty and her husband the other day. "We don't own a computer and up the St John River is where sensible people in their right minds take their vacations—which explains, I dare say, why we are headed for the Minas Basin!" This is their first year with a sailboat and, although she's lived here most of her life, she didn't know where on earth the Minas Basin was. With a frightened look, she asked why we would want to go there. I had done my best not to ponder that question of late. So I told her I didn't know, ask Doug, or someone who listens to gossip in the beer section.

I must have taken on a worried look because she asked me if I was scared. Who me? I didn't want to be sarcastic, so like a politician I ignored her question. I had by now pushed all thoughts of

54-foot tides, a 25-foot boat, strong currents, and harbours that empty of water to the very back of my mind. Then I placed a mental Post-It sticker on it reading, "ignorance is bliss."

I asked her, "This is Wednesday isn't it?"

Looking confused and concerned for my well being, she answered, "Well, yes … but …"

I turned quickly on my heel. "I'll see ya later, I've got to get to the market before it closes!"

The hours of the R&M IGA take a bit of getting use to. Monday, Tuesday and Wednesday they're open 8 a.m. to 6 p.m. You better know if you are out of eggs during those hours unless it happens to be Thursday or Friday, when you can shop until 8 p.m. I truthfully cannot remember what the hours are on Saturday but I do know that when Sunday rolls around you really need to have your act together because your window of opportunity is 10 a.m. to 1 p.m.

I hear people from away ("away" people are those who were not born and raised around here) and vacationers complain about this all the time. But seriously speaking, what person can't give thought to their basic needs of life in the 66 hours a week that they are open? I happen to know why people can't—because we are spoiled. This is what happens when one lives in a society where there are four major supermarkets within five miles of one's home that are open at least 7 a.m.–11 p.m. seven days a week! It's not like any of us are looking starvation in the face. Experts claim that an average person, not overweight, can live 30 days on his own body fat. I figure I'm good for 6 months.

Living here in Eastport one gives up some conveniences in order to be able to walk to the market for a little fresh air and exercise. How many times in this friendly place have I been offered rides while carrying my bags home? It's a novelty to shop where, if you don't bring enough money the clerks simply say, "Don't worry about it! Pay it tomorrow," and slip an IOU into the register.

It was around noon one Sunday morning, a few years ago, and we were having a party. We hadn't intended to have a party (which we find is a major ingredient to a good one). It happened to be a cold, overcast day in October and we had been waiting two hours for my son, Kyle, and our friend, Rafi, to feed us the brunch they had confidently promised the evening before. Doug and our friend, Dan, decided their contribution would be two bottles of champagne so they got some from the market. Meanwhile our friends, David Moses and Jessie, strolled in, and between the seven of us and the lack of anything else to do while we waited patiently for our brunch, we quickly disposed of both bottles. David Moses and Dan headed for the IGA to replenish our supplies. It wasn't five minutes after their departure that our friends, Bill and April, from Florida unexpectedly wondered in, and the party started rolling! Jessie and I looked at each other and raised our eyebrows a tad, making the executive decision. Indeed, we would need more champagne. Jesse picked up the phone and called one of "the brothers, " Roger and Mearle (the R&M of the IGA), who own the store.

"Hey, would you tell the two guys who are there to buy one bottle of champagne to buy two instead?"

"OK!"

And they did!

* * *

I look down at Doug's crossed legs, which are stretched across the cockpit with his feet propped up on the cockpit cushion. The wind is light and the sun is bright. The Federal Marine dock, from which Dana had waved goodbye, is still in clear view. We have been drifting with the tide out towards Head Harbour. The Captain is maneuvering us closer to Campobello Island, hoping to catch a stronger current to take us out into the Bay of Fundy. I had raced around so much this morning with the last of the preparations for a month-long cruise that I felt profoundly relieved to finally be underway.

I'm just sitting back like a baby being rocked to sleep, but trying not to fall asleep in the first thirty minutes of our trip! I squint into the sun and turn my head to see the buildings along Water Street, like sentries, watching over the waterfront.

My eyes always settle on the four-story brick building at 73 Water Street, with its large arched window at the top. It was my home for nine months, some six years ago. The three floors below the part where I lived held a commercial kitchen, a restaurant and a pub.

Many times every day, during the time I ran the Tavern On The Bay, I was asked, "How on earth did you ever end up in Eastport?"

Eastport, Maine
My eyes always settle on the four-story brick building at
73 Water Street, with its large arched window at the top.
It was my home for nine months, some six years ago.

I had three answers to that question: 1) It was a moment of temporary insanity; 2) I had a frequent flyer ticket and this was as far as I could travel within the contiguous United States; and, 3) I was in the witness protection program.

The first two were true, but the third enabled me to cut the conversation short. Most customers just let their mouths hang open and then would divert their eyes to the menu or the painting on the wall. Seldom would I take the time to tell anyone the long versions of the true stories, the highlights of which included moisturizing cream and vodka.

How could I recount to strangers from Dallas, Texas, or Oakland, California, that when I first actually came to live in Eastport, it really did have all the attributes of an asylum for me; or that my days spent here were a mental treatment comparable to sitting in an Adirondack chair on a rolling green lawn and having attendants in white uniforms bring me my meals.

I never felt comfortable enough to look a couple from Dublin, Ohio, in the eye while they were cracking the claws of their two-pound lobster and sipping their Samuel Adams beer, and tell them that, a year and a half ago, three messengers from heaven were sent to my friend, Sydney, in California, to tell her about this weird little spot on the northern coast of Maine called Eastport. No lie! Three totally unrelated people in the span of two weeks time started talking to her about Eastport—the last one leaving her with her mouth hanging open, speechless! At that point, when she left her dental hygienist office, she threw her hands in the air and called to whomever might be listening in the heavens, "All right, already! I get the message!" She began to lay her plans to scout out Eastport, looking for just the right property to buy.

It was hard to tell those who inquired about the hows and the whys of my being in Eastport, while they sipped their wine and rolled clam linguini around their forks, that I accompanied my friend here because my life had recently gone to hell in a hand-basket and I was anxious to get as far from California as I could get.

While my customers sat comfortably in the warm sunshine of the windows overlooking the breakwater and the pristine bay, unable to decide between the Chinese chicken salad or the baked stuffed flounder, I wasn't going to create in their minds a picture of that freezing, dark night in early March when Sydney and I first drove into Eastport.

It occurs to me, as I embark on this journey of thirty days to the Minas Basin, that, like that day in March 1994 when I boarded my flight in Fresno, California bound for Bangor Maine, I don't know if I'm excited, nervous, or slightly askew in the upper storey. Today, like *that* day, I have no idea what life-changing events may occur along the way. Today, seeing as I'm not checking whether or not table #5 has finished the salads so we can serve their entrees while they are still hot and, seeing as I'm not eye-to-eye with some couple from Connecticut who own a summer home in Perry and are anxious to hear my story of what on earth brought me here and why I opened a restaurant, I think I can be candid and tell what *did* happen after I boarded my flight, headed for somewhere in Maine.

To be honest, l hadn't even looked at a map to see exactly where it was that Sydney had been sent by God to buy property. I was just along for the ride … or so I thought.

March 1994

The women at the Hertz rental car counter were wide-eyed when we confided that we were headed for Eastport. Sydney and I had rendezvoused at the hotel attached to the Bangor Airport the previous night. We arrived on different flights because my frequent flyer ticket and the cheap ticket Christine's Travel in Visalia found for Sydney (Christine being her best friend) were on different airlines. We had a good night's rest and then were ready to head to our final destination.

"Hey, Marlene!" *Marlene* seemed to be the one in charge. "They're goin' to Eastport!"

Curious now, we asked, "Why? Is that far?"

All three chattily went on with business and all three seemed to have something to snicker about, so we waited in confusion. Sydney rather impatiently tapped the pointed toe of her new, leather, supposedly-suitable-for-this-climate, boot and arched an eyebrow. We looked at each other and blew out our breath. Our cool, calm, and collected demeanor was fading, even as we tried to look like we knew what we were doing here in Maine, in March, *the March* which, they proclaimed, was to have had the most snow in 50 years (now that I've lived in Maine I know that every winter is the coldest, driest, wettest, snowiest, or iciest in 50 years). One woman finally answered, as if she were rehearsing for a part in a Stephen King movie, "Far? Oh, it's not the end of the Earth—but you can see it from there!" Cheering news!

Another gal, studiously avoiding our eyes, gravely added, "Watch out for moose and black ice!"

The third female wasn't just taking up space behind the counter. She was thinking of the company. "Do you want extra insurance?" Much reassured we set out from Bangor, up scenic Route 1 towards Eastport.

* * *

Later, night was upon us and we were beginning to think all life had disappeared from the planet. We hardly knew what to do— there were no advertising billboards telling us we needed to stop and buy! I felt like Commander Perry planting the flag at the North Pole when I spotted the sign that should've said, "You've finally made it to Perry!" but actually says, "Welcome to Perry, Established in 1763." It was another hallelujah moment when we turned right off of Rt. 1 on to 190 and read a sign that said, "Eastport 7 miles." Momentum had us in its clutches. At 60 MPH we zoomed on. We barely noticed the insignificant sign proclaiming, "SIPAYIK Indian Reservation." Who cared about the next sign, which read "Slow 35 MPH, " and the irrelevant sign beneath that proclaimed, "Strictly Enforced"? The force must have been with us that night! Rumor has it that more speeding tickets are issued in that half-mile stretch in a year than parking tickets in New York City.

Frank's Pizza had the only light shining on Main Street. The snow crunched under Sydney's feet as she returned to the car. With a certain steadiness she advised me that we must have missed the sign for "The Inn at Eastport" as we drove into town. We both looked a little skeptical at that prospect—I was looking as she drove in, and there was not a sign to be seen (and very few plowed drive-ways). With quivering mouth and watering eyes she told me, "The fellow said he thought it was closed for the winter!" She pressed her head on the steering wheel for a blubber or two. She raised her head momentarily, stifling an outbreak of panic and frustration. "But he said The Motel East should be open. Maybe they have a room!"

Backtracking up Washington Street confirmed the address we had and, on closer observation, we saw the top third of a sign. Aided by the headlights of our rental car, I jumped out and with one leather-gloved hand, brushed away enough snow to see that the "Inn at Eastport" was indeed closed for the season, like most of the rest of this Godforsaken town.

Driving back through "downtown" I was about to question the motives of Sydney's three messengers from Heaven, when we saw the lonely but welcoming lights of The Motel East.

I sat in the car while Sydney got out to check the availability of a room—she's a better woman than I am. I pulled the mink collar of my wool and cashmere coat up over my ears and wondered, like all those I met on my flight from Dallas-Fort Worth to Boston, and from Boston to Bangor, had wondered. *Why on earth I was traveling from California to Maine in March?* After the fourth of these inquiries I stared at my ticket and said, "Beats me! I asked for Bangkok and I got Bangor!" And Bangkok was sounding pretty good.

The next morning, incidental civilities taken care of, I headed for the coffee pot in the lobby of the Motel East. On duty was Owen, the owner of "The Motel East, " the establishment completely responsible for saving Sydney and me from mental collapse the night before.

"I hear you are the one looking to buy a house in Eastport!" Oh dear God in Heaven, he has mistaken me for Sydney, whom he heard about through the nighttime attendant.

I stood for a long minute gazing out the French door at what appeared to be an abandoned fish plant, the huge snow-covered granite rocks which gave a foundation to his motel and to the ominously white-capped bay. I turned around to face him and plastered a smile on my face—the smile I might give to someone who had mistaken me for a woman who would carry a straw handbag in the winter.

I assured him that I was not the one who desired to purchase a house here in Eastport—that person was my friend Sydney. I picked

up my Chanel handbag and I adjusted my Must de' Cartier scarf
and I did not share with Owen or Sydney, until months later, what
I thought at that moment; that it would be a cold day in Hell before
I'd ever live here!

Truthfully I didn't know where I wanted to live—my family
had just moved from our home on the golf course in Visalia to a
leased house, leaving behind my garden of 300 rose bushes. I strode
out of the motel and stood in the parking lot and let the tears freeze
on my face.

Finding the right house for Sydney and her husband Richard
became a formidable task. Four days passed. We swished along the
streets and sidewalks of Eastport, brightly colored silk scarves flying, leaving whiffs of Escada perfume behind. Our Dana Buckman
suits and our high gloss lips and painted nails enthralled all those
we met. We saw not a glimpse of a house that would make Sydney's
eyes shine. Our evenings were spent in our startlingly beautiful motel
room moisturizing, sipping vodka and tonics and touching up our
nail polish.

On the fifth day I was busying myself in front of the full length
mirror contemplating whether or not my Donna Karen cashmere
sweater, accessorized with my rhinestone studded Judith Leiber belt,
looked a little too much for Eastport, when the phone rang. Sydney
picked it up and soon informed me that today was the day we were
going to see a house that she thought sounded most interesting.
Built in1805, the Hayden House was a grand old house with a lot
of history.

Betty, the real estate agent, had assured her it was a disaster and
we would instantly run for our lives. "Sounds good, " I murmured
in encouragement, and decided to skip the Judith Leiber belt.

We were greeted by a depressing back door covered with some
sort of metallic insulation. This vision and the obligatory tromp
through stacks of construction material covered by dirty snow is
not the first impression most real estate agents dream of. "You probably ... I doubt ... you don't really want to see this house do you?"
This was Betty's best sales pitch as we neared the door.

Ken and Paula had worked hard at restoring the grand dame of
Eastport and their efforts weren't without merit. It's just that, shall

we say, the ole' girl wasn't quite there yet, and needed just a tad more work before one might put on a proper tea party. With even less enthusiasm than before, Betty gave us the tour of the three-story, 5, 200 square foot house. Amid the scraping, peeling, sanding and stripping and the smell of old musty furniture we saw a lot of large rooms, where a vast multitude of cats seemed quite comfortable. Betty's face scrunched and her eyes ran from the wide variety of fumes. Out of the corner of my eye I detected her hand thrown to her mouth several times to stifle a little cry.

As for my friend and I, we traipsed from room to room not daring to even glance in each other's direction. Once back at our motel room, with showers taken and faces remoisturized, we sat cozily in our wingback chairs ignoring the evening news. I peered over the top of my vodka and tonic glass and said, "So! You're going to buy that house, aren't you?" I knew that look! I was there to give advice, to be a one-woman support group, to be the devil's advocate! But I knew that look! I did my best. "What if it has ghosts?"

The next morning I started toward the bathroom, to give Sydney some privacy for her phone call to her unsuspecting husband, Richard, in California. I hadn't yet shut the door when I heard the first words out of her mouth. "It has these fantastic tile fireplaces and a grand curved staircase—gorgeous tin ceilings ..."

I yelled out to her before shutting myself in for some quality time in front of the mirror, "and a beautiful stained glass window at the top of the stairs!" Just in case she forgot. I checked for gray hairs, dental flossed my teeth and practiced some dance moves before I heard her hang up.

Just before lights out that evening I advised, "Start low. You never know what they might take ... you guys might really like living here—it might be just right for you!" Again, unspoken thoughts ran through my mind. What great philosopher said, "never say never?"

Well I didn't. I just said to myself, "It would be a cold day in hell." I'm here to tell you that in my lifetime, "a cold day in hell" has taken on new meaning!

While Sydney negotiated a price for the house, then the furniture and started shuffling through stacks of paint-color cards, I wandered through town. As I walked, I conducted a scientific study. How does a specimen from sunny California adapt to her new surroundings and keep herself occupied in frozen Eastport?

I spent quiet hours across the street in the beautiful old Peavey Library. I took long walks up and down Key, Shackford, Middle, Boynton, Washington, Sea and High Streets admiring the old architecture and imagining what each house could look like all restored. Walking down Water Street, one day, to the center of town, I was shocked to see a huge cargo ship moored at the breakwater. The tide was up so it floated high next to the pier, dwarfing the old buildings in front of it.

On another day I drove the rental car over the Canadian border to St Andrews By The Sea, a lovely old tourist town with a magnificent hotel called The Algonquin towering over the old homes.

After each day's outings I would stop for a cup of coffee with Owen. One day I said, "I noticed there is a police station here, all decked out with fancy cars, a police chief and the whole business! What in heaven's name do they do here?" Owen shrugged his shoulders and showed me the stack of *Quoddy Tides* newspapers. One was from the summertime when Eastport is at the height of population, "Stolen! Rutabaga from garden on 3rd Street." Another shocked me with, "Lost! Female goose on Redoubt Hill." There were a few arrests for drunk and disorderly—one was because the fellow was pounding on the local convenience store door after hours. I heard in town the next day that the local police even have swat team equipment. I considered this and quickly decided it must be just in case! Just in case the British try to take the island like they did during the Revolutionary War.

I spent many an hour in our comfy motel room gazing out our second story window or bundled up in a deck chair on the balcony breathing the cold, fresh sea breeze thinking about nothing in particular and feeling more relaxed by the minute.

Sydney and I made our rounds to all the local restaurants, which were more plentiful than we had first thought, ten days ago. We found the WACO diner (pronounced "wacko"), La Sardina Loca (literally, The Crazy Sardine but commonly called The Mex), Happy Landings and Captain T's. We indulged ourselves with ice cream at the

Fountain Book Store. I did another thing that I found I hadn't done in a while. I laughed a lot! For Eastport is a funny little place. As our days here came to an end, I realized I was going to be sad to leave.

A plan began to develop in my mind. We still had enough frequent flyer miles to fly the whole family here for "Old Home Week," as they call the local 4th of July celebration. It is supposed to be a real, authentic small-town event. By then Richard and Sydney would be tucked into 17 Boynton Street and the house is so big, I knew we could be there a week before they even knew it!

On our last morning, I still had the covers pulled over my head when I heard something odd—a melancholy sound, I thought in my half-conscious state. But as I lay listening, trying to determine the source, my mood changed utterly to one of peace. I got up and opened the French door to our deck just a crack, and smiled as the Dog Island fog horn sang its regulated warning in the milky predawn light.

* * *

The sun has gone behind the clouds and the wind has picked up. The cool breeze brings my thoughts back to the *Guillemot,* so I go below and grab jackets for each of us. My husband's strong arms trim the sails to catch a gust. We whoosh past Cherry Island Lighthouse. My mind is still flooded with memories and the emotion-charged events that brought me to where I am today. Even 7 and 8 years later the pain of loss still overwhelms me sometimes, causing my chest to tighten, my shoulders to slump and tears to swell. What possessed me at the time? A long series of events—that's what life is, isn't it? There are times when life smacks you up the side of the head and impels you to do things you'd never consider when things are going well.

We both flop to the starboard side of the cockpit as we tack to get around to the other side of Campobello. My Captain looks at me with a bit of concern, "How's my sweetie doin'?" Before I have time to answer, a strong southwest wind starts pushing us out around Head Harbour. I have to hang-on to my hat! The East Quoddy Head Lighthouse is to starboard. The bright sun is sifting through the clouds and shines down upon her as she sits there majestically on the rockbound coastline.

Once we are past Head Harbour it is wind against tide. The waves are coursing in and rearing up and pouring down with a crash. I think they are going to swamp the dinghy. The guillemots, with their little red feet, surround us as though their namesake needed an escort. The Cory from St. Andrews comes into view. She's a large steel cutter that takes passengers on three-hour tours. All of their advertisements show the Cory and in big letters, "SAIL TO A WHALE, " so we assume that is where they are heading. A half a mile southeast of Bliss Island lighthouse we finally cross paths. There is one other sail out here with us, which is passing us on a beam reach just when two large finbacks start spouting. We are jumping, splashing, bouncing, and crashing, with the Cory and the other small boat at our heels. We are sailing right through it all, just en route to our destination, and it's purely a coincidence that we are on center stage for the whale watching boat.

We haven't seen Kim and Darin, the crew of the Cory, since July when they were dressed like pirates and playing their instruments on the deck of The Cannery Restaurant. Suddenly up comes a finback aft and to starboard, really close! Too close, when a 50-foot whale is less than 30 feet away and you are on a 25-foot boat! What a spectacular sight to see a finback whale, the second largest baleen whale after the blue, and the earth's only asymmetrically colored mammal. The left side of its head and jaw is dark, the right side light. Marine biologists don't know why, but it is thought it may aid in the capture of small schooling fish such as herring. The whale swims around the fish to the right in smaller and smaller circles, showing only its less visible white side so as not to startle its prey. As the herring clump together the whale turns into the pack, mouth open, throat bulging and expanding bellows-like to take in his lunch. Then it presses the water out of the baleen plates that grow down from its upper gums and swallows what is left behind-all quite efficient. Being as they can swim underwater for forty minutes without surfacing to draw a breath you never know when and where they will come up spouting.

My heart settles down to a normal beat, although the waves still have us in their grip. The Captain yells to me over the sounds of the crashing waves, "Reminds me of when the *Guillemot* was painted black below the waterline. A whale followed her for about an hour trying to put the make on her."

The GPS tells us we are making eight knots many times, which seems crazy because the Captain always says the fastest the *Guillemot* goes is six knots. I look up at our new sails and silently give a word of thanks that we are not likely to tear one like we did with the old sails last summer. The day is clouding over again and the wind is getting chilly. The first three hours were glorious, but alas my stomach has weakened.

"I'm about at the end of my rope!" I inform my husband. We hit a big wave that about sends me flying.

"What's at the end of your rope?" He yells out over the splashing of the waves.

"Don't ask!" I head for the rolling V-berth. Doug had told me we might have to go in a little early, to New River Beach. Winds like these bring the big surfing waves. Our friend J.C. came by last night for our little bon voyage party and said he would likely be there surfing because he has the day off from boat school. I lift my chin off the pillow and give words of encouragement to keep going if he wanted. "Onward!" I halfheartedly cry. Our goal is to make the Minas Basin, Nova Scotia-world's largest tides! We can poke around on the way back. "1'm good to go!" I'll be okay if I can just crawl back down under the sleeping bag and cover my head. I mutter to my inner self, "This is a fine mess you've gotten us into, Ollie!"

It isn't long before I am sprung from my refuge by a crashing wave that has soaked the cockpit and half of the inside of the cabin. I have to jump up to get the big pop-top hatch down. This task is not particularly easy in smooth water, let alone in a wet slippery cabin and with rolling waves. Eventually my mission is accomplished, but now everything is wet. I grab a towel and commence drying everything off. This type of activity always makes me have to pee. That is a project you have to start early—you definitely cannot wait 'til the last minute. It takes a while to get your pants down and your butt firmly planted on the bucket, with the boat rocking like a ride at Six Flags Magic Mountain. I throw myself back to my funk hole— I put up a good fight for rolling space with all the gear, sail bags, boat legs and sleeping bags. I am comforted by five little friends—

3 Rolaids and 2 Bonine. There is of course only one certain cure for seasickness—sitting under a tree. At least I didn't puke, which is just not cozy on a tiny boat!

Thoughts along the lines of, "I must be stark raving mad!" Begin rolling around with me in the V-berth. I lift my head for a moment to see if the Captain is still gripping the tiller. The sun gives me a ray of hope as it breaks through the clouds. The shadow of a gannet as it flies overhead darkens the features of my husband; intent on his goal of a safe arrival at Dipper Harbour.

I close my eyes and nod my head. Yes, I'm here because I'm a cup and saucer shy of a full place setting. Love does that to you sometimes.

October 1995

Shutters on the abandoned house up the street banged from a gusty nor-easter. I could almost hear music from a Clint Eastwood movie coming in off the street. The sailboat on the sign over the door of The Tavern on the Bay swung up and down so fast it could have made someone seasick if there had been anyone out and around to see it. If Eastport had tumbleweeds they would have been blowing down the street for sure.

I thought at first the wind had blown the door open. A collection of autumn leaves, paper plates which once held pizza, old garage sale notices, cigarette wrappers and plastic Mountain Dew bottles blew in with a bang. But no, someone with a tight grip on the knob kept the door on its hinges and closed it securely. There, in the middle of the little pile of trash, stood my destiny.

Pulled tightly over his ears was a stained, bent and frayed cap. Where his dark hair protruded from underneath it stood almost straight out. The dark shadows of his beard and his thick mustache gave him a Frito Bandito look. A guitar case swung over his shoulder, and clutched tight in his fist was a ticket for a free hamburger and rosemary roasted potatoes at The Tavern On The Bay, one of the prizes I had donated to the boat school picnic.

It was over three weeks before I knew Doug owned a car, let alone a house, in Eastport. Whenever I saw him he was either walking, riding his bike or sailing.

After a sunset cruise on his sailboat and an overnight trip to a beautiful spot in South Bay (which we named the Straits Of The Romantic Boom Boom), I was hooked. Or shall I say, we were both hooked. Now what would we do?

A few nights later, in my loft above the Tavern, I found myself too full of thoughts for sleep. I curled up on my sofa and cuddled under a soft, off-white, knitted throw, purchased expressly for this purpose. I gazed through my wall of glass at the sky, bright with stars. The lights from Campobello Island, a half mile off, were little competition. I decided I would just sleep there.

My eyes opened a while later. For a moment I was startled, but soon I calmed and a happy tear rolled down my cheek. The bright light which I had thought at first to be a space ship, illuminating the entire bay and my loft, was not aliens wanting to probe me. It was the full moon, brilliant on this extraordinary night.

I felt like I had swallowed a pack of those No-Doze the truck drivers use on a long, lonely haul. I was buzzing, and my whirling mind settled again on the subject that had occupied most of my waking hours: the scruffy one—that stranger that had come into my increasingly strange life. That night, as I often do when I need to clear my head and make a rational decision, I resorted to two activities that some have deemed a bit excessive in my life. I poured myself a glass of wine and I grabbed a pen and began to make a list.

I divided the page into pros and cons. The pros and cons of Doug Beaver or the pros and cons of our relationship? I couldn't decide—I'd figure that out later. Normally when my yellow legal pad is filled with a numbered list my heart would swell with satisfaction. But morning found me with my legs tucked tightly under an extra blanket and my mind full of confusion. My pad held no answer to the dilemma of whether or not I was going to continue seeing this person.

1) Pro: He's a singer/songwriter!
   Con: But is that good? A friend had recently looked me straight in the face and told me, "Never marry a musician!"
2) Pro: He is always riding his bike or walking
   Con: If his car doesn't work, why doesn't he fix it?

3) Pro: He owns at least one pair of jeans without frayed knees
   Con: That's a stretch. His utter lack of concern for dress is charming here in Eastport, but what about in the real world? He would likely never be caught dead in a tie. He would probably say, "Why do I need to wear a leash or a noose?

4) Pro: He owns a sailboat and loves to sail!
   Con: This could mean he's crazy. I don't know anything about sailing—so far it's been peaceful and beautiful out there, but also big, deep and scary. His boat is very nice, but it's very small. When we went for our overnight cruise my cosmetics barely fit on board!

5) Pro: He is a naturalist!
   Con: He probably hates my coral-colored acrylic fingernails

6) Pro: He's adventuresome!
   Con: He'll probably want me to hike the damned Appalachian Trail.

7) Pro: He's 34 I'm 44!
   Con: This seems okay now, but I recall the saying, "Better to be an old man's darling than a young man's slave."

8) Pro: The future with this man would be dazzlingly unknowable!
   Con: Haven't I had enough of the unknowable lately?

9) Pro: He already has two kids, so we are in the same position, there.
   Con: His two kids might be horrid. One of them is a 2½-year-old. Is this good or bad?

10) Pro: He seems deeply impressed by my sun-dried tomato torte.
    Con: He seems even more impressed by the fact that I have Guinness on tap two floors down!

11) Pro: I know he has at least $36 in his pocket because he entertained in the pub the other night for tips.
    Con: Sounds like another stretch. He's probably spent it by now.

12) Pro: He owns a house in the middle end.
Con: It needs a *lot* of work and do I really live in a town with a middle end?

13) Pro: He says I'm fuzzy.
Con: When I asked what that meant, he told me, "that means you're not prickly!" What a compliment!

14) Pro: He seems very smart. Just when I get thinking of him as an adorable bumpkin, he comes up with something profoundly innovative and intelligent! He does have a very large dictionary, and what girl doesn't love a man with a big dictionary!
Con: If he has any particular education he's never mentioned it.

15) Pro: He's simple, with simple needs and wants. He is never pretentious or egotistical.
Con: I look around me at all my grandiose antiques, elegant off-white sofa, oriental rug, mahogany bed, graceful artwork and full closet, and I have to admit I do lean, shall we say, toward the luxurious side of life.

16) Pro: He has never been married and says he never wants to get married.
Con: This is okay right now, but do I want to be 50 and be someone's girlfriend?

17) Pro: He seems to get along well with Kyle and Brooke.
Con: But will they ever really accept him? They probably think their mother has lost it!

18) Pro: He's so funny, cute and sweet (I patted myself on the back for waiting 'till the very end to list these attributes, and for the fact that I could have listed them all separately and made myself feel better).
Con: Am I just behaving like a teenager, or worse yet a woman in her mid-life crisis (but even my sensible self melts when I look into those gorgeous eyes).

My trusty list did little to clarify anything! I decided to list the things we have in common!

1. XXXOOOOXXXOOO!!! This is not a juicy romance novel so that's all you're gonna get.
2. We both hate television! We both agree with a quote attributed to Groucho Marx: "I find TV very educational. Every time somebody turns on the set I go into the other room and read a book!"
3. We both love to read!
4. Neither of us has any money.

It turned out to be a rather short list, but maybe it was something to work with. I put my pen and pad down on the coffee table and watched the sun rise over Campobello. I turned the pad over so I wouldn't be tempted to read it over one more time. I had already figured out that any woman with an IQ higher than her bra size would see the ratio of good to bad in my lists did not look very favorable.

An emotional woman deep inside of me played out the scene: In a dramatic spate of tears I tell him face to face we cannot see each other anymore! Soft romantic music will be playing in the background. I will drape myself seductively across my sofa and then throw my arm across my forehead saying, "Alas! We must part!"

He'll ask forlornly, "But why?" Then I'll show him my list! The music dies. I think I have neither the temperament nor the cheekbones for high drama!

I began to get ready to meet my day and fulfill my destiny. By the time I got to the mascara, I felt good about life—I looked at my 44-year-old self in the full-length mirror of my armoire to see if was still the same me. In fact, I was barely recognizable. I now owned jeans. I was now a woman who had drunk a beer out of a bottle in public! I had pumped my own gas at the gas station! I was no longer the woman who tied a ribbon around tubes of tampons to place in the powder room. Then I noticed that I looked happy. I pulled my shoulders back, filled with resolve. I was going for it! I mean him! The world outside looked larger, bluer, pinker, fuller, and muddier ...

By Thanksgiving the *Guillemot* had been hauled and put away for the winter. Matt and Dottie had arrived to take Doug away, back to Pennsylvania, to see his parents, his Nanny and his small son. Doug had made me a rope belt to match his own (this had become serious). We made a date for me to visit PA after Christmas. He wrote me a love song—some may call it a love song—"The Train Song, " Doug's version of a love song.

And the rest does flow like a romance novel! On April 30, 1997, we eloped to Elton, Maryland, following his Nanny and Poppop's footsteps some 67 years before. We listened to a live band in a park near the courthouse play "Third Rate Romance, Low Rent Rendezvous, " which we now say is "our song." After we got married we stopped and bought a case of beer.

August 31, 2001, 4 p.m.

I am pulled out of my dreamy state by the Captain yelling in his best pirate voice, "All clear we are, at Dipper Harbour!" He had to admit that the remainder of the sail, after I excused myself, was the wildest day sailing in his sailing history! He said he had quite a time while I endured, in my sailor's snug harbour of the V-berth. The guillemots, shearwaters and gannets entertained him while he brought our floating home to safety. Tonight, I quietly contemplate what the future holds. Then I suddenly become annoyed because of the loud ticking of our Dollar Store clock. Our good clock got soaking wet today and it reacted badly. At least the cheapy is holding it's own. I jump up and hide it in a drawer. I'm back in the quarter berth looking up and out like Noah in the ark. All I can see is the light flashing at the harbour edge and the sky. Once inside our little nest I wish the windows were clearer so I could see out a bit better—maybe this will be a winter time project.

Before we climb into bed, I ask my dear husband, "Do you think I seem like a wacky old woman?" I tried not to panic while I waited for his answer.

"Eileen, even if you were a man I'd think you were wacky! Old? Oh, I don't know. What do I have to judge "old" by? The rocks?"

In my jumbled dreams of the night, I kept seeing our day on the water, the whales spouting, my husband diligently keeping our boat on course, the many emotional days of my past. I woke up once with my heart pounding. Then I remembered the words of Sir Winston Churchill, when asked what had been his greatest accomplishment: "That I survived."

Day 2

Saturday, September 1, 2001

With as much indignation as I can muster, I jump out of bed, and with half-open eyes I search for the drawer, which holds the loudly ticking Dollar Store clock. It's six o'clock! Which means it's actually 7 o'clock. I'm changing this sucker today, as soon as this thunderous booming sound quits.

The reverberating clanking and clanging of the anchor line and chain being hauled in at the foot of our bed stop only when the Captain's feet pound on the roof of the cabin and he begins hoisting the sails.

We are sailing out of the harbour and the first mate is struggling to find her clothes. I'm concentrating on getting my pants buttoned when my husband calls in to me from the door of the companion-way, "It's started to rain. I'll need my rain gear." I grab his foul weather coat, bib overalls, and Sou'wester hat while searching for the armhole of my sweatshirt. The Captain fusses with the suspenders while holding on to the tiller cursing all the while over the way the bibs are made, "I hate these, I can't wear them. There's no place to take a leak!" Someone pulled the plug on the wind and since we have a coming tide we are being pushed back toward last night's resting spot. Doug goes to start the motor and the electric starter won't work, but after four hard yanks of the pull cord—*bruumm, bruumm,* our little motor saves the day.

I managed a whole five minutes out in the cockpit, suitably dressed for the occasion, when we see a wall of Fundy fog, not a reassuring sight! My Captain cuts the motor and lets the wind take us back around to the Dipper Harbour. We drop anchor, lower the sail, pull in the jib, tie the main sail, raise the pop top again, pull out the stove pipe, put the canvas back around the pop top, tie all the sheets, take off the rain gear, hang them so they might accidentally dry, put the rugs back down—all the while the cabin sole is cluttered with the cockpit cushions because, as you already know, it's raining.

I had just sat my bedraggled butt down after all this activity and leaned my head against the wall of the quarter berth, when Doug asks in a tone so flat it might have been computer generated "What on Earth did you do to your shelf?"

The shelf is down on the V-berth and all my gear is strewn all over. This shelf (my shelf—Doug has one too, just the same except for mine has twice as much stuff on it and his is sturdy) belongs along the wall of the V-berth. This broken shelf (my shelf) does somewhat well on it's own, but unfortunately for me, when you put gear in it, which of course is what it is made for, it falls off. I repack my stuff, meaning jeans, shorts, hairstyling lotion etc. in my backpack and tried to fit it on my side of the V-berth.

You can lay odds that when anything of this sort happens, there is one thing I will need to do—pee!

I have on board, I might as well tell you now, a thing called a Little John. For those of you who do not know, a Little John is a portable urinal. It is bright red plastic. Following years of research, First Defense Industries, the manufacturer, has come up with a female adaptor, transforming it into, you guessed it, a Lady John.

If you, my female readers, do not have one, your life is not complete. Or so says the brochure.

WHO NEEDS "LADY J"? ANYBODY WHO OWNS
A CAR, TRUCK, BOAT, CAMPER OR AIRPLANE! ...
INCLUDING: SALESWOMEN-TRUCKERS-PRIVATE
PILOTS-STUDENT PILOTS-BEER DRINKERS-
TEENAGERS-GRANDMOTHERS-
HELICOPTER PILOTS-GAME WARDENS-
AIR TRAFFIC CONTROLLERS-
RACE CAR DRIVERS-TROGLODYTES-TRAVELERS-
SPORTS FANS-ONE BEDROOM FAMILIES-
FLAGPOLE SITTERS-HOT AIR BALLOONISTS-
CANOEISTS AND STAGECOACH DRIVERS!

For all of you who have just found out you do not have it all, here is the number: 800-362-5757. Now, for the entirety of this journey I will refer to this piece of equipment as the "LJ"

Where was I? Oh, yes, in the middle of all the morning commotion. Doug busies himself finding the tools to fix the shelf and whatever else he may find broken. I make use of my time with my comb and tooth brush. I turn to go outside, toothbrush in mouth and LJ in hand ready to be dumped into the big flush, when I realize I am barricaded into the cabin by Doug's body, while he makes one of his repairs. There is only so much room on this boat to pass by, so I mentally count, "one banana, two banana, three banana ..." at four bananas I am gagging on my toothpaste.

The way is eventually cleared when the Captain, after all this fruitless effort, climbs into the V-berth, pretending to fall instantly asleep after he recoiled the sheets I coiled, restowed the gear I stowed and fixing the shelf I broke—all without a word to me. I won't ask if I did anything wrong. I don't have to do or not do anything on this little suppository of a boat—I can just think and it is wrong. Everything on this boat seems so perfectly obvious to him, and I'm sure this would be true for a great many people. Unfortunately I do not happen to be one of them. I fear I'll never make a sailor, and I sometimes wonder why all men don't just marry men; then they wouldn't have to put up with inept beings like me.

Filled with self pity, I slumped back down into the quarter berth, pulled out my *Basic Keel Boat U.S. Sailing Certification Series Book.*

It has a stupid picture on the front showing a perfect day, everyone smiling, with short sleeves on and Caribbean-like waters. Not only do I hate the picture of the palm trees (as the frigid rain pours down around us) but also the instruction that my face and ears are wind sensors and I should be able to use them to tell which way the wind is blowing. I still have a hard time with wind direction. Our Eastport friend James put up tell-tales made of audio cassette tape for me, and they work well until it is so windy they tear off. You have to understand that on a boat you can't even throw your pee overboard or brush your teeth and spit without knowing which way the wind blows ...

Sardined into the quarter berth with the charts, extra sails, cushions, raincoats, sail covers, as well as any gear and supplies that need to be stowed near the cockpit, I look up to a foggy rain. There is one saving grace, the wind has died down. Last night we rocked and rolled and during that time something on the boat which was not stowed properly became the percussion section for the orchestra, in my dreams of the Ritz Carlton. I never ask what the thud, roll, roll, soft thud, little clang might have been.

I exhale meaningfully and look back to my idiot's guide to sailing. Success comes in cans, failure in can'ts. Getting out of irons, tacking from reach to reach, accidental jibes ... I toss the sailing instruction book back on the self and reach for the novel I've been reading. *Poisonwood Bible* is about a missionary family in the 1950's living in the Congo of Africa. It's a novel based on diaries and historical facts. I have a feeling their plight will help keep my life aboard in perspective. I read on the cover that it is an Oprah's Book Club Choice. I bet Oprah is sitting in her marble bathtub right this very minute! I'd be happy with a Motel 6.

I console myself with an apple. I only have two left—veggies keep better than fruit on board. I tried polishing off the last of the summer watermelon yesterday before we set sail, having an uneasy feeling that there might not be any more fruit real soon. I don't want to get plugged. There are three major things to avoid on a boat—the PPD's—puking, being plugged, and diarrhea.

Doug is really sleeping. I probably kept him awake snoring last night. I wonder if he feels stuck with me. He probably thought I had potential. After he jokingly complained for the last two days about how much food I brought on board, last night I finally retorted, "I'll be happy to let you pack the food next time!"

He just smiled and replied, "No, no, you'll see ... !"I don't want to wait and see. I'm 50 yrs old—just tell me!

Sailing is different when just spending the day or a few days, when you are not loaded for bear, when you don't have a destination that is practically in uncharted territory. World's largest tides, for God's sake! Maybe if I try to stay calm and keep out of the way and give him my air of innocent incompetence he won't throw me overboard. We will surely put to the test the old saying, "true love overlooks and understands." Doug just moved and said, "I'm so sleepy, I must have what you've got!" What have I got? 9 a.m., maybe it's not too early for Vodka. I am on vacation, aren't I? That is debatable.

The skipper just awoke, bounced up and said he felt like he'd slept half a day, though it was only an hour and a half. He is all cheerful-like. Maybe he has been dipping in the vodka. He has decided to start a fire "for his little sweetie." I guess that's me—he must have had a dream that he was married to a sailor.

On a happy note, he is a competent, efficient, and sweet companion. Sometimes I think too competent, efficient, and sweet. I guess I am crazy, for how can you be too competent, efficient or sweet when you are on a boat? Maybe I'm not so bad either because now he's going to fix the light over the stove! Life is looking better.

"Hey, look at this, there's a big coastguard boat, a police car, and a bunch of other cars on the pier, " says the Captain. We wonder if there is a rescue going on or what might have happened. It is still foggy, but soon we can see that someone has just launched a nice, large wooden rowboat. We continue watching and listening closely, our curiosity piqued. Soon we hear a loud speaker blaring a speech by a person we take to be the local mayor. With great exuberance he is thanking all who have come out, telling them not to let the weather dampen their spirits, etc. The celebration commences with tours of the fire truck and coastguard boat. Country Western tunes blare optimistically from a little hut with lobster buoys and lights hanging from its rafters.

The early morning fog that followed us back in from the Bay of Fundy did lift, only to be replaced by a gushing, drenching rain. But our little wood stove is making headway, warming our spirits along with the cabin. I for one am tickled pink not to be out in the bay, thrashing around trying to find a harbour to ride out the storm. From outside our canvas door, there is a loud pop! Barely visible through the deluge is a rowing race in full swing. We find it to be a rather comical scene. From our viewpoint, if it weren't for the enthusiasm of the cheering crowd of about 40, it would look more like a funeral in a murder mystery, all dreary rain, dark clothes and umbrellas. We give our two hip hip hurrahs and agree that the Canadians are good sports to have come out for the festivities instead of staying home and watching sports on the tube. Now there is a clown prancing out to the end of the pier. Calling out to the crowd, "this is such a great day!" he almost knocks over a woman on crutches, in all his eagerness. We shut the canvas door amused by the fact that for the folks here at Dipper Harbour, it is!

At no time in our life on board is my husband more content and dreamy-eyed as when I have something scrumptious-smelling cooking on the stove. Trying to mend the error of my ways from early this morning, I gaze thoughtfully at the leftovers from last night, waiting for inspiration.

Hurrah for sesame oil! I add a little to last night's spicy rice and veggies. I throw in a few more fresh green beans for crunch, add a bit of oriental hot sauce and do a saute number on it. Right when I turn it out onto the plates I add a few more of Rutleys' tomatoes, I can't go wrong there. My beloved Captain gives me a big hug, and as I rest my head against his chest, I think to myself this isn't so bad, really.

Doug waited for me to finish lunch cleanup before he started a few more organizing chores. This is a one-man or one-woman work area. An observer might think he accomplished these tasks with unwarranted enthusiasm. How can two grown adults be so excited over moving the paper towel holder to a new location and installing 2 brass sailor multi hooks for our coats? Understand, my reader, this is the nautical equivalent of having built a new closet.

Nestling in the lap of such luxury in my warm, dry quarter

berth, I sip on my afternoon zest-of-lemon martini. My husband's brows darken as he reads aloud to me the serious part of an act of Shakespeare. I can't help giggling at his performance, and I bet the great playwright himself would laugh at Doug's interpretation.

We are both submerged in journal writing, contentedly enjoying the quiet sounds of the drizzling rain and the cadence of the still cheering crowd, which has now moved to the other side of the harbour. I decide this is the perfect setting for an afternoon nap.

I crack one eye open to see the skipper checking the water level. It is 1 p.m. and we figure (this means, "we guess") it is approximately high tide. We now have 27' of water. We float in 2'4" because *Guillemot* is of shallow draft, and this all adds up to the encouraging fact that we should still be floating at low water. This is something really convenient to know at high water, so there isn't a rush to find a new parking spot. And it is particularly meaningful for me, the self-appointed anchorwoman. I have already pulled anchor twice today, or was it three times, to change locations in the harbour, making sure we are safe and have enough scope. This should help tone my upper body.

I step out into the cockpit for some fresh air. The enormous sky is clearing and fantastic clumps of clouds are outlined against the perfect blue. Returning from the activities across the harbour is the inflatable rescue boat and the *Bay City 1*. Their festive flags swish in the breeze as they tie up next to *The Wife and Kids*. I call my husband out to see the show. Pointing to the stern of *The Wife and Kids,* I laugh and say, "Now there is a name that placates! Even if you change wives you're covered." I read a book a few months back where a young man told his sweetheart, "I named my boat for you." The girlfriend felt flattered but nervous about what type of commitment this meant. The day he took her to the dock, for their first little excursion, she let out a sigh of relief to see that the stern read *For You*.

Such a gorgeous afternoon! I get out my trusty pink weight so I can get in some more upper body workout time. Feeling very pleased with myself for remembering to bring it along and stuffing it in just the right place for it not to roll around or come crashing down on one of us while we sleep, I start doing some impressive curls. I am moving on to underarms and back muscles when I turn to see the Captain standing by the companionway, one hand up on the pop-top, fingers thrumming, the other on his hip, head cocked, forehead scrunched, eyes laughing but troubled, mouth opening and closing. "What?" I say, still bringing my weight up and down then front and back. "I say, what?" I swing the weight over my head, bending to one side, showing off a little if the truth be known.

Then I see out of the corner of my eye that he is giving me that smile! That smile that says I know more than you! "What do you suppose all the people of Dipper Harbour think of a wild woman out here in the cockpit doing all these weird gesticulations with some bright pink thing?"

My husband rows us ashore as four large boats full of locals take off for their Fisherman's Day sunset cruise. A crowd is starting to gather for the "Mizzen Boys" performance. A local we met at the dock, thinking we might be coming in for dinner, recommended the "Fundy Haven." His review was, "It's kinda expensive, but (punch, punch with his elbow) with your US dollar it'll be ok."

We take a long walk to stretch our legs, heading down past the huge lobster pound, which is a caged in area where they keep the lobster in the water before sending them to the market. We venture to the other side of the harbour where the races took place earlier today. Doug decides we should take the rockweed-covered-rock way back. It is very slow going but I manage. It reminds me of walking on slippery Chinese food. We spend some time up on some big boulders listening to the music. The deep blue of twilight is turning black. The sky, now perfectly clear, allows the stars to shine with such brilliance that it makes the two tone color of the night into a magnificent work of art. We make our way back down to the dinghy—the moon rises, the "Mizzen Boys" ballad's ring, and we row.

Dipper Harbour
We take a long walk stretch our legs ... we venture to the other side
of the harbour where the races took place earlier today.

Day 3

Sunday, September 2, 2001

A loon calls to us from our rocking-chair mooring at Black River, New Brunswick. Across the Bay of Fundy, Nova Scotia is light pink in the sunset. The tide is coming back in, and Good Lord, is it sucking in here strong! How come? I gather it is because we are at the narrow opening of this river. It is now 8:00 p.m. and what a day we've had we're already yawning. The Captain says, "Maybe I'll have a little whiskey tonight just to prevent a tooth ache, I don't have one and I don't intend to get one!" I bring out the bilge-cold vodka and add some lemon zest, and we sit back for some reading. Doug pulls from the shelf behind him *Sailing Directions for Nova Scotia, the Atlantic Coast of Canada and The Bay of Fundy.*

There seems to be everything black in the guide: Black Breaker, Black Rock, Black Duck, Black Island, Black Head, 6 Black Ledges, 19 Black Points, actually 18 Black Rocks, Black Prince, Black bill Point, Blackman Shoal, Blacks Harbour but only one Black River. I drop the book from my lap, jerked to full attention by Doug exclaiming, "My God what is it?" I can say things like "Oh my God—

or yipes—heaven help me etc." all day long. But when Doug says, "My God what is it?" I fear the worst! When I get out to the cockpit and all I see is what looks to be a spaceship on the horizon, I let out a sigh of relief. For as long as it lasts we stand immobile. Together side by side we wait, while it changes every second. Our silence has intervals of, "Oohs and aahs!" as its shape changes and our faces are illuminated by colors an artist might try to mix on his palette. We are face to face with an iridescent orange smiling pumpkin. The spell is broken when Doug jumps inside to grab the camera. I sigh as he takes the last picture of the moon, now white and shining brightly over the water. What a beautiful ending to the beautiful day.

* * *

This morning about 6:30 a.m. on the coming tide, we leave Dipper Harbour. The Captain turns the Guillemot left, and we head up the bay. We have clear skies, a good N/W wind and a beautiful sunrise. Sounds great huh? BUT, (there are always buts) it is very chilly, nippy, crisp, brisk, yes you might just say *cold.* COLD. "If the thermometer had been an inch longer we'd have frozen to death." I gazed at my look-a-like on the cover of *One Man's Dream One Woman's Nightmare,* a book about a couple rounding the Horn. My fashion accessories include tights, knee high thermal hiking socks, jeans, hiking boots, silk shirt, flannel shirt, a hooded triple thermal sweatshirt, a cap and a hooded old L.L. Bean down jacket, and gloves. I look down at myself and decide this style doesn't do much justice to a short, round person like myself. I have so many layers on I have to turn sideways to get through the companionway door. Daylight has properly broken and I ceremoniously plop myself down on the cockpit cushion. I am only vaguely enchanted by the prospect of a day on the water.

Thankfully, by noon the sunlight is doing its best to warm us. I take great pleasure in removing one of my hoods, and can now sit next to my skipper without the chattering of teeth.

We pass St. John Harbour, with all its smoke stacks. We waved heartily to the crew of a Panamanian cargo ship. The large white bay ferry heading for Digby Harbour, Nova Scotia looks ominous to us in our little sailing vessel. From this point up the Bay of Fundy, the day that unfolds is gorgeous—we are wonder struck.

The shoreline becomes more beautiful with each inlet and curve of the rocks and cliffs. There is hardly a cottage to be seen, but when we do spot one, we instantly want to move in. We cruise along enjoying each and every nuance of the shore. Gannets plunge into the cold bay for their lunch, their 40-inch wingspans framed by the crystal blue skies. Gannets are spectacular to watch. A system of air sacs under the skin of the bird's breast cushions the impact when it strikes the water. They alternately flap and glide in flight, and the gleaming white of the adult is highly visible as he dives from the height of 50 ft.

I toast bagels in the skillet with a little olive oil, while underway. Spread them with cream cheese and Harry and David's Wild and Rare Plum Preserves—I feed my hungry husband his breakfast. "What is this "wild and rare" business?" I explained that it was the jam that came in a gift basket from Guy and Kev after they visited last month. "Humph! Only Harry and David could get away with that corny name!"

Excitedly we pull out the fenders and tie to the dock when we arrive at Black River Harbour. Here, protected from the wind we strip down to what sensible people wear on sunny fall days. As usual the timetable of the tide dictates what we do next—Jump in the dinghy so we can row upriver while there is still lots of water.

Minus the heat and humidity, I feel like I am in the Fern Grotto in Jamaica. We are immediately beguiled by the lush ferns, and a beautiful rock formation trickling with little waterfalls. We hear a Sora, his very distant musical call setting us to searching, but we can't locate him. We just float and enjoy the notes of his rapidly descending scale. We whisper, and row quietly so not to disturb.

Along the river, not far from the docks, there are what we might call small boat piers. They consist of pilings driven upright in the mud, close to shore, so the fishermen can tie their boats up to work on them at low water. A group of locals have gathered just for that purpose. "How yer makiner, " they greet us as we come up along side.

When we are back at the dock, the fisherman, his son and grand kids are gathering supplies for the labor at hand. Doug asked, "Do you get many sailboats up here?"

Black River
*Along the river not far from the docks, there are what we might call small
boat piers. They consist of pilings driven upright in the mud, close to shore,
so the fishermen can tie their boats up to work on them at low water.*

Black River
*Doug, who doesn't seem a bit phased by the fact that neither the
sophisticated computer charts nor the locals had any knowledge of our
destination, jumps back in the dinghy for more exploration.*

"Nope, you're the first!" The eldest of the group looks to be about 60-years-old and there was yet another, older generation back at home. The only moorings in the harbour belong to the family. When they learned our destination, the fishing crew offered advice about going up the coast. Doug was able to insert a few questions and they all jabbered on a bit.

The oldest son of the clan takes on an expression as if a light bulb came on. "Come aboard, we can look at the computer charts of the Minas Basin!" So lickety split they are in the wheelhouse of his fishing boat.

I busy myself with many jobs, the most important being sitting in the cockpit enjoying the warm sun. I am almost in lullaby land when I hear the crew offering up their mooring for the night or they say we can tie to the dock. The group fears that if we stay at the dock we might have some teenage company.

"What would they be up to, fishing and drinking beer?" My husband asks.

"Yep, that's about it."

"No problem, I've made a career of it!" Doug tells 'em.

Deciding to try out the mooring, we untie the *Guillemot* and as we pull away from the dock I can just hear the youngest of the group, (11 maybe) tell another "nope I ain't never seen a sailboat before!"

After the process of tying up to the mooring is completed, I ask the Captain what the computer charts showed. "Weell! The charts showed Eastport, Black River and everything to Africa, but nothing about the Minas Basin!"

"Ha ha, at least we don't have to worry about heavy boat traffic, ha ha ha …" My ha ha's fade as I think to myself, where in hell are we going?

I keep my mouth shut and concentrate on the sea cows lined up drying their wings along the edge of the dock. These dark, goose-sized birds are a choir making guttural grunts. They are actually called double-crested cormorants. The French derived the word "cormorant" from the Latin words meaning sea cow. The Japanese are said to use them for fishing. They place a ring around their neck to prevent the birds from swallowing. Connected to the boat by a rope, the birds do their natural thing—fish. The fisherman just pulls the fish from their beaks. I'm told the diving birds are given their lunch once their work is completed.

Anxious to get dinner started and to concentrate on something other than the upcoming days of this journey, I make an effort to appear busy, rummaging around in my variety of storage areas. Suddenly, as if we were in their flight pattern, a bunch of bugs come into the boat. I blurt out, "What are all these bugs doing here?" I am satisfied that they have been sent to make my life miserable.

"Ah!" the Captain thoughtfully replies, studying their flight pattern and shapes, "they are just doing their bug thing, mating, reproducing and trying to keep their race going." Next he'll be setting up their trust funds.

Doug, who doesn't seem a bit phased by the fact that neither the sophisticated computer charts nor the locals had any knowledge of our destination, jumps back in the dinghy for more exploration. I watch him row towards the cliffs which were strange looking caves when we first arrived. The tide is rushing out and the current here in the opening of Black River is about as strong as I have witnessed except for around Falls Island in Cobscook Bay where the reversing falls put on their show for all the tourists at Reversing Falls Park in Pembroke, Maine.

With all this action going on around me, I start my choppy, choppy routine. Dinner d'jour is on its way once I peeled garlic and diced jalapeno and sauteed them in butter. I hear some Spanish music in my head, as I continue dicing, swaying, rolling and jerking.

I add thick slices of whole-wheat hearth bread to the saute until they are well toasted and then set them aside. To the skillet I add a tad more olive oil and the veggie mix. Then I topped the mixture with grated extra sharp cheddar cheese and chopped onions. I put the lid on and let it grill the wax peppers, bell peppers, green beans and cauliflower. At the last minute I add the bread to the top of the dinner to warm. When I served this to my hungry man I top it with diced tomatoes—I dramatically present it as La Bruschetta con Verde de Salsa Cruda. He says, "yum yum, you are the best Rock 'n Roll cook in the world!"

Day 4

Monday, September 3, 2001

I awake to a sunrise that is clear and beautiful. Lucky for this first mate the Captain has the wood stove cranked up high, and the cabin is toasty. Doug has been awake for a long while and has busied himself by putting away the legs and adjusting the dock lines.

Yes, we were tied to a mooring. It was about 9 p.m. last night, and the moon had risen higher in the sky, when the Captain deemed it was too roly poly to spend the night where we were, especially since a dock was close at hand and—most importantly, we have legs. Doug had spent at least an hour tying up to the dock and was still out there waiting for the tide to go out enough for us to settle on the bottom so he could adjust the leg, when I glanced at the loudly ticking Dollar Store clock: 10:15 p.m.. I wasn't asked to assist in this operation so I finally crawled into the V-berth and managed to read at least two paragraphs before I was dead to the world.

I was still in this repose early this morning when my husband kissed me. What a nice, sweet awakening. Unfortunately all he really wanted to know was if I had an extra toothbrush because his was lost over the side of the boat in his late night, whiskey drinking excursion with the legs and the dock lines.

I reward myself with a pat on the back and a smug smile for over-packing and bringing extra things the Captain never would hear of. Why would I even think he was being romantic? It's daylight, and I look like a red-nosed, drowned rat. I've been taking antibiotics for a tooth problem. The label reads: "Can cause sun sensitivity." An understatement! Yesterday, although lathered in sun screen, my knuckles, chest, lips and all my lower face got burned almost immediately. I'm saved by the fact that Doug is so thrilled with being here together; he loves everything about it, seeing and experiencing all this—maybe my inner beauty will show through. Yesterday, in all his excitement, my husband took tons of pictures and luckily none were of me.

Keen on the idea of having something to eat and having time to throw on my arctic gear before our departure, I climb out of bed. I feel rather achy in spots that do not normally ache, and my mind searches for reasons why. We didn't get a walk in yesterday; we were merely in and out of the dinghy. In a moment of washing my face and brushing my teeth it comes to me. The boat had rocked so much it was an exercise routine just keeping my balance. I had gotten a workout just cooking and walking from one end of the boat to the other, mostly to empty the LJ. The effort it takes to poop and pee!

I have already explained the LJ so I suppose it is time to allow my reader to fully understand other private areas of my life. We have on board a device whose brand name is the Reliance. It is basically a plastic lid and a toilet seat covering our bucket. Before you use the facilities it is required to dip the bucket in the water and add just enough to make things float, but without making it too heavy to lift on board. After completion of this task you are free to utilize the bucket.

The need for real technical brilliance comes at this point. You are required to discharge your waste overboard (my husband says, "a turd doesn't stand a chance in these tides!"). This is not easy even when the boat is stationary, but when we are underway it takes as much thought, concentration and steadiness of hand as cracking a safe. First and foremost you have to maneuver the bucket out to the cockpit without spillage. Once you have successfully placed the bucket in some area of the cockpit you now have to balance yourself so you can hoist it up and over the side and dump it all into the big flush of the Bay of Fundy, again keeping in mind which way the wind is blowing and the need to avoid falling overboard.

Yes! Mission accomplished, but now you have to do the dreaded rinse, dipping the bucket to add water, swishing it around, and dumping it again. The force of the water and the movement of the boat tries to rip the bucket out of your hands and often feels as if it will rip your arm sockets out.

The first hour of our sail today is a drift. We have no wind; we just let the tide take us out. Thus, we are able to savor the shoreline. The coastline just past Black River is bordered by sand dunes, an unusual sight north or east of southern Maine. The fall weather has not changed the meadows that stretch inland. Further up the coast our vista includes a few country roads leading to 16 homes and 3 churches. Our last glimpse of this little community reveals a huge cliff with a gorgeous beach walk at the base, and no slippery rockweed or unsightly salmon pens.

Despite the lack of wind, the tidally-induced waves in this large bay are enough to nearly thwart my attempt at a couple of cups of tea, but I ride the galley floor like a surfer and manage a couple of half cups. With the sunshine and the lack of wind I'm soon able to happily shed layers of my morning-in-the-arctic clothing. We aren't getting anywhere and the motion is a bit much, but the peace and the sunshine envelop us.

So far the cruise is good and bad, like everything else in life, but when it is *sooo* cold, I really start to question my reasons for being here. A few nights are one thing—it has been interesting, different and tolerable—I could almost say fun. But my mind just keeps pushing ahead to the twenty-some-odd days yet to unfold in this journey. It may well-become colder, and I sometimes have to just stop and wonder why? I am happy to have this time together with Doug, and we do have fun. I'm thrilled we get along so well, but then, who am I fooling?

He wouldn't do this for me. He wouldn't make this sacrifice for me! He didn't want to go to Ohio with me. He doesn't want to go to California with me, even though his parents have offered free flight tickets. He, my husband, the man I love, wouldn't even go to a two-hour company party with me. I feel like I am the one who adapts. He is the one who does what he wants and luckily for me he wants to take me along.

I still don't understand why, as I wrote earlier—a male companion would be more fun and probably more competent. These thoughts are briefly interrupted by a section of fantastically beautiful shoreline. But wait, I'm not finished! He hates to go to motels and B&Bs, so I am always sleeping in the back of the cow car or the van along the side of the road, in gutters, ditches, and in the woods. At least that saves money, and maybe someday when I'm about 65, we'll have a house whose holes he has taken time to patch. I'll be too old to care or be dying of cancer or be falling down and breaking things. Then and probably only then, I will "call back yesterday, and bid time return" of our journey on the *Guillemot*. I will evoke the memory of my younger self, writing with tears in my eyes having finally realized that life is not very convenient and often it hurts. So when LIFE IS GOOD, pull on your mud boots and grab hold— and hold on tight.

Having gotten that off my chest and into my journal, I sit back to calmly try and enjoy the day. I turn and look at my husband smiling indulgently at his nearly hysterical wife, sensing that there is some loud ticking going on in my little brain and some harsh hen scratches in my journal. "The wind is so light, why don't you make some martinis and come over here and sit close to me so I can give you a big hug!"

I keep my distance, pretending to still be observing whatever it is I am observing. He doesn't really think I'm going to fall for that "Let's have martinis—sit close so I can give you a big hug" business does he? I am about to rear up and tell him what's what, but I consider my options and decide to wipe the tears from my eyes, have martinis, get hugs, and save this damn good argument for another day! I make a note in my journal to pick a day to have words with him, to give him my full two cents, then I get up to play bartender.

The coastline just keeps getting better and better, one magnificent beach after another! Cliffs and ledges full of red, gray and yellow mesa-like rocks—the similarity to Zion National Park amaze us. What a difference light wind and warm sunshine makes. We have time to talk and laugh and we make all sorts of plans. Every cute cottage we see, we wonder if it might be affordable, and all the while the tide is swiftly sweeping us to what we hope is our next harbour. Yesterday the fisherman told us that St. Martins is a charming village and figured we could lay up there for the night.

The bay gets narrower as we go up it, so Nova Scotia gets closer and closer—we raise our hands in a mighty gesture, "We can do it!"

"Come hell or high water we'll get to the top of the Minas Basin!" I add, though in the back of my mind I wonder, "How much hell, and how high the water, by the time we get there?"

Up ahead in the far distance we see a headland and what looks like a sail in front of it. It has been two days since another boat of any kind has crossed our path out here in this vast bay, and that was at the entrance of St. John harbour. Our last sighting of another sailboat was when all the whale spouting was going on, four days ago. But it looks like a sail.

We keep our eyes focused on the object, and as we get closer we decide it's a tall bell buoy. Then no, we don't think so. The wind is shoving us along at pretty good pace now so we aren't long in coming close enough to see that it is a hole clear through the huge red bluff! We are overjoyed to discover it and pass the binoculars back and forth. Just as we are getting really close we start traveling fast because of a strong gust of wind, and a moment later we look up to see not a sign of it. The perspective of the entire coastline changes in seconds. The difference is so remarkable that for a moment we wonder if it had ever actually existed. Soon we realize that we must be in front of it—we have no way of telling. Again, as if someone stepped on the gas we jerk forward and we sail along the proper angle again and see it from the other side, and yes, it was real.

Inspiration has plucked my husband's vocal cords, and the happy tones of Doug's best seafaring voice floats across the water ...

Sailing, sailing all me life is sailing
Sailing and bailing, all me freakin' life
Sailing or bailing or pukin' over the railin' …

A postcard scene is ahead. According to the chart and the GPS
this must be the St. Martins Lighthouse. With the aid of our binoculars we see people gathered around the light enjoying the view
and the lovely warm day. But as we look we think there is something slightly amiss. The people are gazing seaward as one would
expect, but there is a little too much pointing and shielding of their
eyes from the afternoon sun. I report to the Captain, "They sure
seem to have a steady gaze in our direction. Probably another group
that has never seen a sailboat in this area," I laugh. Still, none of
them seem to be pointing their cameras at us.

Doug is facing out to sea and I am facing him and land. We
quietly sail along, speculating about St. Martins Harbour. The chart
and the guide predict a turbulent rip up ahead and we spot it. In the
areas between some very large rocks that protrude from the water,
the current is running hard with the now-outgoing tide and, as it
gets lower, the surface is getting closer and closer to the rocks that
lie below—the probable reason for the lighthouse high on the bluff.
We calculate where we are on the tide and we study the area between the lighthouse and the large rocks.

We, and by that I mean Doug, are confident we can make it.

The day is turning out to be really nice. My husband had tried
to get me to wager that we'd be in shorts before the day was out. I
give a doubtful, "humph!" and said, "Maybe if we were on shore."
But truly, I am revivified by the extraordinary day. I keep flashing
my loved one convincingly genuine smiles between my oohs and
ahhs of delight. My mind drifts around with the motion of the boat
to all manner of subjects, some of which are printable and some are
not. My spiritual side tries to keep control. I marvel at the volume
and depth out here, in the sky, the water, the cliffs.

* * *

During the days of preparation for this journey I kept looking
at my stack of. "Eileen's Gear" piled on the landing floor. I really
wanted to bring my Walkman, maybe some favorite music, my

twenty-one hour *Jane Eyre* book tape. But no, I thought, I want to see, breathe, hear and feel God's world.

To myself, I repeated my goal—to find my center! I wanted to try and understand what I'm here on this earth for. Around a month ago, on one of those days when I was doing my best to avoid small thinking, I wrote a quotation on the first page of my journal. I wanted to keep referring to it like the posted and framed *Mission Statement* at the local supermarket.

> *Perhaps the only way to avoid attaching ourselves to some false center, whether a cause, a person, or some aspect of ourselves, is to discover and submit to the authority of our true center, the place where God makes his presence and purpose for us known. To be attached to a false center inevitably leads to division within the personality*
> —Christopher Bryant
> from *The River Within Self-Realization/Eternal Life*

I knew this to be a distinctly unpromising goal for someone like myself—but I figured, miracles do happen! I like the part "where God makes his *presence and purpose* for us known."

Today, I will meditate on what God has for me—to learn, do, believe and act upon! This, my reader, is exactly what I am doing, while my husband sails the course for St. Martins, when I hear a voice calling, "Hello! Hello!" My eyes circle the boat, my husband, then to shore, up to the high bluff. I see from the look in the Captain's eyes that indeed he had heard it too!

"Did you hear that?"

In the same instant that I asked this, my husband's furrowed brow and pointing finger directed my attention to the sea behind me. "Over there!" He jumps up and sternly tells me, "He's down!" I turn and spot a man in the water, at a distance hanging on to an overturned kayak.

I say to myself, "Okay God, I see one purpose you have for my life!" With my heart pounding, I ask my Captain to tell me what to do. With greater efficiency and patience than I thought possible the Captain gives me my instructions and follows his instincts.

As we pull the lonely kayaker from the frigid cold, the first words he is able to sputter are "I thought I was gone ..." With his sunglasses still neatly in place, holding on to his overturned kayak, he'd been drifting with the strong current, steadily being swept into the huge Bay of Fundy and out to sea. He'd hit the rip between the mainland and the rocks and capsized. Although an experienced kayaker, he wasn't able to right himself. After we help him climb on board, he lies gasping on the stern for a few minutes and then we slowly help him move further into the cockpit. We strip off most of his gear and clothes. I wrap him in a flannel shirt, a down jacket, an all-weather raincoat, a Carhart jacket, a blanket, and whatever else I can find on the boat in which to cover him.

Meanwhile, Doug is rowing around in the dinghy rescuing his paddle. The Lone Kayaker is a very clean-cut man with mostly gray hair. He gives me the impression of being a professional type, around fifty-plus. He is a fit and muscular man. "I almost gave up about 10 minutes ago, but something told me to keep trying. I was praying for my wife!"

I choke back tears as his emotions spread through me—I don't know how to reply, so I pat his arm and give him a hug—or try to—around all his layers. As I did so I said emphatically, "I can just imagine that you were!"

He is still gasping and taking deep breaths when he manages to say, "Where, where, did you come from?"

"Well, ah um ..." I considered 'Philadelphia and California' and 'Black River' but settled, instead, on "Eastport, Maine."

He looks up rather startled, "What?"

I repeat, clearer this time, "Eastport, Maine!"

His eyes are wet from tears. He shakes his head and pushes his chin to his chest, "Oh God!" He suddenly starts laughing and crying, "Oh God!" He is still shaking his head and repeating more of the same. I am still standing along side him feeling rather angelic—wondering if, at any moment, large white wings may sprout out of my shoulders. I am anxious to fulfill my duties as his patron saint so I offer him some water.

He gives me another tired laugh and replies, "I believe I've had enough for one day." This little joke is not lost on me—I give him some *Spring* water and I brew him a cup of Jasmine tea. While sipping his tea I advise him to keep maneuvering his toes, feet, legs, arms and shoulders to get the circulation going, though they are all looking good.

On the way in to the harbour we meet another fellow in a kayak coming our way (we find out later he runs the kayak rental and tour shop). He and another boat are part of a rescue team on their way out, hopefully, to rescue the Lone kayaker. This is at least 20 minutes after we have him on board.

Doug and I both look at each other and then to our survivor, head covered for warmth, and shake our heads. We think it would have been too late by the time the crew arrived, especially since he was rapidly moving seaward every minute. When we pulled him on board, the Captain asked him how long he had been in. My first thoughts were I'm sure he doesn't really know. But he gasped as he looked at his watch and said "30 minutes." Doug and I looked at each other, knowing 30 or 40 minutes is max before hypothermia sets in.

Hypothermic death is a gradual and insidious sort of trauma. It overtakes one literally by degrees as one's body temperature falls and all natural responses grow sluggish and disordered. A person suffering hypothermia experiences several stages. First there occurs mild and then increasingly violent shivering, as the body tries to warm itself with muscular contractions. Then comes profound weariness, heaviness of movement, a distorted sense of time and distance, and increasing confusion which can result in illogical decisions and failure to observe the obvious. Gradually the person becomes disoriented and subject to increasing hallucinations such as a misconception that he is not freezing but burning up.

The rescue boat discovers that we have him aboard and then turns to escort us into the dock. There is a greeting party awaiting us. As it happens, a woman on the bluff at the lighthouse had seen him go in, explaining the peculiar behavior of the crowd we had seen there. Those people had scurried to find someone with a cell phone while another kept him in sight—a matter of critical importance in such cases.

But the folks at the lighthouse who watched the rescue were not in direct contact with the rescue boat they had sent. The Lone Kayaker (which we will forever call him because we cannot remember his name) said, "I was calling to God to save me!" when we heard him yell.

"Are you from around here?" I ask.

"I'm from Fredericton, New Brunswick. My wife and I came to St. Martins for the Labor Day weekend."

We notice people and a hoopla going on at the dock, which is where his van is parked. The Captain doesn't think our soggy passenger is ready to meet the press, so to speak, so he veers left, as far away from the main ramp as we can get.

Our only recourse is to get chummy with a commercial boat called, *The Sea Monster*.

"Oh well, we tried, " Doug consoles the Lone Kayaker, when we see the crowd all converge to the dock where we have our lines thrown over to *The Sea Monster*. Two guys are quickly down the ladder and helping us tie up. They are Troy, the owner of *The Sea Monster* and Vic, who had a radio so he must have been part of the rescue crew.

St Martens
Our only recourse is to get chummy with a commercial boat called The Sea Monster.

The third person to reach us is a policeman, seemingly full of self-importance, whipping out his pad and pencil asking very important questions before we can even finish tying up. Taking his job seriously he asks "Name, where you from, and date of birth?" Not the kayaker, but Doug! We roll our eyes and wonder what on earth (or in heavens name) August 5, 1961 has to do with a guy almost freezing to death today?

Next to board is a medical person of some sort. Our survivor is checked to ensure he can walk on his own up the steep ramp. His entourage is ready to escort him off the *Guillemot*. The Lone Kayaker walks by the pop-top area where I'm standing inside, trying to stay out of the way. He stops and gives me a long, thoughtful handshake. I notice once, again, the little strap on his wrist, which read, "What would Jesus do?"

He has tears in his eyes when he says to me, "Eileen (he *remembered* my name), thank you so much and God bless you." I could have just gushed out a big snotty cry.

After he waved goodbye from atop the dock, Doug, with his sick sense of humor said, "You gave him my new flannel shirt!" It was not exactly *new*. It was nine-months-old and already had a few holes in it, but when you are on a boat you don't have a large wardrobe.

I laugh, smile my saintlike smile, and say, "He'll bring it back, for God sakes."

The Capt'n says, "We do the most fun things!" Still full of euphoria, we hug and laugh—we laugh because it's funny; we laugh because it's true.

But folks, on a sailboat in a harbour that empties of all water, there is not always the luxury of time to think of life and death or to bask in the warmth and exhilaration of finally being able to justify your existence on Earth. The tide is going out fast, and we have to get our legs on!

Nothing can ever be easy, so we find that the rapidly approaching harbour bottom is lower on one side of the boat than the other, but it is not the side you would think. Not that I've *thought* much about it—let's just say it's not the side the *Captain* would think. Anyway, the legs will not hold and one of them is caught underneath *The Sea Monster*. Doug unhooks the main halyard and jumps on *The Sea Monster*. With the leverage of the mast he pulls the *Guillemot* upright so we can readjust our legs. Or rather, so *Doug* can readjust the legs.

That leaves you-know-who to hold the boat upright and I am not the type to climb aboard some else's boat, crawl up their window, and pull myself up to the roof of their wheel house (hoping it holds) in order to pull a sailboat up straight (without cartwheeling off the top). All this so that a thin wooden leg can be attached to the rigging and we don't lay over in the mud for the remainder of our stay at St Martens.

I'm telling you, just getting the fenders out and tying the dock lines are enough acrobatics for me and, at this moment, I'd rather be listening to the piano at Nordstrom's, where the hardest maneuvers expected of me would be pulling out my credit card and riding the escalator.

But we finally did it. We are level and all the water is gone out of the entire harbour. Soggy with relief, I drop into the cockpit like a crash-test dummy. I look down to see that my pants are smudged with blue and white paint, bird crap, and at least three weeks of dirt compliments of *The Sea Monster*.

I look up and see none other than Vic and Troy. I am grateful that they weren't here to see me struggling onto the top of their boat. They tell us that our survivor has faired well and, apparently, God has officially endorsed us, for local opinion has it that the Lone Kayacker must have someone looking out for him. It turns out that nobody in the group gathered at the dock for the rescue had ever seen a sailboat come into this harbour, nor had they ever seen a sailboat in these waters. It was a miracle sent from God that we were here, that our timing was perfect for the rescue, and that we have legs!

I consider all this—the facts are there. If we had been a powerboat instead of a sailboat, we would never have heard him calling to God to save him. If we had been one hour later, not only would we have not been there to rescue him, but we would not have had enough water to get into the harbour and tied to the dock. I can think of no better explanation and, besides, who am I to argue with local opinion?

Now it is back to everyday life and, just because I've had an enchanted day, doesn't mean I deviate from my prescheduled personal hygiene. Here I am in a harbour with no water, sitting on stilts, washing my hair in a bucket.

A continuous parade of locals and vacationers are coming by to see the sailboat sent from God! We had left the doors open because it was so hot. We do have a curtain I can pull, so I can stand in a 2' x 2' semi-private area—which I do—in order to strip and clean all the rest of my private parts. I am clean and ready for romance.

The Captain suggests a walk through town and that we should go out for dinner. I have to think about this for about one second. "I'll race you up the ladder!" I say as I push him out of my way. We tromp across the monster that lies beside us and scurry up the very steep ladder to the dock. Our long walk ends at the caves along a red beach. We sit, eating fish and chips and enjoying the children playing on the low tide sand, where, we read, the Fundy Trail begins. What a gorgeous place—I want to come back!

I make it back down the steep ladder and we reverse the trek I'd mentioned before, which involves climbing back up onto, across, and down from the *Sea Monster's* roof, and back to our little sailboat sent from heaven. The Captain starts the wood stove and we sit down for our evening of writing and reading.

We normally love to sit across from each other in our respective quarter berths, but "by the Jesus, " it's hot so we have to move out to the open air. We sit for a long while, the sun disappears and the moon makes its appearance.

"I guess we should plan our exit out of St. Martins, " says my husband. We just got here, I want to shout. Instead, I try to figure out, with my honey, just when is it that we can maneuver our way out of this little hamlet to continue our voyage to Nova Scotia. The plan is to set the alarm for 4 a.m., we will then take off the legs and untie from *The Sea Monster.* At that time there should still be enough water left in the harbour to get out.

It is now 8:30 p.m. and the high tide will occur while we are sleeping, about 2 a.m.. Once out of the harbour we can wait 'till dawn to go the 24 miles to Isle Haute on the coming tide. It seems complicated but, here in the upper part of Fundy, the tide is so strong that if you don't go with it, you don't go.

BUZZ, BUZZ goes the alarm, and we are up and out. I ride out of the harbour on the foredeck, hoping to be able to tell if we are about to go aground. Fortunately, last night we were able to see the harbour when it was dry. We could see a narrow path that was deeper than the rest of the area.

We motor out with crystal clear skies and only two days past a full moon. The light from the heavens illuminates our path. How the Captain knows where that channel is that we saw last night, I haven't the faintest idea. It is a rather perilous venture but the beauty of the 40 gazillion stars and the tranquil early morning makes it a heavenly experience.

We motor 'way out into the bay and, I don't know why, but I say to myself, "Oh yeah, Monica Lewenski? Beat this for a big hot dog of a time!"

My higher self is still wondering about my mental condition when we anchor. To port we have the lights of St. Martins in the distance, and we can see some lights of Nova Scotia. I am so excited about the exit from St. Martins and the hope of Nova Scotia, that I have to do my business.

If I were going to write a top ten list of best places to think, and I fully intend to add this to one of my to-do lists, I would place the bucket, in the cockpit, in the top five. When you have to go #2 (or, as Aaron and Julie's three-year-old son Ty puts it, when you think something is the matter), what better place than out in the open cockpit, peacefully suffused with the light of the stars, the moon, and the faraway lights of the city.

So, here I am dropping the kids off at the pool, when splash, splash curious George the seal, pays me a visit. He looks at me quizzically. "What's up George, I suppose you have never seen a sailboat before, either!" George stayed, we stare, I smile, he smiles, and we bond. "Goodnight George, it's time for a second snooze before we depart on our very own special day five."

Day 5

Tuesday, September 4, 2001

The anchorage is calm, with only the quiet noises of the sea outside. The gentle rocking of the boat lulls us into a good deep sleep. There is no sign of life in the V-berth. Have you ever heard the doors close in Alcatraz Prison? I have, on a tour that included the sound of all the cells pounding shut at once. That sound (which is said to have been used by George Lucas in *Star Wars* for Darth Vader's entrance) echoes to your bones. This is close to what it does to you, to be sound asleep and have someone walk across the cabin top and pull up the anchor, which ends up 4" from my feet.

I jump and quickly flop upside down, squeaking angrily as I rush to push the bottom ends of the sleeping bags out of the way of the wet, muddy, seaweed-covered anchor rode and guide it into its rightful place in the forepeak so most of the mess stays out of our bed! There is no question as to what the Captain is doing now. I hear the pounding of his feet on the roof of the cabin as he hauls up the mainsail. Now, he's moved to the cockpit to unfurl the jib. The only saving grace is that he does not start the motor and now peace has returned to the valley of my soul, despite my having awakened at the hands of the nautical alarm clock that is my husband.

I decide to turn over and go back to sleep.

But, no dice! I soon start to feel remiss in my self-appointed job as anchorwoman and, now fully awake, I also feel some twinges of excitement because we are setting sail for Nova Scotia! What a dud, to be down here and not sharing the excitement of it all with my Captain. Isle Haute is our goal for today—I must gather my strength and my enthusiasm and crawl out of bed.

While finding my jeans, combing my hair, brushing my teeth, taking my vitamins, putting lip balm on my cracked lips, I have to figure out how to chuckle without making my lip's bleed. I ponder, me, an anchorwoman!

If, eight years ago, a fortuneteller had told me that I would become an anchorwoman I'd have surely thought she meant at a small TV station in the boondocks, perhaps one desperate for someone to report the grain silo news. Had I, looking into her crystal ball, seen myself as anchorwoman on a 25-foot sailboat, dealing with 54-foot tides, cooking quasi-gourmet meals in a galley the size of a kitchen cabinet, with no refrigeration, a 2-burner alcohol stove and a sink with a pump, it would have seemed far more improbable.

* * *

Today we are taking the tide, which is going our way. We feel like hitchhikers with our thumbs out, hoping to be taken to our destination by the big flush. While I languished below I wasn't missing out on much excitement, for the wind is light and it is very slow going. I provide entertainment by practicing vocabulary with our trusty vocabulary-builder book.

If this does not sound wild and exciting it was the best I could do aside from reading aloud from the cruising guide about the many Beaver Harbours, Beaver Islands, Beaver Bluffs, Beaver Narrows and Beaver Points there are. Shockingly enough, after a while, the Captain says he has had enough of vocabulary building, as well as the bobbing around. I am grudgingly forced to put away my book and Doug is grudgingly forced to start the motor. We are determined to make our big crossing to Isle Haute so we *bruumed bruumed* toward our goal.

The motor is steadily droning on, and I crawl into my sanctuary of the V-berth. I feel as though I've taken a tranquilizer and again I tell myself I have abandoned the poor lonely sailor. But, before I drift off, I remind myself that he is the one who loves this, he is the one that would rather be here than any place else on earth, and I am the one who would rather be someplace else doing something else ... I think.

To tell the truth it is growing on me—shhh!

My dreams drift into a fantasy land where we have a boat with a shower, a proper toilet with a door, and a little more sitting room. All this is just wishful thinking, for while we do occasionally discuss how lovely it would be to have a larger boat, I don't believe it is in the cards. It is not just the initial cost. A larger boat costs much more in every type of upkeep. Doug is Mr. DIY (Do It Yourself), and is solely responsible for the maintenance of our old cars, our old houses, and our old boat.

You also have to factor in the difficulty of handling a larger boat. The *Guillemot*, as I said earlier, floats in 2'4" of water and our beam is only 7'9". So we can literally go, as now, in a sense, "where no man has gone before." In general a larger boat makes life easier in some ways but harder in others.

I agree fervently, don't I? "Sure I do," says the dutiful wife. The *Guillemot* wins in the practicality race by a head or two. So, here we go, on our journey in living space no larger than most people's closets. Lucky for him, I come from Nebraska and Oklahoma farming stock that weathered the Depression, the dust bowl, the grapes of wrath, and WWII!

A pale ray of sunshine shines through the translucent window, too weak to warm me. I go on dreaming—we go to Isle Haute—it is a tropical island with plenty of food and water and, when we open our sea rations, I find a large supply of Prozac.

Not much more than an hour later we are faced with the ominous sight of the real Isle Haute. On approach to the island all we can see are 300' cliffs. As we pull around to the east side we see the island has an ancient look, and we half expect dinosaurs to step out onto the rocky, half-mile long beach. We find the only possible anchorage, we move four times within it before we pick our spot. At least we hope it's a good spot. My highly developed anchor pulling skills show themselves to the fullest, for when I say we move four times that means I pull the anchor four times. While this seems quite a lot like hard work, at least it means I can keep my bright pink weight hidden for the day. I had nearly lost my will to live when we finally find a hole that the depth finder shows to have 68'.

Thank God, it is time to go for a walk on this island. We row ashore. The sailing directions tell us it is uninhabited. The tide is going out, which is favorable because we don't have to carry the dinghy way up on shore. This would not be a simple task on this shore, for the stones are all shapes and sizes, with some covered in moss, and some invisibly slick for the unsuspecting, clumsy, weak-willed victim helping to carry a dinghy, which I should point out is a difficult task in a flat driveway.

The Captain points out in his being-nice-to-a-klutz tone of voice, "Be careful!"

I stifle the urge to shout, "No Shit Sherlock!" and wonder silently—what I am doing out here in Jurassic Park?

Triumphantly, I make it up the steep beach and the slippery boulders without bodily harm. It turns out we are not the first humans to have discovered the island after all, as we find the remains of a variety of camps. There are logs pulled together around campfires, names and dates carved on driftwood, and even a written log of those who have come before us. The log has been here for years safely tucked in a Rubbermaid container. In this journal of discoverers, someone left a brief history of the Island, which includes the fact that in the early 1600's de Champlain wrote in his log about it, noting a fresh water pond which still exists today.

Doug has his own ceremony to record in the log book along with our names, the date, and the name of our vessel, for he notes with reverence the burial given to a stowaway from the night at Black River. Anthony the dragonfly (named after Doug's old friend who had died just a few months earlier) came aboard and stayed. He died the next day, but he was a beautiful sight and we marveled at his colors.

The first thing we do after we finally make it back on board is to check the depth sounder, and it shows 28'. Good, we are O.K., but then we look at each other.

"An hour ago it was 68'. Are we dragging anchor?" I say with concern. We keep an eye on it and in five minutes it reads 15'! We sit for a few minutes digesting this startling information. Then I look again and it reads 65'. We must be over a hole. We felt we were anchored really well, but with the wind kicking up, it can put a big strain on the anchor and we worry.

That beach and pulling the dinghy around is not an experience I would willingly repeat, but macho man here wants to go back ashore to hike to the highest point of the island where there is a light house tower waiting to be conquered. Climbing 300' lighthouse towers has never been one of my strong points, so I tell him, "Go for it! Sitting here on board taking inventory of the bilge vegetables is better than going up that beach again."

Since what is for dinner reflects what needs to be used before it goes by, I stick my head down and my butt up, to check our bilge. The Captain says. "You're so frugal, you even skimp on seawater in the poop bucket!" Nothing will go to waste if I can help it, and who knows when I will see a normal market again. The entree for tonight's soiree is warm Tempe over a mixed vegetable salad. The dressing also serves as a marinade. It is made with diced Jalapeno, minced garlic, fresh ginger chopped, soy sauce, sesame oil, rice vinegar and fresh lemon juice. While the Tempe is marinating I chop three different types of cabbage, fresh yellow beans, cauliflower, red onion and tomatoes.

My salad bowl is a Rubbermaid bowl with a lid so it can serve several purposes. After I saute the Tempe I will serve it on top of the already tossed salad with feta cheese. A boat cleanup tip is to serve a slice of bread at the end of the meal to wipe up the tasty sauce and the plate. Although the wind is mild, the tide running through here is so strong I am transported to my imaginary cooking show, *Virtuoso on a Skateboard!*

I may get a little dizzy trying to cook, but few people have the views from their kitchen that I have here, under the *Guillemot's* poptop.

I look up from my galley to see Doug coming down off the trail, his face covered with a most genuine grin, and I find myself smiling as I watch him walk the stone beach now much larger due to the going tide. The waves lapping the beach are glittering with dancing spangles in the afternoon sun, like a most fetching necklace.

Our evening is spent in the cockpit, with just light sweatshirts. We feel entitled to have a beer with our dinner. We eat every last scrap and hardly speak, not wanting to break the silence. Our calf muscles ache while we write in our journals and the log.

I whisper "look" and point to the broad sky, which is host to a tomato of a sunset.

Inside now for the remainder of the beautiful evening I see my husband yawning and trying to keep his head balanced on his shoulders. My reader might think that this would be a romantic evening here with my rugged and handsome husband. But with all the activities of the day, Daisy Duck could be in the V-berth with the Captain for all he cares.

My last thought, before retiring, as I peek out of the forward hatch and see the cliffs silhouetted against a harvest moon, is what a very strange sensation it is being the only ones mad enough to be here all alone in this enigmatic place called, The Eye Of Gloosecap.

Day 6

Wednesday, September 5, 2001

My pace in the mornings is that of an elderly tortoise. This morning, however, startled, I sit straight up and bump my head on the ceiling of the V-berth. I groan and rub my head then quickly switch to my jaws and neck. My wake up call is the drill sergeant over head, calling me to attention, "Eileen! Eileen! I need you to coil the anchor rope!"

I manage. "Yeah, sure." I wonder if I have lockjaw? Springing to action, I uncoil my self from my cozy bed to coil the rope that is flying in from the hole on deck. My arms and hands moving as fast as any conveyor belt to expertly fit every bit of rope we have on the anchor back in the fore peak. Our routine is going rather nicely, Doug pulling, pulling, pulling and I'm coiling, coiling, coiling like nobody's business. I am not even given enough time to consider why my jaws and neck ache as if I'd been in a car accident. I keep my eyes fixed, firmly focused on the job at hand.

Finally, there is a lull in the action. My tense muscles relax.

Whew! Overhead I hear a fair amount of grunting going on and some creative use of the Captain's favorite four, five and six letter words. I close my eyes and lay my head face down, arms still stretched for coiling. The strong current jerked the boat, like being hit in bumper cars, and I acknowledge, with some relief, that it was the tossing and pitching to and fro of the boat all night long—not lockjaw!

"Eileen!" I jump to my call of duty. "Eileen! This blankity, blank, blank, is stuck! You'll have to get out here and help!"

Pulling on a partial amount of clothing, I race out to the foredeck and up to the bow pulpit, anxious to be of service. I almost trip on the jib lines when I see my Captain shaking from stem to stern, eyes protruding. Good God in heaven! What can that anchor be stuck *on* or *in* or … *whatever?* No time for a state of panic to set in. I brace my bare feet up against the toe rail, butt against a bronze cleat, and then grab my portion of the rope.

Doug spoke with words of one syllable (stop, go, pull etc.) and neanderthal grunts. I bite my lip unintentionally and pull as if goin' for the triple hernia. We stop, periodically, to relax our clenched muscles. I can hear my heart slamming against my rib cage—Bam, Bam, Bam! Try, try, try again. We feel it start to move—at a glacial pace—but *move.*

I totter back shakily, then collapse, breathless, too tired to whoop for joy. The Captain is muttering appreciatively while he continues to pull our frayed anchor rope and finally sets our anchor firmly in place. Our muscles are trembling with stress. We both stare down at a huge log floating along beside us. We feel strangely honored that this log came up and released our anchor.

We glance up to see the huge, verdant cliffs of Isle Haut looking strangely like Diamond Head—half-covered with fog. "I wonder if this is some grand conspiracy of Samuel de Champlain, leaving this flotsam behind, to keep us from our goal?" The Captain raises his eyes brows several times in a Groucho Marx type gesture, then bounces toward the cockpit to set sail.

I am left alone, stretching my back, massaging my butt, where I will likely have a permanent dent in the shape of the cleat. I wipe the sweat and the warm mist off my brow. I chuckle when I envision the ghost of de Champlain writing his log on the Island. He notes, *Women of a certain age should not be seen pulling a stuck anchor in their undies.*

In silence we enjoy a calm, warm, dreamy drift toward mainland Nova Scotia and, more importantly, *The Minas Basin* (always pronounced with deep bass tones). Our GPS is set for Advocate Harbour today. We have only a breath of wind and we may need to start the motor. With eyes closed, head back, feet up, I set my inner GPS toward my lost beauty sleep.

"Damn!" reports the Captain. Reluctantly I open my eyes, at least I think I have them open. I can't see a blasted thing. Fog has completely enveloped our ship, just like in a spooky pirate movie.

"Eerrr! Where is ya, Matey?" Doug can joke after he checks the GPS to make sure we aren't about to hit land. At least we are moving, if really slowly. Five minutes later the wind grabs us and we are off like a prom dress.

The fog lifts her skirts just enough to glimpse what the chart shows to be Cape Chignecto. We oohhed and awed as we near the shore. Ledges painted red, black, green, and blue-grey surrounds a haven of a beach.

"There she is!" he says, pointing to the shore.

There's a woman out there? I think. But it was just *Ole Sal,* a rock formation adding more dimensions to the breathtakingly beautiful shoreline. The Captain announces that an expedition is in order.

I silently groan—*it is?* My look must have said, *you're out of your ever lovin'* ... because he quickly chided, "Ah, come on ... we may never get another chance. We won't be gone long."

I tell myself—*don't be a wimp!*

We aren't sure of the tide level here but it is likely to be 40 feet. This is a lot of ground to cover in six hours. The height of the tide dictates a very long haul of the dinghy up the rocky, ticklish beach. We can see the water quickly covering the shoreline. With each step I take I feel the gritty rocks move beneath my feet. I fight for balance.

Up, up and still further up, we carry the dinghy. We are always overly cautious. We don't want to get delayed, out on a little exploration, for any number of reasons, only to return and find that the tide has captured our only transport back to the boat.

I am gratifyingly moved by our strolling experience around a pond, finding an old oven from a long ago abandoned mill. I lift my hand to pat myself on the back for not missin' out.

"Oh cripes!" I point back where the *Guillemot* is anchored. We see the water is big and angry-looking. We had better get ourselves back to the boat! Conditions change around here as fast as the current. We vow to return again someday. We are unaware, at the time, that beyond the 600-foot cliffs is Nova Scotia's newest provincial park covering 10, 000 acres and 30 miles of hiking trails through an old growth forest.

I feel queasiness, a sudden sweat, a dryness on the tongue as I crawl into the seven and half foot dinghy to ride in our only option back to the *Guillemot*. The tide and the wind are against us. My white knuckle grip on the gunnels is to stay aboard. How the Captain has the muscle power to continue this long, long hard row back to the boat after our last near-debacle less than two hours ago, is impressive.

Relief floods me as I step aboard. My euphoria is short-lived. The wind stepped it up a notch and together, acting like a wrestling tag team with the current, they pick up the boat, slug it around and give me a choke slam against the cabin wall. Menacingly, my anchorwoman duties demanded my presence forward, while the Captain tried to get the sails ready to get the hell outa here. An observer from shore might have thought the whole scene rather comical—much like a bath tub toy on the end of a slinky.

I wrap my legs around the jib to stay aboard. There is tremendous pressure on the anchor. I am wondering if, sometime this century, I will ever see the end of this rope and hear the *clang, clang, clang* of the chain that signifies I'm nearing my goal of "anchor aboard"—when the skipper yells, "Oh no!"

Dear Lord, I think, what now?

Over the roar he yells—"I lost a sail tie, Eileen! Grab the boat pole!"

Well, *hel-lo!* I'm still trying to pull the damn anchor—I calculate I have about two tugs left in me. The Gods were on my side and I manage the final hoist of the anchor onto the deck. But I know there isn't a snowball's chance in hell that the anchor will stay if I don't get it properly tied. This all takes *time!*

Isle Haute
In silence we enjoy a calm, warm, dreamy drift toward mainland
Nova Scotia and more importantly, THE MINAS BASIN (always
pronounced with deep bass tones).

Cape Chinecto
... staring at the coastline of what looks like an uninhabited country.

Anytime something falls overboard, we try to handle it like a man-over-board drill. Now our sail tie is drowning and being washed away.

Doug calls again, like I'm ignoring him for spite—*"Get the boat pole!"*

I want to yell back—*"You, of all people, should know I can only do one thing at a time and that not very well."*

The boat pole in question is in its little holder attached to the mast, only a few feet behind me. I decide to for it. Then the boat convinces me to stay put and hang on for dear life as it does some impressive thrashing around.

Not wanting to join the sail tie and say "Hello" to hypothermia. I crawl over to the mast and edge my way up. I have the *pole* but now I have to go to the life line, lean over, and reach out with the awkward, hard-to-handle pole in order to hook the "man-over-board" (sail tie).

Doug expertly starts the motor, swings the boat around—I've lost sight of the sail tie (the man), I see it (him). Thank the heavens for strong lifelines—I'm able to bring in the tie.

"Yes!" the Captain cheers me on. "Hurray! Hurray!"

One should never get blinded by one's glory. I still have to reset the boat pole. The boat thrusts up and down, riding the waves. Slap, slap it goes, jarring us as if we're riding a bucking bronco.

I'll guaran-damn-tee ya, there is nothing in my *Sailing for Dummies* book about this.

Our hearts must surely beat as one—when I flop myself beside my Captain in the cockpit. We both started laughing hysterically. I laugh to keep from crying, he laughs because I look like a clown from the rodeo.

"I'm starving!" I announce, wiping my eyes.

"I'm with ya there!" the Captain's eyes light up. "A bagel?"

My wobbly legs carry me to the galley. Stuff is flying all over the cabin including me. We have to have *cream cheese!* A bagel without cream cheese is like a hug without a squeeze. This is like functioning during an earthquake that continues on and on.

Pressing my back against the sink and feet spread for balance I proceed, with slow cautious movements. I pull out the knife to slice the bagel …

My thoughts, oddly enough, sift with the movement of the boat, to the previous evening. Doug had looked up from his log, responding to some remark which escapes me at the moment. He had a far away look in his eyes.

He said in a low voice—"I'm a person who loves and needs to sail. Most of the world that humanity has created can get really boring. It's constantly changing out here. If you focus on nature, it will never disappoint you. Some threads of interest lead me here. If a person has an inkling, he has a direction to take through the different dimensions of life. What more in life do you need?"

Last night, I listened with interest to this autobiographical statement. I came to the conclusion, philosophical genius that I am, that in other words, this is about what *Doug* needs. Staring at my bouncing bagel I realize I don't even know what in the world I need. All I know is, right now it is 9:30 a.m., and I'm caught in the dimension of the stove and the sink.

Twenty minutes later the sun is shining and the wind just did us a favor. I sit down comfortably in the cockpit for my first bite of bagel. Doug is deeply impressed by the fact that I even managed to top them with "Wild and Rare." I give him a cocky cream-cheese smile. A large spray of water comes up over the side—misses the Captain—and hits its target.

I sat there frozen, eyes wide, bagel to my mouth, drenched.

Frustrated tears threaten. I blink them away, take another bite of my soggy, salty bagel and marvel at a yet more gorgeous section of shoreline as we whiz past. This place is amazing! Everything happens so fast that if I go for dry clothes, the camera, and a new bagel, I might miss something. We continue chewing, laughing, oohhing, awing, and sailing.

I can just feature a travel brochure encouraging the adventure of seeing all this, *To experience the salt spray in your face, a cool fall breeze at your back.* Omitted in their fall vacation planning kit would be the picture of me with my burnt chapped face, eating a soggy bagel.

Most treasures that life may bestow upon you come with a price. That price can be time, money, inconvenience, heartache, strife, sunburns, sore muscles—the list can be endless—damn it! I have to face the facts: for the vast majority of my life my motto has been to *avoid discomfort at all costs*! I'm a 50-year-old menopausal tea-sipper. I love Adirondack chairs on a deck. During a storm, I desire to be tucked inside, playing cards in front of a large picture window, sampling scrumptious foods from an organic gourmet deli. Do I want the ocean without the awful roar of it's many waters? The rain without thunder and lightning? My crops without plowing the ground? Well, I mean seriously, *who doesn't?*

My eyes and thoughts settled on my calm, contented husband, bare feet stretched across to me in the cockpit, one foot balanced between the toes of his other foot, staring at the coastline of what looks like an uninhabited country. *I know who doesn't.*

My funny, resourceful husband is driven by some alien force that disallows ego and shallowness. He once told me (when discussing travel and exploring), "Show me something that makes me wonder why I want to see it—something that makes me really feel strong emotion, whether that emotion is one of wonder, shock, euphoria, sadness, love, fright. I don't want to live life comfortable, but numb."

The Captain has his reasons for this journey. Would I be here if he weren't making me? Well, he's not forcing me, but I couldn't in good conscience let him be out here all alone! After all I saved the sail tie, helped unstick the anchor, fixed his bagel! It's almost out of morbid curiosity that I'm here. What if something horrible happened? What if I miss out on something really amazing? A by-product might be that I accidentally stumble on my center!

I stretch my neck and look up to a clear blue sky. Out of it comes a burst of exhilaration and excitement for our goal. We both shared a *simply awesome* over yet another colossal rock formation. I'm a fool in paradise! I suck in a contented intake of breath. The blood of my English homesteading ancestors cursed through me— no struggle, no progress—no pain, no gain.

After the morning fog and strong winds, the weather turned to one of those unexpected warm afternoons. We are nearing Advocate. The bright sun is shining down on my copy of the *Nova Scotia's Dreamers and Doers* guide. Pleased as punch, I managed to sneak it past the Captain's inspection. The Captain's theory is that the charts and cruising guide are enough. He wants to be surprised. Thus, this guide is dated 1980 because our friend James found it at a yard sale. There has to be a certain amount of valid info in it. Some things don't change.

For instance, it tells me Advocate is one of the oldest towns in Atlantic Canada. The Acadians who settled here built extensive dykes between the shore and the barrier beach to recover rich farmland from the sea. This natural barrier beach extends from the rocky promontory of Cape Chignecto to the harbour entrance, below the cliffs of Cape d'Or.

In the three miles before the entrance of Advocate Harbour we see a magnificent array of huge piles of tide-cast driftwood. We have never seen anything like it! Excitedly we start the motor for our approach into the harbour. We have checked the chart and the cruising guide and computed all the information at hand into our little brains. We estimate it is approximately an hour before the high tide. We figure there should be enough water to get into the harbour and enough of the coming tide to take us there.

Most approaches to a harbour have a channel and most of the time this channel that gives you some extra depth is marked. In nautical dreamland the approach is marked by buoys of a certain color and shape. A can is always an odd-numbered green buoy with a flat top, which is used to mark the left side of the channel when entering or returning from seaward. So when you leave the harbour, the can marks the right side of the channel. A nun is an even-numbered red buoy with a painted top, which marks the right side of a channel when entering. I always have to run the little saying through my head each and every time to remember this vital information. *Red, Right, Returning!* Again this reverses when you leave to seaward. The nuns mark the left side.

Are your eyes crossed? I give this tidbit of information to explain that we do have some guidelines upon entering a harbour anywhere.

We smile like it's Christmas morning when we see the harbour dotted with red and green buoys. My body is almost limp with relief that we made it and we have water and buoys! My expert Captain has all my confidence in almost any situation, but this, has to be a relaxing, smooth putt putt into a quiet harbour. La la la la, I casually comment on the style of the houses, the sea scape gardens. We anticipate a walk around town before dark.

There was a stunned silence for a moment—a soft thud stopped us. I cut my eyes over to the Captain—gauging the situation—wanting to know if I should begin to worry. I detect a mood change. I ask with a note of pleading in my voice. "Do think the tide is still coming in? Do you think we will get enough water here to float?"

His eye brows went up—"I hope!"

Ah fa God's sakes—what'a we do now? Complaining gulls swarmed overhead like vultures. We did what we could do, wait. I have this unusual habit of pushing my nose down with my forefinger of my right hand and rubbing my upper lip on it. Perhaps it's not the most attractive pose. "I can tell you're thinking." My husband observes.

"Yeah, I have a feeling there is more than one pair of binoculars focused on us!"

I took action. I did what any normal vain woman would do when she thinks she's center stage. I adjusted my sunglasses, fluffed my hair and held in my stomach.

We were very relieved that we did float. We made it to the town pier but we had no idea of what others would think of our achievement. We never even started to imagine, while planning this cruise to The Minas Basin (again, always said in a deep bass tone—it's important to the drama of the story), that we would be launched into the world of a "celebrity hood." The first of our onslaught of visitors were at the dock to greet.

We receive and give the pleasant salutations one expects when you float into town and meet new people. This steady stream of pleasant, well-meaning new acquaintances offered much more.

A retired fisherman paused from time to time to take off his glasses and rub his eyes, "You know, the water empties outa here, you know?"

Another man with an open rough hewn face which reflected a lot of years on the water, said, "There's only two hours on every tide to get in and out of here, an hour before and an hour after."

One fellow blew out his cheeks thoughtfully, "Do you have a

keel on that boat? The water is emptying out right now and you will keel over! That's five hours on this tide and five hours on the next, before you'll float!"

My husband, a very patient smiling man, tried to explain to all we met, that we have what we professionals call *legs*. This information gave them no tangible proof that we have not absence of mind. One woman laughed outright while her husband narrowed his eyes. The Captain gave them a brief demonstration. They would watch, listen, then shake their heads.

All agreed that we could not be planning to go further into the *Basin* could we? Some regaled us with powerful and personal accounts of the currents and turbulent waters. Ship wrecks back two hundred years.

Another, pointing to the steel gray water covering their harbour, laughed till he cried, recalling seeing us an hour earlier aground next to a green buoy. With tears running down his face he tells us, "Oh, yeah it should be red! But they ran out of that color! Ha Ha Ha!"

There are lots of throat clearing and sharp intakes of breath, preceding comments like, *Isn't this just the livin' end. How the dickens did you get here? What in the sam hill are you talkin' about, LEGS? What in tarnation do you think you're doin' here in a sailboat?*

I have had enough. I escape down into my rabbit hole to straighten our cabin from today's folly. I'm goin' for a slice of civilization. Doug can stay here and put our leg on. We are tied to the dock; he should be able to handle this on his own … ?

I pull out my four-and-one-half-inch mirror and … ah bloody hell!

Day six and I look worse for the wear. I work at arranging myself for a walk into town. The conversation overhead goes on and on with our well wishers, looky loos, doomsayers, and advisors. My ears perk when I hear mention of a bakery, invitations for tea, offers of laundry and showers! My cracked lips smile!

I set off in a determined pace for fresh bread. I try to assimilate all the bits of information I overheard from below. My ambassador of goodwill husband can be very entertaining but I'm the detail person. I would have asked about the bakery, directions for the cuppa tea, and the showers.

I walk for a very, very long time. I am very vague on my facts. I begin to look around for another well-wisher to confirm my compass bearings. Where are they when you need them? Eventually I happen onto the Calder Convenience store. I thought I heard the info-givers say the bakery was next door. I was very charmed by the bucolic setting—cows and large round bales of hay all around—but where's the bakery?

Like most little stores in a rural setting, it tries to cover the basic needs of the locals—a two pump full-service Irving station, a small market, baked goods, sandwiches, pizza, ice cream cones, liquor, beer and a pay phone. I ask the girl behind the counter if this is the only store around.

"Yep!" she confirms. "Unless you want to walk to West Advocate!" she adds with a very wide stretch of the arm indicating a long distance in the opposite direction. I smile inwardly at the correct way of pronouncing the name of this little hamlet. *Add-vo-cate,* long o, vo, and long a, cate.

I inquire about the bakery. "Sure!" she tells me, "raight next door!"

Hum. I give her an eyebrow lift. How did I miss it? I walk back out the same way I came. I look right, then left. "Where?" I ask, peeking my head back into the door.

With a sorrowful, can't you see anything shake of the head and a heavy sigh indicating patience, she says again, "Raight next door!"

So, back out I go.

Sure enough, upon closer inspection, I do see a little house. It has a dropped-down-from-Wizard-of-Oz tornado look. In the corner of one window, I spot a tiny 2" x 4" sign telling me to *Come in.* "Where?" I thought.

I did a solo circumnavigation of the teeny house. I found one door but no indication of a bakery. No entrance sign, no posted hours. I knock—nothing.

I try the door—unlocked. Moving cautiously inside, I stand still to allow my eyes to refocus to the dim light. Sure enough, there is a counter, but, no food.

"Hello! Hello!" No response. I turn and stop, forgetting my quest for fresh bread.

Beside me stood a two-person table draped in kitschy red-flowered plastic. Three 1950 vinyl chairs, a lot like those I grew up with, surround the table which showcases two large boxes that once held breaded chicken parts. The chicken (long gone) has been replaced with *TV Guides* and the latest crochet project.

Elevated above all this, each in its own exalted spot, sit a variety of decorative items. *Grandpa Is a Kid's Best Friend* is artfully displayed in plaster of Paris and a plastic wood grain plaque tells me, *The Lord Giveth and the Government Taketh Away!* My eyes follow the wall around to find another sign, wood-burned this time, *The Definite Age Has Come Where I'm Too Tired Too Work and Too Poor to Quit.* I hear the low hum of a TV in a back room, I decide I should try again to alert them of my presence.

Slowly a smiling sweetheart of a man walks toward me. I notice, at his approach, that he is one and the same as the framed newspaper article dated June 1993. The *Oberon Press*'s "Where to Eat" article chose this little restaurant as one of the top 500 best in all of Canada.

"Yes, " he points proudly to the wall, his hazel eyes merry, "I ran a restaurant here until I had my open heart surgery." He then explains that it stood in front of his house. Sadly, they tore it down. No bread today, just cookies—one kind.

"I'll take what you have, " I assured him. I grabbed my bag, clutched it to my breast, thanked the kind man, laughed at the picture of him and his wife photographed with their favorite WWO Wrestler and opened the door. I cocked both my pistols and stepped out into the street! NO! NO! I'm getting my stories confused. That's a Steve Earl song.

I did step out into the bright warm sunshine and removed a layer of clothing. I had way over dressed for my venture onto shore. I look up and down the road from whence I came. No Captain Doug to be seen. I have a few moments to myself to enjoy the freedom of being warm and on shore.

In a rare, frivolous mood, I dart toward the store and its ice cream counter. I waited while the attendant dawdled toward the two lonely pumps which protruded from the ground. When the customer was fueled by gas and gossip, she returned, at a snail's pace, over the long distance of the gravel parking lot. She checked the pizzas she had been cooking, sold some cigarettes, chips and jerky then turned to her tourist.

The sun melts my ice cream in record time so I fight to keep up. No thought of sacrificing one minute of this warmth by sitting in the shade. Despite the pure joy of the moment, I am not so self-centered as to not even consider my husband. I'll give him some cookies. I wonder what the delay is? I sit licking and looking down the road. Will I walk back to the boat and find it lying on its side the Captain stuck underneath?

It is good to see my husband smiling. Looking calm and confident as he approaches the Calder picnic bench. The leg is on, YES! We have some time before it is urgent to be back at the boat. The Captain suggests that one should never, ever, pass up the chance for pizza. I whole heartedly agree, feeling like a naughty child who ate her dessert first.

I feel obligated to call Bill and Jean, Doug's parents, to advise of our location and mental stability. I need a new phone card. Mine is an US card and not cheap in Canada. I wait for the attendant to return from washing windows and for Doug to order his pizza. I ask her if they have any Canadian dollar phone cards. Then I make use of the WC (water closet).

I occasionally can be of some real help to the Captain. I give my report on the time frame for the pizza, the comical bakery and the vital news that, while using the WC, I jotted down in my trusty notebook—the possible life-changing info of the tide chart for Parrsboro, our next intended destination. Why in the restroom? Beats me. I guess if you are going to meditate while doing your business, what more contemplative thought than the 115 billion tons of water that flushes in and out of the 186-mile length of the Bay of Fundy every six hours and 13 minutes.

I sit, stiffed back, poised like an efficient secretary with a pencil over one ear, ready to give other tidbits. Moosehead beer is twice as much an eight-pack here than in St. Stephens New Brunswick and (I pause for effect then add a slight smirk) the pancake mix I have on board (the Captain stowed it out of its package) is one cup mix to 3/4 cup of water!

"Thanks for the information," he says, "but I cut the instructions from the package for the pancake mix and placed them inside the plastic container."

It is? I hadn't checked. Damn! "I did remember to check for the Canadian dollar phone card; no luck, no phone call. I can wait till Parrsboro." Finishing my report, I haughtily stick my pencil and pad in my backpack.

"Oh, by the way, Eileen" he starts talking with his forearms on the table, hands clasped, as if praying for patience, "when you are in Canada, it sounds ridiculous to ask if they have Canadian dollar phone cards!"

This struck me like a rubber band. This man, whose stage name should be *faux pas* for his naughty behavior—like singing irreverent songs at my friend's catered cocktail party—is telling me I've commented a travel *faux pas?* This man, who has only been to Canada, Tijuana, and Puerto Rico, is telling *me* how to ask for something in a foreign country? I give him a look of someone constipated.

"I'm sorry! I just forgot! It's not a crime—as though I should be placed in an unmarked grave! For crying out loud, we happen to live on a Maine and Canadian Border. Where, if you remember, we find ourselves regularly, for good reason, specifying if we are paying in US or Canadian dollars."

I was furious. I told myself to get a grip, but I will get a grip later! I let him have it—how did I ever manage to travel these last twenty years to seventeen different countries without his guidance? I may be an ignoramus when it comes to sailing but ... I want to gibber on but my eyes start to itch, a sure sign that my nerves are as frayed as our anchor rope. I stomp my feet on the seat of the picnic table, my elbows on my knees, my fists clapped on both sides of my jaws, my back to *the Captain*. I wanted to run away and leave him behind like a bad habit.

I peeked out of the corner of my eye. He sat there wide eyed, like what the hell's come over her! I sat for the next five minutes, my head hid in my folded arms. He had time to calculate his next move. Calmly he concedes. He is the Captain on the high seas but I need no instruction on land.

My heart starts to warm to the fellow—no better thing that a man can do than to admit to being wrong! As well, there is the issue of the pizza. Then my anger flares again—he can take that pizza and ...

I have not one iota of space left in my intestines after the pizza. Of course, I ended up *eating* the pizza. What kind of punishment would that be—not to eat the pizza?

The mood between us was still a bit frosty, so I tested the waters. I ate my pizza with a knife and fork! My husband has long proclaimed this to be a disgusting habit, not at all the proper way to eat a pizza.

The long walk back was made in companionable silence. We had talked enough for one day. Halfway back I stopped and stared at a gravel driveway. Could this be the house where someone offered tea, showers, laundry? I think this is a reasonable question.

"I don't remember." He looked anxious, "Can you walk and talk at the same time? I need to check the boat!" He went on to confess that there was so much chattering about blue pickup trucks, the house with a barn and two large trees next to a garage, one mile this way and straight up a gravel driveway and around the corner, that he couldn't remember what was what.

I just kept smiling and shaking my head. I was too stuffed and tired to care at this point anyway.

The huge harbour, as far as you can see—which seems like miles—is mud. The dock is bustling with fisherman, locals, summer people and tourists. A curious lot really, but with one thing in common, all were there to see the sail boat with one leg, sitting on the mud. We see all kinds of chattering and arm waving going on. A photo journalist could have a hey day.

Back on board, I stretch my neck muscles, for the hundredth time today. Now even more stiff from the need to continually look up from our cockpit to the side show up on the dock.

A couple in their 70's who appeared to be married but looked strangely alike, stood simultaneously shaking their heads. Up and down: "Yes. we've lived here all our lives." Right to left: "No, we've never seen a sailboat here before!" (I might add with a keel)

Mr. Dirty boots and flat cap probed his teeth with a tooth pick, studied us as if we were a new planet, "Powerful currents around Cape d'Or!"

Advocate Harbour
The huge harbour, as far as you can see—which seems like miles—is mud.

Never a dull moment—one salty fellow brandishing a knife for emphasis instead of a pointed finger, warned with a half growl, "Stay clear of black rock, strongest currents in the world!" I gulped

A younger fellow, hands tucked in the back pockets of his pants, laughed over and over as if we had said something terribly funny!

The dude with the most unfortunate hat listened to the continual commentary, some of the stories had a long untidy sprawl of information. Waiting beside him was a dog of an indeterminate breed. As if riveted by our conversation, the dog cocked his head and panted.

"You know, I've been around here a long time, " he paused then spoke a few more words of local knowledge, then stopped. His pauses were so wide the Queen Mary could have passed through with room to spare. So where's he headed with this? Finally, he tells us, "You're gonna need two of them there legs!"

All afternoon and evening we heard a whole lot of *calata'n* goin' on about when we might have enough water to get out of here tomorrow morning. We take into account what they *reckon* and what we *figure*. Then we set the alarm on the Dollar Store clock. The windows of this sleepy town glowed red with the sunset.

We called it a day. Cardiovascular speaking, it had been a long frigin' day. Two a.m. will come all too soon.

Advocate Harbour

Day 7

Thursday, September 6, 2001

I sit up and peek out of the forward hatch. Unmistakably, it is my husband motoring the *Guillemot* out of Advocate Harbour. After the two o'clock alarm, I dropped back on the sleeping bag as if given an anaesthetic. When I woke to the rumbling of the motor I wondered *where, when* and *why?* It's a bit of an eerie feeling to be all cozy in my hidey-hole and realize I'm being removed from where ever it was I last remember being.

I call forward to the Captain. Once again, he assures me that my technical brilliance is not needed at this early, dark hour of departure. I'm rather enjoying being thought of as generally incapable of safely rendering us out to open waters. Not often are we able to see our path entirely empty of water, to know there are not huge rocks lurking, ready to place an unneeded hole in the hull of our little wooden boat.

Seemingly to celebrate the setting of the anchor and the relief of Captain Cold Butt slipping back into bed, a bugle sounds. *The*

Washing Machine Olympics have begun! We are out here in the throughs of things. The large waves from the wind and the heavy current behave like an agitator, whipping our heads and necks back and forth, back and forth, like nothing we've experienced before. I comfort myself by thinking, perhaps, it is firming the ole' jaw line.

There is something to be said for being absolutely exhausted. As much as the conditions tried to prevent sleep, we were able to dose.

"You've got to get out here and see this!" the skipper sounds excited but not stressed. This is always good. I fling myself out of bed and sway, unable to focus my eyes, as if I were trying to find an exit sign after stepping off the Magic Tea Cups.

"What is it?" I question.

"Just get yourself out here!" he replies. I obey direct orders from the Captain. I grab a down jacket on the way out of the zippered companion way door. I half stumble out into the cockpit. The Captain's face is lit pink and orange. Is he sick? He didn't sound sick. He points behind me. I clumped onto the cockpit coushion.

Magnificent, is an inadequate word. We stare, our mouths agape, the sky is ablaze with reds, oranges and pinks. The interior designer in me let loose—knockout orange, papaya, rumba, delicious melon, curry, chrysanthemum, kimono violet, azalea pink, vivacious pink, Eros, ethereal, daybreak! The colors swirled with the bold clouds moving quickly across the horizon.

Now that I'm up, I might as well stay for the full show. To port is the Cape d'Or lighthouse. It fulfilled its duties of warning sailors of the promontory and the rough waters in front of the lighthouse known as the Dory Rips from 1922–1989. Remembering from yesterday's commentary, the area is almost always turbulent because of the violent meeting of the currents from the Minas Basin and the Bay of Fundy. The trusty old guide book tells me that Samuel de' Champlain named this the Cape of Gold in 1604. The rocks that appeared to be gold actually contain veins of copper. They say you can still find copper close by, on the beach of Horseshoe Cove.

Cape Spit is to starboard. The sunrise makes it glow like it's lit for a holy ritual.

Ahead of us, in the far distance, we see what looks to be a scallop dragger. Perhaps it is one of our friendly visitors from yesterday, who mentioned keeping his boat at Spencer's Island.

Gee, look at the time—10:45 a.m.

Even though the sun is bright and the sky is showcasing a few sparse clouds, I'm still wearing my arctic gear and we just hit 8.1 knots with just the main sail up!! "This is fast for this little boat!" the Captain confides.

"So tell me somethin' I don't already know."

Passing Greville Bay we have wind against tide and 8.7 knots. Doug has renamed it *The Bowel of Glooscap*. I would tell you about the legends of Glooscap but it will have to wait. We have some real action goin' on! We're not in Kansas anymore. I am lying on my back with my legs braced on the seat of the cockpit, writing; my trusty pen in hand, recording this for you, my reader. You are likely to be reclined in a lounge chair in Florida or snuggled in front of a fireplace with a hot toddy. Wherever you are, buckle up your seat belts on your easy chair.

Fascinated, we look at the ominous opening of the Minas Basin. Looks harmless enough from here. My husband decides a picture is in order. Oh, the camera? That means I have to let go, stand and move around, balance—the whole business. The skipper sees no problem in this. He can hold the tiller, trim the sails, read the chart, drink a beer, spot something interesting with the binoculars, look up a bird in the Audubon Bird guide, check the G.P.S. and take a picture, all while the boat heels over in a wind that would have blown our old sails to smithereens.

Before I move for the camera, I affirm to my husband, "Sure do like having new sails!" Then blah, I just got a mouth full of sea water from over the side.

Amidst the crashin' and the splashin' Doug looks up to the clouds, "Do you see what I see?" Usually it takes me awhile to see the artwork in the clouds, but this time, I see it immediately. We both chuckle at the sight looming overhead, that of a perfectly formed snail in his shell.

Ah oh, the wind whips and takes my neck with it. I brace myself for the continuance of Mr. Toad's Wild Ride.

"There is an Age of Sail Heritage Center at Port Greville," I read from the guide book. We think how weird it is that at one time, when lumber was exported, a hundred huge sailing ships were built here and sailed all over the world. Now, 120 years later, generations have not seen a sailboat come into their harbours.

The Captain just said the most pleasing-to-the-ear words in the sailing dictionary. "Soon, my sweetie, we will turn and *go downwind!*" he assures me.

"Yes!" I cheer. "*Downwind.* That's what I'm talkin' about!"

I hear the words *downwind* and a smile comes to my poor blistered lips and a tickle flutters up my spine.

Ahead of us there is an enchanting valley. We are hugging close to shore, not wanting to miss any of its beauty. There are a few people roaming the beach and lying around in the warm sunshine. No sign of a road or houses—we wonder how they got there? Lucky ducks! They are in the lee of the wind, so this bright sunshine is beating down warming them! They are probably wearing shorts! Damn Them! I grab the binocs and pull the collar of my down jacket closer around me to protect me from the cold wind blowing over this cold, cold, water. I moan a sigh of relief, at least they aren't in shorts.

Down wind! All righty now! Peace has returned. Now I can say to all those ashore eat your hearts out! I can calmly tell myself what a rarity it is to see this fantastic shoreline from the water. Every turn reveals beauty and around every bend, a marvel. The coastline makes us believe we are in a land that time forgot. We see miles of beaches without a sign of people or houses. Now that I'm calmer, my excitement level increases—weird huh? Just the way I operate.

"Talk to me, Magellan!" Doug orders our G.P.S. (Global Positioning System). "No greater way to spend a 100 bucks!" he speaks with conviction. "Hey look up there!" He directs my attention to the top of a high cliff where some people are stopped on the road, probably to take *our* picture. With the help of the binocs we see they are on a Goldwing. It is the couple that was part of our retinue at Advocate Harbour. They traveled from Massachusetts on their motorcycle and were staying the night at the Cape d'Or lighthouse— now a Bed and Breakfast. The plan was for us to pass by at 9 a.m.,

Minas Basin
... every turn reveals beauty and around every bend a marvel.

their scheduled breakfast time, and they would take our picture. They have all their meals served to them. Umph, I liked them anyway.

The Captain continues all afternoon with his series of comments from the cockpit. "Trim me, trim me, you lazy bastard!" It's the sails' turn to comment as they are flapping and luffing. But as soon as we do trim, the fickle wind comes out of another valley from shore and swishes in both directions. "The wind has its own personality." He struggles to keep his hands on the tiller.

"I believe I learned the methods of sailing in heavy currents in Cobscook Bay." he informs me. Cobscook Bay is Passamaquoddy Indian for Bay of Boiling Waters. We have spent many a day sailing in and around the reversing falls. Sailing there where, *Yankee Magazine* recently proclaimed that you have to be very foolish or very brave to sail, prepared him for sailing in these huge back eddies and rips up the wazoo.

"My eyes are feasting!" he announces. Then he said. before long, "My eyes are gorged! Like when you eat too much and are full but pleasantly satiated. If you can come to the Bay of Fundy and not be awed you might as well just watch the Discovery Channel."

Naturally the wind gives us a kick in the pants just when I take the helm and we enter a heavy current area. The Captain just keeps saying, "Hold her to it! Hold her to it, Eileen!" We are flying. Doug keeps his eye on the sea and the GPS. I feel quite pleased with my self. At one point we hit our maximum speed yet at 11.5 knots. Eeegadds!

We are nearing the dreaded *Black Rock*. I'm happy to hand the tiller over to the expert.

Well, ladies and gentlemen, with a wind behind us and a fair nine knots of current, we make it past Black Rock going 14.8 knots!!!! We had a high ole' time of sailing.

We hang a left at Partridge Island. The spectacular beaches and rocky cliffs set the scene for the Ottawa House; the site was originally an Acadian trading fort built in 1770. In the late 18th century it turned to a dwelling house and Inn. The former prime minister of Canada and Father of the Canadian Confederation, Honorable Sir Charles Tupper used it as a summer home. Today however, it stands white and imposing and according to a brochure I saw in Advocate is used as a museum highlighting the shipbuilding and commercial history of the region.

Onward we sail up to the Farrells River, past a charming light-house and a wharf which looks large enough to take cargo from large cargo ships. Parrsboro looks small and picturesque from the water, although our cruising guide claims it to be the largest com-munity on the north shore of the Minas Basin. The warm sun and the excitement of pulling into town, enhance our difficult 50 tacks upwind and up river. Sailors' patience brought us close enough to row ashore.

Tucked up the Farrells River, close to town, surrounded by marshes and birds we decide to anchor. As if in a choreographed movement, a fellow fishing and a Great Blue Heron jump up from the shore and both move quickly toward us. The bird eclipses the sun as it flies directly overhead, gives a hoarse guttural squawk, then glides down to the edge of the marshy pool. He tucks his five foot wings to rest and watch for fish, frogs and the—what the hell is *that* doing here—a sailboat?

The fisherman, a modern day version of Tom Sawyer, white t-shirt, frayed cut-off jeans, is now standing as close to us as possible and not be swimming. The wind whips up and blows his rather longish, frantic-looking hair, while he waves his arms yelling lengthy welcomes, advice about anchoring and the latest news of fishing striped bass. We try to concentrate on his conversation and not seem rude, but we have to get the anchor down and the sails tied! He moves quickly from one barefoot to the next, spurting out knowl-edge of the weather, the history of his family and the town. He stops, leans against his fishing pole, motionless and silent for a breath or two, then with a burst of energy, rests his fishing pole against his chest, waves his arms frantically, and continues his narrative of how many generations his family has lived here, the years they ran the Ottawa House and something about a summer cottage. He is still rambling on and on as I head down below. I leave my husband to sharpen his social skills by nodding his head at the right moments while coiling the sheets.

I chuckle as I peer out my plexiglass window at the strange man still gesticulating wildly. I'm wondering if he could be some kinda out-patient. I change my shirt, peer into my 4-and-one-half-inch mirror, apply medicine to my lips and wonder if I will be judged harshly for not remembering anything he has told us.

All at once my attention is riveted by words flowing out of the mouth of Mr. Wild Hair-barefoot-cut-off jeans. These words transformed him into my super hero from a parallel galaxy. I ran out to the cockpit, smiled as if I'd won the lottery, placed my hand in the air to halt the continuing dialogue, "What did you just say, before the bit about fishing lures?" Pushing the graying hair out of his face, he cocks his head in thought.

I couldn't wait, "… the part about the bath tub!"

"Oh! I said if you would like to take a bath," he uses his fishing rod to point toward town, "my house is right up there behind those apartments." God Bless this fourth generation Parrsboro man!

"Thanks! I'll be there!" Not even glancing in the Captain's direction.

Port side, Brian bid us adieu, satisfied we had been lured and hooked into a bath and more conversation. I scramble below to grab clothes and my shower bag for our expedition ashore. I drop the shampoo from my bag and quickly bend down to pick it up, in my haste I knock my head on the table—there is hardly room to bend over in here. Moaning, I don't stop, I'm on a mission.

From the starboard direction I hear a small motor approaching. I step out to see a fellow in a small skiff fumbling with the motor and the boat.

THUMP! THUD! His skiff clunks into the hull of the *Guillemot*! The twenty-something guy looks at me, then Doug. In a state of shock I look from the fool to Doug. The Captain speeds over to check if there is a hole in the boat. I expect the dude to start gushing forth apologies.

Instead he leans forward and peers questioningly and anxiously into our faces. He asks, "Have you ever sailed a sailboat before?"

For a brief tense moment, I thought my wanna be pacifist husband, might just throttle the stooge. I was totally confused at what might happen next so I busied myself with my best pushing-away-the-skiff-without-having-it-smash-my-leg routine.

The Captain leans over the side of the boat, sees the big deep scratch—no hole—takes a big, deep, controlling breath, and replies, with interest, "Yeah. Have you ever motored that boat before?"

Steve, we discover, is not so much a jerk as an excited muddle head. Wondering, like those visitors who came before him, what on earth were we doing here?

I let out the breath I didn't know I was holding when I saw that, indeed, there was a Victorian style house awash with flowers up behind the apartments where my tub lived. I felt a warmth toward Brian when he greeted us at the door. I listened patiently to the information, freely given, about his Grandfather who lived in the house for many years; about the story of their constant state of remodel for the last three years; the tour of the kitchen, living room—a quiver of anticipation ran through me—here's the tub and towels.

Resting in the lap of luxury, I take a long contented breath and give a nod of approval for the roomy, clean bathroom of the man who yelled from shore some 45 minutes ago. I thank the Spirit that watches over me—there are still people left on this planet who have not developed a healthy sense of distrust.

I comb my wet hair, reluctantly looking into the small mirror over the sink. I actually laugh. I should have taken a before and after picture. Clean hair and clean underwear does wonders for a woman's disposition.

Then, a nice bit of luck, Ruth came in the back door, home early from her nursing job. Likely wondering who put the ring around her bathtub—she greets us all sitting around the kitchen table. Brian, a lean energetic soul who talks so fast that I'm still trying to digest the first sentence while he's waiting (briefly) for a reply to the last. Ruth, in contrast, is a tranquil woman, with a face of a cherub.

Be back in a tick, Brian assured us. He and the Captain of the up-the-Farrells-River *Guillemot* shut the door behind them. Silence! They were off to check the water level. How will we know when it will be exactly right to tie legs to our little home in the marshes unless you are on board? There is not a tide chart for this exact area up the marshes. How fast does the tide run out way up here? Like most inlets, there are usually sections that empty of water quicker than others. Doug has put both the legs on only once by himself in a trial run back home on the rocky shore of Broad Cove.

What a busy evening this turned into. The boys, all patience and consternation, ran back and forth and back and forth checking the boat; finally they stay aboard and wait 'till it hit the rock, gravel, mud or whatever is under there. The Captain really thought he could handle the leg ordeal on his own. This being our first dry run (and I do mean dry) of our journey and not being tied to a dock or *The Sea Monster.*

Ecstatic as a kid at FAO Schwarz, to have a sailboat up the river, Brian came to the rescue of Doug's semi-competent first mate, by being there, on-the-ready, to assist in whatever way the Captain needed to be assisted.

Joy and relief spread through me to have a quiet few hours talking face to face (not from low in a boat to someone high on a dock) to Ruth about houses, gardens, kids and remodeling (not tides, boats, fishing and our irrational sailing behavior). The hours are lovely and she's so sweet that I have an urgency to confide something, anything.

I can't even think of anything to confide until our little tour commenced of their kitchen redo-project in the rear of the house. I see their undertaking closely resembles the in-need areas of our Eastport home. I make a comment to that effect. Ruth, her hand gripping the stair railing faltered a little bit, protesting, "it can't look this bad!"

I confided that, "Yes, indeedy. It did."

Car tires crunch softly on the driveway. Shawn, a friend of Brian and Ruth's, from Halifax, pays a surprise visit. Shawn, a youthful looking man, is an environmental biologist at the Halifax airport (I never knew they had such things). He's here for a "little fly" weekend, wanted to let them know he was in town, then rushed off for a "little fly" before dark. The fellow seemed so intelligent and sensible, I presumed he meant in an airplane.

The two from the marshes returned, reporting a successful legup job. Doug reported, when all was said and done, that the twoleg job is positively a two-man job. The minute Brian is told of

Shawn's visit, his eyes sparkled—yes—I would say they positively sparkled. Then he turned on his bare heels, "Let's go watch him touch down!"

Doug was caught in the grip of his contagious enthusiasms and followed his host out the door. "What could be so exciting about seeing a plane touch down?" I ask stable Ruth.

Paragliders are what they call themselves. We're talkin' jumping off cliffs! Brian, as it turns out, is like an assistant instructor to his friend, Michael Fuller's, local paragliding school. He and Brian even host the *Atlantic Fly In* weekend in May. When Brian, Doug and Shawn return, Brian speaks with evangelical zeal to his captive audience about this flying gig. His insatiable feelings, seemingly instilled from a superhuman source, flowed, as he showed pictures and videos. This guy is off the charts.

I have an uneasy feeling ... don't tell me ... it's too impractical ... inconceivable. Out of the question! Doug is not getting the fever is he? This fellow, as helpful as he is, should be kept in quarantine.

Somewhere between all this commotion, Ruth serves up a tasty dinner. I relish the time in their comfy home, around their kitchen table. Doug has played a few happy tunes on his guitar. I can see the Captain is fading. Discreetly checking the time, we share the look of "it is positively time to go!" Our 2 a.m. alarm, our washing machine Olympics, our sailing at record-breaking speeds since the crack of dawn, the warm room, good food makes us droopy-eyed.

Standing at the front door (I love front doors), we finish with all the "delighted to meet ya business." Doug dons his tall rain/mud boots. Brian, out of the corner of his eye, gives me an uncertain look and asks, "Eileen, where's your boots?"

I draw a blank and looked to my Captain for help. I gave a light laugh. The trouble with light laughs is they don't always come out the way you want them. I gave myself a mental slap-on-the-head. What was I thinking? Answer? I *wasn't* thinking! This is what happens when you're peeling an empty banana.

But, my husband/Captain is supposed to save me from these tactical errors. I pause here for a moment to let you imagine—as I did—if all the water is gone from Farrells River to wherever it goes. If our floating paradise is sitting on its legs like a 4, 000 lb. woman, precariously balanced on one pointy high-heel, then there must be a world of mud out there. Ah, my cruel and relentless fate! There is a sizeable distance between the high water mark on shore and my sleeping bag.

Brian spotted my quivering, stiff upper lip. He coughed and cleared his throat (I'm starting to get sick of people doing that!) and leaves us standing at the door; me with my shoulders slumped, arms to my side, my backpack already on my back. He reappears with a pair of flat, black mud-smeared boots.

"See if these fit! They're Ruth's. She hates to wear them."

Mere words were inadequate. I gave them both hugs.

"Are you sure you don't want to spend the night?" the perfect host and hostess ask in unison. They are obviously people of high moral fiber. What a delicious thought! I look longingly down the hall. I close my eyes and smile in of memory beds and toilets. My too-tight boots squeak as we exit their cheerful home.

The path to the sweet Victorian with its halcyon garden, which housed my tub, is by way of ditches, bushes, high marsh grass, gravel slopes and muddy rocks. All this didn't seem so bad this afternoon. As matter a fact, I barely remembered walking to their house. I was single-minded then, as visions of bathtubs danced in my head.

Tonight, however, exhausted and in the pitch dark, my life changed.

Doug never seems to need a flash light. I always carry one in my backpack because, frankly speaking I would just as soon not twist my bad knees in some dark ditch. Most of you out there in normal land have street lights and porch lights in your everyday world. I don't seem to benefit from those inventions much these days.

I let Doug go ahead. I like to go at my own pace, slow and careful. Half-way back to the boat, in the dark, I trip into a bramble patch, I keep my groans to a minimum. This is a lot more than should be required of a sweet loyal wife, but ahh, the paths of love never run smooth. When I arrive at the high water mark, I see the silhouette of the boat. I survey my next steps with utter dismay: lots of slick muddy rocks leading to the mud.

With loads of luck I make it to the mud without falling on my patootie. Eeehhhhuuuuuyyyuuucccckkk!!! It is a foot-slogging *splat,*

splat, splat. The mud is so deep and gooey it pulls off my too-tight boots. My husband stands at the stern of the boat, checking my progress. He seems to think this is somehow hugely amusing.

I arrive at my destination with an air of subdued triumph. I certainly have no intention of doing that very often! Doug pulls the dinghy under the tiny boarding step on the stern, in a chivalrous gesture. I can now step on the dinghy and take one giant step for mankind up to the boarding step and try to hoist my bod aboard.

I find this somewhat similar to mounting a horse. Denise and Paul, our friends in North Carolina, provided me with the gentlest horse they owned. The downfall was that it was also the biggest. Me and my short legs! God forbid if I'd worn jeans that weren't suitable for a yoga stretch.

"WOW! What a day," my husband echoes my thoughts as we cuddle in the V-berth, laughing. I'm thinking about my bath. He's probably thinking about ... well, I'm not sure if I want to get into what he's thinking about. Let's say for the written record—we'll continue with the sailing theme. Evidently Brian had seen us go by the Ottawa House. Surprised, and as if following the circus into town, he ran all the way along the path to meet us here in the marshes. Brian, in all his elation, insisted that we stay on another day, to enjoy Parrsboro.

The tide gives no man a break. We do our calculations then set our alarm for 4:30 a.m. We will do the preliminary check of the water level and make a guesstimate of when we might settle on the river bottom and reset the legs.

At lights out, a mocking bird is singing energetically. Exhaustion overtakes us. We listen silently. All we can manage is a weak-willed *Hubba Hubba!*

Day 8

Friday, September 7, 2001

I shiver as I pull on my long johns. My goose bumps calm themselves as I layer the clothing. I stretch my new boating gloves over my hands, like a surgeon preparing for an operation! As if sterilized, I hold my hands in front of my face, palms in. I check my grippers. I note the time, 6:15 a.m. I burst through the flapping plastic doors of the companionway, ready for operation LEGS UP!

At 4:30 a.m. the Captain rose to check *Guillemot's* condition and her vital signs. She was only five centimeters dilated, not ready for delivery of impact, she still had plenty of water to keep her happy. Reset the alarm, crawled back in bed.

We stand at attention, waiting to be on hand for delivery. Wait-Wait-Wait! As in most occasions of my life when I've forced myself out of bed early in the morning and then forced myself outside, I find it a gratifying experience. Today I find great beauty in the noiselessness. There is a difference in soundlessness and noiselessness. Noises represent sounds made by motors, car doors, talking, radios and so on. This crisp clear morning is noiseless but not soundless. I hear the gentle wind, the swishing marsh grasses, the fish splattering and the pandemonium of the birds, all of which are amplified by the noiseless hush of the village.

"Stat! Stat! Code Blue! Here she goes!" I stand on starboard, holding tight to the halyards (thrilled with my gloves, or my hands would freeze, I see patches of ice everywhere). I lean as far off the toe rail as I can safely render myself. The delivery doctor is to port, setting and tying the leg. When he gives word, "Reverse!" I race over to port and he to starboard to set and tie the leg on this side. I say race, but as in an operating room you move swiftly and steady as to not upset the patient. *Voila! Stilts!*

The Captain stays on duty. He checks the strain on the ropes every few minutes. He loosens or tightens the ropes according to the shift of the boat, the wind and the level of the ground underneath.

I'm sure you all perfectly understand what I'm talking about— whatever! I'll let Doug write the technical manual for using the legs— all I want to do is go back to bed and sleep till the crack of noon.

I have secret dreams of a lavender scented linen closet until I hear my husband's very best, not soothing, you've-slept-long-enough tone of voice!

"Cow says Hello!" he yells as he climbs aboard. He stuffs the cold beer under the bedcovers. Now what? I jerk violently, push ... What's with that? Cow? Don't test me, I'd fail the test!

All I can think is, Cow? Is he talkin' about a Canadian relative of our beloved and cherished CowCar?

Our dear CowCar was (it has since gone to the by and by) my extremely reliable '79 Buick station wagon. I drove that sucker for five years—best car I've ever owned. I've had Mercedes', Jaguars', Porches, Corvettes and Volvos (all plural) just to mention a very few ... but the CowCar was the best car I ever owned. We pulled her out of Frank and Colleen's cow pasture in PA. She spent two years of her precious life with the cows who shared her home. They kept her company by licking her brown paint with their sand paper tongues. She was not much on looks—inside or out—with sun-rotted upholstery and her paint job of matte finish in cowlick brown, but she ran like a good ole' girl.

I've gotten rather use to my husband's tendency to get up close and personal with the bucolic life, but the conversations do not normally include salutations to me or the beer he is happily clutching in his hands.

My eyes focus—9:30 a.m.—Clancey's Beer. Beaming, he reports, "Cow is a real character. He gave me a beer!" I can tell he has really taken a liking to whom or whatever this *Cow* is because he classifies him as a real *character* who gave him a beer; which both rank high with Doug!

"He was a drummer in a rock band in Toronto!" I am slightly amused. Who else, I ask you, besides *Captain Beaver*, Captain of the sailboat secured by two poles in the mud of the Farrells River, can be given a beer by a rock star named Cow, by 9 a.m. on a Friday morning?

The Captain stayed awake after the early morning operation. He managed to do about 10 fix-it jobs while I slept like a drunken sailor. He mudded ashore and found, not far from our place in the marshes, the MV KIPAWO.

"What?" I ask, "A strange new marsh bird?"

The MV KIPAWO he explains, is the last of the Minas Basin's ferries. The name of the ferry was taken from the places it stopped— Kingsport, Parrsboro and Wolfville. A group rescued it from salvage to house a summer theater. The maintenance man for the theater was busy this a.m. putting the final touches on the closing of the theater for the season. The maintenance man is none other than *ROCK STAR COW.*

I am hell bent on doing the laundry, on this 8th day aboard. I am merrily collecting our two loads from the dark recesses of our floating closet, when we have three visitors. Number one is Brian, arms flapping at his sides, anxious to see if the children have gotten themselves into any trouble. He offers his washing machine. Says he doesn't have a dryer but a clothes line. Tempting, but we make the judgement decision to get it done all at once—we are walking to town anyway.

Number two and number three almost appeared to be the same person except one is taller. Both stand ashore examining us, as through a microscope. Both call an indefinite number of knowledgeable questions to the Captain. Both stand, hands behind their backs, feet spread almost at attention. Both gentlemen are pushing or past the 80 mark.

We've had enough of this divergent way of conversing and we were going ashore anyway so we splatted in their direction.

Both friends grew up in Parsboro and left at a young age to pursue their careers at sea in the oil business. Both returned home to Parsboro, when given leave, to their homes, wives and children. Both traveled world-wide and thought Parsboro the best of all of it. Both retired 20 years ago, back to Parsboro, after their 30-year careers. Both were named Robert—no, I'm just joking. I don't even remember their names, but both offered tea and laundry at their houses. Both pointed to a lovely spot overlooking the town harbour. Both had eyes which were wide and knowing with life beyond North America. We thank them ever so much. I would love to hear of their travels and their life here in Parsboro.

Maybe later, but at that moment we were on a mission. *Get the damn laundry done then we can play.*

The warm coats and gloves of the early morning is only a vague memory as we walk the shore to the road. What a day! By this time the sun was well into the sky and had gathered some heat. In our shorts and cottons shirts we are almost skipping along, ready to enjoy even the duties of laundry in beautiful Parsboro. A sparrow keeps circling us while she "tsiped" her monosyllable sound.

We stop. Before us stands the MV KIPAWO. Yesterday we had seen the building, but from the rear. From our vantage point then, it looked more like a warehouse.

From the wings of the theater steps a ghostly apparition with a black leather coat flung open like bat wings to his knees. I jumped back, slightly shocked, until he blessed us with his broad smile and cheery, "Hello Mate and welcome Love!" Cow was a blast of unruly hair and goofy enthusiasm. His handshake felt like a tourniquet. Beaming with pleasure, he gives us a tour of the theater. His commentary on the workings of the theater informs us that the *Ship's Company Theater* offers a unique venue to perform Canadian plays with an emphasis on new works from the Atlantic Canadian Playwrights.

He left us to poke around and enjoy the sounds of the echoing empty room.

His eyebrows are hoisted high, when he returns. He is so pleased that fate has thrown us together that he has devised a plan! A plan, even more shocking, that he has already put into effect! He has called a taxi! We assure him we like to walk.

"No, No, Oh No, too far!"

"Too far to where?" We ask.

"Too far to the beer store!"

I assure him we weren't going to the beer store. I look at Doug—at least I wasn't!

"Too far to the beer store and then up to my house!"

My husband and I look at each other and do some eye rolling. We need to do the *laundry*, we tell him again. Grinning with satisfaction and waving his hands as if he were playing an imaginary set of drums ending with a cymbal crash. "You, my dear friends, can do laundry at my house!"

Doug laughs and pats him on the shoulder. "Thanks a lot man, but we just want to get it done and ..." he broke it off. Cow has a disappointed look on his face—as though he'd been bitten in the leg by a close friend.

In a wild cloud of dust and loud noises our taxi pulls up and slams to a stop on the gravel driveway. Neatly tucked in the passenger seat are two 8-packs of Labatts Bleu.

We are in the taxi on a beautiful ride in the opposite direction of town. We make a fast sharp right up a steep hill to Cow's Barn, or, as it turns out, a charming little house. We stop by a garage door.

Cow jumps out, races out of sight and leaves us, Andrew (the taxi driver) and the beer behind. Doug looks quizzical when I check for his reaction. Doug asks if this is Cow's house?

"Yeah!" Andrew assures us.

"So this is where we're going?"

"Oh yeah," Andrew pats the beer. Doug looks my way and does the arms out, palms up, for, *I dunno?* I fidget in my seat. We wait. Doug asks Andrew about driving a taxi in a small town like Parsboro—I don't even listen. I give my "mate" the wide-eyed, brow-furrowed look of *what is going on?*

Minutes later ... well by golly, Cow returns, gives Andrew the money for the ride and the beer. We are free to get out, ransom paid.

Cow leads us through the house, past the kitchen where Rosie, Cow's wife and the artist in residence, has painted cows everywhere! He points to the back deck, Taa Daa! A fantastic view! The sun is hot and the sky a clear, burning blue, like the blue you get by scattering salt on the fire, blurred at the edges with heat haze.

The nourishing sounds of the beers being popped only improve the moment. I want to sit in full view of the trees and the Minas Basin and yet not have my face and lips exposed. My Tilley's hat, Blistix, and sun screen are in place but YEOWZA! Am I burning! The clear intense sunshine of this 7th day of September is just too much!

I choose my seat and flash Doug a shocked expression; he caught me before I fell over into the steep embankment. I had sat on a less-than-stable portion of the deck.

Wanting to be the perfect host, Cow directs me to the basement laundry area. The gyrating motion of the washer makes my neck hurt. Our host directs my attention to the back of the basement, filled with memorabilia of his rock days. Surrounding his drum set are all sorts of novelties, including a 5'x6' poster of Mr. Bean and a computer-printed photo of a biker dude with his face ripped off. There's an assortment of other photos of friends, fans or whoever, most of whom appeared to be the type you wouldn't mind meeting face to face, once you were comfortably behind plexiglass.

We heard loud noises coming from his stereo, which was meant to be music. He is the self-proclaimed biggest "Rush" fan in the world. Funny—I thought my son Kyle was.

He tries to show us a rock video but we keep edging our way back outside for more blackberries from his yard and conversation with his pet turtle dove.

In between beer and laundry, Cow entertains us richly with stories of Toronto, his family from England, and his real love, Nova Scotia. He stopped periodically to assure us, with his infectious smile, "You guys rock, you're brilliant!"

Rosie came by briefly on her lunch break. She works at the hardware store. "Do they have mud boots?" I anxiously inquire.

"Oh, they surely do. Baffins even!"

I don't want to admit I have no idea what a Baffin is. Rosie, a diminutive gal, as sweet as can be, shyly presents me with a delightful pin. A tiny piece of wood intricately painted with the image of the Parsboro lighthouse.

Once our comrade is a bit in his cups, we stop him several times from sitting on the over-the-steep-side-of-the-embankment-part of the deck. He tells us of his brother's death a few years back, which produces tears. He displays his emotions as visibly as wash on the line. Hair standing on end, his rheumy eyes watering, we both give the big guy a friendly hug.

We hate to be party poopers but the laundry is completed, the beer almost gone. We begrudgingly leave the sturdy part of the deck and our big teddy bear of a host. The fact is, we do have several things we need to accomplish while here in Parrsboro.

This is the picture I choose to hang on my mind's wall. The two of us drunkenly tromping down his steep road, swinging our large bags of laundry, our faces covered with broad grins. We wave back at Cow, still carefully balanced on his deck, shouting at the top of his lungs, "You rock. You're brilliant!"

Nothing could be more absolutely certain than that we are enjoying ourselves!

The long walk back to town was shortened by hearty laughter, boisterous talk, and the unbearably beautiful day. I was transported to a tropical island, the slightly humid breeze and the tranquil roads were so delicious we didn't want it to end.

There she is! The "G" is floating serenely upon the water. The dinghy is securely tied to her stern. My husband walks ahead of me, his laundry bag thrown over his shoulder, beautiful marsh grasses surrounding him. It's a Kodak moment not to be missed!

It is not until the camera has clicked and I hear the sound of the film advancing that I really observe what my camera has captured. Hum. There is something very wrong with this scene. I stand unmoving and wait. I watch my husband move toward the edge of the shore. Suddenly he stops, puts the bag down, places his hands on his hips, gives a look to the sky for encouragement. He does a few shakes of the head, grabs his bag'o laundry and follows

Parrsboro
*There she is! The "G" is floating serenely upon the water. The dinghy is
securely tied to her stern ... Hum. There is something very wrong
with this scene. I stand unmoving and wait.*

his footsteps back up the grassy hill. He has a look on his face of a person calculating his next step on a tight rope.

I watch him come toward me. How do we deal with this crisis, if a crisis it be? I gaze hopelessly back at the boat. I inquire of the Captain what should we do? I stick out the lower lip do a little nod toward our home upon the water.

The skipper's eyes are twinkling. "I have a secret plan!"

"You mean you have to swim out to get the dinghy?" I ask.

"Probably!" he laughs!

"We can't just wait till the water leaves and splat out to retrieve the dinghy?" (I have a short second of unreasonableness).

He patiently explains, "If we wait for the tide to go out, not only will it take at least 5-6 hours, but, we won't be on board to set the legs. She'll be lying on her side for God only knows how long before she floats again."

I have to agree with this flawless logic. Like a dimwit I forgot for a moment about the *legs*. We burst into a peal of laughter. I didn't bother reminding the skipper that I'd mentioned the dinghy upon our departure (to the place where people have machines that plug in), only to be told we would be back "in time."

Our brains are way to fuzzy to devise some cunning plan for getting back on board, until we have some lunch. I quickly scribble a note to Ruth and Brian explaining our predicament and that we went for lunch. We place our laundry and note in their foyer next to their note, telling us to "help ourselves" and the hours they would likely be home.

Up ahead the streetlights hold banners commemorating Parrsboro's famous geological find of the world's smallest dinosaur print. At Main Street we see a little restaurant to the right. The window beside the entrance holds numerous signs. One caught my eye; in large bold letters it reads "T-Bone $.25." The line below this reads, in small letters, "with meat $15.00."

"Pon, me soul I'm dryer than a corn meal fart!" Doug quotes our new friend, Cow, as we take our seats at the counter. Waiting for our fish burgers, we sip our large glasses of water. Judging from their friendliness with the waitress, the two guys down the bar are locals. A weather-beaten, squinty-eyed fellow talks with his buddy next to him, a dude with short, cropped grey hair. Mr. Squinty-eyed wears a navy sweatshirt with the arms cut out, which tells us he is someone's Uncle Bill. He informs his friend and all those in ear shot, "Most of these tourists act like they get their money for free."

Plaintiff noises issued from the TV (held in high esteem by a bracket on the wall), points out the latest way the government has decided to spend our money. The woman newscaster with black saran wrapped hair is trying desperately to say the same things she said yesterday in a new way.

The room is dark and cool, but we've had enough TV and being inside on this gorgeous day. We survey the remains of our lunch, we haven't left much but what we left we took.

I glance at my list for our big shopping spree, I read aloud, "Postcards, lip cream, food, clock and boots."

Mr. Optimist/Tightwad pipes in, "Clock? What if our old one starts working? Why spend money on a new clock when the loud ticker is still ticking? Besides if we are really desperate (he means if I get really desperate, the Captain never seems to be desperate) the GPS shows the time!" See what I have to deal with? I roll my eyes to the back of my head and cross 'clock' off my list.

A block before Ruth and Brian's house is a nifty bakery. I buy a scrumptious looking dessert for them and cookies for us. "Hooty Hoot," we call as we invade through the front door. Brian, the man of many resources, comes through to save the day again! He has a canoe. Happy happy happy!

Doug rows out to retrieve the dinghy. I, on the other hand, have some important research to do with the water closet. Brian insisted that I document in my journal what it feels like to take a bath two days in a row! I note, for scientific purposes, that it tends to induce hypnotic trances.

I tiptoe through the rooms as though I might disturb someone asleep. The house seems so large and quiet here all alone. I shiver with excitement as I brew a cuppa tea and casually poor it into a proper tea cup with a saucer, perfectly balanced, nothing sloshing. I walk, calm and poised, to a room with which most of you are familiar.

The name escapes me.

You know what I'm talking about—sofa, lamps, coffee table, fireplace, artwork, large window—the whole business. I settle myself in on the cozy sofa, for a nice read of a magazine.

No, I don't want to read about paragliding, I'm not interested in what chemicals you should (or what I think should not) use on your lawn, no travel articles with beautiful people in fancy hotels. I'm not interested in who is screwing whom in Hollywood ... Oh, here's one! Recipes. I just ate so it's safe to look at food.

Ooooh! Next page is about rockweed! In the system of bays around Eastport: the Passamaquoddy, Cobscook, Whiting and several others, there is so much rockweed you start to get sick of it. I know, I know, there is a huge eco system that lives in there, important to the life of the bays. The big news is that they want to harvest the rockweed and ship to Japan or wherever. Shock, Shock, they want regulations *before* they start harvesting! Not after they've depleted most all the resources and changed the eco system in the bays forever!

In the past I've taken a few bags of dried weed off the beaches to my garden to enrich the soil but, holy smokes, this article really raves on. It's a rich non-polluting source of natural organic minerals and trace elements, amino acids, carbohydrates and several essential plant growth hormones. Wow! If that's not enough, it increases the capacity of the soil to retain water in times of drought and acts as a soil conditioner! I have a whole new respect!

The little town appears like a tour video stuck on fast-forward. We are whiiizzzing through in Brian's pigmy of a car. Omi-God! There is the giant statue of The Mighty Glooscap! Doug and I try hard to keep a straight face when our tour guide points it out as one of highlights of the town.

Sometimes, I casually say (actually, often this I must admit) that's the funniest thing or that's the stupidest, dumbest, ugliest (you get the picture) I've ever seen! Doug calls me on it—THE STU (STOOOO) PIDEST? THE UGLIEST! YOU HAVE EVER IN YOUR LIFE SEEN? You mean in your whole ENTIRE life, Eileen?

I'll fix him. Now I say, THAT'S *ONE* OF THE MOST RIDICULOUS THINGS I HAVE EVER SEEN! Anyway, for the record, we both agreed, The huge statue of The Mighty Glooscap

Parrsboro
The huge statue of The Mighty Glooscap *was/is probably one of the craziest things we have ever seen in our entire lives. It gave us huge laughs—what more do you want from a statue?*

was/is probably one of the craziest things we have ever seen in our entire lives. It's like this paper-mache crinkle thing. We have a picture with Doug hugging its leg for dear life. It gave us huge laughs—what more do you want from a statue?

We can see the cliffs where they'll be jumping. High atop the cliffs is a giant wind catcher. Even from the main road you can tell a whole lot about the wind. Why get yourself and your gear all the way up to the cliffs if there is not some fair wind? We hang a quick left onto a dirt road. I hold tightly to the arm rest to keep from flying over to the driver's seat. Fifteen minutes later we evacuate the car to trudge up MaMa Mia hill.

Brian, a healthy 56-year-old, leads the way carrying a very heavy bag with his kite and all his needed gear. I try to not appear winded when we reach the jump sight. I say, taking deep breaths, you are in great shape—that bag must weigh a ton. I tried to lift it and barely got it off the ground.

Mr. Kite Man tells us he used to have terrific pain from his varicose veins, which we can see bulging from his legs. He proclaims, that after making this trek regularly, his legs feel 100% better!

Brian explains, in the stifled tones considered appropriate in consecrated surroundings, "This is part of their instruction weekend for a higher level of certification. They are to decide on their own when they should jump. Michael asked me to hold back so it won't influence their decision." Brian goes on to explain that once you become expert, you can pick your own jump and land locations. Shawn, his buddies, and Michael, their instructor, have been up here for a long while waiting for the right conditions.

The beautiful day and fantastic views make my afternoon complete. We waited, talked and waited some more. No jumping. Humm, jump and land locations? I have time to ponder all this. Jump location. You have to be able to get up to the cliff with all your gear. The wind has to flow through that valley to take you to your 'perfect' land spot. The property owners need to be in favor of this little drop from the sky and finally, and foremost in this day of litigation, are they liable if you happen to go splat on their land? I don't know.

I ask one of the fliers for the time. He has a watch big enough to call the mother ship. There is only one 'fly' in the ointment here—we are starting to get a little antsy about the boat and when she might hit hard.

Darn, we really want to see someone jump. At least, Doug wants to see someone jump—it all makes me nervous. We can't wait another minute. We really have to go! We run down the hill, leaving Brian to ride with his friends. We jump in the miniature car, seatbelted in.

I prepare for take off. Ahh Oh! It doesn't start.

The Captain/mechanic opens the hood, fiddles with the battery cables. Nothing. I'm silently calculating the time, the tide, the ride back, the row in ... the little mite of a car refused to sputter. I console myself with the fact that Doug has seldom ever failed to tap, probe, prod, flick or somehow caress any car in just the right spot to get her engine to respond! Yet. Could this be *the* time, his Midas touch doesn't work?

I silently think positive thoughts. I call on the powers of the Universe to get us there on time. Twenty minutes later ... Snort, Snort, the roaring-small-engine-noise erupts, she comes alive. Brian's car seemingly darts off the hill under its own power. With many bounces, jumps and crashes over a few ruts and rocks, we make it down the hill, off road, run. Once on the main road (at least we think it's the main road) we pray it is the right road back to town.

I strain to look up out of the car window, Yes! There is the wind catcher, we should be on the road to town. Still, no flyers. Looking way up at that huge steep cliff, I remember the beautiful views, the tension amongst the flyers deciding when they should jump. There must be something missing in part of their brains—maybe a large part. A carburetor perhaps? I can tell you all, with my hand held high and never before with so much fervor, unless someone pushed me off that cliff, the winds would *never, ever* be right!

We speed along. It is like a race to the hospital; the labor pains are frightfully close together. When we approach our little hideaway in the marshes, we peek through trees, houses, buildings and apartments trying to glimpse her condition. To the uninitiated eye, she appears as any other boat, bobbing gently. We sigh with relief, still bobbing. We know that within a very few minutes she will lie over on her side and perhaps poke a nasty rock in her belly.

As close as our mobile will safely render us to the edge of the marsh, we squeal to a halt. We practically slide down the rock-strewn slope over nameless slimy objects.

"Hang in there ole' girl. We're coming!" the Captain soothes. "We would not forsake you in your hour of need."

As though in response the current gives her a little jerk. My assured, practical, self-reliant Captain rows to her faster than I would be able to get the oars in the oar locks. All the while, I'm timing contractions, checking all around me for some indication of how much time before she hits the hard. Focus, focus, I say, as we the midwives rush aboard. Deep cleansing breath, slow exhale.

I half-expect the Captain to start yelling, push, push! Instead his orders are to, man the toe rail!

We have a much needed tranquil evening aboard. After our big midday meal, we decide on merely an evening snack. The old Maritimers would call it a bed lunch. We are quietly reading and writing. From where we are sitting, here in the marshes, I see no visible signs of mankind living in the 21st century.

This gives me a sense of this place when occupied by the *Mikmag (Me-Mac) Indians*. History tells us that they were possibly the first to live and hunt here. Archeologists have found implements from a caribou hunting camp dating 6,000 years before the building of the pyramids of Egypt. Isolated finds of fluted-stone spear tips confirm the *Paleo Natives* were in the maritime region 11,000 years ago. Thoughtful of the natives and dinosaurs that wondered here before us, we watch as the sun descends into the cloudless sky. We soak in the solace of a safe beautiful autumn evening.

Day 9

Saturday, September 8, 2001

From the arms of Morpheus we awaken, refreshed. There are privileged nights in which we can sleep with the forward hatch open. Most September nights, at least up in the Atlantic Provenances, are not buggy. The insects have gone their merry way to hibernate, lay eggs, die or whatever they do to prepare for attack in the spring. To enjoy an mild evening in September is an extreme delight. We can lie in the V-berth and the open hatch frames the stars. At one point, in the middle of the night, we awakened to find it perfectly framing the moon. We call it our TV.

The beautiful morning has only the distraction of my swelled, cracked and bleeding lips. Now I'm really look'n good. The placating Captain tells me I still look pretty. I notice deep wrinkles around his eyes as he squints in my general direction.

I have very little time to primp anyway, because its *leg time.* I dress well enough to keep from exposing something no one would want to see—better safe than sorry. I rush out to the deck, only to *wait.* While we wait, I help to adjust the boat by pulling on the anchor line and tying the cleat tighter to keep us from changing our location as much. The wind circles around us and we swing toward the bank. In an attempt to keep us away from the bank, we use a leg as a lever against the boat. Poised for action, I wait, wait, wait.

Finally, she hits the bottom and it is operation *legs up.* I hang off the toe rail like I'm on a cable car in San Francisco. A thought occurs to me, at this moment—a thought which does no good for the state of my mental health. Under slightly different circumstances, I could be doing this same maneuver at 3am in heavy winds and cold rain. Oh joy!

"Ahoy Mate!"

A voice from ashore gets our attention. From below, we check our clock. It is already 7am. What took them so long? We step through the companionway to see our familiar apparition.

The Captain calls to Cow. "Best time I've ever had doing laundry!"

Cow inquires about our departure schedule. Maybe today, we tell him. He sighs like there was no reason to go on living.

Doug asks how the rest of the day and night treated him after we left. Cow shakes his head, calls out to us voice full of amazement, "It's a night I'll never remember!" We all laughed and then Cow followed up with, "I was right out of 'er."

From here I can see he is bleary-eyed and dead for sleep. He turns to galumph his way home from his Friday night festivities. He stops, waves, and with a robust and hearty voice, he calls, "You're brilliant! You really rock!"

At 9A.M. our patron saint of tubs and canoes, Brian, solicited our attention. He inquired of our schedule and well-being—as though he receives an hourly wage to watch out for us. He calls from ashore, "How about breakfast at the Little Lighthouse Café?"

Hey, when opportunity knocks I'm ready. I don't want to be left below finding my socks. With success proportionate to my efforts, I splatted ashore. I hate having an audience for my award winning performance. I trudge up the rocky embankment and through the marshes to Brian's squirt of a car.

Yesterday, in a newspaper article clipped on the counter in their kitchen, I read about the death of Brian's father a week ago. Here at the café, the conversations and greetings went from, "How's your Mum doing?—Your Dad was a good man.—The fishing been good this week?—Been golfing lately?"

Brian orders a cuppa tea. He had porridge earlier, then entertains us while we pick the ham out of our cheese omelets. He pulls out several stacks of photos of his trip last year to the South of France. Super shots of a Provence and Monaco that I missed. Could it be because they were from the air, attached to a kite?!

Doug's interest seems piqued. Oh, heavens to murgatroid! I make a mental note to make sure I order more life insurance.

This man is one of those people who shouldn't be allowed to drink caffeine. It is when we step outside the café door that we realize Brian isn't finished with us yet. Driving us to a beach within eyesight of the light house, talking as fast as a person can talk and not be a recording on the wrong speed, he has time to tell us of the hitchhiking days of his youth. For many years he went all over Canada and the US, but always returned to Parsboro. When he parked and scurried out the car door to the trunk of his car my husband and I had no idea what we were in for.

He has his flying gear strewn all over the beach. The announcement comes—it never occurred to me, on this mild September morning, that Doug would be in for his first ground lesson for paragliding. The reflex movement of my husband's eyes revealed surprise. I am pleased as punch he never considered inviting the likes of me to participate. The huge tides provide acres of beaches for practice and landing. Mr. Loquacious Instructor's eyes take on a dreamy look as he tells us that autumn brings some great winds, which they call magic. It is magic when the warm wind comes off the land and produces gusts, which take you up and keep you there, for a rip-roaring ride!

I can see the joy in that. I feel, possibly, where and how I landed might suck the fun out of everything.

Driving back to the boat, we mention Cow and his brief visit to the boat. Brian chuckles when he tells us he saw him woe bawling home this morning so he gave him a ride. Rosie, probably figures he can't get in too much trouble around here. Doug feels it is likely a

Parrsboro
—it never occurred to me, on this mild September morning, that
Doug would be in for his first ground lesson for paragliding.

good idea that he has never had a driver license. I decided right then and there, that just maybe the reason his nickname is Cow is because it stands for *Can only walk.*

Just seeing my Baffin boots waiting for me in the ditch makes my tummy flip. I wish I could only walk! Walk in and out of a front door. What happened to my life of brick walkways and automatic garage door openers? I do have to laugh when I remember modeling my dream-come-true Baffin wader boots for Ruth, her sister-in-law and her English-accented mother-in-law. Cinderella is proof that a new pair of shoes can change your life. I pranced up and down the large hallway like a model on a Paris runway. "I feel confident that tall rubber boots are sure to make a comeback," I tell them, "If I only had the attire to complete the ensemble! One of those trendy shirts with a polo player on my chest, my collar up turned casually, as if the wind blew it in that position, and some khaki pants (which would be dirty in three minutes) would contrast nicely with the deep blue of my boots. Quite honestly, ladies, I've shopped in Paris, Rome, New York and London—never have I purchased anything that I've needed more!"

I listen to two birds engaged in a domestic standoff. In a pathetic attempt to document the last few days in my journal, I don't look up. Fifteen minutes later I allow myself the privilege. The world is shimmering. The tide is rushing in and has filled the bath tub around me. This is the first time I've been aboard on the coming tide. It is shocking how fast it floods. Our legs are tucked away, we are in five feet of water ready to set sail.

Our new friends sit in very much the same location where we spotted Brian, three days ago. Ruth sits serenely, Biggs (their dog) always included, Brian casts his rod. They wait quietly for our departure.

With solemnity, excitement and the magic wind at our backs, we set sail out of the Farrells River. It is a blissfully warm day, savoring every millisecond of the moment, I stay forward after I weigh anchor. Brian, Ruth and Biggs disappear then reappear down river a few minutes later. Many photos are taken as we pass the town pier. All three are there perched for viewing along with many locals. We give our big boat wave and say the last of our thanks and good byes.

Our buddies call their final salutations of—*have a wonderful trip, we'll send pictures, please come back!*

It is a dear sweet scene. I should have taken my own pictures. There are moments that are not to be broken by the rush for the camera—the sound of the film advancing, the zoom lens focusing. Better to be captured in my heart.

There are precious few times in your life that you meet people with such kind and generous spirits. These two Bluenosers have given us the traditional Gaelic greeting *CIAD MILE FAILTE*—One Hundred Thousand Welcomes!

Leaving our little smidgeon of civilization, we turn East past the lighthouse toward our next destination, Five Islands. Again we stick close to the shoreline enjoying our slow-moving nature show. We are the only ones on the water so we have our own private viewing. We gasp over the layers and curving colors of the carved cliffs. We wonder what geological events took place to sculpt this shoreline? How could any artist capture all this? I certainly cannot with my words.

We are absorbed in our own thoughts as we sail quietly along. We hardly turn our heads, not wanting to miss the nuances of the constantly changing shadows and sunlight. Intermittently we see a house high on a cliff. I wonder what the eyes of the shore sees? Just two tiny bits of creation bobbing around in a small tub? Two dots of insignificance amidst all this grandeur? We humans think we are so powerful, smart and in control. I'm here to say, when you see, feel and try to survive in 54 feet of tides, you are nothing! We ask very respectfully, for the wind and the tides to take us to Five Islands.

Our greeting party of one fisherman, one dad, two kids and three dogs ask if we need a hand? We go through the where, when and whys of our trip. When the Captain launches into the explanation of the legs, I head down below, to start dinner. The dad calls back in a jovial manner, "Come on up to our little cabin, we have some homemade wine!"

Dinner is about to be. I carefully check our provisions, then I come up with a menu. The last of Rutlee's garden yellow squash is put to good use by slicing and then sauteeing them in olive oil with wax peppers and a little shaker seasoning. I pull them off the heat

Sailing To Five Islands
We gasp over the layers and curving colors of the carved cliffs. We wonder
what geological events took place to sculpt this shoreline?

Sailing To Five Islands
Intermittently we see a house high on a cliff. I wonder what the eyes of the
shore sees? Just two tiny bits of creation bobbing around in a small tub?
Two dots of insignificance amidst all this grandeur?

while still firm and top it all with diced green onions, tomatoes and feta cheese.

My husband requests a hearty slice of our whole wheat bread, to mop up both of our plates. Full, but taste buds still crying for more, he wolfs down a couple of double chocolate chip shortbread cookies from the Parrsboro bakery.

The tide is out, the legs are up. We find we have our very own private beach shack. The offer of friendship and homemade wine is very tempting, but we opt for a peaceful evening alone. We stroll, hand-in-hand, up the road towards the Five Islands Campground. The warm breeze ruffles our collars. It is the big Saturday night in the campground. We hear music and jovial goings on around the large campfire. Several other campers pass us by, flushed with the success from their fishing expeditions. We reminisced about summer evenings years ago, me on the West Coast at Pismo Beach and Doug on the East Coast on the Jersey shore. We are content to be alone; we talk quietly to the moon and the stars. Off in the distance we see the silhouettes of the Five Islands for which the area is named. Goodnight, little lighthouse.

Fatigue overtakes us. I strive to write my journal; the Captain his log. Hardly able to form the words, the Captain looks up and tells me, "Now all I have to do is write about tomorrow. I mean yesterday. I mean today!"

With an almost aggravated tone he adds, "I loose track of time. Time is not rigid like that blasted clock that is tick, tick, ticking" (loudly I might add but you are the one …) "Time exists in gusts; time ceases to have real meaning. There is not *time*. It is just a measurement, a way to chalk off the days. Maybe time comes in waves and it can accelerate as fast as a space shuttle or break and float like a very slow river? It is not a monotonous thing; it can be fast, it can be slow. If there is no wind, does that mean there is no time? There are lulls, updrafts, downdrafts but it is not linear. It's a shame to mash and force time into structure, like we do with our children when we force them into school. How long was 30 minutes to the lone kayaker?"

I contribute with, "Remember Albert Einstein's *time passage* when he discussed *relativity?—When a man sits with a pretty girl for an hour, it seems like a minute. But let him sit on a hot stove for a minute and it's longer than any hour."*

I ponder all this insightful information. I guess it is all relative to what you're doing. If the appearance of time as fast or slow happens because time is an illusion we invented to carve up the oneness, which is indivisible, then we really should not care what time it is if we are living and enjoying the here and now.

We laugh at our ramblings, we step out in the cockpit to stretch and suck in some warm fall air. I, for one, am really lovin' this weather. We have given our little wood stove a holiday for the last five days. I admit, I'm a California woman who never knew what cold was until I moved to the East Coast. A ski vacation is a big difference from living with it all.

Away from man's artificial light, the two tone sky is mega huge and bright. Our big plan for the morning is to sail over to the Five Islands. I say to myself, whatever the day may hold, I'm beginning to look forward to it with enthralling pleasure instead of apprehension. I also say to myself, Ha! This bunk comes from a woman safely tucked in a quiet marsh, her own private beach, with a light breeze and a full tummy.

How my life has changed! But to live is to change. A friend once told me, that adaptability shows intelligence. If this is true, I must have a much higher IQ than one would recognize at first approach.

Day 10

Sunday, September 9, 2001

The crash of the waves on this rocky beach breaks the wordless silence. The whisper of the soft breeze increases its breathy voice to a gust. Speaking or making a rustle of any type is disruptive, making unsolicited clatter in this silence. The scratch of my ink pen begins to sound like thunder. The *kip-kip-kip* of the of the common tern directs my eyes to his black cap and red bill as he gracefully soars over the water searching for some krill. The Caspian tern follows, singing his low hoarse *kraa* and the shorter *kow*. All are likely to be heading to Florida or South America for the winter. These sounds, along with the soft rhythm of the endless waves rolling into this quiet cove, seem to fit and not disrupt. The most wonderful thing about being out here amongst these beautiful Five Islands, is the privacy. They are uninhabited and inaccessible except by private boat.

Doug has rowed ashore to explore the roundest Long Island I have seen on a chart. The privacy allows me to surrender in the

The Five Islands "Islands"
Doug has rowed ashore to explore the roundest Long Island
I have seen on a chart.

The Five Islands "Islands"
The crash of the waves on this rocky beach breaks the wordless silence. The
whisper of the soft breeze increases its breath voice to a gust.

open-air cockpit. We have begun to call using the ole' reliance at this location "surrendering." Doug found the tiller to be the perfect toilet paper holder. When the breeze blows, the tiller sways back and forth and gently unfurls the paper, making it wave a white flag of surrender. I barely have time to finish *surrendering* before Doug comes back aboard booming with excitement. The silence is utterly disrupted by my childlike husband who performs like an animated puppet as he provides me with a full description of his walk and the huge thunder holes he discovered.

The clouds above us are pulled apart like cotton candy. We quietly sip our peppermint tea and munch our ginger cookies, grapes, cheese and crackers. There is an unexpected mystery surrounding these islands which astounds me. Is it because of their magnificence? I tell my husband of my preternatural feelings and he agrees that there is a strange spookiness around here.

Doug, not one to dwell on the uncanny, breaks into song. The Captain's rich full voice entertains me with his own rendition of the Doors. *I'm going to Love you till the stars fall from the sky!* His voice then becomes a one-man-band of a trumpet, trombone and drum.

A pacing bird, pausing for a quick waltz, makes me laugh. Honestly, I start to feel all melty-gooshy. This man, among men, makes me go *Oohh La La*. I let my guard down and there is a powerful jerk from the wind. A gust that should be reserved for hurricanes, nearly landed me and my peppermint tea overboard.

The eeriness returns. I don't know if it's being here on Five Islands that's giving me the creeps or the whipping of the wind, reminding me of 4 a.m. this morning.

I'm desperately trying not to be a fanatical timekeeper! I really am! I try the "time is relative" bit. I rehearsed it over and over and it was was pretty much settled in my mind until this morning. Time *is* relative—relative to how dark it is and ... what in heavens name is he doing? I am baffled until I feel the masculine movements beside me in bed. The firm, cold movements are those of legs sliding in beside me. Optimistic, I rolled over to greet the new arrival only to find that my husband is gone and his "replacement" consists of the boat "legs"! This is when I find the blasted clock.

I am still trying to push the cold, wet legs to their own side of the bed when I hear the pounding and clanging of the anchor being hauled. Inharmonious thoughts echo menacingly through my brain. This is enough to drive one mad, enough to provoke a saint, enough to make a preacher swear, and finally, this is enough to try the patience of Job. Much to my consternation, all these perfectly justifiable thoughts are being drowned out by the sound of the incessant droning of the motor and the boat hull pounding through the water. Our interim anchorage out in the deeper water of the bay, thrashed us around a bit while we waited for some daylight.

Fate was only playing games with me when the boat stabilized and my quiet sleep resumed.

I take it personally when I'm in a deep sleep—in a totally anaesthetized state for a whole 30 minutes—and I hear the setting sail routine come round again. The anchor pulled, the main sail hoisted, the jib unfurled. AAHH! At least he didn't start the head-splitting motor. I only check the time to decide if I would feel guilty if I went back to sleep, I rationalize that 6:30am is not too early to get up but not too late to go back to sleep. The princess in me is still debating when the wind grabs the sails abruptly enough to give me whiplash (if I hadn't been lying down).

We are blasting across the bay towards Five Islands close hauled. *Crash! Boom! Bang!* I am twisted and tossed, rocked and rolled! Rehearsals for the Chubby Checker video were set in motion. My decision is made, I stay in bed.

When living on a sailboat, one can usually assume that if your normally cheerful, loving partner is in a bad mood, it's because said partner was tossed out of the wrong side of the bed.

AAHH! But that was a long time ago and I've had a few minutes of perfectly eerie tranquility. As in most good moments in life, they don't last and now the wind is really putting on a show. The Captain asks if I'm up to my "AW" duties (Anchor Woman)? We have to move because of the wind and the current.

Note that the Captain doesn't just ask this once or twice or even three times. In the last two hours I've pulled anchor four times. I'm too stubborn to give in and admit to being the namby-pamby some may think I am.

Speaking of stubborn, the Captain has just given orders for one last pull of the anchor. We are to set sail at 1PM for Stubborn Head—9.3 miles the GPS informs us. That last pull took something out of me—the wind and the tide set me up for a teeth-grinding anchor haul. I will soon find it difficult to slip my shirts over my bulging muscles.

Tumult: 1) an uproar 2) a state of confusion and agitation.

Yes, I would say tumult was the general word for the day. The "crossing," from one side of the Minas Basin to the other, was a rough one. The tide was so fast and the water so shallow that the waves went *slap, slap, slap*. The strong wind pushed us like a bat out of hell. Now, the reader who is still with me and has followed this narrative closely will know what this means. The Brilliant One … She Who Rocks …does *what?* Naturally she went down below to ride it out.

I thrust my hand to my mouth in an attempt to stabilize the movement of my crusted, split and bleeding lips. My arms then stood guard, keeping anything being tossed to and fro, from coming near my face. Improvising a positive attitude, I thought, *at least this isn't the 38 mile crossing back to New Brunswick*. If it were, I'd just have to say, pass me the Ol' Bushmills (then I'd try to forget everything until it was over).

Meanwhile, on *this* little excursion, not even Bushmills would help. Between the medication Ruth gave me for my lips (she's a nurse), the lip balm that concerned Cow gave me, and the stuff I bought at the pharmacy, I have glopped and licked off so much topical medicine on my poor lips that I'm half-poisoned. I try not to laugh (it hurts) while lying here, burping up ointments.

I envision a slogan I will have put on a tee shirt: SHE ROCKS.

Forlornly, I again check the clock—5:30pm. I have lived in a world of constant thrashing, memories on which I don't want to dwell. From behind the scratched windows I can see rolling hills and green pastures. The change from one side of the Minas Basin to the other is so remarkable that I wonder how many days have I been asleep? The wind and tide have de-escalated enough for me to valiantly stumble out of my asylum and take a survey of our new surroundings.

The chart tells me we are in the Copiquid Bay; my eyes tell me that we have entered the world of chocolate milk. This fanciful bay and the powerful tides work like a blender. The churning, sloshing, and chopping don't stop until it purees the mud and pours the iced mocha into the larger Bay of Fundy. The Captain proclaims we will not be anchoring until around 7pm, using the entire flooding cocoa brown tide to get us there.

I feel it prudent to begin preparations of my craved meal. The grain silos, farms and fertile growing land stimulates my appetite. My fondest memories of childhood are of time spent on my grandparent's farm in Curtis, Nebraska. I gathered corn, potatoes and carrots and assisted my Grandma Bailey in putting supper on the table.

The sail has now slowed to a normal escalator pace. Carefully, knives in hand, I start dinner. I sit in the cockpit peeling potatoes, mesmerized by the swirls of chocolate milk and reminisce. One year, when I was 12-years-old—I'm sure of this because any year we visited could always be divided by four (our family only had the money to drive to Nebraska every four years). At this mature age, a neighborhood family invited me for dinner on Tuesday. With 18 children under their roof, the Ennis household was always full of action and fun. Mom Ennis was large, round and happy. Two of the 18 were twins my age, Inez and Ilene. I had never known any twins before and never anyone with my same name, even though she spelled it different. I was secretly thrilled to be the only one of my family to be invited. I am the youngest of eight children and lived a rather sheltered childhood. I had never been invited or allowed to go solo anywhere before. I carefully dressed, checked myself in the mirror, and then walked down the road all by myself.

I entered their house by the back door, pleased to have made it unscathed, only to find that I had *missed* the whole thing. Their "dinner" was my "lunch" and their "supper" was my "dinner." It wasn't until I met Doug that, like him, I sometimes call dinner, supper, mostly just for fun. Today I'm cooking a good old fashioned "supper."

It is so refreshing to peel in the open air. You can just throw your peelings overboard in the great digestive tract of the bay. The Captain has finished putting the boat to bed and I'm in a mouthwatering state. I cut the potatoes into small chunks so they will cook faster. I added some sliced garlic to the pressure cooker where the potatoes have been soaking so they wouldn't turn brown. I closed the lid tight, but without the pressure cooker knob, for our quick mashed potatoes. My other pan awaited corn on the cob, cut to fit, and chunks of carrots. When the potatoes are soft, but not too mushy, I drain part of the water, add a bit of butter, powdered milk, salt and pepper and stir. I recap the lid to keep them nice and warm while I strain the veggies. I realized, at this very moment, that I'll need to cut the corn off the cob because of my lips. Shoot, good thing I can keep the potatoes warm. My slight scowl turns to a lip-cracking smile as I dish out our plates. I remember, with delight, that a favorite of my youth was mashed potatoes with corn stirred together! This, of course, is the low-cal version of my grandmother's kitchen, where we always had fresh milk, cream and butter. I was a stupid kid (not that things have changed much) in that I never liked milk with cream layered on top and the fresh eggs I enjoyed so much gathering. They all had funny tastes and colors.

I eat my meal with complete and "utter" enjoyment, remembering, with each bite, my wild exertions at cow milking. A puff of wind blows the smells of the farm, the wheat, grain and manure. I breathe deep and I can see the cow's large liquid eyes, the foaming white milk flowing into the pail. I had learned to admire their kick while trying to maneuver that heavy pail.

Indelibly impressed on my memory was the freedom I experienced on the farm. It is my only memory of freedom from my childhood. I would rise and dress early, before anyone else in my family was awake, open that kitchen door and run. I would run through the cornfields, run to the pigpen and snort, chase the chickens doing my best grandma, "cluck cluck," then stand on the fence railing and "moo moo" to the cows. I still vividly recall holding tight to my grandpa's overalls, bouncing wildly along on the tractor, my hair flying in the breeze.

It makes my heart ache that I can't go back and live it all over again. The farm may still exist (I've no idea) but I haven't been back in 23 years. I think of it today only in my memories. Back in Pennsylvania, we have an acreage way behind our house where there are still large cornfields. We often take walks there. As everything in life, it is never the same, of course, for life changes as fast as the tide runs.

Speaking of the tides, momentarily lost in my thoughts, I forgot where I am. I look up to see the far side of the shore, velvety in the distance. Will this slow down? Here we sit at anchor and the dinghy is putting on a show as though it's chasing a boat going 6 knots. With the heavy current cutting through here, we want to make sure we are really caught. Suddenly, as if to demonstrate all this, the boat whips and jerks around, pulling tight on the anchor and showing us it is doing its job. I silently hope there is not another log thrown in by de Champlain. The episode with the log at Isle Haute shows you can be anchored too well.

After supper we laid our plans for our first night in the Shubenacadie. Did I happen to mention that this river is a tidal river? I can thank the aforementioned Brian from Parrsboro for this one! He is the one, as nice as he is with a bathtub and all, who informed Doug that if he truly wanted to go to the top of the Minas Basin/Bay of Fundy, he should go the 17 miles to the top of this river. I remember the two of them talking and pointing at the charts, discussing canoes, rafts and such. I wasn't in on the confidential conversation that this is a world-famous tidal bore. The only tidbits of information I remember my beloved sharing were: 1) it is really pretty; and 2) it has lots of wildlife.

So I said, optimistically,"Sounds good ... let's go for it. We might as well because we may only be here once!" (I was trying to sound brave).

Yesterday, when the conversations with our greeting party at Five Islands came around to our next destination, I just managed to hear a fisherman remark, "You're gonna *sail* up there? That's a world-famous tidal bore!"

What does this mean to me/us sitting here in a sailboat, I really don't know! All I know is Tidal Bore doesn't sound like something I should willingly want to do in a sailboat! Last night I forced myself to remain calm. Why ruin the evening? So far everything has been just fine! Don't get your panties in a bunch, Eileen.

This knowledge (or lack of) brings a *new* sense of insecurity.

This evening, as I sit at the mouth of the Shubenacadie River, I take inventory of my available information. I think it is high time for a proper list. I'll pour a glass of wine and make a list. I always feel better when I make a list.

1. I don't even know how to say Shubenacadie. Doug and I are already tired of trying. We have nicknamed it the Shooby. We took the name from Shooby Taylor, a hipster from the 60's, who found a little fame in the early 1980's. He was called the human horn. He entertained in clubs with wild gibberish, called scatting or vocalesse. He sang a jazzy gush of babblement, like, *Sprawl Dabba Sprawl,* to all sorts of tunes, including "Here Comes the Bride"!

2. I check our navigating directions, dated 1990. They are the first, and only ones in print, for the top of the Bay of Fundy. With only four pages for all the Minas Basin, I was surprised to read that it does, in fact, mention the Shubenacadie River. It has one sentence and tells me that the Shubenacadie River is navigable by boats, at low water, for about 13 miles, within about 2 miles of the village of Shubenacadie. *That's it* for God's sakes! What kind of boat? A canoe? A raft? A sailboat with a keel?

3. My old *Dreamers and Doers Guide to Nova Scotia,* dated 1981—nothing!

4. I have a dictionary on board. Nothing

5. I search for my tiny computer dictionary and thesaurus. I enter tidal bore. It blinks Correction! Correction! Then it refers me to teddy bears!

This all thrills me to no end. Around Eastport, we sail in and around the St. Croix River. It has brackish water. The tide goes up and out of it. Never heard anything about a tidal bore. I think this through—a tidal river, inlet, or stream—means the tide fills and empties. Now I have an idea. I look up bores (bore). The fourth definition is: a tidal flood with a high, abrupt, front. Well, there you have it! This is all I know.

I feel like jabbing my index finger at him! *Him,* being my darling adventuresome husband (love being in every syllable). I want to cry—I want to ask, "Have you lost your wits?"

I refrain from the crying and jabbing finger business.

Doug is not bothered by, as Tennyson so aptly put it, our *"Blind and naked ignorance."*

Mr. Oblivious is out in the cockpit giving his guitar a hard pounding and singing along in a volume to match. He is telling all those on shore, who I'm sure are wondering what the big flusher brought in on high tide, *"My girl is red hot! Your girl ain't diddily squat!"*

I'm not too hepped up about venturing into the unknown of a tidal bore river. But what do I do? Set on shore until the Captain gets his jollies running the *bore?* What if he needs me? We can't, and I for one, don't want to, visualize what the bore will do or when it will do it.

I have to face the facts. I'm STUCK, here. That's it. But can't I trade for what's behind Door Number Two instead?

It is dark and we are tired. We stop talking, to listen. The current sounds as if it is slowing. We check the depth sounder. It shows 12 feet. We have anchored at the side of the river. If we happen to be in a deep channel we may not ground out.

The Captain devises a plan. We set the depth sounder alarm at 5 feet. We'll get up and check the water situation. At that height, no matter how fast we lose water, we should *(should?)* have enough time to ready the legs before it is "heel-over time."

I whimper to myself. I'm scared and exhausted. I just want to sleep in a normal bed, miles away from a tidal bore. Maybe I can come by tomorrow and look at it. Maybe. Maybe?

How can I handle this situation?

Perhaps detachment? I said, detachably. "I didn't even know the depth sounder had an alarm. Besides, I thought time was an *illusion* we invented to carve up oneness and all that?"

Detachment wasn't going particularly well.

We instinctively hug for dear life. We don't know what mishap, or rather, *adventure* lies ahead. It is 10 p.m. and the tide has slowed down to a trickle and we still have a decent depth.

I'm now too tired to feel extreme trepidation as we lie in the V-berth. I try to sleep. Nietzsche's words keep running through my head, *"Love your fate."*

Right! He was never in my shoes (Baffins), in a tiny sailboat, getting ready to sail up a tidal bore river! The sedative of sleep takes over.

To think there are people out in normal world, concerned if their martinis are shaken not stirred!

Day 11

Monday, September 10, 2001

You cannot discover new lands without consenting to loose sight of the shore for a very long time. Many years ago I used this quote in lectures speaking about business. Believe you me, when you are on a boat it is very comforting to see shore unless you are too close to the shore, heading for rocks, out of control because you're riding a tidal bore. Discovering new lands, new self, new lessons, new goals, new patience in waiting, is not all it's cracked up to be. According to some spiritualists, they think (supposedly) that he who waits poorly turns time into punishment, which materializes into further loss in the future. This is a lesson in wise living. Take a vacation from control. When you have no control, trust that the greater power is in control.

It is 9 a.m. and I have managed to turn time into punishment, I have no control and this is no vacation! The one and only thing I've discovered is that if I were on vacation, I'd need a new passport picture.

There is an old saying, *if you look like your passport picture, you're too sick to travel.* I just gave a quick glance in my 4-and-one-half-inch pocket mirror. I'd give up martinis to look as good as my passport picture. I mean, I've never necessarily found looking in the mirror a pleasant experience—but now that I'm 50, I know damn good and well that I use to look a lot better when I looked horrible!

I brush my teeth and mumble about old passport stamps. All those wonderful places. The days I use to travel by planes, trains, automobiles and luxury cruise liners. Those vacations where my luggage was filled with beautiful clothes. I would spend my days shopping, touring museums and sipping cappuccinos. Evenings would bring the major decision of the world's finest restaurants and my favorite Chardonnay before returning to a grand hotel (I'll never take clean sheets and clean fingernails for granted again).

I put my head down next to my 12-inch sink with a pump and give a tiny groan for all those beautiful beaches with margaritas served to my beach chair.

I make my bed which consists of two sleeping bags, one on top and one on the bottom. Last night I must have adjusted my side of the bag 20 times. The idea is to stay on top, without ten 3 inch rolls under me. Early this morning I found myself exhausted, my short fuse getting shorter. Full of self-pity, I wanted to scream four letter words and do some major stomping and pouting.

Then I came to my senses—self-pity, is such an unsophisticated emotion. I indulged in a silent tantrum.

Thank the almighty, the power of the universe! There are moments on board that make you almost jump up and shout, *whoopee!* Self-pity now tucked safely inside with my pocket mirror, I stepped out of the companionway. I slipped my stretch jeans onto the cockpit cushion and the world smiled. The beauty of the scenery and the warm sunshine almost took me to a height above a normal vacation. Our view rivals most resorts. This helps to mollify the night we had after the depth sounder alarm was set and we fell asleep in the V-berth.

Doug smacks his lips telling me, in a joyful voice loud enough for the cows to hear, this is the best blueberry jam ever! The jam was included in Ruth's departing gift. The *good luck* package included special seeds from her garden with growing tips, the scrumptious jam she and her grandson concocted a few weeks ago, and cream for my lips.

As an afterthought she handed me names and phone numbers of friends along our journey's way. Then she looked as though her lips moved in a silent prayer when she added the words, "just in case …"

The Captain's attitude can really be annoying. He is not going to let a near sleepless night and our foreboding future get in the way of enjoying every minute of his adventure! His eyes literally dance with contentment and anticipation. If he were to be taken out by this tidal bore at this moment, he would be swept away with a smile on his face. He is really in his element. Whereas I'm more on a heating element, wondering if I might spontaneously combust!

A helicopter zooms low just over our heads. It looks to be the same one we saw land on a beach a few days ago. He just missed the *Doug at the Spa Show.* Doug had decided it would be a good personal hygiene day. Clean underwear and clean tee shirt in hand he stepped out into the cockpit for a little privacy. "Oh, clean underwear and a shave," I raise my eyebrows and purse my lips, "you must be feeling frisky!" He looked at me blankly and closed the canvas companionway door.

My Captain, while in the privacy of the daylight and open-air cockpit sang as he cleaned. *The birdies know that the best time to sing is in the morning … !* His bath is a study of time and motion—he gave me a running commentary. Just when it was towel-off time, the sun hid behind the clouds and a very cool breeze rolled in from the foggy Fundy. I gave a satisfied chuckle. He was completely dressed when the sun shone brightly and the wind changed and blew warmth off the land.

I can't say in the words of Cow, *"last night was a night I'll never remember!"* It is *vivid* in my memory bank. With a very unsympathetic blast, we were torn from our sleep. The alarm on the depth sounder shrieks like a WWII air raid horn. We got up and checked. It was 11:30 and we had 5 feet of water and the tide was still going out! We went through the same routine of alarm and back to sleep.

Then, at 1 a.m., our little pleasant sounding alarm tells us to watch out! We are in only 3½ feet of water! We discuss our little situation ... we decide to get completely dressed (we slept half-dressed to begin with) and be ready for action any moment. We figure in 20 minutes we will either go aground or the tide will change and we'll start to float in deeper water. How we came up with this notion and, better yet, how we convinced ourselves, is kinda amusing to me now.

My prior foreboding seemed to float away with the rest of the tide, when we took our waiting party out to the deck. The moon is shining its half smile. The light shone out where there was once a river; now only sand bars. Our eyes adjust, we move forward and aft, starboard to port. We think we see a channel and, you guessed it, the only place there is water as far as we can see, is right where we are anchored. We ponder the possibility that the tide is all the way out and it merely lowers about a foot or so every hour because of it trickling out and seeping into the sand?

We kept thinking that she'd finished lowering and then she'd lower some more. Out on the decks we moved back and forth like hovering clouds, waiting for whatever it was that might still happen. The trickling sounds continued. All that trickling made me have to pee. I purposely didn't drink anything and still I must have gone five times since 10 o'clock.

Then ... oh geezzz Louise ... surely not now! I whimpered. Something is the matter! This may seem like a small thing to all of you, but stay with me ... I thought, sure as the world, I'd go below and sit down on the reliance. Then we'd hit hard and I'd have to fly out to man the toe rail. I winced at the picture.

In the moonlight the Captain sees the expression on my face. "Quit pinching and go for it!" he commands. Having little choice but to follow the Captain's orders, I stood and felt a little woo woo from holding it so long. I raced to the bucket. I believe there is some cosmic force that protects.

The sounder ultimately shrieks out its alarm—2½ feet of water! It is 3:30 a.m. and we've been waiting, holding our horses, keeping our shirts on, since 1:00 a.m.

Okay. We agreed ... this was really it. We sat quietly; the trickling sounds have stopped. We listen ... nothing. We don't lower any more. The tide must have turned. We go inside to stare at the depth sounder, checking for any change. The Captain decided that we'd better lower the pop-top, remove the canvas door and bring out the boards which slide in to close the door. *Batten down the hatches*, so to speak.

With the tide change, the bore may be coming! Will it bore here? Maybe it's too wide here, at the mouth of the river, and it will bore at the narrow part of the river, if there is one (we have no clue).

His philosophy is, "better to be prepared and not need it, than to need it and not do it" (or something to that effect).

We sat in silence except for the loud ticking of the dollar store clock hidden in the drawer. The Captain starts to say something— I hold up my hand. We both concentrated on the sounds outside the boat. I thought I heard something. We think we hear it again. It sounds like a soft roar. We stare at the depth sounder.

The sounder has an 8-inch screen, which conveys a variety of information including the depth of the water we float in (minus about 6 inches) and the voltage of our battery (recharged by our solar panel). It shows a nice assortment of other images, like seaweed, fish, rocks, mountains and valleys. Mountains and valleys are about the only things you can identify for sure. The screen starts to blink its little eyes, as if in despair. Our little friend, Stephan the Sounder, starts to dim, no longer blinking. It gives us one last silent blink, then a line of darkness slowly creeps across the screen.

We both cock our eyes back and forth to each other and back to the sounder.

In all my years of being ballast aboard this boat, I've never seen my Captain show this expression of nervous awe. We've *never* seen our little friend act like this before. Eee gads! What could cause this?

I kid thee not, a minute later it gives a flicker of life. We hear a roar and a swoop and Stephan reported, on his brightly lit screen, 15 feet of water.

Doug couldn't get the wood slats off the doorway quick enough for my liking. He was first out the doorway, into the cockpit. I hear a Zippidy Doo-Daa Zippity-Aah! I raced out to be beside my Captain. We steadily fixed our eyes out into the moonlight. I nearly wept. All the sand bars had disappeared; there was water all around us.

I mean how cool is that? Arm and arm we stood mesmerized by the beauty of the moon shining on the rushing water.

Suddenly life seemed hopeful, I felt at peace with the world; doom, doubt, and derision gone. I feel I need closure. I tell the Captain, "I'm going to sleep. Stick the fork in; I'm done."

My confidence and peace of early this morning seems far away. I keep my mind and body busy with preparations for an early dinner. I've had three different types of mung beans soaking overnight. To this I add some barley and spices of sea salt, bay leaf, white pepper, red Indian pepper, split coriander seeds and fresh ground pepper. My good old pressure cooker will cook our *Last Supper* (if our last supper it be) quickly and preserve the flavors. If we survive this ordeal, at least we'll have had plenty of fiber. I'll add some diced vegetables at the end so they'll add some texture but won't overcook. If we were back in Eastport, I would garnish the dish with fresh chives, cilantro or parsley from the garden. With eyes swimming I stir my concoction.

I want to turn and shout at my husband, "Okay! Fun's over. We can justifiably say we made it to the top of the Bay of Fundy. Let's turn this sucker around and head back to my little garden in Eastport!"

I don't. Some thoughts are best kept silent.

It is 2 p.m. we have had all day to see the changes around us. The water is so muddy it's red. The day, weather wise, has been resplendent. I have managed, most of the day, to keep my fears and emotions in check. There have been good moments, but bad quarter-hours.

Out of the *Complete Works of Shakespeare* book, I read a line meant for me today, "*Nothing routes us but the Villainy of our fears!*" Alright Willie, I'm going to take things as they come, roll with the punches. Who cares if I'm waiting here to be swept up a river by a tidal bore? I'm not going to go with the flow like a cinder block!

I hastily snatch *my* trusty old *Dreamers and Doers Guide* from under the nose of my Captain, as if it were some sorta grand achievement. I open up to what our chart shows as Maitland. Then, at least in 1981, the population was about 400 people. The township was named after Governor Sir Pereguine Maitland (nice name, I hope there wasn't a Junior) in 1828.

Way back before Pereguine showed up, the Mi'Kmag favored the area. They hunted and fished from their traditional summer camps along the Menesatung. The Indian name for this area means *healing waters.*

"Guess what?" I tell my husband. "I found something about Shubenacadie! First of all, it is pronounced Shoo-ben-ack-a-dee! Secondly, and most helpful in our situation, is that it means, *place where wild potatoes grow!*"

This is vital information to add to my growing list about this tidal bore.

"Oh, here's another nice bit of luck. The pronunciation of Cobequid Bay, (Cob`-a-quid) which has almost completely emptied of water and is starting to refill, and it means *end of flowing waters.* Not far from here," I continue to read to my already bored-with-my-facts husband, "is a Kobelawakwemode (Ko-bel-awak-we-mode) which, you might figure, means *Beaver Harbour!*"

"Along came the Acadians in the 1600's. They settled along the shore, building extensive dykes which, as I mentioned before, turned the tidal marshlands into fertile fields.

"After the deportation of the Acadians (long, sad story) the land was settled by the New England planters, many of whose ancestors still live here today.

"Nova Scotia is Latin for *New Scotland.* I recognize some of the names around here from places my kids and I visited in Scotland. There is a Dunvegan (Dun-vay`-gun) named after the castle of the McLeads of the Isle of Skye, and Dunmaglass (Dun`-ma-glass) from around Inverness. There are a few French names they retained, like Brule (Broo`-lee), which means, *burnt land.*"

One of the hot topics of this journey has been the *Mighty Glooscap.* I'm sure you are all wondering how he fits into the clanship. Way, way, way, before the Scots, the French and the English, these waters were claimed by the *Mighty Glooscap.* This legendary man-God of the Micmac (both spellings are correct) Indians of Nova Scotia, lived on the shores of the Minas Basin, on Blomiden (Blom`-id-dun). Legend says it was named by Portuguese navigators—Blow-m-down—and is one of the finest vantage points in all of Nova Scotia. The man-God could see across the waters of the Minas Basin to Advocate. He lived there in almost perfect harmony with the animals. The animals were all his friends except the insolent and mischievous beaver (of course). The beaver came to taunt his people. The Mighty Glooscap's voice rose with the wind and he cast five clumps of mud at the bad beaver—and Five Islands rose from the sea. He left Blomidon to settle near Advocate and Parsboro. He made his herb garden in the fertile soil. He set out feasts for his children. It is said that Mighty Glooscap scattered glowing jewels along the shore for Nogami, his grandmother. Jasper, agate, onyx and amethyst (the eye of Glooscap) can still be found today.

The beaches in front of us are glimmering in the sun. Doug has left me to go on an exploratory excursion. He stands and waves (all joyful like) on some of the beautiful packed sand. I can see from here that the beaches up the far shore are swirls of deep red, light red, tan and gray. What a fantastic painting!

Holy guacamole! I've got to get back to the future! If I have one! The time is 3:47 p.m. and we have 4½ feet of water. I know the *time* means nothing to all of you, living in the moment. I would just like to know when my life, as I know it, may be ending.

It's changing, it's changing! Nothing happens like it did last night or this morning, whenever *that* was. Just when we thought we knew something. Go figure?

Now, here's something new: a Zodiac raft with a 60 HP motor and three people is coming toward us. We can see the raft following the channels of water from the last of the receding tide. Now they have stopped. Are they waiting to ride the bore up-river? I stand up; my stance is as stiff as a soldier. If all this weren't bad enough, this must be an adventure ride up the bore! I'm not feeling good about this.

A fellow gets out of the raft. He is walking toward us. He must be the guide, I get the binocs. He has this shocked look on his face, he's shaking his head and looks puzzled!

I can't stand this, I better sit down.

He reaches us here, very few salutations are exchanged. "What, whhaat, do you intend to do?" he asks.

With exuberance, my smiling husband, responds, "Sail up the river!"

Mouth of The Shubenacadie
The beaches in front of us are glimmering in the sun. Doug
has left me to go on an exploratory excursion.

Our visitor steps back now, as if we were an infectious disease. Doug raises a dark eyebrow, then interjects, "I'm about out of beer. I wonder if there might be a beer store up river?"

My husband likes to have a sense of *purpose*. The poor kid really doesn't know what to take seriously. He looks to me, half-amused, half puzzled. It's possible, if he didn't live in Canada, that he wouldn't be old enough to buy beer.

I just keep shaking my head and smiling, as if I were a bobble head on a dash board.

The young man finds his voice. Sternly, he tells us, "Not, not ... for," he stops and looks around at the mud banks. He changes to a chokey voice, "Not ..." he stops again.

(I don't know where he's goin' with this, but I hope he gets there before the tide does).

He finally continues, "... for a very long, long, ways!"

I keep one anxious eye on the rafter kid and the other on the wise ass. "We're pretty desperate to get there!" Mr. Smarty gives him his piano key smile.

The young, befuddled guide tells us he has to return to his customers. He says, in answer to my question, "Yes, in fact there are many tourists who ride the bore. Most start further up river."

I almost jumped out and went with him. I'm not young and resilient! Why can't I just be a wife at home yearning to fulfill myself?

Suddenly (it seems *suddenly*, even though we have waited all day—see how time flies?) the Captain calls for his anchorwoman to *pull anchor* and get ready to ride the bore!

My emotions were so clogged they needed a drain. My brain is blurry. I changed my mind ... I'll wait on the bank. But no time!

Here it is. Too late!

I use my Wonder Woman strength to pull the anchor. How much sand had swirled around it? Just as I have the anchor set and tied, wobbly I stand, to go aft and hide in the cockpit. The Captain gives orders to stay forward and *hold tight* in case we need to drop anchor in a hurry.

In other words *I am in charge of the brakes.*

It is very disconcerting not to have a nice pedal, in a convenient safe spot, to apply quickly as needed. *Stay forward?* I repeat to myself.

I look down to see only the thin lifelines between the bore of the Shooby and me. I do not have my life jacket on!

I look over my shoulder to see that my diligent, absorbed, husband has enthusiastically and with passion already set sail up the Shubenacadie River.

Focus! Focus, Eileen! What was my intent for this trip? To find my *other awareness*—that which enlightens and enlivens my being? My journey to my center, where the immanent God dwells? To fight to continue that journey, no matter how many *obstacles* are thrust in one's path?

All this looks good on paper, written in one's journal.

I snort, then snort again. (It's really difficult to weigh snorts in the balance, but I do believe this second one has it over the first by a small margin).

All this before one meets a certifiable lunatic, with a tub, who happens to jump off cliffs for fun, and who gives *local knowledge* of the area. All bunk, I can say! Bunk, bunk!

In all honesty, the only words that seemed appropriate, while riding forward into the tidal bore, were those well-said words from *Butch Cassidy and The Sundance Kid,* when they jumped off the cliff into the rushing water … OOOHHH Shit!

Day 12

Tuesday, September 11, 2001

I decide upon a French braid today, with a few little cute bangs. I squint into my four-and-one-half-inch pocket mirror. I ponder the possibility of a remake of *The African Queen*. This time starring a Doris Day look-a-like—me!

Outside my Darling Doug is calling to me, "If this isn't cool, I don't know what is! I'm a river boat Captain!"

Doug's baritone voice gives gaiety to the moment.

Hey, Hey, Criplecreek Ferry, the sun's goin' down.
It's a mighty cool bree'eeeesse!

My independent nut case is digging our keel out of the mud.

My water is boiling. My cup is clean after brushing my teeth. My tea ball is packed with my calming tea mixture: camomile, mother's wort, mint and lemon balm. This mixture is to help those in menopause. What about those in menopause in the Minas Basin?

An extra special mixture is needed for those in menopause in the Minas Basin, stuck in the Shubenacadie river, close to Stewiacke! Or maybe I'm *in* the Stewiacke river? Wherever I am, I'm really ready to be soothed. I pour my tea.

I hear my name … "Eileen. Can you come and stand on the toe rail and help me pull the ropes for the anchor line?"

The ingenious Captain has it stretched all around, back to front, to help pull the boat free. The mastermind of this operation has been up since the crack of dawn … masterminding. All these efforts are working toward a goal.

And a worthy goal it would be, on anyone's *My Goals List.* Our goal is—I clear my throat as I say this—is to try and pull the boat *free*, as in able to *sail, motor* or *whatever*, at high tide.

Aahh! Nice warm sunshine and a cold, calming cup of tea. I do some yoga stretches, deep breathing—suck *in* positive energy, *out* with the negative energy.

I take a sip of tea. Slosh, slosh, my tea sloshes all over my private tea room, with a scupper, called a cockpit. The Captain, Doug, has come up with the ingenious idea of shaking the boat to see if the mud might loosen its grip on our keel. What makes men love this so much? Get down and dirty—the more challenge the better!

Women, I almost think scornfully, we love tea, hair, toilets and washing our faces—all the meaningless things in life. Speaking of which, I didn't finish checking my 4½ incher before coming out to meet the world. I check my reflection in the plexiglass window. Gosh! My hair looks as fuzzy as a cloud; maybe it is a cloud?

It is always good to have someone else to talk to when your spouse is having a menopausal moment. Doug does his best "Moo, Moo." He has the attention of the cows having their breakfast high up on the bank.

"We are from Bucks County Pennsylvania. How's it goin'? We've got some nice grass down there. You should come down sometime. We've got lots of you girls down there!"

I asked and he explained—"Heifers are females before they calve and they are cows after that." Oh, I didn't know this.

We hear the sounds of the tide approaching. We hear its churning and swishing as it makes its way up river towards us. The loud ticker says 8:00 a.m.

I glance down at my cup of tea and I wonder if I could read tea leaves like Nanny Winner, what would these leaves tell of my future?

The Captain has all his gear in place. I head for my appointed position on the toe rail. We are deluged by the racing water. We are on a mud bank. We wait for the top of the tide to hit. Here, close to Stewiacke, the water rushes in, stops, and then, not as quickly, flows out.

We do not wait long before the realization hits ... *Sur-prize! Sur-prize!* (in my best Gomer Pyle impersonation). We are officially still stuck in the mud. The tide level today is about a foot lower than it was last night when we arrived at our destination and landed, like Noah and his arc, on a mud bank.

My wide-eyed look spoke for itself.

My spouse starts doing the tapping-of-the-finger-under-the-eyeball-gesture, describing, at very great lengths, the technical plan he has devised in his swift-as-the-tide brain. I will spare you the details, until I understand them completely, of just what is to be done about our little predicament, especially since it involves the high tide around 9:00 p.m. tonight.

I go below, making no comment, and brew another cup of soothing herb tea.

I slump and bury my head in my hands as the water boils. My eyes blur with tears. I cannot focus on my teapot. I swallow hard. I let the tears stream freely down my mud-speared cheeks.

I've just looked at the tide chart for Eastport—the only one we have. The accuracy of times and levels is not the same for the Minas Basin, but the over-all levels, with the gravity pull of the moon, are the same.

Same moon, same earth.

It may be, if Doug's blueprint in his mind doesn't work, that the tide may not be high enough to pull us off this mud bank for 30 days!

An odd sense of sanity-preservation commands me to get out my journal and tell of our sail up the Shooby to our exalted state here in the mud.

I'll think positive thoughts—if I made it through that—everything will be fine.

Just so we are all on the same page, I was riding forward, about to disintegrate into a tidal bore river. I was left with no possible option other than to ride it out. It's the honest-to-God-truth. I decided right then and there—might as well make the best of it. I put on my semi-smile—not too excited and certainly not scared—my "I'm a salty woman smile!"

My muscles were flexed. I'm rough and I'm ready! All those wimps riding in the Zodiac rafts will think I went to Nepal for my summer adventure. I just stopped on my way home to ride the bore! My white knuckles weren't visible, as I clung to the bow pulpit, because my sweatshirt sleeves were covering them. Which reminded me of my anchor gloves? Damn it—I forgot those too. I hadn't been wearing them lately because my hands were so burnt (the antibiotic thing again). My hands sweat inside my gloves which makes the stinging so much worse.

So there I was, hanging on for dear life, with hands that I can barely use.

Actually—thinking back—I was in such a state that I hardly noticed.

The first leg of the rush upriver was very fast but, as it turns out, not really that scary. I became fascinated by the shoreline. Like the rest of the Minas Basin, it is beautifully carved by the turbulent tides. I had read, in my trusty *Dreamers and Doers,* that Nova Scotia has the largest population of Bald Eagles east of the Rocky Mountains. So I wasn't surprised to see some Bald Eagles but I was shocked to see so many, and so close! All along the river were beautiful farms and beckoning cottages, tucked back on hillsides.

We had enough water level to be swooshed into paradise. I relaxed; the waves aren't that big. Like most times in my life, I worried over nothing. The afternoon follows through by giving us, out-and-out, perfect weather!

I thought to myself (we can't converse, the raging water is too loud), this is fun. I was just suffering from the mountain/molehill syndrome. My shoulders relax, my mind is going over the clichés: veritable piece of cake—as easy as picking low fruit from tree—not much different than riding in a San Francisco cab without a seat belt. My hands, however, stayed clutched.

We rounded the bend. My eyes and brain focused. Whoa boy! There, ahead, were *power lines* swinging over the river. What's the problem? I have seldom in my life worried my little punkin' head over being too tall. The *Guillemot* is a small sailboat and sports a mast proportionate to her size.

From my vantage point, or should I say my disadvantage point, these lines look uncomfortably low. On most charts they show clearance and bridges. We are practically in uncharted territory. A rafter, canoe, or fishing boat wouldn't care. They don't have high protruding objects sticking out of their deck.

Another factor is, "How much water are we sailing in—3 feet or 33 feet?"

It's a handy thing to know. Even if the charts showed the clearance at high water—when and what is "high" water *here?* Are we too high for these lines? Even if I had dropped anchor at that moment, would we stop in time before we electrocuted ourselves and/ or, with the power of the current pushing us against the lines, would this cause the mast to break or snap? Hence, thrusting us, like a rubber band, to who knows where? Wouldn't that be a double whammy?

There wasn't time for my heart to react, so a heart attack was averted. The *Guillemot* swished right past. Power lines were something I hadn't even considered. What other obstacles may lie ahead? I gave this serious consideration, I guess we'll cross that bridge …

The river wound its way like a brown sinuous muscle. My breathing slowed to that of an out-of-shape-marathon runner. We rounded yet another mysterious bend—they all seemed mysterious because you can't see very far ahead.

Great Googaluga, can't ya hear me talk'n to ya? I turn to see if my ever-ready Captain had the look of a man going into hyperventilation. He seems calm. Ahead is not a bridge to cross, but one to go under!

Ahead of us, before the bridge, were two sets of Zodiacs filled with tidal runners, or whatever they call themselves. We see that one of the guides is the one and the same stupefied kid. He shook his head, still in a state of perplexity. "Where are you guys from, anyway?"

The other guide, who was older and gave gestures of being the boss, yells to us, "Are you here on purpose?"

Mr. Captain Wise-Ass took no time for snide remarks and called, "Do you think we have enough clearance to pass under the bridge?"

In my opinion, the fellow in charge gave us a very unqualified, "Yes! Plenty!"

The Captain turns our sailing raft around to let her back through. I knew it was just in case we need to haul our too-tall asses out of there. We could possibly start the motor (rarely starts on the first try) and hopefully our 9.9 Johnson would have had enough gumption to pull us out.against the tide (not likely).

The tide runners must have thought we decided against the bridge situation but were sucked under anyway!

The very unique bridge has a high point in the center and that's where we headed. I reminded myself to breathe as we passed under the lovely bridge. I turned around and gave my Captain the thumbs up.

I turned to see what lay ahead; what we couldn't see until we pasted the bridge. I saw what some may call a tidal-rafters dream but what I quickly placed in a category of my nightmare.

Holy cannelloni! There are the big ones, the slam-dunk, crashing, splashing, zip-roaring waves. Everywhere! There's no way around them, we were headed straight for all the action, right along with two Zodiacs full of tourists.

I turned wide-eyed back to the Captain. He smiled and raised his eyebrows.

The rafts were on either side of us, their eyes more on us than their experience.

Shoot! I missed the market again. I should have sold tickets—better than anything showing at the theater. The guides, I'm quite sure, told their groups that this was the inaugural *sail* up the Shube (now we know what they call it) for this century and probably the last.

Lips slightly parted and my upturned chin, I gave them my best salty woman profile for all the photos.

The motorized rafts ran through the rapids, surfing down waves and skirting whirlpools. We went right along beside them. All those years of living in California—going to every amusement park in existence, riding every fast ride as many times as they would let me on—finally paid off. The ride was unexpectedly thrilling! We were having fun! How could we be having this much fun and it be legal?

Way ahead of us, in a large, straight section of the river, the guides veered their rafts to the right and up to a wooden ramp. They let their tide runners out and I saw them heading up a hill to a cabin. As we passed by, our young friend, the-not-for-a-very-long-ways/where-you-from-anyway, guide stood waving. He was laughing his head off. We gave our big boat wave. The Captain yells, "*Now* how far is the beer store?"

Shaking his head, eyes full of cheer, he yells back to us. "At the fork in the river, go left!"

This all happened extremely quickly because the tide and the wind were still speedily pushing us toward the fork in the river and the beer store. My general feeling that death was imminent had passed. I was feeling pretty darned exuberant!

The river continued winding its way up. The scenery became more beautiful each minute. We rounded the next corner and my life changed. Suddenly, locating the deepest part of the channel became deceptive. There appeared to be a sand bar ahead. Doug headed the *Guillemot* toward starboard, the wide part of the turn, where the deeper channels usually lay.

THUD!

What a strange sensation! We went aground hard. We were moving at a fast speed.

"ANCHOR!" the Captain yelled.

For a brief second, I was dumb struck. The tide was pushing us over and roaring in and around us like a mighty monster trying to stamp us out!

"ANCHOR!" the Captain yells again. He was still at the tiller trying to keep control.

In seconds we're on our side, water coming up over the gunnels. I'm on the high side, struggling to stay on board. We are being pushed onto a sand bar.

It took every bit of strength and finesse I had, in my limited capabilities, to stay aboard, untie the anchor line and drop the anchor. The second it hit the water the rushing tide took control of it. The chain ripped through my hands.

The Captain yelled. "CLEAT! CLEAT!"

But I was powerless to stop it! The rope was taunt and raced out of the forepeak, burning and chaffing my hands as it went. I gave it all the power I could muster, using my legs, arms and feet to try to get enough give in the line to be able to cleat—all the while trying to not *follow* the anchor line into the rushing water.

Doug is able to maneuver forward and together we fight for the almighty cleat of the anchor line. We did it! After the anchor hooked, we kept pulling on the line, trying to lift the boat off the sand bar and into deeper water. Every second the rushing tide gives us more water to float.

Muscles straining against the power of the water and the weight of the boat, we were able to inch our way down the rope and pull her off the sand bar.

She started to sit upright.

Do you get the picture? I may not be explaining this the way the Captain would, but *Holy Shipwreck,* that was pretty gol' darn scary! It all happened so fast that I didn't understand for sure, until it was over, what it was we were trying to do.

I know it will come as shock to most of you readers, but I was an inexperienced anchorwoman in a tidal bore racing up-river. I let out the scope *without cleating.*

This revelation, of what *not to do* was not in my *Sailing for Dummies!* I should write to the publisher—it's a handy thing to know.

I sat on the foredeck, panting, holding my hands out as if I just burned them on a hot wood stove. Tears trickled down my face. I felt weaker than a sunburned snowflake. But I knew, if I wasn't a strong, squatty, stubby, flexible 1st mate at moments like this, I'd be in deep doo-doo.

I was just experiencing with the ability to breath normal again when the Captain gave orders to man the tiller.

The look, I gave my Captain—oh Lordy! Yes, in fact, he had seen that look of resentment and pain on other occasions. Aahh, but never so piercing! It was a waste! I mean total! Mr. StrongMan merely moved forward to pull the anchor, buried in mud, to continue our swish up river, as if he were returning to the back nine.

Once the skipper was back in control of our tidal raft/sail-boat, I assess the damages of my hands, back and nerves. We quickly move deeper into the Amazon—I mean the strange phenomenon of the Shubenacadie River. I put on my life jacket and anchor gloves and found my way back to my post, up forward. I was hoping they would serve as an umbrella might—if you have it you don't need it.

The further up-river we sailed, the water at the front tended to slow down because of the narrowing, but the water behind was still rushing up at normal speed. One more (of many more) idiosyncracies we were to find—as the tide changes to go back out again, the bore still has its momentum going up. So it meets *itself.*

Did I explain that right? I nod my head as I reread these sentences. Yep, I think that's right!

The shoreline along the way calmed me. I recovered. No major surgery is required after all. The only damages were to my hands. Now they really hurt, on the bottoms as well as the tops.

On we go and up, up, up—past rolling hills with cattle lazily grazing beside farms with as many as five grain silos. Beautiful cliffs, summer homes and horse ranches. The sun lowers, the sky darkens, our ride becomes slow and dreamy.

We took the fork in the road, we made it up river at dusk, 8:30 maybe? Who knows? Who cares? All this tends to wear one down! We were weary beyond awareness.

The tide was absolutely high but, naturally, we had no way of knowing this. All we knew was that we wanted to anchor, go aground, get the blasted legs down, close her up, and collapse (in my case have a nervous breakdown) ASAP!

We moved around again, like the rest of this trip, trying not to be too close to the bridge because of the traffic. Then we wonder if the hole we found will be deep enough? Will the current be too strong? The list of factors involved made my head hurt and you know how I love lists?

We somehow ended up in this seemingly perfect spot to anchor. We were really shallow. It would touch bottom in no time. This is great! No waiting and wondering all night if, and when, she'll hit.

Yes, Yes, Yes! Triple Yes! We hit the hard, put the legs on, we are smiling, laughing, kissing, hugging and finding the beer we have stowed for special occasions … when, aah ooh!

We went *flump, squish*—our keel started to sink into the mud. We have another rather impressive *flump, squish* and we sank some more! We sat at our little table and stared at each other, in synchronized movements we took big gulps of beer. No words were needed. Just how far would this go?

We sat and waited, gulped, waited. We seemed to be just slightly easing down, as if in a big cushy chair. It wasn't too bad, our nose was in the air but … we could handle that … with an ultra large *woosh,* we sank a considerable amount more. Then we stopped.

I gave a laugh—my threshold of laughter was low. I nod my head forward. After a quick assessment, I remark, "I guess we'll have to sleep with our heads forward and our feet aft!"

The Captain believes I have a genius for underplaying the obvious. We gave a toast and smiled. Might as well smile; imagine everything will be all-righty. What choice do we have?

There is an opening to the V-berth where you crawl in and out. There are two small walls on each side. When we finally crawled into bed, our heads were close enough together to hear each other's thoughts and at least 4 and 3/4 inches from the forepeak where, as you all remember, the anchor makes its home.

Last night, in our little love nest, the only thing we hugged was the haul of the boat. Our feet were braced against the small wall on each side to keep from slipping right out of bed. Our diagnoses? A bad case of inverted V-berth (sounds like a female problem). We entertained ourselves with *sleep and slide* all night long!

Between yawns, I put my journal away.

I do feel better having gotten the story on paper.

I think.

I look on the bright side, the Captain isn't out there singing the old sad song, *My Sweetheart Went Down With the Ship!* The bad part about writing the story was that it brought back the vivid memories. Tears sting my eyes and my muscles are tense. I'm sick of acting like some crybaby!

I turn my lips up into an evil little smile.

I can just blame it on menopause.

The mirror is not my friend today either! Screw it! I try to concentrate on what I need in order to walk out my front door. My backpack is a given.

Now let me see ... large boat bag, check; hiking boots, check; shopping list, check; extra socks (in case my others get wet), check; drinking water, check; money, check; mud boots, check; shorts (in case I have to wade), check; Tilley's hat (it is pretty sunny, plus it hides my hair), check; lip stick, check; chap stick, check; sun screen, check; sweatshirt (in case it gets cold), check; mud towels, check; bag of garbage, check; and loud ticker clock, check.

(Did I ever tell you why I don't wear a watch? If I didn't, I feel there is some explanation needed. I have to wear a solid gold watch or it breaks my arm out. I do happen to have a rather ostentatious-looking, solid-gold watch from my old life, but it is not waterproof. It quits working if I sweat, let alone climb on the boat. Doug hate watches and refuses to wear one. So there!)

I do my big climb down out of the boat (no water, remember). We muck through the mud, pulling the dinghy behind us, over to the side of the river where there *is* some water. We pile into the dinghy and row a long way around to the other side of the shore, avoiding the high spots with no water. The tide is lowering, the bank is steep. Like it as not, we have to pull ourselves, along with the dinghy, up the embankment. The mud is sticky and thick. I'm trying to help Doug pull the dinghy—he sees a disaster waiting to happen.

"Just get yourself up," he advises, "I'll handle this."

I don't want to seem like a shirker, leaving all the transfer of gear from the bottom to the top of the mud bank to Doug. So I grab some stuff and, as he prophesied, I did fall. I look down to see half of my body is coated in only two inches of mud.

My darling husband, the extremely capable one, has to handle everything. We make it up to the tractor path and I roll in the dry grass a bit to remove some of the mud. I remind myself, "Yes indeedy! I used to have a life. Sadly, it is still on lay-away at Neimens."

Although I look extremely fetching in my Baffin boots, we change to our hiking boots and place our mud boots upside down and at a slant. We don't want our boots to fill with water in case it rains.

Now, by George, we are ready for our walk to town. It can't be far, we tell ourselves. But we don't *know*. Actually, the only thing I *do know* is that I've never, in my entire life (yes, I did say entire), have known less.

We follow the tractor path up the hill. We cross over and pass some mobile homes in order to get up to the main highway. Walking up another large hill, we walk under the overpass. We cover our ears to ease the pain of the thundering noises coming from the trucks and cars racing overhead. As remote as I felt last night, in our little inverted V-berth stuck in the mud palace, all the noises from the two overpasses—one over the road and one over the river—and the rumbling of the train tracks, along with the fact that were obviously nestled under the approach to the Halifax airport, added to our unrestful night sleep. Down in the river, surrounded by the high banks and farm land, we are in a parallel Universe to all this fast track of life.

To have found our Mecca, we felt like true pilgrims. Our Mecca, with a large dumpster out back, is more than one could ask for. Doug ceremoniously dropped our bag of garbage into the wide opening. To relieve our ten feet of living space on the boat of our garbage gives one a feeling of satisfaction.

Now it is on to our shopping.

I bet you, the reader, can guess what is first on our list! Great, the door is unlocked, Open! We weren't sure of the hours. We think it is around 10:30 a.m.; the loud ticker is tucked away.

The booze store seems very clean, big. When one has been on a muddy boat for two weeks, one becomes deeply impressed by clean and big. It is as quiet as a funeral home. What's the matter with all these Canadians? This should be a happy place! There are two fellows standing behind the counter, but they have the look of two who just finished paying their taxes. Doug and I seem to be the only ones needing beer at this hour.

We care-freely stroll through the store, admiring the water cooler that can instantly chill your wine—maybe we'll get a bottle of wine too! Eee Eee—we quickly notice that the prices seem a little steep. Here on land, in this store, I can put all my problems into one little box at the moment. That box held two problems. How much is this going to cost and how can we lug it back to the boat? These problems don't seem to me insurmountable, but certainly thought-provoking. Where there's a will there's a way, Doug's Nanny always says.

I am on one end of the beer aisle, Doug on the other. As usual, there is a radio station playing softly in the background. As usual, we do our best to ignore it. The dang store is so quite we are having difficulty doing so. I catch a news report—that is, what I can only assume to be a news report. This has to be fictional, a joke, a bit of news from the past, an old radio show, like, George Orwell's *War of the Worlds*, or something!

Doug and I look to each other's eyes, silently saying, "Did you hear what I heard? World Trade Center, planes, both towers, collapse?"

Then ... something about DC and Philadelphia. We can't hear it all. We both turn and walk over to the two fellows talking in low serious tones. We speak together, "What is that we just heard on the news?"

They shake their heads, "Bad stuff going on down there!" They start to explain. My mind races—we have been on a boat for two weeks! Anything in the world could have happened!

Yes, almost anything in the world could have happened, but, *We, The People*, who are protected, pampered and exhaustively governed, never thought it could/would happen to us. This the first news we have heard in two weeks and the shock of it turns out to be the disaster which will likely change irrevocably what it means to be an U.S. citizen.

"Many acts of terrorism," they explain. "Two planes, both Twin Towers, Pentagon and Philadelphia area."

As we hear the commentary, I lean against the counter. I don't speak. I'm not able to because of the big lump in my throat. My mind reels. I glance at the clock on the wall—it would have to have been at least 8:30 a.m. when it all began. I considered the number of people at that hour in the financial district in New York. My soul mourns; this would have to mean thousands are gone.

We stay gripped to the counter, as the conversation continues. I don't remember the rest that was said. We turn, slumped shouldered, back to the gin aisle and hug instinctively. We stare at the aisle laden with sedatives in a variety of choices. Decision made! Enjoy, life while you can. We'll buy a case of beer and a bottle of gin! We remember we are in a small town in Nova Scotia, when one of the two fellows offers us a ride back to the *Guillemot*. We are very grateful, but not really ready to return. We leave our booze with the kind souls running the liquor store. We will be back in an hour.

We are happy to step outside. We take deep breaths of happiness to be alive and able to walk freely around this sweet, safe little town. I see a pay phone outside a bar/pizza joint. We decide we better try and call home, to Pennsylvania. We wonder about the world situation as we saunter along. This will probably mean war, conflict, or whatever they decide to call it. Doug recalls when the Gulf War broke out, he and his son Nate were listening to the radio in our cottage in Pennsylvania. Myself, I was with my family on a crater on Kona, Hawaii, so close to an active volcano I could smell the sulfurous fumes and see where the slow flow of lava made steam as it oozed into the ocean.

As I wait, attached to the phone for my call to go through to Doug's parents, my perspective of our little plight changes. We are merely trying to get out of the mud in a safe, quiet, bucolic setting of the upper Shube/Stewaicke river. Our little situation of the stuck business and the possibility of 30 days will remain our little secret. Doug's parents will have to read about it.

Hey, in a river, as well as life, you never know what is around the bend.

"There's a TV on in the bar, if you want to catch any news," my husband tells me. Naah! We both shake our heads. We would rather enjoy some fresh air and ponder the reason for our existence.

The ride back to our life in the mud is swelled with contemplative melancholy. We find comfort in talking to the kind fellow, in the pickup truck, about his life in Stewiacke. This seems to be a common scenario. Simon left in his twenties, only to come back 30 years ago to settle down. He tells us. "I would bet it has been over 30 years ago since we've seen a fishing boat up here and I'd wager money, it's been a hundred years for a sailboat. Nope, not since the days they were built up river on the dry and then sailed them down into the bay!"

"Do they do much fishing up here," Doug asks the nice guy, thoughtful enough to be driving our booze to the mud bank.

Simon gives us a rather forlorn look, "Oh, there use to be tons of fish up here, salmon, bass, smelt and roe. Like everywhere else, people thought it would never end. They don't stop until the bounty is pilfered and depleted. Some of the problem could be chemicals. I don't know for sure."

The fellow speaks more about the goin's-on of Stewiacke. My mind drifts to tomorrow's headlines. I don't even want to ponder that. The headlines that flash across my mind, are headlines which might help our world *situation—Let's Go Back To Simple Living! The Us Against Them! Greedy Attitudes Need to BE Eliminated!*

Nearing the river, our discussion turns to the erosion problem. Simon recalls, "My dad owned property along the river when I was a kid. The erosion cut off a slice of land, creating a small Island. This started a fight between my Dad and the neighbor. The neighbor wanted to claim it!"

"And, what became of it?" I prod.

"They fought and fought until my Dad finally gave up and let the neighbor have it!" he replied.

It strikes me, as he spoke, that life is the same world over only at different levels. I compare this neighborhood feud with our situation in the Middle East. How did our oil get under their sand? We've had alternative renewable energy technology for 30 to 40 years. We have chosen to ignore this and continue our quest for oil. Will we continue fighting over it until someone gives up or until like the fish, until it is depleted?

The tension of the day is broken by a good chuckle. We all see our stuck-on-a-mud-bank sailboat. Simon kindly drops us off at our boots and we wave good bye. The dust on the tractor path has not even settled when we remember #5 on our shopping list. The marsh grasses hide our bounty. We march back up the hill, under the overpass to just past the freeway. There, we find a convenience store and gas station. We hope they have what we need. They do and we whine a little over the price. I was happy to save another walk to town for our needed disposable camera. Our good camera didn't like the crossing from Five Islands any more than I did. It is still pouting next to our good clock.

Across the road and up another hill we spot Clem's Farm Fresh

Produce Stand, just waiting for us. Never in my life has grocery shopping been so difficult and yet so gratifying. We stroll through heavenly stocked aisles. The Magnificent Mile in Chicago never brought me this much shopping joy. We gather, from all corners of the indoor produce stand, all sorts of neat stuff. We keep in mind the three things on my provision list. 1) Where can we store it? 2) How long will it last? 3) Can we get it back to the boat?

We stop high on the bank to take a photo before we start lowering our provisions. Darn! I miss my zoom lense on my sick camera. We will likely not be able to see what on God's green earth or, in this case, what in God's red mud I was trying to photograph.

During the few hours between the time we slopped up the embankment and now, our slop down the embankment, the river has made good use of its time. It has continued draining and preparing for the next show. To the people in town, or to those on the train and in automobiles, this means nothing. To us, however, it means we have a very large area of wet gooey mud.

Okay! Let's go, let's get this dinghy loaded!

Ha Ha Ha Ha Ha. I could Ha Ha the rest of the way across this page. But, instead, I'll attempt to describe what it takes to do this. If you homeowners ever had to experience this, you wouldn't be so complainy about market day. What a life of Riley (I always wanted to be Riley), to drive to your market, load your shopping cart, stack it all in your easily assessable vehicle and quickly drive home. Once home, your spacious pantry, refrigerator and freezer await you. No problemo!

We face the challenge ahead of us with the vigor and vitality of those who have new provisions. The swell of emotions of the day serve to enliven the moment. We almost kiss the mud we walk on. Gung Ho, we work together going up and down the embankment. We slide, we climb. After many trips we have the dinghy loaded. We slop over to the area where we still have water pulling on the painter line, the dinghy behind us.

We pile in as before and the Captain starts rowing. It doesn't take long to figure out that the shallow water gets more shallow with all of our weight and gear in the dinghy. All this adds up to the familiar word for the day, *stuck*.

This presents the next obstacle in our little venture. You can't begin to understand how much finesse and effort it takes to remove your mud boots and jeans, then replace them with shorts, all the while sitting in a dinghy packed to overload, till you try. The goal is to do all this without getting covered in mud, squishing the groceries, tipping the boat and—God forbid—the booze, over into the muddy river.

Doug has transformed himself into my Egyptian slave. He performed the previously described task with much more success and poise than I would have, so I sat still. All I had to do was laugh and try to balance the boat, then slip into my role as Cleopatra. My slave drapes the painter of the dinghy over his shoulder to pull our cargo through the muddy Nile. I am transported along as he sings the old spiritual, *Twelve Gates To The City*. I give my most provocative look and promise him a bed of roses when we return to my palace.

All too quickly, however, I am expunged from my royal position, to slop back on board the *Guillemot*. My slave is there, on the other hand, to take my Baffins off my feet as I take my giant step aboard. My slave hoists everything up while I stand aboard loading it into the cockpit. I busy myself stowing, while Doug slops through the mud for a bucket of water. I have the job of sorting and stowing. The Captain has the job of wiping out the dinghy and all things that have mud on them (which is any solid object we have) before it all comes aboard.

I grin often at my husband while we each perform our duties. I thank the Spirit of the Universe that we are healthy and alive to experience all this together. I'm old enough to know that, in the future, when musing on *"The days that are no more"* (Tennyson), I will surely love to tell the story of "Once upon a time in the Shooby Taylor river."

Since necessity is the mother of taking chances, we are willing to try almost anything to get us off this mud bank. Captain, Sir Douglas William Beaver, the Factotum of the Universe, has, for the last two hours, worked flat out. Together we have pulled every tool, rope, pulley, line and hitch out of the boat. Both anchors are strategically placed up on the grass banks. Every line we can come up with leads from the boat to the anchors. This production involves various physical laws, which I don't understand.

I still feel like I could be in Egypt as I look out to the grasses on the riverbank. Beads of sweat on Doug's dark skin make him appear Egyptian. This operation looks as complicated as building the pyramids.

I fan my humble self as I scan the farmlands. I have to remind yours truly that it's September, way up here in the North. Suddenly, I become somewhat deflated when my idle mind scans the events of the day and our possible 30-day stay on a mud bank. My head and shoulders start to twitch and I spasmodically walk over to the galley and fix tea. I try my philosophic composure routine. I will sit down and confidently practice my very best "taking tea" manners. I will not say, think, or write anything negative. Two minutes into this sit-down-composure-routine, I hear from the mud side.

"Can you hand me that small brush?"

I finish the request with, "You mean the one that is stuck way up underneath the 1/4 berth? The one where I practically have to stand on my head and remove ten objects to get to?"

"Yeah. That's the one," the Captain grins.

From the mud side, "Will you put this away? Will you clean this? Pull that?"

I do as I'm asked, the sweet obedient stuck-in-the-mud wife that I am. At least his requests now involve stable, inside-of-the-boat stuff. This morning, on the a.m. tide, my job was to hang from the boom, out over the water, and then swing into the dinghy, remain standing while maneuvering around the boat, and all this with the tide rushing in! This may sound easy for some ole' water dog, but we're talk'n a mere *polliwog* here.

Other days aboard, when we aren't stuck in the mud, this polliwog makes herself useful at times. There is always something. "Chart, please," "How about the other chart?" "Would you get my other hat?" "I don't know where it is, try under the guitar case." "Orange cushion, please." "Would you move the reliance inside?" "GPS, please." "Where are the binoculars?" "Are the sailing directions on your side?" "You better add this to your list." "Can I have some water/beer/cookies/tea?" "I could use a snack." "How about some chips to go with this sandwich?" "Sunglasses, gloves, heavy coat." "Would you take the tiller? I have to pee" "I'm hot and I need to take off my long johns." "Would you put away my coat?" "GPS instructions." "Pump the bilge." "Lower the centerboard." "Raise the centerboard." "Go forward to anchor." "Lower the pop-top." "Raise the pop-top. "Snap and unsnap the canvas around the pop-top." "Hand me the WD 40."

Well, you get the picture. I can tell you, this galley slave keeps busy.

As I look out on our world of mud, it comes to me in a mud-smeared flash—I'm letting all this go to waste! I could go for an herbal body pack—let me bake in the sun—then let the soothing *Menesatung* (healing waters) cleanse me. It would be slightly freezing, but that would be part of the treatment.

From the mud side, I hear. "Can you get me the mung towel?"

Dear Jesus, Mary and Joseph, (might as well include the whole family) I almost forgot to list the *sacred mung towel*. Doug has been wading around in ankle-deep water for around four hours now. Two mud-globbed t-shirts later, I hear a series of clangs and crashes as he discards his tools. His work-grimed fist hauls a bucket of water (muddy water) (that's all there is) up and clunks it aboard to wash his feet and legs. He swings around and dries them with the mung towel.

The Mung Towel! The filth this towel, (Towels, I must add. We have two. While one is rinsed and drying, the other is in use.) has wiped up, I can't even begin to describe. The mung towel, (I say this with reverence, because I can't imagine our life without it) gets its name from a year ago last summer while playing 100's around the kitchen table in Eastport. Nate (Doug's oldest son) was spending 12 weeks with us. He was the encouraging source of this beer-drinking card game. We had several days of rain, wild guitar playing, Scrabble and 100's.

When playing 100's, a towel is needed (at least when he plays with his young buddies and we wanted the tradition to remain) for the rituals of cleaning up split beer, puke or general slobber. Thus, here on the *Guillemot*, we now call our "muck" towel, the mung towel.

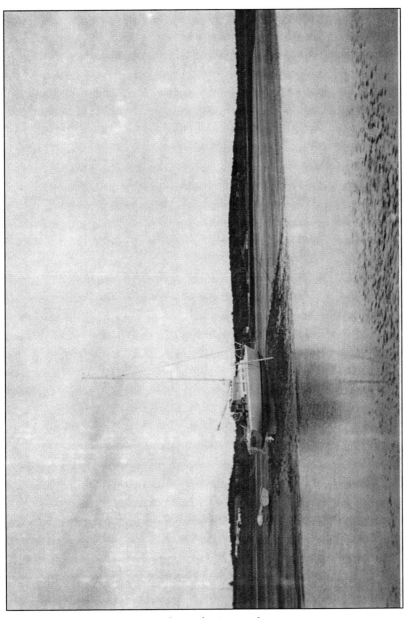

Stuck in The Stewiacke

Yes! He's set all her lines running from the anchors ashore to the jib winch.
Tonight, at high tide, he (the factotum of my dreams) will turn the winch
handle with all his might. He thinks this might dislodge her.

The factotum of my dreams gives me a satisfied nod. He's convinced he's done everything in his power to successfully pull her off her exalted place. Doug will use purchase, he explains to me. *Purchase?*

Yes! He's set all her lines running from the anchors ashore to the jib winch. Tonight, at high tide, he will turn the winch handle with all his might. He thinks this might dislodge her. For all intents and purposes we are set. We just have to wait for the tide.

We will see ... a man never knows ... a woman never knows.

We await our fate in the cockpit, soaking in the peace and quiet. We realize, now, that North America has stood still. All the trucks, planes, trains and automobiles from the previous evening are silenced in the wake of the terrorism attack. In our case, it is the silence that makes us realize the abnormality of life. Meanwhile, I wrap myself in the normality of life. I start to prepare dinner.

All the fresh local produce makes our taste buds tingle. We smack our lips and discuss the farmer who called to us from the shore earlier. Surprisingly, he was not one and the same as the farmer who owns these cows we've been conversing with all day. "No," he tells us, he would be the "bass farmer" from up around the bend in the river. Bass Farm?

Yesterday evening about dusk, when we were slowing meandering up the river, we passed his farm. He tells us that while we were observing we were also being observed by the one and only bass farmer in all of Canada. The Stewiacke/upper Shubenacadie, is the only river in all of Canada where the bass still spawn. Research shows, because of conservation, that there are more bass here these days than 45 years ago. The Captain and I agree; this is progress.

I asked the bass farmer if it might have been two large fish jumping that we heard as we rounded the bend? "Don't think so," he tells me. "There are two large seals that hang out in that area. They probably jumped off the bank when they heard the big monster, they weren't use to, come upon them."

I rest in the cockpit enjoying the last of the warmth of the day. I drink a beer. My mind says I need more than this to relieve my tension, but I tell my nerves to settle down on their own. I can't be plastered and lie down, comatose, in the V-berth. The Captain may need me.

The last two weeks aboard have served to heighten my senses. Now that we don't have a real camera, except for our 27-picture throwaway (which I hope I don't just throw away the pictures), I feel an urgency to look hard at each aspect of the day. I feel a calmness come over me as I take possession of all around me. I want to see (really *see*) and remember the reflection of the ducks in flight, all swooping down together to land on the river.

We sit waiting, cozy in our respective spots reading and writing. We stop occasionally to discuss the state of the world. We speculate, wonder, and vent. We vent our anger, sadness and worry. How pitifully stupid mankind can be—-greed, power and religion. Can we ever change? *"Through our feast of reason and our flow of soul,"* (Pope) we lament on the mentality of one nation against the next, instead of all of us trying to complete the miracle of our lives on this planet. This planet, the Earth, whirling through space at a thousand miles per hour in the infinite Universe!

On the stern of most boats, the home port is printed. On ours we just have *Guillemot*. The Captain feels if he ever does make the change, it will not read Eastport, ME. It will read EARTH!

The tide swam to us like a serpent and rolled over us. Facing west I can only see the cows and grain silos silhouetted against the fiery sunset. My personal slave is still mumbling all sorts of tidbits to them as he gathers the anchors and coils the ropes. The technical plan in question was, as it happens, successful in pulling the *Guillemot* off her pedestal of mud. It is now 8:40 p.m. and we are floating, ready to move to our new, just-right spot, for an evening of needed rest. Whew!

Drinking in the sunset, I realize we are some of the few persons incommunicado with the world and all the gathering dark clouds. We have spent the day preoccupied with our own personal survival. We knew New York was burning, but we did the only thing we could do—we just kept trying to get out of the mud.

Life continued; I cooked, the cows chewed, the bass hatched, the seals splashed and the tidal bore rushed.

Bonsoir cows. Goodnight cruel world!

Day 13

Wednesday, September 12, 2001

We had a sweet, gentle, smiling, golden sleep. As our traveling companion, Shakespeare, put it, "a sleep that knits up the ravell'd sleeve of care." My wonderful-got-us-off-the-mud-bank-husband just rolled his eyes when I told him of my latest list. That list being: To what I attribute our great night's sleep. "All right Listy, let's hear it!"

1. We are still floating
2. Zero leg drills
3. We didn't have to change locations
4. Perfect weather
5. The rushing water is fairly calm way up here towards the top of the river
6. We didn't play sleep and slide all night
7. It was quiet. The trains, planes and trucks were still almost silent in the wake of yesterday's terrorism

Yes, last night we had a hint of familiarity from our old sailing lives. Until 6:30 a.m. Doesn't the person up there know I *really* want to sleep? Why does it sound like I'm underneath a helmet upon which a mean person is building a house? Peeking out, I hear and see a scene that could not fail to bring a smile to the most tortured face. My Egyptian has returned, sporting a white-toothed grin. He is rigging the entire boat with the sheets he just cleaned in the bucket. While he cleans all his gear used to remove the ole' gal from her lofty position, he is bellowing,

Sailing, Sailing, all me life is sailing . . .
sailing and bailing all me friggin' life.
Sailing, sailing, pukin' over the railing . . .

The menestung mud covers all; the ropes, handles, pulleys and every tool he used in the big lift off. The penetrating brown mud covers almost every square inch of the *Guillemot*'s decks. My fastidious husband will make sure it will be clean if it is cleanable.

Alas! His finished product leaves our little boat a new shade of taupe. All of our chores are finished in time for breakfast and tea before we embark on the next leg of our journey. My right eye twitches. After a short, shuddering look down river, I consider where we'll be heading as the tide turns, riding the tide that journeys back all the way down and out to the Copiquid Bay, then all through the Minas Basin, then out to the upper Bay of Fundy, out to the Grand Manan Channel and Gulf of Maine, and then finally to the North Atlantic Ocean. I turn to my more-confident-than-I husband. He cocks an eyebrow at me, then gives me a wink.

I've got to think positive. I try that for a while and now I'm positive I don't want to do this.

I am well aware that most of my prayers have been manifestations of my intentions. I have full intention of surviving the ride down this river. I let God know, early this morning, that I will write down all the valuable lessons of life I've learned and have yet to learn on this journey. I'm hoping he buys this and thinks I'm worth saving, at least for today. There are times, however, when the message from the pit of my stomach tells me that the power of the Universe is busy with more important things than me.

Applying lessons in life reminds me of my mother. She was not a woman of many words. I remember, all those years ago, her giving me some bits of insight. At the time I thought she was just a woman trying to keep her daughter chained to the sofa during those years of my life when some would have deemed me temporarily insane (while others would simply categorize me as a normal teenager).

She said, "Eileen!" (for I was no longer "Little Eileen." Then she gave me a stern look and held her hand high (Doug can blame my mother for that one).

"Eileen, Los Swan!" (I still don't know what that means), "*Never, I mean never do anything for the first time!*"

Thinking back, this was *sound* advice. However, I've never quite figured out the tactics I need to follow her words of wisdom. Today I can say, for example, if we'd run this river many times, seeing how the tide flows in each little area, then we'd be, some might say, playing with a "full deck."

Later, in my teenagerhood, I found myself in a little predicament. "Eileen Mary!" she said, looking at me over her glasses, shaking her head, kneading her bread dough as if it were my head. "Eileen … *like most things in life, it is easier to get yourself into something, than it is to get yourself out.*"

"Mama," I said now, looking heavenward, with sentimental, scaredy-cat tears swelling, "I hope in this case you weren't right."

At high tide, as we watch closely for the first sign that the tide has turned, we throw our dice on the table. We start the motor and head down river. The roulette wheel of the river is spinning. The tidal bore is completing its destiny as it always has every six hours. Unconcerned with us, we are mere jetsam. I hope lady luck is not snoring.

I'm jolted out of near-sleep by the squawk of about fifty crows taking flight, chasing two bald eagles out of a tree. I watch as they swirl overhead. Then I relax and lay my head back down on my arms, resting on the coaming of the cockpit. At times, during the first couple of hours, the ride was tense. We had to read the current and the depth of the river, rounding each bend before crossing over the more shallow parts to get to the deeper channel.

All seems so peaceful, quiet and warm.

I relax.

We're going down river perfectly. At this rate we should make it out before the top of the river goes dry.

The sounds of the water and the call of the loons lull me into a smug complacency.

Geez! It's so hot! This life jacket and anchor gloves are boiling, sting-y, itchy. I'm going to take this jacket off until we get at least a breath of wind or we move into the shade. I wonder what this raging river must look like in the winter. I see a charming camp ahead, I wonder if they are there to see it that way—banks covered with snow and all the frothy water. I let my mind drift along with the river. I'm almost relieved not to know more about the consequences of yesterday's terrorism.

We round another bend in the river when our seemingly slow, lazy river suddenly changes. The river here is very wide and turbulent. We can't see the channel. We make a split-second decision to get over to the other side, where the channel should be, this minute! And while there is still enough *water* to get us there!

In this section of the river we are not deceived. This river is raging, emptying with more force and speed than we thought possible. Here, the depth changes with every passing second.

Somewhere in the shallow depths of my mind, I recall being given a bit of rather profound advice, *"Expect the unexpected and you're never surprised."* I will never get that through my thick head. I should have it tatooed somewhere.

The depth sounder changes quickly. We are jerking and moving around spasmodically (the Captain, I'm sure, wouldn't call it that but it sure seemed spasmodic to me). We search for a deeper part of the river. The ebbing tide changes so quickly that it fails to show the heavy rapid-like waves that a flooding tide does.

We are losing control of the boat and, more alarmingly, the speed with which we need to get to the deeper channel. With each breath I take (and I am breathing fast and heavy), our depth lowers—it hits—THUD!

One never forgets this experience, as hard as one may try. Blast it! Gosh darn it!

We've gone aground again, again, again!

Characteristically, I would like to like to scream bloody murder.

My panic button has been pushed but fearing that my Captain might try to stuff something down my throat (or throw me into the descending river), I silently mutter, *"Eeeck,* we're *done* for!" The water is descending now and there's *no chance* to get her to float.

The boat is heeling over, water is splashing up over the side and general tumult has commenced.

The Captain, calls for … for … I'll give you *one* lucky guess! "Anchor!"

I climb to the high side of the boat feeling very much like a roofer on a slick, very slanted roof only a few feet above a raging river. Having made it to the forward deck, I wrap one leg around part of the bow pulpit to keep from sliding off—you're likely familiar with the routine by now. I grab for the anchor, untie, release it from its hold.

You can all give me a big cheer now! Miracles never cease! Despite my panic, I remember the all-important rule of anchoring in a tidal bore!

Cleat! And cleat *before* you release the line into the pandemonium below. The rules are—if there were ever any written—*anchor*. Then, once stationary, perhaps we can pull ourselves upright and into deeper water. Good plan, but (there are *always* buts) the anchor *will not hold.*

I do my job of *cleating* and *uncleating* the anchor line, while hanging on for dear life. I turn to see if the Captain approves—I don't want to disappoint him.

I realize he doesn't expect *much,* but still I didn't expect to see my Captain stripping down to his skivvies. What the hell? Then …he lowers himself down *into the water.* I want to scream, "Come back! Don't leave me here."

The water is rough, loud and turbulent, but not deep. I tell myself, well *that's* a plus.

Well, duhhuh! That's why we went *aground.*

The Skipper works his way to the anchor, then fights his way through the water hoping to find a place where the anchor will hold and work for us so we can pull ourselves to deeper water. The Captain has the anchor rope to hang on to so he won't be swished out to the now-full Copiquid Bay.

If I fell in … (no life jacket again!) but let's not talk about stupid stuff. I continued to adjust the scope to no avail.

At this point an event happened that shocked the two of us and would have shocked anyone who'd been there struggling with us. The tide was swirling around us with such tremendous force that it began to dig a hole filled with *water*.

And we began to turn *upright* again.

Before long we were floating in our very own lake *Guillemot*. All of our harsh exertions were fruitless—we simply watched in awe. The water receded, red sand appeared, and there we sat bobbing in our little lake.

Both of us were huffing and puffing. I'm wide-eyed. Doug is shaking his head smiling. I won't allow myself a smile yet. Doug made himself decent and we set the legs to hold us upright as the water seeped out and gently lowered us into the sand.

We stood, hands on hips, and surveyed the terra firma. It is time to consider our options, or, as I feel now, the lack thereof.

I didn't bother with my trusty pen and pad.

The Captain placed the anchor in the deepest part of the channel in order to pull her (hopefully) in that direction later, when the water returned.

Yep! That was our only option and we took it.

Now, crew, make yourself comfortable in our boat-made lake. We have all day to wait. All damn day until the tidal bore will come to pay us a visit around 8 p.m. tonight!

Well, well, mercy me! Another beautiful spot here in the Shube. Very quiet—the squeaky cackles of the bald eagles are the only noises around me. The clear warm sunshine dries our underwear, tee shirts and towels hanging from the lifelines. I like it when I have laundry hanging from the lifelines instead of me.

I squint into the sunlight to take in the view of acres and acres of packed red mud, my *sea of troubles* (Shakespeare), that surrounds us. Despondently, I go below to prepare some needed nourishment.

My husband does his "*Yum-Yum-Yummy-Yum-Yum*" routine over our lunch: thick slices of 14-grain bread spread with spicy mustard and million-dollar relish, slices of cucumber, red onions, tomatoes and sharp cheddar cheese.

As I clean up, however, my mouth starts to turn up on the ends.

I look over at my husband's unconventional pose. He is lying in the middle of the V-berth with his legs elevated and propped against the open hatch, spread like butterfly wings, resting and stretching his poor sacroiliac. He reads aloud from an act of Shakespeare.

I am hell bent on not laughing. I grab a beer. He can't make me laugh if I don't *want* to. I want to cry! It is a woman's prerogative to cry, drink and laugh when she wants to. I stood there a long while, exercising my prerogative. I felt a bit better—not a lot, but some. My husband knows to duck when I start tossing around my prerogative.

Doug is sleeping, I pull out the gin. I figure I'll have a little Cape Cod (I know it's made with vodka but I only have gin). A psychoanalyst peering over his/her pad, would remark, "Does this *really* solve any problems?"

I would sneer and answer emphatically, "No, but it is providing me serenity to accept what I cannot change! I just need to calm the ole' nerve—after all, I only have one left! You see Doc, *reality* has set in. You know—the *total* of real things and events. The current *reality* is that I'm stuck in the middle of the Shube in, likely, one of the most turbulent sections, in a hole of our own making, waiting for the tidal bore to hit at between 8–8:30 tonight. I have way, way too much time to think about what will happen to us then. To top the whole thing off—it will be dark! So, what if it swishes us up against a cliff? What if it turns us over, we flood with water and mud, and have to swim for shore? What if we can't *find* the shore (remember, it's dark out)? If I *do* find the shore, then what will happen if I happen to survive? I could be four miles up river and my husband half-buried in *mud*, who knows where? We know we can't hear each other call over the roar of the tide. And, if we *did* happen to survive, we'd be penniless, boat-less, shelter-less, and freezing to death. Anyway, Doctor Know-it-all Analyst, I'm in menopause! So, even if I once had a handle on life—it broke!"

Mark Twain, perhaps not the most sane person on earth during his life, said it like it was. *He had arrived at that point where, presently, the illusions would cease and he would enter upon the realities of life—and God help the man/woman who has arrived at that point!*

Doug has just turned over from his little nap and said, "I Love You My Little Sweetie Pie!" Gulp! Gulp!

Just because I said "I Do" I find that now I'm *here!* And all this *waiting* is driving me up a wall. All sea rations should include tranquilizers.

I prefer to remain in my normal state of denial, but yesterday, at Stewiacke, we picked up a brochure that included advertisements for the river runners! *Big Mistake!* This knowledge is in no way helping my state of mind. The brochure encourages you to encounter the "power of the advancing tide" overtaking the natural flow of the river.

> *Watch in awe as a small stream reverses into a turbulent river. Then the wet and wild adventure begins, as we ride the roller coaster rapids over and over. Ride the famous tidal bore and ensuing tidal rapids … [get this]* generating waves from three to sixteen feet *[emphasis mine] depending on the phase of the moon. You'll feel the rush of riding the tidal bore and eight sets of rapids as the tide thunders up the Shubenacadie. Rare in the world, the tides of the Bay of Fundy can rise up to forty feet in just three and half hours. Tidal Bore? Who needs a roller coaster? Take a ride of a lifetime, surfing down waves and skirting whirlpools, rafting on Fundy's famous tides. Don't let the name fool you. The tidal bore is anything but! Come with us on the journey of a lifetime and experience the incredible POWER OF THE BAY OF FUNDY!*

The day moved along as fast as evolution itself. I gave a little forlorn sigh of despair and then climbed off the boat. I waded through our mini lake and set out on a walk across the beautifully packed, red spirally sand. While sitting aboard, the weight of the world from the events of yesterday and the unknown state of our future caused what I diagnosed as *anxiety neurosis.* Now, let that roll off your tongue a few times. For a while I thought it might be *anxiety psychosis.* I thought this through in my foreboding state.

In my view, the difference between a psychosis and a neurosis is this: a person with psychosis thinks that 2+3=4. A person with a neurosis knows 2+2=4, but it *bothers* him. A walk was sorely needed. Cheapy camera in hand.

I walk out alone, counting 666 steps (how doomsday is that?). I walk on to 700 steps and turn to take a picture (I count so that I can have a perspective for the picture). How silly we look out here stuck in the middle! I have to laugh. If I pretend I'm having a good time, it might just work.

Suddenly, dread floods me again … even if we get out of *this* situation, it could be the same thing just around the corner. I sit down in the sun seeking composure.

I hear Doug thunder out at the top of his lungs,

"I got one good cell where there use to be a brain. I've got one good lung so I guess I can't complain. She tells me that she loves me, somethin' tells me she's insane"

How romantic, he's singing *The Train Song!* Just for me. I really am *the only one who can make his whistle blow!*

Willing the lump from my throat and the tears from my eyes, I'm losin' it! *The Train Song!* My love song. A happy, happy song which reminds me that being out here, waiting for the bore, is not unlike being tied to the tracks … waiting for the train to hit.

I am such a fool. This whole situation proves what the late P. T. Barnum used to say, that "there's one born every minute!"

As evening closes in, steadiness and presence of mind are no longer options. I can't see the fun or the beauty in this unnerving situation. I feel shrouded in uncertainty and trepidation. Each minute the loud dollar store clock ticks, it gets worse. We have the hatch tied shut and the companionway boards slatted shut. Everything is as secure as possible. The Captain doesn't let me indulge in my moody fears. I should have been given complaint coupons at the beginning of this journey. Aahh! The nitty gritty is that I would have probably already used them all anyway.

I remain below, contemplating my future—if, indeed, I have one. I peek out the scratched plexiglass window to see that Mr. Confound Eternal Optimist is having a great time. He is taking one more walk on the packed sand.

I have decided that a bit of fresh air may help, the Captain joins me in the cockpit. He slings the guitar strap over his shoulder and sings, as loud as humanly possible, *The Mean Eileen Song.* Normally, his music would be a salve for the wounds of my soul. Today,

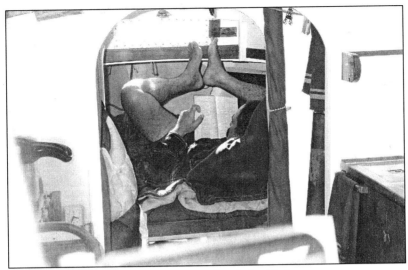

Stuck in the Middle of The Shube
I look over at my husband's unconventional pose. He is lying in the middle
of the V-berth with his legs elevated and propped against the open hatch,
spread like butterfly wings, resting and stretching his poor sacroiliac.
He reads aloud from an act of Shakespeare.

Lake Guillemot
How silly we look out here stuck in the middle! I have to laugh.
If I pretend I'm having a good time, it might just work.

however, it's salt. As I watch this character (who is supposedly my "soul mate") sing with wide-open mouth and closed eyes, the hilarity of the situation does finally begin to strike me. I think to myself that it's a good thing he doesn't have cavities.

My own personal *Hee Haw Show* is now made more absurd— we both look up to see we have an audience.

I see his raft parked in the deep part of the channel. The river rafter guide is walking our direction and he's laughing his head off. So, this is a new one to add to our list as we hadn't met up with him yet. Introductions behind us, he tells us, "Oh yeah, I heard all about you two!"

Taking on a more serious look, he asked if we'd heard the news of yesterday. Doug described the Stewiacke beer store run. I asked if there was anything to add to the first four traumas. Apparently the world had held its own.

I inquired, with a masterly attempt at indifference, "Just what time do you think the bore will hit here?"

He looked at his watch, checked our exact location, and replied, "Approximately in 40 minutes."

I sighed as though my worst fears had been realized. I think I had the brief hope that this *bore,* that has faithfully come and gone, for who knows how many thousands of years, just *might not* tonight.

The fellow had to go. Had to get back to his job. It seemed a woman awaited him in the raft and her job was to take shots of the rafters and then sell them their pictures. I wanted to jump out and tell her to keep that camera pointed *away* from me!

I fought the urge.

I had been *simmering* all day, and now my emotions were coming to a boil. Take a cleansing breath and a pattern breath—expel breath. Calm.

Calm, yeah, calm! *Screw* calm!

By God, I was gonna be prepared *this* time! I threw down my pen and pad to don my very best survival gear! Instead, for the *two* seconds that it took to circumnavigate the boat, I paced. I went down below and paced.

Then I started with the gear. Minutes later our ole' *paesano* from our first run through, Wally (the other guy told us his name), stopped by to pay his respects before we were buried in the mud of the Shube. I stuck my head out of the companionway, as a turtle would out of her shell, and then I tucked it right back in.

I checked my four-and-one-half-inch pocket mirror—now *that's* depressing. I shut my eyes and concentrate on deep breathing. Finally, I step out to greet Wally.

He asks if we'd heard the big news of yesterday and we confirmed that indeed we had. We shook our heads and discussed the ordeal a bit. Then Wally speculated, mildly, about when and what the bore might do to us here.

"Might just swoop you up? Might not ever get your anchor unstuck? Might heel you over," he suggested, probing. "You got me? Did you find the beer store?"

The Captain proclaims that, "It was worth the trip." Wally kept glancing my direction. Was he checking my mental condition? Checking to see if there is a homicidal glint in my eyes? I am greatly relieved not to have all my nightmare survival fatigues on. Wally's expression was complicated. Surprise? Curiosity? Just a touch of admiration?

Could it be admiration and reverence for a woman who's on her fourth day in the Shooby Taylor?

Wally cocks his head philosophically. Then he looks my way and pops the question. "Were you pissed the other day when we first saw you go up river?"

I think—what—where?

"My boss and I," he continues, "were wagering that you were *pissed* at being tossed into the tidal bore. That's why you were so far forward on the boat—to get as far from this SOB [pointing to Doug] as possible."

Huh? Pissed off?

"Oh, no," I answer.

Not that I am a salty, brave sea wife who really knew her stuff? Oh no! Not an ever-ready anchorwoman ready to save our sorry asses by riding *forward* for the anchor? So they thought I was pissed! Well, truthfully, that is pretty much how I feel now. But not then! Then, I was true salt! Then, I was *ignorant!*

This makes the whole event worse because *no one* thinks *I'm* salty! No one believes I'm rough and ready! Face it, they thought I was a fuming candy ass!

Breathe, Eileen. Practice what you learned in those Lamaze classes all those years ago. Breathe—cleansing breath—pattern breath—expel breath. They emphasize distraction as their primary control technique—then breathing. I don't recall anyone ever really *mentioning* the pain. They conveniently never thought to *tell* you the length or the severity of the pain. They circled around the subject, phrasing it in terms such as *labor sensations*. Nope ... they just came up with this great plan to *breathe* with speculations that you will receive emotional and physical *support* from your labor coach. Your dedicated and concerned coach will say, "Trust Me!" (we've all heard that one before). You are to maintain a calm, relaxed atmosphere and keep focused. I sat in those dumb classes, nodding my head mater-of-factly. How can you not feel confident, when you know women out there have been doing this for ... well, you know a long time? I focused my attention on nutrition, how much weight I gained, the wallpaper in the baby's room and swelled ankles.

That was the *first* time through. Back then—I was ignorant! With the second baby, reality sets in. You know there is no breathing or spiritual solution to this little problem. This time you scream for drugs. No one gives you credit for having your baby naturally. Tonight, I'm screaming for drugs, so to speak, and I'm gonna fix a stiff one—just a little somethin' to see me through the ordeal.

My preparatory study for tonight's festivities tells me it is getting chilly and the mosquitoes are out. All my gear lay on the quarter berth cushion ready for Showtime! One by one I layer, as though preparing for battle. First, my hooded thermal lined sweatshirt. Next, my life jacket. Then my windbreaker, also with a hood, and last but certainly not least, my gloves for the chaffed anchor-rope hands. I pull the hoods tight so you can only see a few inches of my face. Hey, the mosquitoes are big in this river and they haven't disappeared yet! I'm just getting over two weeks of blistered face. Last summer I stopped counting at 160 bites at one time, so I'm taking precautions. I check all my gear one more time and then, of course, I have to go pee. So I strip off enough gear to do so and then redress.

Okay! This is it! I guess I'm ready to *watch in awe as this small stream turns, again, into a raging, turbulent river!*

I step out into the cockpit and darlin' Doug just about splits a gut! He's laughing so hard that I thought he was gonna pee his pants. I send him a poisoned look full of daggers.

I admit that I look like an astronaut ready for Mars. But, I exclaimed, *"Who* in the hell is going to see me?"

Doug is happy as can be at the prospect of the tidal bore overtaking us. I am a devastated wreck! He's still laughing at the sight of me and I was almost (almost) infected with the humor of it all, when, suddenly, "who in the hell is going to see me" comes floating up right next to us.

Naturally, it's a raft full of tourists (we have enough water for that now), and I groan when I realize that I am certainly staged front and center for the lucky viewer.

The cool Captain of the stuck-in-the-mud-*Guillemot* climbs up to the deck and does a surfing routine for our spectators. He yells over the roar of the motor and the rushing river.

"Yes!" he shouts, pointing to me. "Yes, she's having a *great* time!" Oh, OOOOOHHHH!!!!

I glower at him. My burner is now on high heat! I can usually stop short of actual violence. I feel like one of those broads on the *Jerry Springer Show!* I am seized with an intense desire to throttle him—only my vanity stops me. I can't possibly move gracefully in all this gear! I call down all curses I can think of on the head of my surfing Captain. An arm's distance is where I need to be.

He's having a lifetime experience and I want to scream, "Get me *out of here!* I mean the boat, the Subenacadie and the Minas Basin!"

Then! Then! Let me tell you all ... all women who have ever had PMS or been through menopause, you'll be with me on this one. Then! *Then!* He had the *audacity* to say, "Only a damn woman could be here, with all this happening, and not enjoy it!"

I gave him the look of a gorgon.

Well, that did it! I'm going to ... and then ... the bore overtook us.

* * *

Because my adrenal glands are still pumping, even now, I have a fierce determination to finish writing about the course of *events* that followed my last sentence. I choose *events*, rather than incidents, because the word *incidents* denotes a matter of relatively slight importance.

A divine spark leads me to confess, while my emotions are still being replayed on the screen of my mind, that my old-fashioned projector, empty now, still rolls. The end of the tape on my reel-to-reel continues to flap, flap, flap. My mind does the fast, noisy rewind. I wait with anticipation, just as I did in every classroom of my childhood, while the audiovisual operator makes sure it is threaded perfectly.

Now, once again, I will roll the film. It will be slightly distorted from poor audio and age—not like the clear DVDs of today. Am I capable of an accurate account? Hardly! But I am prepared to try. I have only to find the play button.

Here it goes! Lights! Action!

∗ ∗ ∗

. . . then the tidal bore overtakes us.

The bore rushed upon us. Roaring, splashing, trying with all its might to move us out of the way. The *Guillemot* hangs onto her anchor for dear life in an attempt to keep from rushing up, up, up, to—who knows to what end? She was like a scrawny tree, hanging on by its roots in the middle of a flood of rushing river.

The current and waves thrash her, lifting her up and flopping her down, to and fro. We waited and waited. With each jar my throat became more parched. There was only darkness in this ominous night. There seemed to be no sky, no clouds, no starry firmament, no heavens, no promise. Endless, seemingly endless, roaring.

Finally, we felt the tide begin to slow, enough, we hoped, to pull anchor and move over to the deeper channel and out of the rush of the river. Our plan was to spend the night and take the outgoing tide tomorrow morning. Tonight would be like trying to grope our way out of a knotted maze. I knew it was too dark to navigate. I just hoped we could find the *channel.* We've had hours of pressure and build-up of mud on our anchor but if we don't pull now we'll be stuck again—possibly for another night or day? Who knows?

My mission, which I was daft enough to accept (but I had no

real choice), was to try to *pull* the anchor. The Captain was at the tiller doing his best to control the boat, motor running, hoping to be ready to maneuver her across the rushing water to the channel.

Forward I pulled and pulled with increasing intensity and urgency. I kept thinking that if I just pulled harder, faster, longer, used more/different purchase, got a different grip, braced my legs or *something,* the anchor would eventually come loose. I felt it was my responsibility to pull and release us from this horrendous ordeal. Doug kept trying to use the motor to help with the leverage. My fierce energies kept me going.

The roar of the motor and river was deafening, I could hear no instructions from my Captain. Likewise, he received no reports from me. When you are facing forward, your back is aft and your hands are gripping with all you've got. You can't use hand signals or yell, like a scene in a lurid romance novel, NO! YES! SLOWER! FASTER!

Despite all my efforts, I just wasn't getting it, so we switched places. The Captain gave me a quick lesson of what to do with the motor and what he was trying to do with the anchor line. We decided on head signals, which didn't work at all because it was too dark and you can barely see anyone's head when you're groveling on the deck pulling your guts out.

I guess I failed at the motor, as the Captain motioned that we should switch again. We all know by now that I wasn't in the gifted program at First Mates' school and I have all the technical knowledge of my smallest skillet.

I can't tell if I'm being any help or not. At this juncture in our routine, my *anxiety neurosis,* which I'd pushed far to the back of my head, comes unstuck (unlike the anchor). It surfaces right smack dab in the center of the aqueducts of my eyes. Tears stream down my face. I can't see to get forward so I just feel my way. I'm glad it's dark and the Captain is too preoccupied to notice or care.

We go through it all again—over and over again. How many times? How long? I have no idea. My film becomes fuzzy at this point. This is the *time is relative* bit. It seemed like an eternity. I was only conscious of my back-breaking, gut-busting, futile efforts. The Captain came forward and advised, "Don't pull your arm sockets out of joint. Let the motor do the work."

Yeah right … just to keep hold and continue pulling at all was taxing my lifetime supply of super-human force.

I just kept giving it "all I had," over and over, endlessly, until some interminable amount of time passed. Then I focused my eyes and suddenly Doug was there by my side.

I was using "purchase" while he was pulling frantically! I mean, *frantically!* I don't care if the Captain wouldn't say it was frantic! It's *my* story, *my* book, and believe you me, it was *frantic!*

All of a sudden he yells, "CLEAT! CLEAT!" (I'm beginning to really *hate* that word). I fumble because my hood has fallen forward covering my running nose and wet face. I can't get it *cleated,* at least not *fast* enough. He could feel the anchor start to come!

He pushed my face, not knowing where he was pushing—he was struggling (frantically) to get me out of the way. I fell back on my butt. I was panting, gasping and crying my eyes out. It took many tries to pull my hood back so I could get some air.

The Captain eventually maneuvered the cleat. The anchor was loose! He handed the line over to me to finish bringing her in. He ran back to the motor and I was left there alone. I got her up, gasping hand to mouth, and then tied her off properly. With the pressure of the running water, it was probably the most difficult thing I ever accomplished.

My tears and nose were running as hard as the tide. There was no throwing my arms in the air to signal a victory or touchdown. No "Yahoos!"

The Skipper motored to a better spot and I didn't even look to see where we were. With an aching heart and a body in exhaustion-overdose, I went inside and flung myself face down on the V-berth. Lucky for me, the sounds of the motor and the water drowned out my wail of woe.

Now I sat inside in my hideaway, listening to all the commotion going on in the outside world. The Captain has dropped anchor in many spots only to pull it up and continue looking for just the right place for us. I feel very disconnected. I need to plug in my cord to the spiritual outlet; to recharge my energy with the force that gives life, the force that causes the sperm and the egg to bring forth a human being, and that bring the acorn and the oak tree into existence. The same force that cannot be tamed or controlled. The force which causes the tide to flow. That formless, infinite energy that is non-understandable.

It is much easier for me to journal the *facts* instead of my *emotions*. Not nearly as rewarding, but easier. I now analyze both. There are days, hours and moments in which we become acutely aware that time is precious and that we will not live forever. The world and life seem flimsy, like tissue paper in the rain. Today, I came to grips with the reality that *nothing* lasts forever—not lives or empires. I was frustrated, scared and sad, not just for our situation, but for the whole world. I wanted to go back and live under the illusion, as I did years ago, that life was stable and predictable. I wanted to believe that I had a safety-comfort zone. I wanted to be close to our children; for us all to be tucked into a cozy little nest, safe from the volatile world and Mother Nature. But it was not to be. The *now* of it is that I am unable to be with our children and family. I am, and will likely always be, helpless in my attempts to officiate the world. I must accept and respect the power and forces of the raging tides.

I hear the anchor go down one more time, The Captain is making the sounds which indicate that it's time to get the boat ready for a long-needed rest. I stepped out of the companionway to the cockpit. Once I recover my ability to speak, I feel I need to try and explain my behavior to my, probably by this time, bewildered husband. However, I don't know what to say. Well, maybe I do but I don't know *how* to say it. So I just start quoting what I've just written in my journal.

As I speak, I realize I have no sense of what his response will be. I search his glistening eyes, hoping for even a brief moment of understanding. I grope for more words when, suddenly, he stops me by pulling me close, stroking my head and hugging me tight. Aaahhh, just like a good Captain should. What followed was a warm flush of hope that felt much too good to be a hot flash.

So the Captain and Moaning Minnie are both relieved at having, quite literally, kept our heads above water. We are out of the meshes and toils, at least for tonight. We smile as we work together, putting the boat to bed.

With the nurturing protectorship of my husband, we snuggle close in the V-berth. I feel almost unburdened and purged. I am dropping off to that wonderful world of quiet oblivion when a sudden, curious noise alerts us. The sounds of a space ship are coming from outside. Telepathically, I tell the aliens out there, "If you have come to take my husband back to whatever planet he came from, you'll have to take me too!"

I burst out laughing at the sight of my Captain, scantily dressed in only a down jacket, disappearing out of the companionway door. He tightens the main sheet and the weird noises coming from the rigging stop.

I fall asleep with visions of Joseph Campbell, in one of his videos, telling me, "There is no security in following the call to adventure!"

I shout back, "Damn straight!"

Sometime in the middle of the night we will surely need to do the leg drill. I assume the Captain knows when.

Day 14

Thursday, September 13, 2001

There is a strange quiet surrounding me. Only the sounds of being here—only the water, the land, the rustle of the leaves and the songs of the birds harmonizing. My ears hear what they desire to hear. I cannot detect one man-made noise.

Sometimes this natural quiet stimulates, sometimes it mellows. Stimulated I put my trust in creation, which is made afresh daily, and I am mellowed at yet another glorious day of warmth and sunshine. The fleecy white clouds, bright blue sky and the lush green landscape all seem intensified by the clean air renewed by the wind and the tide. The morning has dispelled all dreary thoughts. The sunlight transformed the foreboding shapes of the night. The sense of urgency that was driving me the previous night has left me.

Just as the wave can not exist for itself, but is ever a part of the heaving surfaces of the ocean [or tidal bore] so must I never live

*my life for itself, but always in the experience which is going on
around me*
    —Albert Schweitzer, 1949

We have a fair tide. We start our (hopeful) final descent out of the Shubenacadie. My renewed spirit makes me want to smile and appreciate each hour, as if it holds 60 little diamonds. Our ride out is really relatively simple when compared to the last five days. We stop along the way at a beach, located at the base of an entire cliff full of gypsum. We grab a hunk to take back home, our very own eye of Glooscap. Doug climbs a large crevice in one of the cliffs. We give reverence to this world of the Shube River. Reverence is a way of honoring life.

The knowledge comes to me; nothing is the same as it was yesterday. Not this crevice, the wall of gypsum, a tree, a rock, this sand that moves beneath my feet—all are beautiful and fantastically rich. Each is complete in its incompleteness.

Midway on this river adventure, there was supporting evidence that I was to learn a few unexpected, highly specific lessons. At the time I thought they'd not be particularly useful, at least not in my "normal," not up the Shube life. But I found that goin' the Shube is a lot like life. The mysteries can beguile you. The ride can be heart-swelling scenic, suddenly heart-thrilling exciting, then as though entering a right of passage heart-expanding smooth. You're filled with the false assurance that you are in control. You're confident that your schemes, strategies, smart and careful decisions will achieve your goals and provide you with the life you planned. And sometimes they even do!

Then, when you *least* expect it, you go around a bend and suddenly you find yourself utterly out of control and, before you know it, you've gone aground. You are ripped, pulled and jolted. The tidal bore of *real* life swirls you around and rocks your boat. It grips you in its powerful, emotional snare. You fight, struggle, resist, and suffer. You are torn. Life thrusts you in a direction you never intended to go. There are twists and turns in every river of life. The bottom line is that goin' the Shube and life are about as easy as taking candy from a gorilla!

Shubenacadie
Doug climbs a large crevice in one of the cliffs. We give reverence to this world of the Shube River. Reverence is a way of honoring life.

The half-mile wide opening to the river seems very calm and expansive. We turned left toward Maitland.

We sailed past what they call flower pots! These "little islands" have been washed away from the mainland as a result of erosion from the tides. They sit surrounded by water, nodding their green furry caps in the wind.

Hot diggedy dog! The Captain has announced that we'll have a nice, calm, relaxing day! Just a short sail to Maitland. The French author, Henri Etienne, was right when he wrote, *"God tempers the wind to the shorn lamb."*

I wave goodbye to the Shooby Taylor. The river and my past are both behind me, like our wake. Just ripples. I turn my face to the future.

We can just see the Lawrence House Museum as we sail into Maitland. The cloudless sky allows the sun to shine, ever so brightly, on our happy heads as we plan our day. I pick up my *Dreamers and Doers*. I love this book! I slip easily into my ex-travel-agent mode. We decide that a little stroll through town and a tour through the

Cobequid Bay
We sailed past what they call flower pots! These "little islands" have been washed away from the mainland as a result of erosion from the tides. They sit surrounded by water, nodding their green furry caps in the wind.

museum, to soak in some history, sounds good. We both are intoxicated by the sun. We busy ourselves with anchoring, fixing lunch and doing a cleanup job on our floating abode.

The fact that the Shube mud may stay with the *Guillemot* until we sand and paint did not affect our free and easy mood of conviviality. Our sandwiches are scrumptious. The "Million Dollar Relish" and mustard beans I added were both canned locally. Our list for town reads: bread, chips, another disposable camera, and a dreaded newspaper. I shudder to think of it. Do we really want to see and read about all the pain and anguish? Two days after the terrorism, the papers have to be filled with the aftermath. Our isolationists' period will be over. I'm goin' with Goethe on this one, *"Nothing is worth more than this day!"* So I'm not going to let the wretchedness of it oppress me.

I head back to my live-in closet. I need to select an ensemble befitting a tour of a historical grand home of a wealthy shipbuilder! Goody, goody! I get to wear my reasonably clean jeans (the ones which aren't coated with mud), a clean tee-shirt and I'll take my clean flannel shirt if I can find it. Here it is! It was scrunched under the pillow and sleeping bag. I look down at my once-white sports shoes, now Shube brown. I'll wear them like a medal of honor. I stuff my sweatshirt in, always, just in case.

We are sitting pretty now. Our "legs" are on and we are not far from a long wooden walkway leading to the gravel part of the shore. I turn to see the Copiquid Bay starting to empty. Before long, the entire bay, except for a few ponds here and there, will be red mud.

We pull the dinghy way, way, way up to the high grasses of the marsh, just in case we get detained in town. I giggle to my husband. "This place looks so itsy bitsy. I hope they even *have* a general store."

We change out of our boots on the wooden walkway—I'm liken' this wooden walkway bit. We look down to see our little grubby and mucky hands and our grubby mucky boots. The Captain then directs our mini-expedition down to the very end of the walkway. There is still a tad of water left there to wash our hands and boots.

A feeling of equilibrium comes over me as we walk on solid ground, heading up the hill to the stately home of William D Lawrence. I fix my eyes on the architectural lines of the home. An enclosure has been added to the front door, probably for wind and rain. I see movement at the doorway. I believe it to be a woman standing in there, facing our direction. As we approach, she steps back and it appears that she wishes to remain in the shadows. I sense something I'm unsure of—as though we're crossing the threshold into an imaginary "other" world.

We tromp up past the entry of the Victorian home to take in the panoramic views of the Copequid Bay. High on the hill stands a photographic outdoor exhibit, a parking lot and picnic area. We stop to soak in the sunshine and the view of the large empty bay. My peripheral vision spots movements from the house—a head in a window, perhaps, but when I turn to face the house, it's gone.

The outdoor exhibit informs us of the history of W. D Lawrence and the house. He was every bit the enterprising fellow. This Irishman, born in 1817, came to the new world to try and make his dreams of being a shipbuilder come true. He built this house in 1870, when Maitland and other towns in Nova Scotia were prosperous ship-building communities. He was already a prosperous ship builder, when, in the fall of 1872, the keel was laid for the largest full-rigged ship ever built in Canada. Her overall length would be 272 feet. Right here, Well, not right here where I *stand*, but right where we are anchored—I mean legged.

Two years later, the launch of the W. D Lawrence was witnessed by a crowd of 4, 000 people. The part of the story I like best is that W. D had eight profitable years of sailing in world-wide trade, during most of which he sailed as a passenger, before he sold her to a Norwegian concern.

While reading the exhibit, my eyes kept glancing house-ward where I caught the surreptitious movements of someone peeking through the curtains. As we move over to the picnic tables, I told my husband that, "I have this weird feeling of being watched."

"Well!" he replied, with a mock, horrified expression, "Tourists can't look out the windows of a historical house?"

The eerie, clandestine observers positioned themselves to follow our movements to the entrance of the museum. I describe them to Doug as we walk. I said, with a preternatural shiver, "Don't look, but they have moved from the back to the side, now overhead."

My husband just does a head shake and laughs. I am feeling pretty brave, having just made it out of the Shube. Otherwise, I might have yanked him by the shirt collar and put tracks between us and the haunted house. Visions of a mummified old lady in a rocking chair plague me.

We stop at the entrance. "Well, do you want to go in or not?" he queries.

I give him a brow furrow. "Aahh, of course! I have to find out *who's* in there."

So we step inside the entryway and let our eyes adjust from the bright sunlight. Two demure, older ladies greet us. (I say older–sixties or seventies? Older than me.) We proceed through all the proper greetings including the current and future weather reports. They calmly (*raight cam,* as they say here) explain the self-guided tour. We pay and then they point us to the guest book, requesting our signatures. We move toward the book. They both follow. We sign our names.

I tend to vacillate while deciding on Maine or Pennsylvania as my residence. There have been times I sign PA. Doug signs ME. We finish and when we turn I almost hit her with my backpack, she's so close. Behind her gold-rimmed glasses, her eyes are full of excitement. I laugh good-naturedly.

We leave our packs in the entryway and proceed with our tour. There is a central hall leading to five rooms. We go in one room while the "ladies" stand in the hall—monitoring, surveying, scrutinizing—whatever is that they are doing.

I smile again. This time my smile says, "Okay. You have my attention. Now spit it out."

We move to the next room and the "ladies" hover, close behind. We tiptoe to the next. We stand *far away* from anything breakable. I'm starting to get a bad case of screaming meemies. Could they be upset because I dropped our bag of trash in their rubbish bin? When I turn to look, though, their smiles are sweet, not like a couple of schizoids.

Do we look suspicious? The town seems very quiet but it is on the Nova Scotia Glooscap trail. We are only about an hour or so from Halifax and we can't forget all those tourists wanting to ride the bore! You'd think I had signed New Jersey, after having driven into their parking lot in a town car with tinted windows.

An excited squeak finally comes from one of the guardians of the old house. I turn to face the door, just in case a quick exit is required. With eyes full of amazement and an infectious smile that showed she could hardly contain herself, she blurted out, "You came in on the *sailboat!*"

A small sin really in a wash of great ones . . .

In a high, strangled voice, the other woman said that when they saw our boat, they ran straight upstairs to the second-floor telescope.

So that was it. They didn't think we were here to rob, pilfer and vandalize.

Doug is often mistaken for a dubious character. I, on the other hand, am normally greeted and treated as a proper lady—which I used to be.

I exhaled meaningfully, "Yes, yes, we are on the sailboat!" I shake my head in relief!

We get so busy trying to preserve our sanity, haul the dinghy and slop through the mud–we forget how very charming and foreign all this appears, especially way up here at the top of the Bay of Fundy.

The impeccable ladies, with breathless enthusiasm, relate *all* our morning activities. One tells me, with amazement in every syllable, "You fixed your sandwiches and ate in the sun." Then she really grew ecstatic, "You got your dust pan and broom out and cleaned all the decks!" She went on in varying degrees of awe and wonder.

"Oh! We heard reports that you sailed through here on Sunday evening!"

There was a stunned pause and I guess we looked bewildered.

"That was *you,* wasn't it?" the ladies chime together.

We look at each other. Sunday? Was *that* Sunday? Seems like a coon's age and a few gray hairs ago to me. I visualize my journal. Okay, this is Thursday, Day 14 September 13th, "Yes," I reply, "I suppose it *was* Sunday."

Ms. Eyeglasses stiffened her spine and tipped her nose up a fraction of an inch. "Yes *siree!* We are sure it was Sunday!" I should just hand them my journal and let them fill in the blanks.

Mystery solved, we continued our tour upstairs. Yep, there it is—the shipbuilder's telescope. We found it, still focused on the *Guillemot* and the ole' reliance standing guard in the cockpit.

Tour completed, hoofing it up the road which appears to lead to town, we find ourselves in a marsh. We have a chuckle over the good ladies at the W.D Lawrence. We couldn't be a more rare breed or more astonishingly observed than if we had come in on a space-ship.

A sign tells us the marshland was made and preserved by Ducks Unlimited. Searching, as we amble, for wildlife and varying vegetation, we almost miss the most unique specimen along our quaggy way. The luxurious marsh almost obscures a group of signs, which appear to have been painted on someone's back porch to lure their customers onward. The once-perky flags now drooped like plants without turgor, badly in need of water. Through the thicket we read large numbers "1 2 3." The three signs were stacked one on top of the other, "1 stop, 2 shops, 300 yards ahead."

Laughing, we pick up our pace. Walking with all the vitality I can muster, I actually break a sweat on this fine warm day. I feel like I could jump up and do a little side kick of pleasure. I am so happy to be on a road, walking, "1" step in front of the other, "2" travelers with "3" hours to do nothing! The quiescent town lay ahead; the perpetual motion of the tidal bore lay behind.

We look to our left. There are three women engaged in social fulfillment in the warm afternoon sunshine in front of the two shops. To our right, as we approach the center of commerce of the little hamlet of Maitland, we see yet another intriguing sign, this time leaning against a telephone pole. It takes a certain amount of concentration to read the tastefully inked artwork which beckons us to *The Swallowed Anchor—Goods and Wares*. We feel genuinely beckoned all right, but to where? We look up and down the road and, then, up and down the next road. Nothing appears to have swallowed an anchor so we move onto the general store. We are excited to see what we may find to fill our packs.

Reminding ourselves how short life can be while waiting in line—chips, bread and dreaded newspaper in hand—we decide to treat ourselves to ice cream cones. I rationalize that one more ice cream in my always-on-a-diet-life won't hurt. It will simply serve to make this day more special than it already is.

There are times (rare) when we do make prudent decisions. We made the wise choice of *small* cones. These cones were so huge, we'd have had to be direct descendants of Glooscap on steroids to have been able to hold up a large cone.

The words from our docent friends at the museum reminded us of an interesting old cemetery. Between greedy licks off our cones, we walk in that general direction. I feel heady with happiness, wolfing down my cone, strolling up the hill of the dreamy little town. Without ice aboard it is heaven to have something really cold on this warm day.

There are only our voices. We, are the only seekers of momentous solitude, reading epitaphs in the quiet cemetery. The old trees provide welcome shade. We decide this must not be the older section we were told about, although the location and the dates make us feel we could be in the 1940's; nothing modern, no car, person, or house, to change that illusion. We sit beneath a tree on the edge of the grounds that looked welcoming. We unfold the newspaper and our time capsule collapsed; September 13, 2001. We brace ourselves for the shock—headlines, photos—when suddenly we are attacked! A swarm of mosquitoes, hungry and probably freshly hatched in this warm weather from the swamp below, found us in 30 seconds flat. Not being ones to dilly-dally and donate blood to the tormenting stingers, we jump from our honeysuckle vine seats and march hastily back down the road.

Appearing unexpectedly as if dropped from the clear blue sky, my eyes frame a scene I would like to have as a painting. A woman, perhaps in her thirties, leans back in an antique chair, surrounded by tall grasses and wild flowers. The intense sun illuminates her brightly colored textile bandana that holds her wild dark hair. With an old house in the background, her trendy, vintage-style clothing makes her fit our illusion, a few minutes earlier, of being caught in a 40's or 50's time warp. Carefully, she balances herself in her chair, intent on her magazine. Silently we stand, looking in her direction as though admiring artwork. Slowly, she looks up, bids us "Good day" and offers an invite to the world of *The Swallowed Anchor*.

The grounds of the property slope and the basement of the house opens at ground level. Just inside the opening is a stone arch. The last of the wild flowers leave shadows on the outside walls. A fellow in a 40's-style brimmed hat enters the scene from behind some bushes, board and hammer in hand. He adjusts his hat and the pencil over his ear gives a precarious tip as he greets us, then gestures toward the door of their little shop.

We step inside, our eyes adjust to the cool darkness. What we find is a chance discovery of pure charm. All around us is an eclectic mix of artwork, gift items and antiques. All are nebulously lit by white Christmas lights. The center structure, full of character, the *pi'ece de résistance,* is a brick-oven fireplace.

Dapper Dan, in his brimmed hat, passes again by the doorway. More tools and measurements must be required for whatever project is in progress. He stops, looks at our packs left at the doorway, pushes his hat back on his head, and asks, "Are you two on the trail?" Not waiting for an answer, he goes on, "Use to do a lot of walkin' about myself, across Canada ..."

We stop him. "No," we say in unison, "We just walked into town. We came in on a boat."

"Stop right there!" he orders us.

His pencil falls off his ear, his arms start flapping, and his head rotates in disbelief, "Holy *Cow!*" were his next words, when he was able to speak. Then, as if we didn't hear him the first time, *"Holy Cow!"*

I turn to look behind me. I suppose there might be one in this little shop.

"Carolyn!" he yells, still gesticulating like a wounded bird trying to take fight. *"These ..."* he motions our way, "These ..." he says emotionally and excitedly, "These (he repeats) are the *sailboat* people!"

He might as well have said, "These are the *aliens!"*

Now, how do ya figure? The two of them are a few blocks from the water, without even a *telescope view* of our Reliance, and he's this excited. I start to inquire if they knew what we had for lunch but, before I could fit a word in edgewise, we are being introduced to the unique bandana woman and we have a Ten Penny beer in our hands.

We are flopped down into a couple of old chairs, around the thankfully cool fireplace, and our interrogation commences under the bright lights of Christmas!

I become inherently suspicious whenever I spot a magazine rack on someone's wall with several issues of *Wooden Boat Magazine* proudly displayed. The puzzle pieces of Paul's (Dapper Dan's) hogwild excitement find their little slots and start to fit perfectly together.

I make inquiries into his interest in the magazines I see displayed behind his head. The Captain's eyes light up like a proud father. He tells our energetic host that, indeed, our precious little *Guillemot* is a 46-year-old wooden boat.

Paul ceremoniously gives us the cheering news, "Oh. Yes! I have almost every issue!"

He shares this news as though this accomplishment is one that every self-respecting citizen should achieve. Thanks for sharing.

I bow my head and close my eyes in silent exasperation. *Oh geez.* I give up! Not, I choke, *not another one!*

Between Doug and MacNaughton, the subject of conversation is seldom diverted from that into which they pour all of their time, thought and money. They live, breathe, and sail wooden boats. Dan Mac Naughton (our good friend in Eastport) was an original editor of *The Wooden Boat Magazine* and still contributes articles. A few years ago we enjoyed a big party, held on the grounds of the magazine's headquarters and school, which commemorated its 25th Anniversary. And this fellow has almost *every* issue?

I will never get out of here!

So, our day flew by like a kite catching a 30-knot wind. It was 1:30 a.m. when we hoisted ourselves aboard (no water). Dapper Dan is *still* talking, outside on the walkway, and has barely noticed that we said, "Good Night, we'll see ya tomorrow!"

The dollar store clock tells me it is 2 a.m. when the last part of the chitchat touches a subject that finally warms to my heart—an invite for a shower. *Ooh Ahh!* I have the energy for a little whoop! I have a new best friend.

Day 15

Friday, September 14, 2001

"If you want to take a shower, you better get up and get moving!" I am removed from slumber land by the Captain, calling to me from the cockpit. "I want to be ready to leave on the 10:30 a.m. tide."

Now, even if I were in a drug-induced state, the word *shower* would normally ignite a quick, spasmodic movement—enough to cause structural damage, getting out of the V-berth.

Today, however, I am in a deep dream. In front of the Maitland Cemetery, stands Rod Sterling, *They walked into the town for ice cream and they entered the ... Twilight Zone!* All night long, Paul's voice was accompanied by the eerie music from *The Twilight Zone*.

Yesterday, in this minute village of Maitland at the mouth of the Shubenacade River, we found Doug's twin. Carolyn and I deduced, they must have been separated at birth.

Paul Fraser—roll your "r" with a bit of a Scottish *flurrish*—a Canadian, fair and lean. A twin to my husband is not something that would register at first glance. You might wonder just how well can you get to know someone in 12 hours? But if that someone never quits talking, a lot of history and information can be procured!

Paul studied history at University, so there is a wealth of information stored under that hat. He loves accents, which he reproduces with exceptional entertainment value. He took dance for many years and can perform a one-man stage show. He is an original Bluenoser, born and raised along the North Umberland Straits of Nova Scotia. Paul and Carolyn were both living around Moncton, New Brunswick when they purchased the house where they live and the Swallowed Anchor resides, last December.

All last winter they spent shoveling, not just snow, but mounds of junk accumulated by the previous owner. The piles outside almost hid the house. The commercial gray carpet was pulled off the tacks, the walls, trim and ceiling originally painted a lovely shade of dark gray, were given new coats of light colors to transform the dark gloomy house to its new personality, bright and cheerful. The 1850's home is sparsely, yet tastefully, decorated; splashed here and there with Carolyn's vivacious and colorful original artwork. Other frames, throughout, hold photographs taken by one of their obviously unusual friends. Their only children are the harum-scarum brothers— Jake and Hank. Jake, a poised Brittany Spaniel, and Hank a once-orphaned/abandoned, slightly traumatized but eternally happy Chesapeake Bay Retriever. There is a lot of action going on from these two rambunctious wards.

Yesterday, the afternoon gave us as much pleasure as one might expect out of an afternoon. Paul talked and sometimes we talked. This seems to be the type of company we tend to attract. We toured their home and tipped the beer. My tipsification kept me heading towards the WC. My need to relieve myself—beer always does this to me—was not the first and foremost reason. You see—well, of course you don't *see*. But I'll tell you as clearly as I can that their washroom is adorable. You walk in and straight ahead is a lovely window with views of their garden. Soft light filters through the window and makes you feel right at home. To the left is half of a claw-foot tub. Seriously, it is the *cutest* thing ever! There is a tiny old porcelain sink, great colors, unique artwork and a nice clean toilet! I could live there.

Here at Day 15, there is something profoundly comforting in having a flush handle at your fingertips. I was, quite literally, flushed with joy. Thankfully, the first time I headed this direction, Paul let me know the house WC rules. *If it's yellow, let it mellow. If it's brown, flush it down.* The water level in their well, this fall, is uncomfortably low. These clear, sunny days have left them almost in a drought. I often vacillate when using someone else's facilities. Is it offensive *not* to flush? Usually yes. I really feel that it's wasteful to use five gallons of water for a little pee and TP. While living aboard the *Guillemot*, we've only used about 10 gallons of water in the last two weeks. So, now it seems an atrocity to use all that water on one needless (although it feels so good at the time) touch of the lever. I was "Throned on highest bliss" (Milton), just to be there, even if I didn't have the opportunity to use the handy lever.

Carolyn and I quickly found common ground. Our unions with these two meant that, in many respects, we were cut from the same mold or cloth. Whatever it was, we agreed that all was not conventional bliss, although life was never dull. As the day moved on, stories stumbled out as the beer bottles went around. After the deep-seated reverence for wooden boats was established, we detected many similarities in our respective spouses, I should have discretely made a list. One thing, however, which became immediately evident, was that this duo liked the same type of beer—both quality and quantity.

Our sunny day turned to late afternoon and finally, much to our chagrin, we discovered that we were out of beer. Since we are human beings, (at least Carolyn and I are) and are possessed with a natural desire to have more of a good thing than we need, we decided that we needed more beer. My eyes and appetite were steadily drawn in the direction of the stove. Carolyn has a scrumptious-smelling cabbage soup brewing. However, it was probably her heart for hospitality and not my hungry gaze, which enticed her to invite us for dinner. Accepting the invitation, the Captain pipes in that we will buy the beer! My husband lifts the bottle and announces, "I'm clutching an empty wish here." My first thought was that we have beer on board. Then I realized that he actually wants a beer rich in yeast and hops, certainly not the cheap swill we already have.

Doug and I look at each other and nod our heads confidently. We were sure that it couldn't be as harrowing as our last trip to the beer store. "Yes," I concur happily, "let's do it! We'll go get beer."

Our host, however, seems to sense a dilemma here. "Well, let's see," says Paul, rubbing his chin. Then he scratches the side of his face and his two-day-old beard. He and Carolyn look at each other. "Aww, no! It's *Thursday!*"

"What's the matter?" My side of the twins asks, "The good people around Maitland don't drink beer on Thursdays?"

Regretfully, Paul explains that the closest beer store is 20 minutes away and they are … you guessed it—closed on Thursdays!

The bad news—that it happens to be Thursday—doesn't faze me! I have more important, life-sustaining thoughts going through my little mussy brain. I cut my eyes toward the aromatic soup on the stove top. The delicious idea of having someone else's cooking combined with my half-a-sandwich, five hours ago, dictates *something must be consumed* besides beer. If not, then Dapper Dan may need a wheelbarrow to get me back to the boat.

Speaking of Dapper Dan, his eyes just about popped out of his head. With his now-typical, sudden enthusiasm, I'd have to guess that he has another idea. "Have you seen Turo yet?" he asks.

"Why no!" we reply. I do recall, from my old tour book, that Turo has a racetrack, museums, a 1, 000-acre park in the center of town and a Salmon River. More importantly, we are now told, Turo boasts a beer store which stays open late (even on Thursday).

With the exception of the pot of soup, we packed up everything needed for our departure. A feeling of gusto comes upon us. Doug sings the B-double-EE-double-RR-U-N, "Beer Run" song, as we pile in Paul's pride and joy, a VW van. He tells us that his 1966 pop-top camper van is "in *great* condition." Paul lovingly pointed out many of her finer points and we assured the commander of this expedition that we loved her. Paul was still calling our attention to more well-designed aspects of his vehicle when all three of us nod in agreement. We really shouldn't *linger*. We need to set our GPS for Turo. Carolyn finally gently points this out to the jabbering Paul.

Paul is one of those open-book type guys—a book with many, many pages.

We sit and listen to details of trips they have taken in the VW van. Carolyn gently touched on the subject of starting the engine and continuing this commentary en route. We had all but given up hope, when Captain Paul finally inserted the key in the ignition. We waited expectantly, but heard—nothing! The Bobbsey twin mechanics then made the executive diagnosis that the battery was dead.

This is but a small difficulty. We will go in Carolyn's car.

With the boys in the front seat and the girls crunched in the back—happy to have short legs—we embark on our journey in Carolyn's tiny, economical, something-or-other car. We all enjoyed non-stop laughter and jabbered along the way. Before long, Carolyn and I are almost cross-eyed from hearing one or the other of them (*them* being those who talk incessantly in the front seat) discover yet another event or opinion that confirmed their likenesses.

We took Route 215 south and in half a jiffy were in South Maitland. The road parallels the narrow part of the Shubenacadie, providing a different view of some of the farms and landscape we had seen from down below. Turning left on Route 236, we cross the Shube Bridge. My throat tightens when I see it, remembering the bridge as a foreboding sight. We strain to see if there are any tidal rafters surfing down the waves and skirting whirlpools of that twisting gauntlet.

How simple it all looks from here—just a river, just a bridge and just some water.

Heading towards Turo, our guide points out the Shubenacadie Wildlife Park which protects the many native mammals and birds in the area. "Indeed," Carolyn adds, "they even have a few exotic species thrown in there."

So, are we to miss seeing the 50 acres of natural woodlands? Doug and I don't waver from our goal. We have lived alone in a small space for two weeks and we have our priorities firmly in place. After this life-threatening adventure together, we are soul mates. Our current, most pressing priority is simply to get to the booze store before it closes!

Paul (as does Doug) drives slowly. We enjoy the views and pull over, occasionally, to let those speed-demon Nova Scotia drivers who are up his ass, race by. A little 4-foot woman in a huge car zooms around us, head barely showing, just white knuckles on the steering wheel. At times, Doug drives so slow that it takes a week to get anywhere, unless we happen to be in a caravan situation, driving to and from Maine. Then he's so anxious just to get the ordeal over, he drives like a normal person, not remembering his wife is driving an old car behind him.

Paul continues on, driving the sometimes-sputtering teeny, tiny auto, with a contented nonchalantness. This drive is not just to satisfy our quest for beer. This drive will also take advantage of his captive audience so that his new friends should know and understand all the vital info of his younger-than-I and much more fun-packed life.

One story concerned Carolyn's purchase, new and right off-the-lot, of her June Bug of a car. True to the character of his twin, who rides shotgun next to him, Paul says one should never buy a new car! Reasons? A) You can hardly ever work on them yourself; B); they lose value the moment you drive them off the lot; and C) they have no character. The twins nod sagely, in agreement. Hey, if they are still solid after 20 years then they have great bones and are good for the long haul. "Yes," they both agree, Doug slips in his opinion, "I'm more concerned with how *long the car will last,* not how *fast* it will go." Why, Doug *still* has his 1973 Land Cruiser he bought used when he was 17-years-old.

Squished in the back seat, I listen quietly and think to myself that this pretty much sums up our relationship; by marrying an older woman, I was already tested for the "long run."

My taste buds do their salivating, jumping bit when someone mentions basil, in a brief reference to a pesto processing facility ahead. I almost gave our driver a yank on his ears in order to turn left at the herb greenhouse. I refrain from doing so, knowing we have a goal already. I wave at the Stewart House B&B in Beaver Brook and we continue on in, *hast like a snail* (John Heywood), toward the hub of Nova Scotia and the beer store.

We all continue to babble and ramble on. Every once in a while, the front seat twins remember their insignificant others who are still cramped in the back. For a moment, they direct their attention our way. We learn more about Turo than we ever thought we'd know or want to know. I note, with growing wonder, that Turo must have everything!

This is a very qualified statement. I now categorize my life as *BD* and *AD*—Before Doug and After Doug. *BD,* I would have said that San Francisco and Los Angeles had everything. Now that I'm in my *AD* stage of life, I can say, with all the sincerity of a woman who has simplified and reduced her life to a 10 x 4 foot space, that Turo has everything.

I'm in awe as we drive through the town which is bustling with activity. *All this,* if I were to fling myself out of this motorized cart, I would have at my *fingertips.* I am amazed at my self-control.

I just sit back, serenely enjoying Turo's solution to the problem of Dutch elm disease, which seems to have plagued half of the Atlantic coast. The once-enormous trees have been reduced to stumps which are a problem to remove and normally an eyesore. This pleasant little town was given lemons but went on to make lemonade. Wood carvers have put their talents to great use by transforming these dead trees into colorful characters of Turo and Nova Scotia's fictional and nonfictional past.

Carolyn made the sign of the cross as we finally pulled into the parking lot of the long-awaited booze store. We all unfolded ourselves out of the vehicle. Rarely have I seen a group move with such speed and purpose! Once inside, the crew separates, each to his or her own purpose. We meet back at the register and Carolyn scurries off to the market at the end of the strip mall for some fresh bread, leaving her selection in the safe hands of Paul.

As we wait for Carolyn to return, happily goofy-faced, we all agree it is an exceptional evening. I am still riding high on the emotional experience of being *out* of the tidal bore and performing some normal, recreational activities. I can stand here and laugh and talk and no one knows how close I came to succumbing to my all-too-human frailties of anxiety, fear, and exhaustion.

Awh Huh! Here she comes, strolling back from the market, grocery sack in one hand and a four-pack of Khaluah drink in the other. The boys pay no notice. They are still going on about something they built, or saw being built, or maybe want to build—whatever. I wonder, on the other hand, where the four-pack came from? I thought you could only buy booze at the state-operated or, here, the province-operated booze stores?

Carolyn is smiling. I give her an I-give-up shrug of the shoulders.

She explains. It seems that, while contemplating the bread section at the market, she was approached by the liquor store attendant, four-pack in hand. He'd overheard her say that she was off to buy bread and he thought that she'd forgotten her booze. Of course, we all know it was Paul, being so gung-ho on his beer and his non-stop dissertation of wooden boats, life and its meaning, who forgot her drinks.

You do feel as though you've left the other world behind when you can come to a fairly large city and have the liquor store clerk track you down in the bread aisle, four stores away, to deliver your beverages! Why, that young man deserves a medal of honor!

Testifying to his astonishing power of recall, our host does remember we have a boat that must be tended. Now, the Captain of the *Guillemot* is starting to get ants in his pants about the tide and the leg thing. Dusk is fast approaching. We take a quick spin around town and then head out for home. This time we will take the expedient route home.

Paul is all "Ooh gaw," over the fact that we will drive right past the sunflower fields. What a sight it is—fields and fields full of sunflowers. I can only imagine their full glory in the bright sunshine; we are barely able to see their large nodding heads in the twilight.

We zip and bounce onward to Maitland. Experience tells me that I should be concerned with the condition of our water craft, especially since my husband is visibly, at least to my eyes, on pins and needles. However, the chasm between our last meal is now in direct competition with my concern over our floating pad. Carolyn should be glad she placed the bread bag (for our supposed supper) in the trunk or I might have embarrassed myself and tried to arm-wrestle her for it.

We girls are pleased as punch to disengage from the Dyno Duo, who go off to tend the boat. I think she's still floating I can barely tell it is so dark. Just before driving off, I hear Doug open a beer, in celebration of making it back in time. He quotes Ben Franklin, "Beer is proof that God wants us to be happy! "

We head to the house and warm the blessed soup.

Two hours later, Carolyn and I have sustained ourselves by all but licking the platter on which she served the hors d'oeuvres. Yes, we ate them all! Forget *them!* With the soup and bread only a wishful thought, we decide that a walk on this fine evening sounded good. We might as well check on the progress of Tweedle Dum and Tweedle Dee.

Flashlight in hand, we stroll along, engaged in easy conversation—even though, by now, we practically know each other's life history. Coming upon the homeland of the *Guillemot,* we see and hear a slapstick comedy goin' on.

The laughing Captain and the wanna-be wooden boat sailor are trying, in their own drunken way, to level the boat. Paul is still talkin' balderdash. He is wading around in the water where, in his own cockamamie way, he attempts to maneuver the boat.

Why? This is anyone's guess. He must be as loose as a bag of suckers, because *I've* never been asked to perform this task.

They both assure us, in so many slurred words, that they will be along shortly.

We both laugh with the shared understanding of how we could have fallen for their infectious charms. We turn and head up the hill, to the main road, where I see the W.D. Lawrence house sitting like an aged woman, with a smirk and lifted eyebrows. Just audible are faint wails of laughter wafting down from the second floor. The ghostly caretakers of the night must be getting a real kick out of the telescope, watching the shenanigans of the Captain and his ole' mate.

We enter the quiet town—no, this is not just *quiet.* This brand of silence borders on a post-nuclear horror film. The town, so charming by daylight, has disappeared and shadows hang moodily around us. I have no interest in a slow walk back, so I pick up the pace while my new friend follows. I don't know what she thinks—perhaps, that I was afraid the bread would be stale by the time we finally ate. I'm greatly relieved to see the lights of their house as we high-step-it up to their front door.

I welcome the sounds and commotion of Hank and Jake. It is most disturbing to feel this way, especially when I have no idea why. I head immediately to my favorite room where my friends await me—my toilet and half-a-claw-foot tub. I feel the need to cleanse myself spiritually and physically, so to speak. Safe inside, I meditate, as one should in a place like this.

Eyeing the tub, I make myself laugh by imagining a large man tucked inside. I like to laugh, it is good for the soul. Then I realize that the doom and gloom of all the newspapers I read today was weighing on me. This light and airy home and fun new friends, brought with it several newspapers they had collected over the last several days. The terrorists have done their job, I'm afraid, even in this quiet, peaceful town. All the potential attacks, all the potential chemical warfare, have come to haunt me. What good does that do? None at all, except to ruin a perfectly wonderful day, a perfectly wonderful *now*.

I shake the ole' head, the brain, the gray matter I use for thinking and worrying. I remember that the Minas Basin is flushing itself, right at this very moment. So I ceremoniously flush my thoughts, without even touching the lever of the convenience upon which I sit. I depart and close the door behind me.

I hear the lollygaggers coming up the front steps. I watch, with unholy glee, as Carolyn dishes up our plates of soup. I can't let these moments slip away, unsavored and under-appreciated! I open a beer and begin to enjoy our highland fling. The Captain has brought his guitar. We laugh and yawn, eat soup and bread, and all the while we watch Paul dance the Scottish jig.

Paul can still carry on a conversation while dancing, so we continue getting to know all the important parts of his life. Then the crazy Scot did something that made me feel aghast—well *practically* aghast.

It all began with an innocent enough conversation about clambakes. We mentioned the great spring clam/mussel bake at Harry and Martha Bryan's house on the Mascarene Shore of New Brunswick. Right in the midst of a foot tapping—*I'm so happy—little spin*—he stops, dead in his tracks. It's as though the music just clicked *off* in his mind.

"Do you *know* Harry Bryan?" he suddenly demanded.

Before it occurred to me what this revelation could mean to someone in Maitland, Nova Scotia, Paul dropped down on his knees and bowed, like a Muslim, to the east. He was utterly speechless. I figured I was experiencing a first as he offered silent reverence, not to us, but to his idol—the Great Harry Bryan.

I put my elbows on the table and head in my hands. Oh, that's right, the magazines! Harry and his boat designs have been featured on the cover of the Rolling Stone a few times (Yeah, right! Actually, he *was* featured on the cover of *Wooden Boat*). They've had several articles about him, his home (which he built himself) and work-shop–all powered without electricity. A fascinating man, to be sure, but I'd think a rather obscure celebrity in anyone's eyes.

BD (before Doug) I had *heard* of wooden boats and even seen some. I never would have guessed they would be like the tidal bore and overtake my life. I am almost too tired to enjoy my brief recog-nition as one who's rubbed elbows with the *créme de la créme* of the wooden boat world. I merely close my eyes and silently agree with E. B. White. "*If a man must be obsessed by something, I suppose a boat is as good as anything, perhaps a bit better than most. A small sailing craft is not only beautiful, it is seductive and full of strange promise and a hint of trouble.*"

We sway, somewhat, back to the boat (yacht, being we are talkin' high society here, even though Harry Bryan has to be one of the most humble human beings I've ever met). The Captain and I laugh as we listen to Dapper Dan planning our action for tomorrow, fol-lowing us back to our floating hotel. We splat aboard, listening to the non-stop, running commentary of our host.

I feel entranced to have entered the "*wonderously strange*" (Shakespeare) world here, at the very top of the Minas Basin, where the flowing waters end. Our day and afternoon had turned into an accident that happened perfectly.

My Captain gives me my second wake-up call, yanking me out of my dreamland of yesterday. Reluctantly, I agree. I'd better get my butt moving. I am hell-bent on providing our new friends an op-portunity to display their *true* hospitality by allowing me a shower. This act of kindness shines even brighter in the light of their cur-rent low water level.

I am in a tremendously good mood. Why shouldn't I be? I made it off the boat and up to the road. Each time I survive this ordeal, without injury or embarrassment, I feel it to be a triumph worthy of mention. I turn to head town-ward.

Suddenly, there he is—Dapper Dan, in all his exuberant glory. He gives me the look of the wild. He bares his teeth in a grin—a grin a child might make when caught out by his parents in the midst of some project.

He is pedaling a 1950s bike and wearing an outfit out of the jumble box. His hands and arms are not the least bit concerned with steering the bike, as they are clutching a large thermos and three pottery coffee mugs.

Before he even dismounts, he starts into a story. His eyes grow wider and his eyebrows grow higher but I have a hard time concentrating on his broadcast. I have a tide clock *ticking loudly* in my ear.

I hold my shower bag up in a halt gesture. My facial features changing, I have no doubt, to that of an old dowager duchess who had just swallowed a sorbet the wrong way at a ball. "I'm sure it is a gripping narrative, full of action. One that should be put to music! But I'm tellin' ya buddy ... don't stand in a Lady's way when she's headed for you know where, to do you know what!"

At first his face was a study in perplexity, tilting his head to one side, then jerking as if lightening had struck, Paul quickly removes himself, thermos, mugs and his bike from the path. In a chivalrous gesture, Dapper Dan bows from the waist twirling his hand in front of his chest, allowing her highness to pass.

To have all my private and public parts clean makes this woman smile. After my few moments of heaven in their upstairs shower, I walk to the kitchen for a quick cuppa tea with Carolyn. I do not want to leave their cozy kitchen, wonderful herb tea, and her refreshing companionship, but steel invades my soul.

Suddenly, I'm out the door, racing toward my beloved husband and the next leg of our journey.

I round the corner. I see the *Guillemot* is still there waiting for me. My Captain still wants me as his first mate to continue our adventure! I rush toward my husband, arms wide, lips slightly parted,

Maitland
I round the corner. I see the Guillemot *is still there waiting for me.*
My Captain still wants me as his first mate to continue our adventure! ...
I head down below to stow my bag and clothes. I leave the Captain
and Paul happily enthralled in their coffee dreams.

my heart pounding like a drum. "Hey relax!" He calls when he sees me. "The schedule is too tight. The wind is howling from the north-west just a bit too much. We'll stay for another day." As you all know at this point, it is *now* or *never* for our departure. We need the full tide to safely render us to our next harbour.

I head down below to stow my bag and clothes. I leave the Captain and Paul happily enthralled in their coffee dreams. The conversation goes on and on while the sun shines brightly. I think I hear lunch at their house. I walk out to join the two crazies. I give a little whine—I know that *look*. Paul's eyes are filled with nautical glitter. It appears that Doug has offered a little sail to Paul and Carolyn this morning.

At high tide I pull anchor.

I have frequently observed that those who have never been on a sailboat with me, believe, somehow, that I am every bit the sailor. While swishing around in the iced expresso bay, I bestow approving looks when they try to help. Confidentially speaking, I thrive on the short-lived moments of *acting* as though I know what I'm do-ing—being loved and admired by one and by all.

Paul is all but foaming at the mouth to buy a fixer-upper. He is an avid kayacker, so he understands these currents. He can't wait to try his hand at sailing and, more importantly, sailing *these* waters. Ha-Ha-Ho-Ho! I watch, inwardly laughing. He has the look of a reverential disciple at the foot of his master.

Paul's look of enjoyment is contagious. I feel it my duty to tell Carolyn of all the positive aspects of sailing. She has never laid eyes on me before, she doesn't know I am barely recognizable as the woman I use to be. I won't tell of my battle scars. Anyway, it's not as if this sickness-with-no-cure had not already invaded her house-hold. I can't be held responsible. After all, Paul had every issue of *Wooden Boat* before we ever arrived!

"The verdict's in, right?" I ask my husband as we stroll into town for our promised lunch.

"Oh, without doubt! That guy is crazier than a shit-house rat. I should have been making a list!"

I look, amazed and unbelieving, at him. "A list?"

"It was eerie," he continued, "how many times we discovered

that we've done, will do or would like to do the same thing. For your sake, sweetie, I should have been keeping track."

I'm not surprised at their camaraderie. My husband, of all people, cannot object to eccentric behavior. I offered a silent prayer, however, thanking the God almighty that my side of the duplex doesn't talk as much as his extraneous twin.

I felt a surge of optimism and well-being as we stepped on their porch. The thought of food does that to me. "Knock, Knock. "Hello... Hello!" Not a peep.

The house sounded as hollow and empty as a beer closet. Usually, the continually barking dogs greet you as soon as you step onto the property. A strange hush seems to have come over the old house. I think, "Maybe we are in an episode of *Twilight Zone!*" I half-expected some elderly man to enter from stage left. He would act bewildered at our appearance. When we asked about Paul and Carolyn, he'd look pensive. Then, with eyebrows furrowed, he would inform us that those two hadn't lived here for fifty years!

We enter and walk quietly toward to their kitchen, as though not wanting to disturb the dead. The wild and weird world of Doug's counterpart is missing. Nothing cooking and no evidence that anyone is expecting company. This is way too spooky for me. It all looks perfectly placed—a bit sterile, almost like a movie set.

I turn to my husband who's staring out the big picture window of their kitchen.

Gulp! We stand silently, side by side. "Did ... did ... you notice that yesterday?" he asks.

"No. Did you?" I answer, somewhat trepidaciously.

No. In fact, neither of us recognized it. The large picture window perfectly frames the oldest part of historical Maitland's burial grounds. There are grave sites ten feet from us.

Yesterday we must have been so engrossed in conversation—the half-a-claw-foot tub, the soup and the beer—that we failed to notice this.

I start to get in one of my emotional moods. "Are you sure he meant lunch? Maybe he said dinner but meant supper?"

Doug tries to defend himself, "Well, what did *you* hear? Weren't you there?"

"No," I reply. "I was busy down below. It was one of your multitudinous conversations." Then I brightened up a bit. "He's *your* twin. What would *you* have said?"

This is just too much. I turn my back to the old tombstones and begin to check the kitchen for evidence that this is one and the same as last night. Same table and chairs, all 50's style. Same stove, refrigerator and toaster, all 1950's. Simple kitchen, no modern convinces such as dishwasher, garbage disposal or trash compactor. I was in a vague area of uncertainty that we hadn't stepped back in time.

I looked for a calender. That's what they always do in those scary movies. I half-expected to see some eery-looking wall hanging with September 1951 starring at me—but no calender.

Ah-hah! A microwave! *Everyone* has a microwave! I'm searching. When I turn to Doug, I note that he's looking at me as if I were a cup and saucer shy of a full place setting.

"Check the refrigerator!" I order. He's baffled now, not understanding the force that is driving me. He opens the fridge obediently.

"For what?" he asks, hand on the handle and head tucked inside.

I didn't want to say "For evidence that we aren't in the *Twilight Zone*," so I just said, "For the leftovers from last night!" He still isn't getting why I'm so emotional!

"So what if they're in there?" he reasons. "I'm not going to warm it up and eat if they aren't here!"

"I know, I know, I just want to know if it's there!" I railed! Yes, it is not too much to say, that I railed!

"Just find the soup!" I admonished.

He could tell it would mean a lot to me to find the soup. Why, on the other hand, he wasn't sure.

After a few minutes of panic and prayer, searching in every cabinet and closet for the microwave, I caught something, or should I say *someone* familiar, just out of the corner of my eye.

It was right outside the small kitchen window, which overlooked the side yard and side street.

"Doug!" I shouted. He jumped and slammed the refrigerator door shut.

"What now!" he says, losing patience with his emotionally unstable wife.

"Is, is, that," I ask, voice a-tremble, "is that ... *Paul?*"

On the side road, we see a man, dressed as if it were at least a hundred years ago. He's riding a—well, ahh, he's riding a *weird* bicycle.

It's one of those jobbers you might see a clown ride in a circus. Or a normal person ride around ... what? The turn of the century? Maybe 1908? I have no idea what you call it. It has a front wheel as tall as a man's head and a tiny back wheel. It's steered with funny-looking handle bars—way up at the top.

If you could frame a 24-hour-day in a single moment then ours would be this scene we view out the window.

"There is a dangerously unbalanced mind at work here," the Captain intones, solemnly.

I momentarily forget my quest for the microwave and we set out to find some answers.

The fellow tips his hat and says, cheerfully, "Good day!" Then our host offers a Cheshire cat grin. "I'm practicing for the *parade* tomorrow. I need to be able to get on and off the cycle with these clothes on!"

And my, my, now didn't he look quite the dandy in his beaver hat, vest, white shirt and old-time trousers. In half a jiffy, the performer dismounted. Flushed with success, he honored the occasion with a little tap dance.

"Is it hard to ride that thing-a-ma-gig?" We both want to know.

"Ah ... it's not the *riding*. It is the "on and off" that seems to be worthy of profanity. Mark Twain claims to have invented all the bicycle profanity which has since come into general use," he says.

Little did we know that, in fact, tomorrow is *Maitland Day*. Each year they commemorate the launching of the William D. Lawrence—*you know*—the largest wooden ship built in Canada. As it happens, there will be a parade with townspeople in period costumes (I surmise there won't be many riding a contraption like Paul's). The small village will celebrate with crafts shows and church suppers. All will gather on the beach (where we are currently legged) to launch a model of the ship.

"Hey, you guys want a beer?" Says Paul, abruptly.

"No, no, no, a thousand times no! Well … why not?" We reply.

He began to divvy out the beers, while providing us a constant, running commentary, about the cycle (it's from a museum), how we should stay for the Maitland days, and the joys and the woes of living in a small town.

I held a shaky finger up and pointed towards the window. With infinite casualness, I say, "I hadn't noticed you have such a great view out your window."

He stops moving, dancing, and orating. He sat on a stool and crossed his legs. He did a lot of respectful tongue clicking, while nodding his head in the graveyard direction, "Just a gentle reminder," he tells us. He performs a few more respectful tongue clicks and nods sagely, "Just a gentle reminder."

My long training as a *respectable* guest, prevented me from demanding, "Where's the food, damn it! I'm tired of counting the ways you both appear to be controlled by some alien force. I'm tired of reading a book in the living room, listening carefully for life signs upstairs. I'm tired of placing myself strategically so that my eyes might flicker with the reflection of the refrigerator in a last ditch effort to get my promised lunch!"

Two hours after my first beer, Carolyn makes her entrance. She floats downstairs, refreshed after a nap. She's showing off a new spiked hairdo and smelling of expensive bath products, her fashionable clothing cleaned and pressed. I whimper when I look down at myself. I look spectacular too—spectacularly wrinkled.

I muster some dignity and join her and the extraterrestrials in the kitchen. I console myself by thinking, "At least now we'll have lunch!" She calmly sits down and joins the two fellows who are, as usual, conversing cozily.

But no choppy choppy. No checking the fridge for supplies. She does make a sweet inquiry about our schedule. Doug and I look google-eyed at this point—late night, no food and, already, too much beer.

This is a trifle embarrassing. Maybe we should tell her that we simply came by for a "gentle reminder" from her graveyard window.

Then we could just get up and leave for lunch at the boat. I tried taking on a hungry expression, a bit like a dog regarding a distant bone. This situation clearly called for initiative and resources!

Drawing on my fine command of the language, I said, "Great Scot!" Paul actually stopped talking. He listened, with what I considered admirable patience, so I continued. "Paul invited us for lunch, but if we don't eat soon I may … I may …" (I give considerable thought to this conditional threat. I *may* … faint? No, no that would be so Victorian of me. Then they'd know I'm not made of pure salt. I *may* … blow away like the wind? They'd shake their heads and laugh, considering my sparkplug figure.) "I may just go down to the general store for an ice cream."

Paul jumps to attention. I grab the teetering stool. He now stares into space, with his arms crossed over his chest, seeking further inspiration from the ceiling. Then, as if a long-forgotten idea had just popped into his head, he opened the fridge and pulled out the (well-hidden) cabbage soup. Carolyn had a half-amused, half-puzzled look.

We both agree while we cut the bread and looked for the butter, that these men really should have come with a manual. We broke bread and devoured the soup. All the while I wondered … then finally I asked, "Carolyn, do you have a microwave?"

"No," she answered, "Why? Is your soup cold?"

I'm not sure if I'll ever consider myself normal again, but I felt half-normal after the food and a large glass of water. Before I could stop myself, I invited our friends for dinner, moonlight on the water—or mud—you know the whole experience of the eating-and-cooking-aboard routine. My mind asks me, "Do I really want to do this?" Sure, I tell myself. At least I'll have some control over our eating schedule.

My darling angel of a husband shifted his feet and wiggled his ears (yes, I'm sure I saw his ears wiggle). He piped in, "No one in the world eats better than I do!" I felt the need to clarify—at least on our budget and on a tiny boat—but why spoil the moment?

Out in the bright sunshine, I swayed a bit. I gave Doug a bleak look. "Are you okay? Are ya gonna make it?" He looked alarmed, wondering if he'll have to drag me back to the boat.

By way of explanation, I mutter, "I believe my system can only stand so much beer and cabbage soup ..." He nodded gravely, in agreement. Grim and resolute, I head back to the *Guillemot,* no detours.

I had a private meeting on board with the old reliance. I can see why that old Hollywood diet I tried, all those years ago, was such a sure fire way to loose weight. That cabbage flushes your system faster than the tides flush the Bay of Fundy! After the episode with the bucket, nothing seemed to matter—the dinner, the boat, the Shube mud, or the schedule—only a warm, drowsy, peaceful, afternoon nap.

I jump, after about the fourth call to attention by the Captain. We need to get the ship in tip-top condition for our dinner guests. We must make things appear to be clean and uncluttered. So we sweep, stuff, sort, and stow unconvincingly. While participating in this effort, I give some considerable thought to my menu. Even when I'm in a normal kitchen, where I have room for skillets to fly and elbows to move, I like to serve meals where most of the preparation is completed in advance. I have certainly learned the lesson of not being to futsy about my house!

At this point in my commentary, I feel the need to explain and pay tribute to my old self—the BD (Before Doug) era. Those were the days when I would jump through hoops; when I donned the hat and apron of *Hostess Extraordinare.*

* * *

In those days, before I even considered the menu or thought about the napkins and tablecloths, the crystal, silver and china, I would head for the children's rooms. Once there, I'd plow through, removing all objectionable matter. I'm not sure why this was so important, except that if I didn't do it then, I never would. So ziplocks filled with half-eaten lunches, composting midnight snacks and old spelling tests were given their rightful home.

Then, brow furrowed, I headed to the hamster cage and later, once the shower grout was scrubbed, I moved on down the line.

The largest entertaining obstacle I encountered during my 25-year career of playing hostess, was *The Dog From Hell.* Our "pet," Jean de la Valette, was named after the hero of Malta, a man who helped defeat the Turks in 1565. This ever-so sweet, white, tiny, fluffy and yappy Maltese always had his timing down perfect.

We paid an arm and a leg for this little demonic fuzz ball, but my family *had* to have him. It is an absurdly inadequate cliché to say he was *more trouble than he was worth* ...

Our old resident calico cat, Patches, (fat, hairy and feisty) hated him. When their paths would cross, (which was frequently, since Jean de la Valette never stopped following her) fur would fly, literally. Sounds like something from *The Exorcist* would drown out the classical music I played to calm my nerves.

Then, when Jean tired of inflicting terror upon our quiet cat, he practically wriggled with excitement at the thought of possible punishments he might bestow on the rest of the household. The bedroom of whichever child happened to be away for the day would receive a visit from Jean. In a most aristocratic pose he would proceed to pee all over the feet of their antique beds, as if they were his favorite trees. Then he might puke up his latest chewed object, along with his lunch, on their chairs, pillows and clothes.

I had the job of taking him to the groomer, so he always planned special revenge for me. The insolent mop would take liberties. Whenever he managed to find an ink pen—watch out! He would immediately head for the off-white (hideously expensive, but we bought it used) sectional in my living room where he left his "signature"—ink sploches in many special corners.

The lovely-but-ink-stained sofa sat atop a large, signed oriental rug. There were special spots woven into the design which evidently appealed to the hairy rat. Repeatedly, he'd cold-heartedly do his business on those same locations.

No amount of discipline, punishment or retributive suffering changed his evil tendencies.

At some point in our relationship, thoughts began to occur to me (on a frequent basis), involving luring Jean to a quiet spot, away from neighbors and family, where I could inflict serious violence. But he had an intuition about such things. He knew when he'd pushed the envelope of my patience and he'd behave like a drama king. He would literally throw himself at my feet and whine, looking pitiful and begging for clemency.

I would lock him in the side yard which held fences and gates built especially to imprison him. Of course, he would still manage to get out, and expend his pent up energy chasing golfers and terrorizing the neighborhood. Once, I tried locking him in Brooke's playhouse. The level of destruction was unbearable.

I would put him on a leash in his spacious area. He would yelp so loud and long that the neighbors called the SPCA. I should have had his walking papers ready then.

One fine evening, the yappity-yapper (which yap he did incessantly, whenever a person dared venture upon the property) provoked me to my limit. One of his favorite tricks was to pay homage to the Persian entry rug. He checked my social calender and saved all his resources for the precise moment of impact. Unwittingly, Kyle let our company into our lovely, spotless home where a grandiose arrangement of fresh-cut flowers from my garden greeted them. The aroma of gourmet food drifted through the house. Fine wine from our wine room (we had a large interior room, previously occupied by an elevator, which we turned into our wine cellar) was carefully selected according to the preferences of our guests and the menu. Both—white wine slightly chilled and the red uncorked to breathe—awaited our visitors, nestled snugly beside our fully stocked bar. Hors d'oeuvres by the pool, salads in the sunroom, entré at the dining table, after dinner drinks and desserts in the living room. Yes, we promised an evening of not only atmosphere, but scrupulousness—food perfectly cooked and served with military precision.

I checked the condition of the entry rug like clockwork. I was prepared and in control.

When "it" happened, however, I turned into a "beserko" Sherlock Holmes, tracing my guest's footsteps from room to room through the house. I clenched and unclenched my fists—this pooch was finally in imminent danger. My eyes were full of unshed tears! If this mutt was going to live to see his next toenail clipping, things in this household *were going to change.*

I put my foot down (carefully, of course, checking first) and took a strong stand! It was either Jean de la Valette or me!

I braced for the worst but this story had a happy ending. Mike, our handyman, took Jean de la Valette to his widowed mother. She doted on his every move. He was King of her World. The last I heard, she dearly loved her sweetie lambkin.

The moral of the story is that these experiences finally altered my opinion of what has to be done before we have company. For years after that, my home was always under some sort of construction. This is truly the perfect excuse for everything. I learned to clean only the toilet the adults used. All doors to the other rooms remained closed. I made all invitations for either dusk, dark or out-of-doors. Casual and spontaneous invitations are also good because expectations are lowered.

Other tricks of the trade? Candle light and dimmer switches provide atmosphere and hide the dust balls. I learned to love *dimmer* switches. All rooms need dimmer switches.

I decided that my home was not some fancy restaurant or B & B striving for five stars. Many times, when I struggled so hard to make entertaining so fancy-smancy, the act was too hard to follow, the recipients of all my endeavors wouldn't bother inviting us to their homes.

* * *

So life is much better! Gone are the days when my entertaining eyes lack a healthy hearty sparkle.

I look at my stack of vegetables and my herb basil linguini, I feel the cooking-for-those-who-love-my-food enthusiasm curse through my veins. I do enjoy creating something to stuff in someone's mouth.

* * *

All those years cooking for the darling children, who complained about sticks and twigs in their food, tend to make one's smile droop. They were always questioning me. "Why do we have to have a *croissant* or healthy *whole grain* bread? Why can't we just have a *plain* tuna sandwich on *white* bread?" Kyle, my son, had the taste buds for the finer things in life, but could still be picky. Brooke, however, when younger, (not now, thank heavens) once cried real tears when I made an apple galette with pine nuts and candied lemon because all she really wanted was a *pop tart!* I didn't know, until she was an adult, that she always craved just a plain chocolate cake for her birthday. I always felt it my duty, as a loving and caring mother, to provide anything and everything *special* for parties. Back then, I never knew how unappreciated my perfectly luscious, triple layer with raspberry filling, topped with champagne frosting and chocolate shavings, cake was to a kid.

Now I know better. I should have just said, "Shut up and eat! In 10–15 years, you'll be coming home for a good meal and telling all your boyfriends and girlfriends what a good cook your mother is."

* * *

In our household, whether I'm cooking or Doug is, we can always add another bean to the pot for whoever happens to walk through the door or, in this case, slop through the mud and up to the companionway.

Eastport is a quiet little island city, but in our kitchen, at times it can really be rip-roaring. My country kitchen has several windows, where I can look out onto my tangled blooms and our resident birds bathing and feeding. The room is full of artwork and antiques and a large, ancient table that was salvaged from one of the old canneries which prospered many years ago in Eastport. Surrounding the table is a hodgepodge of chairs, stools, and benches which are usually filled with a variety of singers, musicians, philosophers, and energetic applauders—a flowing stream of bohemians of every age and gender. My kitchen, like Paul and Carolyn's, could be from another era. Before arriving in Eastport I knew, positively, that I couldn't function without a garbage disposal, dishwasher and a trash compacter. Now, I have none of those, but I do have a microwave!

One memory of entertaining in our Eastport kitchen never fails to bring a smile. Molly, Kev and Guy, our friends from Pennsylvania were staying with us for a week. We had several gorgeous days of sailing, which left most of us a little sunburned. Molly however, was the worst. The tops of her feet were blistered and swelled.

General chaos had commenced in my kitchen. Several unexpected guests dropped in; all good friends who'd come back to Eastport for a visit. I was busy dishing up pasta in large wooden bowls. I turned to see Molly, not one to miss out on the dinner and all the fun of the party, lying on the floor, trying to stay out of the cook's and harm's way. Her long legs were stretched upward, balanced protectively against my kitchen hutch. There she lay—singing, eating and wiggling her tender toes to the beat of the music.

✳ ✳ ✳

Seagulls shriek overhead. Holy smokes, look at the time! I still need to sauté the squash and dice the tomatoes. The beautiful evening will allow us to leave the canvas off the companion way door, This means, we'll have great views of the mud. Actually, it does look rather picturesque with the sun glistening on the swirls and ponds.

The Captain works on the logistics of getting our guests into our legged palace. They can slop up to the dinghy and leave their mud boots in our mudroom, (AKA the dinghy). Then they'll take a giant step up to the dinning room on the bay. I gaze with considerable satisfaction at my menu and the ongoing preparations. I thank the Lord, I don't have any cabbage that needs to be eaten.

Paul reminds me of a real-life version of Tigger from *Winnie The Pooh*—always excitedly pouncing from here to there.

Hmmm, I muse. Here come our guests, but there seems to be something wrong with Tigger. Carolyn appears to be her normal cheerful self, happy to be slopping up, onto our sailing vessel. Paul however, I deduce, is not feeling any too good.

Our guests are seated according to my seating chart. I quote the menu as though I were a waitress, then offer a "lemontini" (since our guests brought ice). Carolyn has a wistful gleam in her eye. Paul's lack sparkle. We cheerfully toast, deciding Martini is just a longer word for joy. I serve the hors d'oeuvres, in this case, bruschetta. My bruschetta is just the classic recipe—toast your bit of crusty bread, cut a garlic clove in half, rub the cut side hard on the toast. That's it. You don't need to add olive oil or butter because the heat in the bread draws out the volatile oils from the garlic, along with the aroma. It's topped with goat cheese, marinated sun-dried tomatoes and toasted pine nuts.

Paul declines his cocktail and hor d'oeuvres. I'm really starting to view the situation with concern. I wonder if his batteries are starting to run low?

We all try to ignore this, munching and talking happily. All seems better, so I move into the spinach and tomato salad with basil walnut dressing. Suddenly, Paul rose quickly, and moved to the outdoors for a bit of God's air. He was back before long, however, and ready for salad. He took one bite and made his exit again.

So ... on and so on ... a few bites and an exit! Some people do have unusual eating habits, like putting the fork down between each bite or chewing each morsel a hundred times, but I've never seen this one. A less secure cook might think it was her food.

As I warm the main course, something else strikes me as unusual. Carolyn is talking rather a lot. Carolyn is animatedly telling us a story. Paul, on the other hand, is hardly speaking. He still takes tiny bites and then the sunshine fades from his face and he's out to the cockpit. He's now pacing like a caged cat. His runs his hand through his hair; it stands up in a tousled mass. His stomach lodges a formal protest that we all heard very clearly.

"I've got to go! Literally, I have to go now!" A look of panic spreads across his features.

It was not too much to say that we all looked baffled. My face registered deep concern but inside I was controlling a fit of laughter. Then he went, scuttling off toward home. What should a host and hostess to do? Offer up the ole' *reliance* and vacate the premises?

Carolyn looked like the cat who swallowed the canary. "Paul has already informed me," she confided, "that I'm not allowed to make cabbage soup again—ever!"

At this announcement, I nudged Doug under the table to keep quiet!

Paul returned later, squiggly-eyed but looking much relieved. We finished the meal with the last of the cookies from the Parrsboro Bakery and I tell them my mantra, "Eat two they're small!" We receive four thumbs-up from our friends as they splat toward the walkway. We can hear more talk about Paul's gastric juices as they stroll home.

There have been frightfully few times in my entertaining years when I thought there might be a need to bury the bodies in the morning. Tonight was a close call.

How would I ever have convinced the good women at the W. D Lawrence Museum, that it truly wasn't my doing?

Day 16

Saturday, September 15, 2001

Why didn't the Captain, my husband and supposed protector against harm and stupid mistakes, just say, "Don't do it!" He should know, when asked his opinion, when to say, "No, don't do it!"

I awoke today to yet another gorgeous morning. I was refreshed—my skin glowed with rest and nutrition. I sat in the cockpit reciting my positive thoughts for the day—the *this, of life is what I make it. This is it! Enjoy the moment!*

Behind the lenses of my binoculars I scan the mud flats. I see a sandpiper in search of his breakfast. He is really hard to spot in his dull winter plumage. In the spring, the guidebook tells me, he shows off his bright chestnut courting attire, curved bill and white rump in Siberia, where he breeds. I smile contentedly, nature whispers of hope and happiness.

My inner-peaceful self is saying "I am happy with all the blessings of the universe." My unconscious-self banters away, "Shower, shower, phone calls, phone calls! Hurry, hurry, go to Paul and

Carolyn's before departure time!" My inner-being speaks up, "Meet life's challenges with calm and confidence." My unconscious-self retorts, "It takes so long to have Doug get the dinghy, he's busy with many projects. Then you have to muck up to the boardwalk, clean the yucky boots, change the shoes … I'm sick of that! It will be much easier and quicker to …"

My inner-peaceful-self groans.

With pinched lips and wrinkled nose, I survey the on/off situation of our legged boat. Yesterday, after our whirl around the bay with Paul and Carolyn, we pulled far up into the marsh. The bow is currently positioned in such a way that the embankment looks close—hardly much different than climbing down onto the dinghy. I asked the Captain, "Do you think I can just climb off the bow of the boat? Then we wouldn't have to get the dinghy, muck up to the boardwalk, and all that?"

The Captain looks as though he were drawing a comparison between me and a cuckoo—the immediate advantage going to the bird.

"Eileen, it's up to you. If you were to ask me if I think *I* can do it? I would say, 'Probably Yes!' Now, I can get the dinghy or you can go off the bow. It's up to you."

I eye the situation again and remember all the trouble it is to get to the road. The marshes are … so … so (I peer down from above) so … *convenient.*

"Whatever your decision," he calls, "make it so I can have time for a shower, too!" These are the Captain's last words.

So, my husband lowers me by my arms but—oh my—it is quite a bit further down than it looked. Once I'm hanging (literally) from the bow, I must consider my "landing" options. Since there's no way to get back *up,* somehow I have to go *down.* I manage to fall-jump-land… whichever … and, upon impact, my knee goes out.

A sound issues from my mouth that I could spend a week trying to describe. How do I put words to a sound? I'm surprised half the village dogs didn't start barking.

The "scrubby" marsh grasses were actually quite tall and this created the illusion of the bow's proximity to solid ground. It was, however, a nice cozy, hidden, muddy spot in which I could writhe in pain. I ignored the passing group of beach strollers and their perfect timing.

During a variety of memorable moments in my life, my knee does me the favor of simply "going out." Most of the time it manages this feat without anything like the help I've just given it. I quickly assess the situation and conclude that this one is a doozy!

I look up to see a pained expression on Doug's face. He gives me a minute to recover before asking my condition. Several places were shooting with pain and, at first, I feared I'd fractured an assortment of limbs. But, with dreadful determination, I try to stand. It is a wobbly success.

I look around me, a bit dazed. I wiped the tears streaming down my mud-coated cheeks and made an effort to brush the Copequid Bay mud from my body and backpack. I don't even look back at the Captain. I'm sure he's judged me 10-degrees-short of a half-wit. I must take courage!

Am I going to let *this* keep me from my *shower* (which, now I *really* need)! I stretch my bruised body and conclude that the worst is my knee. Well, I've lived with this many times before and I start walking to town. After all, I have to consider our hurry-up-and-wait-schedule of the tides.

Woo boy! Not my idea of a good time. I know from experience that I might as well move it and use it now, because tonight it will be stiff and swelled, no matter what. I think about living with a bum knee on this tiny boat for two weeks … EEEHHHEEE!

The distance between the boat and my shower, walking along with my injured knee, increases by tenfold. Cars whiz by. I stop along the side of the road, covered in mud and frowns, and fight back tears of discouragement.

Darn it! I used to live a life of comfort, if not *luxury*. How did I get myself into this? What *day* is it anyway? I close my eyes and see Day 16 written in my journal, right next to all the happy and contented babble of this morning.

Bah! This is like being on a 30-day diet and all I've lost is 15 days.

By the time I arrived at the doorstep, I'd worked myself up into an impressive state of indignation, my disconcerted tears leaving mournful streaks through the mud on my cheeks. I felt old and clumsy, like I should just crawl back underneath my rock. Paul answered the door and confronted my frustrated, muddy visage. Obviously I stirred his deepest feelings, because he backed up, proffered the international gesture of "be my guest" and pointed up the stairs to the shower.

The fragrance of Carolyn's bath products greets me like an old friend.

I search for words, now, to describe the three phone calls I made after my shower. I'd say *most disturbing* just about covers it. The calls managed to undo any relief I'd garnered from showering and donning clean clothes. With a sinking feeling, I headed back to the half-a-claw-foot tub room for quiet and solace. As I shut the door, an overwhelming sadness flooded my soul. I sat on the throne, elevated my leg on the tub and let the tears run down my freshly scrubbed and sun screened face.

The first call was to Brooke's home in Wisconsin. Her phone was disconnected. When I called from Parrsboro and received the recording, I felt it was a mistake—out of order or something. Where could she be? I spoke with her just before our departure and all seemed fine. She made me promise to call and tell her how things were going. I didn't have a work number or friend to call.

I then call Kyle and just caught him. He has no idea about what's up with Brooke. Kyle has been living in Orno, Maine, going to school, working and living with his fiancé. I discovered that he, too, is living out a drama. After a four-year relationship, he and Anna were splitting up. His plans, now, are to head to Europe. He spent a year at University in Austria and now he's set his course that direction once again.

I should have stopped at *this* call—but, oh no! I'm a glutton for punishment.

I punched in the numbers for Doug's parents. The good news, PA-way, was that Bill, my dear sweet father-in-law, must have yet another life-threatening surgery to add to his long list of frailties. My throat went dry; the sharpness of life took a painful poke at me.

Carolyn offered a cup of herbal tea to soothe the nerves. Both Carolyn and Paul interrupted their busy morning to sit and listen to a brief outline of my day thus far. They listened with passion and concern. The window's gentle reminder helped put my life, and its twists and turns, back into perspective. So, with a brave smile and an ungainly knee, I gathered my belongings and directed my course back to the floating world.

Slowly I limped back to my sea-way of life. Two seagulls squawked overhead. Step by step, little by little, the dark clouds disappeared. My herbal tea and friends did wonders for my mental state. I reflected on what I've read and experienced in the Japanese Tea House with its formal ceremonies. As I hobble along, it dawns on me how the Tea House rituals parallel, in some ways, living on the water. The teahouse and our old wooden boat reflect certain standards of simplicity, restraint, and harmony. Both provide a temporary detachment from the world. The teahouse almost always has a garden and water of some kind outside. The boat and the teahouse delight in their proximity to nature and natural materials. I always enjoyed the symbolism in the rough, unfinished, vertical posts of the teahouse. They serve to remind man of his own imperfections and oneness with nature. Finally, both offer a respite from more mundane routines.

The sun is once more shining upon me. In the distance, I see my faithful paladin of simple living, waiting anxiously. His expression is one of relief. So, is it because I'm walking? Or, rather that he didn't have to shanghai his first mate back on board. In any case, my heart warms; there's nothing better than having someone genuinely glad to see you.

I can tell you folks, I have something to brag about. With the help of my Captain, I was able to get back on board. I felt a sense of accomplishment to have made it back and happy to place a mote between us and the rest of the world. I took a moment to probe the tender spots of an imperfect world. The Captain had a strange, soft, light in his eyes when I told him of the phone calls. My hero took me into his belly and gave me a big hug. We took a broom to the mental cobwebs and swept them away. After all, life always brings a few glitches.

The bay is full of rushing water. I flopped myself onto a cockpit cushion to wait for the top of the tide to float us off the high marsh

anchorage. The Captain modified the schedule and scratched his
shower—he just had one yesterday. The whole "famdamily" has
showed up at water's edge to wish us *bon voyage*. They are seemingly
unconcerned with today's business—the large festivities planned for
Maitland day or potential sales from all the extra people in town.
For the next hour we all wait for "lift off." The dogs play gleefully,
swimming, running and retrieving sticks.

The perspective up here is different from that on the shore.
Waiting for the tide on the boat is like being in the highest seat in
the Ferris Wheel.

At last we are off and floating, setting sail out of the *wonderously
strange* world of Maitland, the Copequid Bay and the Shubenacadie.
As we wave goodbye, I'm struck by the faith and inherent goodness
of those we've met. We arrived as strangers and now depart the best
of friends. Paul, back to his old self, is telling us something of great
importance and, no doubt, to the enlightenment of mankind. As
we float away, I call out, "Write us a letter, using one side of the
paper only!"

We had such a good time, it's hard for it all to end. But the hem
of heaven is behind us as we head out into the now descending bay.

We thought it was possible, out in the bay, that the wind would
be against the tide. Therefore, we could reasonably go or stay. "We
aren't on some sorta structured death march to see all of Nova Scotia
on our planned 30 days," declared the Captain, "like on a tour bus
seeing it all behind tinted glass." He gave me a large happy smile.
"We do give up certain things to have this type of flexibility in travel!"

I moaned, rubbed my knee, and thought to myself, if I hadn't
given up list-making, then this would make a good one. I swore off
yesterday in an indignant fit when Captain Doug rolled his eyes at
my latest list and said, with a bit of devilry, "That's only *three* reasons, Eileen. Now you can do better than that."

I had to put my hand over my mouth to stop from making a list
of why I make lists. I gave him a jab in the gut, where it really hurts,
and the *curse* of curses, "May your bilge beers go skunk!"

In all seriousness, we decided we'd better head for home. Late
fall in the North Atlantic can unexpectedly turn to the nasty and
blustery side. We weren't far into the Bay before we knew this ride

back to Five Islands was going to be wind against tide. The westerly is beating against us while the outgoing tide pushes us up from behind. As we slammed and dunked, my nautically-trained mind took over. I refused to be impressed when the wind escalated, seemingly every second. What should one do in these circumstances? I begged my leave from the cockpit and swayed and bounced back to the V-berth.

Two factors were on my side: I managed to get my swelled, stiff knee into the V-berth with no one to witness my act and no one in my way. I settled in, nursing my knee, fighting for rolling space and praying that I wouldn't have to get up and do #1 or #2.

All you sailor types may be wondering how fast the winds were blowing, how the sails were trimmed, the depth of the water, or how many tacks we made? Sorry. All I can tell you is that I felt as helpless as when my goldfish was sick.

I must have fallen asleep because the next thing I remember was the Captain's call from the cockpit, for help. I jumped like I'd just received electro-shock treatment. I scrambled to get myself out of bed, Good God, that hurts! My knee slammed against everything possible, twisting and going out and slipping back—someone might as well be pounding it with a baseball bat. Every movement makes me sicker and sicker.

"Eileen, hurry! The depth sounder just went out!"

I don't like the sound of this (no pun intended).

When you are in an unfamiliar bay that habitually relinquishes its title of being a bay (I don't know—is it still called a *bay* if it doesn't have water?), you really *need* your depth sounder to do just what it does best.

I grab hold of the tiller and brace myself with my good leg to keep from flying over board. I fight to keep control while the Captain pounds on the depth sounder.

Now, everyone knows that this what *I* would do. The Captain, on the other hand, goes about the task of "pounding" in a calm, systematic way.

Now, I can't say that the lack of a depth sounder, in this instance, was quite as crucial as some other predicaments we shared. What makes this one seem so untimely is the scene in its entirety.

Doug reported that we had gale force winds, which means 32 to 63 mph. When that kind of wind is pushing you up against 8 knots of current, there is a *whole lot* of shaken' goin' on.

It's dark clouds—impending doom. You know—the whole business. If I could write in my journal, I'd say it's one of those times I thought about getting dead.

The waves crashing up over the side of the boat are strong enough to blow the fins off a fish. The Captain did his magic on the sounder and I am so relieved and excited, I started shouting like some sort of psycho cheerleader, "Hip, Hip, Hurray! Hip, Hip, Hurr—blaah!" A big wave hit my open mouth!

Why does this never seem to happen to the Captain?

After what seems like an aeon, we finally make to Five Islands. Halfway there, I reminded myself that I loved him. Really.

Once here, we have no choice but to anchor outside the protected inlet, to await the tide change. We fix whatever we can shove in our mouths for dinner. I'll spare you the rolly-polly details. As the day wore on, my body made its complaints heard. I ached in a variety of lesser-known places.

Sometime after dark, the armor of my hero went *chink-chink* as he pulled anchor and gently motored us past the Wooden Pepper Pot Lighthouse and the Sand Point Campground to our refuge in the marshes.

EEEgads, what an effort it takes to do anything with this stupid knee! I know, I know. It is not a stupid knee. It just happens to be attached to a sometimes stupid person. For 50 years my trusty knee joints have absorbed the pressures of my weight and I've given them a good beating. Ski accidents, knee surgery, tennis, aerobics, power walking and not to mention all that dancing! Yes, my jointed friends, you have served me well. Just please hold on for another few weeks, until I can get off this floating tiltyard.

If, someday, a kind soul were to open his lips in a toast of goodwill to me, I would be deeply appreciative if he would say, "May you never be dead enough between the ears to try jumping off the bow of a boat again."

There is one factor in this scenario that gives me a glow. My vacation mishap hasn't been told before. Readers have probably heard endless tales from intrepid travelers of Montezuma's revenge and hemorrhoids. I have a friend who fell off an elephant in Kashmir. But I can say, with absolute certainty, that I'm the first recipient of the "*Good Job*" award for *jumping off the bow of a boat!* Yes, indeed, the first woman to have jumped off the bow of a boat while it was resting on stilts in the Minas Basin.

We sit in the cockpit, quietly viewing the marshes and shoreline from our own private beach pad. The clear sky and the multitude of stars cause us to suck in our breaths with admiration. I understand, more than ever, Cicero when he said, *"There is liberty in tranquility."*

In this quiet close of the day we hug tight, my Captain almost asleep in my arms and exhausted from our difficult sail.

My lower lip trembles.

"Will you love me," I ask, "when I'm old and crippled?

"Of course I do!" he replied.

Day 17

Sunday, September 16, 2001

The gulls swoop and soar in the updraft; they float by like leaves in a stream. This might make some people want to spend their days riding the wind (not me, not today). The birds quickly change direction and soar low overhead, sounding like a school bus full of third-graders. My nerves are jangled; memories of yesterday's sail, the phone calls, the terrorism, and my hurt knee, nibble around the edges of my mind.

Usually sleep is very restorative, but alas, I did not sleep well. Throbbing knee and busy mind kept me from ignoring the unignorable. The Captain gave an early wake up call. We are to set sail in just a few minutes on the very near top of the tide. For a half an hour I have drizzled tears in a disgusting manner all over my shirt. I just want to sit here all day. To read quietly, write, sleep, cook and pamper myself. No talking, no walking—just a chance to contemplate life. Not an outlandish request! I simply don't want to go sailing today.

I bow to the fact that it is not possible to get everything I want. Most everything I want is either too expensive or too fattening, anyway. I do pretty well, I think, in keeping my want list to a minimum and squished on my side of the V-berth! Especially someone like me, who in my BD life (I know it is low of me to admit this) wanted almost everything and wanted it gift wrapped.

The Captain announces that the tide has turned! My artificially wide smile deserts me when I stand upon a pair of legs that don't feel like mine. I tuck my thoughts and want-list away. We wave goodbye to the sleeping campgrounds and our own little beach, now covered with the flowing waters.

Once out into the Minas Basin, we see it's to be another beater of a day. Man-o-man!

The Captain made an *executive-Captain-type-decision* and announced, "Let's turn around, while the turning is good."

This means while we still have enough water get back to our favored place in the marshes. Thank you! In no time our legs were on and our little beach appeared. Heaven!

We nibble breakfast in solitude. We have a chance to savor the blue mist created by the last of the sea lavender on the salt marsh edge. Up the hill, the sun shines on a thicket of calico asters, a shrubby, tiny daisy-like flower of pale purple (I call it euphoric lilac), around a yellow center. A moth flutters atmospherically against my chest, giving me a consoling pat. Here, in our protected marsh, the air moves over us in a warm, gentle, moderate breeze.

I have an open air galley, plenty of time and a steady boat— what more can a cook ask for? Umm, a pinto bean and barley soup sounds tasty. I give my sailor companion a little wink, "If I were a bookie, I'd lay odds that before this soup is ready for lunch (with help from my trusty pressure cooker), we'll have company."

The relief engendered from a morning of rest and quiet, with time to enjoy our beautiful surroundings, was enormous.

Mr. Beach House "come-on-up-plenty-of-homemade-wine," Roger, his young son Nolan, and their happy-go-lucky dog dropped by for some friendly salutations. After the talk of Five Islands, the Minas Basin and, last-but-not-least, the Shubenacadie was behind us, Roger made two points very clear: 1) We must come by their

Private Beach Shack next to Five Islands Campground
We have a chance to savor the blue mist created by the last of the sea
lavender on the salt marsh edge ... Here, in our protected marsh,
the air moves over us in a warm, gentle, moderate breeze.

little house for a visit; and 2) We must try some of their homemade elder flower wine. We can't bring ourselves to dash his cup of happiness, so to speak, so we mark it on our social calender.

As the waggish group pranced playfully away, I came to my senses. I called out to them, "Do the campgrounds have shower and laundry facilities?"

"That they do!" Roger informs me, "But, being you are not campers, I doubt that they will allow you to use them!"

Shoot!

It is moments like this that I see my husband's true worth. He volunteers to go on a one-man scouting expedition up to the campgrounds. My knee is decidedly sore and stiff so walking for the next few days needs to be reserved for special occasions. I'm not sure if I'll participate, but it is always good to know one's options.

While I have a few minutes alone and a few extra inches of space, I decide to take inventory of our provisions. My decrepitude forces me to perform this task by practically standing on my head and keeping my leg straight. Once down, I discover that righting myself—without banging my head and/or hurting my knee again— proves to be challenging.

Screaming in my mind, I look up to see the Captain returning with a smile of joy and glad tidings.

Is this really worth hauling myself off the boat, through marshes and up the long road, to the top of the hill? Bemused, I direct my attention to our stack of dirty clothes which are so filthy from Shube mud, they should only be handled with protective gloves. Doug recognizes the dilemma and volunteers for laundry duty.

I then came to a swift decision. Experience, the greatest teacher of all, tells me this is going to hurt so good. Ooh aahh! A shower!

It wasn't long before the excitement of clean clothes and a shower wore off and I began to moan and groan. Muttering under my breath, "What I wouldn't give for a normal *front door*."

Struggling with my portion of laundry and shower gear in hand, we turn to see a youthful-looking couple on touring bikes, large saddle bags draped across their rear wheels, struggling up the steep hill. The young fellow politely stops to talk. He tells us, in broken English, that they are from Germany and are biking all over Nova

Scotia. I notice the young girl looks slightly irritated at the interruption. Can't blame her, she probably had her momentum going.
Was the campground their goal for the day, I wondered?

One tends to notice the slightest grade when on foot or pedaling a
heavy load. Their sweaty faces held smiles when they said good bye
and lifted their monster thighs to place their shoes to the pedal.

Glancing over my shoulder at our cozy little *Guillemot*, nestled
safely, I brightened up. I trudge on in a determined manner. I cannot visualize me doing what they're doing—bad knee or not. That
type of activity would limit my travel aspirations pretty drastically.
In double-quick time, I decide sailing is a more desirable method of
travel.

These men and their adventures. I envision the handsome Ger-
man boy speaking to his sweet Fraulein, eyes sparkling with ardent
zeal, "It would so romantic to bike all over Nova Scotia!" I stumble
over a rock and cut warning eyes at my husband. "Don't ever think
I would want to hike the Appalachian Trail!" (Just in case—I want
to nip that idea right in the bud.)

On our way, we pass Roger's curious beach house. "Further-
more, under no circumstances would I want to be 'attached' to my
brother-in-law. We don't see eye to eye!" This was the 'Roger Reason' for the way his house is built. Walking past his little house
(which doesn't appear to be that little), we finally see what he meant
by "almost attached."

Both houses are two stories and share a portion of the roof at
the top, like a bridge. An appropriate two-foot space is provided
between the walls. This is his way of getting around the zoning laws
which prohibited two separate houses on the lot. Roger's mother's
cottage, a little pinch of a thing, stands to the right, as though she's
the referee.

We arrive at the camp and give "three cheers' for the kindly new
campground owners. Like the rest of the Minas Basin, the near-
drought conditions have left them with a very low water level. Worried that the well would go dry before the end of the season, restric-
tions were enforced for the usage of their pay showers and laundry
facilities. When the well is dry, you know the worth of water. People
have a deep respect for that which you cannot buy.

However, our title of "the sailors from only God knows where" permits us an exclusive invitation.

The new owners tell us proudly that they're just finishing their second season. They must not have stopped to take a breath in two years! The list of their accomplishments is as long as the walk up the hill, and chief among them are new shower and laundry facilities. We never lack in conversation with the campers, being we are "The Sailors."

The wooden Pepper Pot Lighthouse is not far from the laundry so we pay him a second visit. This cute little guy, for being just a lighthouse, gets around. Born around 1913 he is now in his third home. This fact alone brings an awareness of the extent of erosion on this shore in the last 90 years. If I were to be a lighthouse I would be pleased with this view.

They say life is not to be measured by the number of breaths you take, but by the number of moments that take your breath away. A breathless, stunned silence overtook us. We gazed upon the magnificence of Glooscap's Five Islands: Moose, Diamond, Long, Egg and Pinnacle. Turning to our left, we see the Five Islands Provincial Park. The cliffs, sculpted by the tides and exposing millions of years of geological past, makes me weak with reverence. Suddenly an exuberance erupts through my body and joins the energy that created this beautiful world. The sheer beauty was too intense, too vivid for my mind to translate. It seemed as though the air held its breath.

A very large flock of greater scaup flew over our heads. It is likely their winter compasses are set for the Gulf of Mexico. I feel a strange kinship with these migrating birds—little and big. I imagine what it must be like for them to forsake their familiar earth for the gray ocean, an ocean perhaps that a little sandpiper, warbler or the greater scaup has never seen. How easy "migrates to South America or Siberia," rolls off my tongue! What a gesture of ancient faith and present courage such a flight is; what a defiance of circumstance and death. My heart beats faster for them; my eyes swell with tears. I can imagine the fading land behind, the unknown and the distant horizon ahead. Their first migration may be the most exciting moment of their lives, like a rite of passage; the experience they've trained for and now, ready or not, here we go.

The breeze blows clusters of clouds by, as if heading the same direction as the birds. How many different times in my life have I felt this, recent and past? Perhaps these tiny birds, seemingly so defenseless, are like me, and say ignorance is bliss. Or maybe they figure, "Hey, other birds all over the world are doing this, some with a lot greater distance over open waters. I just have to close my eyes, hold my nose and jump!"

The scrumptious trail of bean and barley soup is wafting through the air and over the water, ready to reach the nostrils of all nearby. Rick, the fisherman we spoke with last time, follows the trail. He and Doug are deep in conversation, discussing "what's what around here." After my achy-breaky shuffle back on board, I feel my number is about up for my stiff knee. It's yelping louder than the two men.

I claim sanctuary in my private place, the V-berth, four feet from where they are shooting the bull.

My hopeful day of solitude on a steady boat has turned into a day of talking. I may have to quit talking to be sure of what I know. I know that I need to meditate and contemplate life. I want silence and privacy. An old adage springs to mind, "Focus on what's right and what you have, not what you want." Here goes ... I have a beautiful, uncomplicated day, out of the Shube tidal bore. I am fixing lunch with no fear and without the boat's inclinometer registering 30-40 while the bilge water fills the starboard side of the cabin. In my rather humble state of living, I have no bells, whistles, alarms, telephones, faxes, voice mail, no time clocks, no traffic, no hurry, no money worries and no deadlines. Out of the world of consumer delights, I have no TV or radio commercials, nail polish, outlandish merchandising of holiday decor, broken pool sweeps, computer viruses, flat tires, or deafening sounds of weed eaters and lawnmowers.

Encouraged by my new list—a list even someone like my husband would appreciate—I jump up, forgetting that I'm getting old (gotten old?). Ouch! I turn off the soup, ease back into a more comfortable position and massage my hip. My hip in now throbbing from walking all that way favoring my hurt knee.

But that's okay. I close my eyes—this meditative business is going pretty well. I may just go on to find my center and complete the journey to my enlightenment. I think on this for a while. Do I find enlightenment and then I'll find my center or vice versa? I guess I'll know when the time comes.

I close my eyes and take deep breaths. I can hear the voices going on, jabbering about bait and paint. I tune them out. I imagine myself being like "Deep Thought," the computer in *Hitchhikers Guide to the Galaxy.* Maybe I'll find the answer to life, the Universe and everything? I might as well, I rationalize, go for it! "It" being the ultimate questions. If I'm going to do this, you never know, I may just come up with an answer. I laugh heartily when I remember that Deep Thought took a mere 7 million years to come up with an answer.

My husband turns and asks, "What's so funny?"

I call back, "42!"

I wake up from the most wonderful nap. I smack my lips as if I'd just eaten a scrumptious dessert. I can't believe the peace I feel. I'm so relaxed, it's as if a doctor had just administered two martinis and 5mg of Valium.

The boat is quiet. The Captain must have gone ashore. The splendid isolation of it all. My eyes close for more of the same.

I wake. I do feel as though I'm in some kind of altered state. I grab my 4-and-one-half-inch mirror. Yep, it's still the same shallow me. Inside, however, I feel *changed.* I feel presence—a higher level of being here.

I prop myself up on my elbows and stick my tousled head out of the front hatch. I take a reading like that of a submarine periscope. I see sections of the marshes that have turned to fall. I am lost in the viewing of the perfection of nature. Wow, this is nifty. I am still alone. Shucks! I want to tell Doug all about the new me. You'd think a few more minutes alone would be equivalent to a mother locking her children outside her bathroom door. We've spent so many hours, close enough to touch, sharing everything but toilet paper, that we almost know each other's thoughts (at least I think I know his and he should know mine).

The truth is, I don't want to miss what he's seeing and hearing at this moment because he inspires me. Or, shall I say, he pushes me to delve more deeply into my own consciousness, to begin to find that other awareness that enlightens and enlivens my being.

I know there have been many times and probably will be still more, when I feel that life with this man of unsound mind is enough to cause me to retire to one of those spas to take the cure. My rational self, seeped in the conventional world, tells me that I should have married someone sensible, normal and established. Fortunately my irrational self usually wins and tells me that would have been as dull as dishwater. Looking again into my four-and-one-half-inch mirror, I doubt that I'll ever take my place in polite society again, which might be nice occasionally. Little by little, I'm enjoying my life of not chasing business rainbows. With society's emphasis on things and money, we tend to loose our reverence for the sweetness of everyday life.

I hear my husband bouncing aboard, "Hey, my sweetie, you've got to see this!" With a look of inspired and happy puzzlement—a look formerly associated only with starry-eyed returnees from alien abduction—he nudges me and points out our forward plexiglass windows. I ask myself what could be so weird outside our plexiglass living room, but he can't be this excited over nothing.

So I look and see two men taking a teeth-chattering swim. The scene is one you might find in the San Francisco Bay, where I've observed the ceremonial daily polar swim. But, this is much colder water. Doug continues laughing and squinting out the window. "Here they come!"

I drag myself out of bed and get ready to welcome their sporting spirits.

Laurel and Hardy in swim trunks is my first thought. I take the liberty, here, to share that these two look to be in their 60's. Although quite different, the two men have several things in common: 1) they both are eccentric enough to be swimming in these frigid waters; and 2) they both sport strong, athletic builds.

Quickly, they moved from Laurel and Hardy to "has beens" as in "has been everywhere." Andre, tall and thin with gray hair and goose bumps, gave his salutations in a very thick French accent. He immediately placed himself on the highly-esteemed "Most High" list. He knows the *Guillemot* is a "Controversy" and was likely built and designed in the 1950's by the Mt. Desert Boat Yard. This design was so controversial, that the original boats were actually dubbed the "Controversies." Recently, Dan MacNaughton (Dan who wrote the introduction and one and the same as the co-editor and author of *The Encyclopedia of Yacht Designers*), in a lecture given at Mystic Seaport, proclaimed this design the coastal cruising boat of the 20th century.

But how this Frenchman knew, I never found out. His plunging pal, Bill, moved right into the inevitable questions—the "who, what, and where" of our trip.

Bill, with the constitution and fur of a husky, offered stories of his sailing life and childhood here in their beach house. Andre, weak-willed and half-frozen, wiggled the tip of his blue nose and darted toward the house. Bill stayed to make himself useful with information about the local waters. He has a catamaran (which sounds large, fancy and perfect for these waters, because it has no keel) being refurbished in Halifax. While Bill continues on and on about sailing, I slip away to turn on the burner and reheat the soup.

Every time I go below, I overhear something that perks my ears. Bill tells Doug about his several ocean crossings to Europe with his wife and daughters.

I stifle a laugh when I join them back in the cockpit. I should have kept a photo journal of this journey. Here he stands—hairy chested and in swim trunks! I find my teeth start to chatter. Shiver me timbers, but that water must be cold! I question him about sailing to Europe, but he always brings the conversation back to his vast knowledge of the area. I can tell from the conversation, thus far, that he feels it's his duty to try and save our lives (or at least, enhance our trip).

I start calculating when the tide will come in and he'll be forced to move away from the boat so we can have our lunch—I'm starved. I break down and invite him for beer and soup.

"No, No," he protests. He has lunch waiting for him at his house. "But, hey, why don't you two come up after you eat for a beer and a look over the charts?"

Mais oui! We'll be there. He then turned his heels toward his weekend beach house.

I wanted to hear more about the canals of Europe and cruising the Mediterranean. I feel spineless! I've cruised the Mediterranean and the Aegean Sea too—on a large luxury cruise liner!

It's sun and soup in the cockpit of our beach pad. We sit silently, making only sounds from slurping our soup. An imaginary curtain lifts and a winged symphony performs in perfect harmony and natural rhythm. I am warmed to the cockles of my heart to realize we have the best seats in the house.

I clean up lunch and give a friendly smile to a silent, green-glossed head of a Greater Scaup, which stopped by to say good bye. Beyond him is Mr. Teeter-tail, a Spotted Sandpiper, endlessly bobbing his rear end. While here for the winter he changes his identity by losing his spots!

"What do ya need to do before we go?" My husband asks, as he readies the boat for our time on the shore.

I sit back, stretch my neck, close my eyes, circulate my shoulders. "Oh, I need to reconsider life."

"Before we go?" he asks.

"Yeah." I stand my ground. I'm into this feeling my being … awareness … what have you.

"Well you better get to it then," he says. "You've got five minutes."

Long legged, suave Andre meets us at the door. I have a feeling I've met him before. Perhaps it's the typical (but alluring) *savoir faire* shared by so many Frenchmen. We climb the winding staircase, Andre in the lead. As he speaks, I want to interrupt (now, that's something new) and ask him several questions I've had on my list since this morning.

Bill told us the story of their meeting. Once Andre had hightailed it back to the house, Bill confided, "He's a separatist from Montreal."

Oh no! I think, hand to my chest.

However, Bill says this in a tone meant to assure us that he likes him anyway. They are fast friends.

I, personally, have no opinion, I'm not sure of the politics of the idea. I just know that sometimes I'd like to be a separatist from Eastport.

"My wife and I were on a ferry, touring Alaska's inland passage and doing the driving/ferry hopping thing." Bill tells us, "I saw him on one of the ferries. I pointed him out to my wife and said, 'He's a separatist from Montreal!'"

To prove this fact to his wife, he swaggered over and struck up a conversation. "Andre prides himself in swimming the coldest waters in the world," he added.

I thought to myself, "That's not on my list, but to each his own."

Bill continued, "I asked him, 'Have you swum the Minas Basin?'" It seemed that the culmination of that ferry boat meeting in Alaska was what we observed today—their frigid swim in some of the coldest waters of the world.

I'm quailing over my knee by the time we reach the upper level of their house. Beautiful views—long, long, steep stair case.

Bill's wife, Suzette (I have named you Suzette because, unfortunately, I can't remember your name, and I like the name Suzette) is a quiet, kind, and attractive woman. She is likely use to Bill dragging people in for a beer. I sit back to enjoy the views and the cold beer straight out of their ice chest! Oooohhh!

The boys commence in spreading the charts of the Minas Basin and the Bay of Fundy out over the large table. Their conversation never lulled. Our conversation, never lulled.

It seems that when Andre, the Montreal separatist, is not dipping into the coldest waters in the world, he enjoys another cold climate sport—black ice sailing!

I tell you, I never *knew* their were this many lunatics in the world. Paragliding? Now, black ice sailing? I nodded and helped myself to a cracker. His stories, albeit interesting, were lengthy. I enjoyed all the taps to the head, clicks of the tongue, smiles of joy and expressions of pity. Andre, I discover, not only enjoys freezing sports but likes to warm up his bones at his apartment in Coco Beach, Florida (which always reminds me of *I Dream Of Genie*).

I tap the theme song with my foot as he tells me that, while in Florida—are you ready for this?—he sand sails! Black ice sailing and sand sailing are two activities my best friends would not recommend for me.

I ask Suzette a few questions about their sailing and traveling. This includes the southern waters in the Caribbean, Central America, Alaska, Greece and other parts of Europe. Figuratively speaking, I could say I'd been almost every place mentioned. Without suspicion, I could join in the conversations. They knew I'd been up the Shube River in that skateboard of a boat. I didn't have to own up to my previous method of travel—bedecked and bejeweled on cruise ships or staying in the finest hotels. I will walk away and they will never know that I'm a hothouse-grown, artificial California girl.

The group offered another beer, but we decline. We are mindful of their schedule and their drive back to Parrsboro. As for myself, memories of the winding staircase, the rocky footpath, the marshes, the rocks, the goo and the gunk, the row to the boat and my precarious knee, stopped me from over-indulging. I envisioned how a situation could arise that was fraught with embarrassing potentialities.

Walking down the path to the road, Bill follows and tells us that he built the new house himself. The original, in which he spent his childhood summers, was torn down. The new home is nice but unfinished.

I know his type—extremely talented, with numerous interests which send him in many different directions. We say our thanks and good byes. I kinda hate to leave. I know there is more to learn from these three. I know, without a doubt, you can meet the most interesting people in the most unusual places.

* * *

While traveling in the South Pacific, around eight years ago, my friend Susan and I were on a small island called Aitutakki, which is part of the Cook Islands. We were seated in front of our thatched roof home, watching a large lizard crawling in and out of the multiple holes in the roof which, by the way, due to some strange engineering feat, never leaked.

We could see the swaying rope bridge, the only way onto the tiny lagoon island where the accommodations were built. On the island, (which we took to calling *Fantasy Island* from the popular TV show), every few days "The Plane! The Plane!" would arrive on a runway built during World War II. The airport consisted of a tiny thatched roof and picnic bench. The new visitors would be hauled to the swaying rope bridge by the local chicken truck, the same way we arrived a few days before. Today, two women caught my attention. The eldest walked ahead bearing golden brown skin, pure white hair, a large walking stick, bare feet, and a face full of wonder with eyes intent on not missing a thing. Her companion is a woman gaily striped and patterned, built for economy and utility, coconut husk hair surrounds her happy cheeks which reflect optimism and high character. Following close behind is a huge Maori native, clothed only in cutoffs. Hoisted upon one shoulder was a huge suitcase; on the opposite shoulder he carried a bag of traveling gear including snorkeling equipment, cameras, etc.

Susan and I exchanged a look, eyebrows raised, I said, "I betcha, those two women have some stories to tell!"

Evening found us in an open-air, thatched roof, dinning area. Guests ate in a communal setting. We were served the same menu and seated as in a school cafeteria, taking the first available seat. As luck would have it we were seated directly across from these two worldly ladies. I was so excited I could hardly contain myself.

"Okay, you two! You must some interesting stories and I'd like to hear them!" were the first words out of my mouth. The eldest held up a finger, knobby from arthritis, then cleared her throat.

We enjoyed three days with the traveling duo. Claudia and Sarah were a pair of wild women, who, with encouragement, regaled us with many of their often hilarious adventures. Aittutaki, was merely one stop on a tour of many South Pacific Islands. Over the past ten years, the two have shared many daring (or so it sounded) hiking, fishing, snorkeling, diving, and boating trips. Claudia, then 76, was the first woman to take a tour group to China in the 70's and has since been there 75 times. Sarah, a 65-year-old married woman (married to a less-adventuresome husband), joined Claudia on one of her Silk Road excursions where their friendship developed. Claudia, now 84, is still packing her bags and heading for China and other unusual destinations.

I often reminisce about my three weeks in the Cook Islands. It was my first real exposure to off-the-beaten-path travel. I went on a whim. I was selling travel and they offered it as a FAM (familiarizing trip—really cheap), and billed it as Hawaii 50 years ago. Hum— it sounded intriguing. I'd been to Hawaii a few times and was ready for something different.

Different, I got, by golly! Little did I know that I was being *familiarized* alrighty! Familiarized for my new life in Eastport, Maine, and the likes of Doug Beaver.

I've often called Eastport, the Aitutakki of the Northeast. Lately we have taken to calling the crazy island of Eastport, our *Fantasy Island* because we never know what wild and crazy people will show up there.

* * *

Out in the bright sunshine, I'm feeling more than a little woozy. We stroll toward Roger's (not "attached" to his brother-in-law's) house. Our nice quiet boat setting, off to our right, looked really tempting. I'm wondering, how did we end up with two social engagements in this tiny place? And on my day off—so to speak. We pose this question and remind ourselves that we've been invited twice and when temptation is there, we're not ones to show restraint.

I'll split the difference—it's homemade wine and probably not that great. I'll take a few sips (usually gives me a headache anyway), be harmonious with our new friends and then head back to the boat and blissville.

A more exuberant welcome we have seldom experienced. Sitting amidst their ice chest, sleeping bags and makeshift kitchen, we uncork the wine. Their jovial contentment was contagious. We toast to new friends and the beautiful Five Islands. The wine is excellent! Or maybe it's the atmosphere ... I can't analyze a good thing too much.

Roger and Connie excitedly tell us of their plans to build a new house on some property they just purchased down the road. It appears to be only about 300 yards away but, I reason, 300 yards is better than two feet, away from his brother-in-law. Connie explains her effervescence over the new plans.

"Our new house will have electricity, running water and an indoor toilet!" She crows.

I looked Connie in the eye. There was no end to my commis-eration. Granted, she did live in one of the more beautiful places on earth, but so is the 17-mile-drive in Pebble Beach, California. I have friends there who need to clean and provide fresh towels for their seven bathrooms.

The happy parent's eyes light up when their little Nolan arrives to greet us. His arms are full of—what? It's big, but what is it? Some sort of missile?

This diminutive, cute lad with a gigantic smile is more than slightly struggling to show us their archeological find from a nearby WWII testing site.

Doug is an immediate friend to all children so he coaxes Nolan over for a closer peak. Our energetic little pal entrusts Doug with a grip on the heavy (for 6-year-old Nolan) missile. With the weight of it now completely in Doug's hand, he dramatically gives a sensa-tional drop to his arm, as if a 50 lb. weight had unexpectedly been placed there.

All of us widened our eyes in question? Nolan's initial shock was replaced with a loud infectious laugh. With bravado, Nolan took it back, only to place it again in Doug's hand. The little guy uttered renewed howls and explosive sounds at my husbands' trick behav-ior. Nolan gleefully reenacted the scene a few more times, his body limp with amusement. This causes us, cultured fine wine connois-seurs, to be thrown into a fit of unrestrained laughter.

Roger further refines the moment by opening the squeaky ice chest. Out of it came our hors d'oeuvres. He places a large hunk of cheese upon an old board and proceeds to brandish a saw-back fish knife, cutting large slices. He hands me my portion off the exceed-ingly sharp tip of his blade—great cheese!

We again toast to our fanciful moments together. I wanted to clap my hands with the fun of it—so I did. When the last drop of precious wine is poured, this alerts our host that this occasion war-rants opening another bottle of wine. Wiser counsel might have advised that a single bottle was more than adequate. But, those who know the Beavers best, know that we're not ones to put a damper on someone's party. Like most travelers, we believe that vacations are not a time for soberness and self-control.

From this point on, I garnered every ounce of concentration left to concentrate on the answers to my questions—I really, truly wanted to know how to make this wine, which was affording me such great pleasure!

Our hosts, we find, use this cottage as a weekend retreat and are packed to head home, over the hill. But this, nor the fact that Connie has to go to work tonight, did not hinder the festivities.

The back door opens and Kricket, their twelve-year old daughter, enters with a sweet, shy smile. She stands tall and thin, holding her latest treasure, a new shell. She talks easily of her activities and friends here in Five Islands. Many of the campers stay for several weeks and return each year, so there are always new and old friends.

The whole family gathers at the door as we prepare to leave, we promise a return visit some day. We step outside, armed with our very own bottle of elder flower (or was it elderberry?) wine and a bag of pretty shells, compliments of Kricket. As we start to move away, they follow, still talking. We are at the edge of the road.

"Do you need some help loading the pickup?" We ask, not wanting our time together to end.

"No, but you can stay for moral support," they replied.

We did.

Nolan is still waving and calling out the back window with the exuberance only a six-year-old can offer, as they set forth on their drive back to their RR#1 Springhill, Nova Scotia home.

Like two migrating birds, we glide through the marsh. The setting sun gives the marshes a new shade of autumn. We clutch our wine, vowing to guard it and drink it at a special moment, commemorating the family and place that pierced our hearts.

Half-way back to the boat we stop to enjoy our surroundings. I dedicate myself to search for more glimpses of the peace and contentment I found earlier today. We hug and cling to each other. We sway in our happiness.

I don't know about happily ever after with this man, but right now I'm happily.

I sit alone in the cockpit. My husband is sleeping soundly. I listen to the rhythmic flapping of the waves against our floating beach house and recall Nolan's infectious laughter. What a privilege to laugh, till the tears ran, with our new friends. Seems like most of us, as we grow older, forget how to laugh freely. I'm going to start practicing, like my deep breathing in yoga.

I peer up to the skies, as the stars fill the night, and wonder what it possibly could have looked like in the Triassic period. Here, I sit, in this segment of time, just one night in the millions and billions that have come before me.

Day 18

Monday, September 17, 2001

Eyes still closed I perform a reclining spinal twist and smile at the sounds of a musical chuckle coming from the salt marsh. Yeah, I suppose you would chuckle even harder, I think to myself, if you could see me move into the spider, the fish, the bridge and finally into the through-the-hole stretch (as much as my stiff knee allows). I repeat a mantra: *I inhale life's positive energy and exhale negativity. I am centered. I am relaxed. I am at peace.*

So there!

With my short series of before-I-get-out-of-the-bed yoga stretches out of the way, I stick my head full of knotted hair out the front hatch. I search for the Semipalmated Plover who laughs at my rather optimistic goals for the day.

Ashore, I see my Captain sitting on the sandy beach, toes dug in, jeans rolled up around his calves, a coffee cup in hand. The sun illuminates his smiling face and the rough-stemmed Canadian goldenrod which surround him. The scene couldn't be more delectable if I'd ordered it off a menu.

The up-slurred *chu-weet* of the plover whistled.

Yes. Perfectly perfect.

"Some good day, eh!" We both laugh at my effort to speak Canadian. Having immersed ourselves in the world of maritimers, we've decided that their way of speaking is smarter than most of us. There is usually a lot of "Eh!" (pronounced as a long "a) going on; this is an umbrella phrase covering all sorts of responses and statements.

My observations of the meaning of "Eh" include (I now provide you, my well-deserving reader, with another one of my trusty lists): *Do you agree? Don't you agree? Isn't that right?* It also covers the Americans' *Huh? Right! Okay? Do you get it? Get the point? What's the point? What?* and *What do you think?*

Some other expressions we find amusing are, "Some good!" which appears to mean *great* and *fantastic!* "Some Bad" and "Awful Terrible" means (logically) *very bad* or *awfully terrible.*

A caressing breeze cooled my cupa tea and we both exhaled, savoring the quiet. "I could stay here the rest of my days," I murmur.

Doug agrees but queries, "I wonder how long it would take them to decide we aren't Canadian? I don't think we're *nice* enough to be Canadian!"

"Speak for yourself!" I reply. "Truthfully, it'd likely be your Philly accent that would give us away."

We took a barometric reading this morning by looking to the west and feeling the air. Often, during the autumn months, a mild high-pressure system (fair weather) may become entrenched, bringing pleasant "Indian Summer" days. In any case, there appears to be no low-pressure system (cloudiness, high humidity, stormy weather) on our horizon.

Many hours will pass before we can set sail at the top of the flooding tide. I am satisfied to have my place in the sunshine, to muse over the bubbles on the water. "Did you hear the kids call them fish farts yesterday?" We both laugh, remembering our fun day. I feel a little younger this morning. Where is it written that your glory days can't be the ones in front of you? Or that your best memories can't be bested? We are in the waiting room of paradise.

All morning I wallowed in an exquisite existence, enveloped in

Next to Five Islands Campground
Many hours will pass before we can set sail at the top of the flooding tide. I
am satisfied to have my place in the sunshine, to muse over the bubbles on
the water ... we are in the waiting room of paradise.

a deep inner peace. Finally Doug tapped me on the shoulder and delivered news of the high tide. My sailing first-mate genes kicked in and I gave a big, gleaming smile to my faithful Captain. I know, now, that we're "Two minds, but with a single heart—two hearts that beat as one!"

We sail out at slack tide going nowhere slow. The Queen Ann's Lace seed pods wave goodbye from the shore. I look to port side as a cloud moves in front of the sun, its dark shadow passing across the cliffs and rocky beaches like a hand across a face.

"I feel blissed out, man!" I tell my husband in my best hippie voice.

When things are going well, you need to be sure and notice it. A sailor who's experienced the vicissitudes of the open sea learns to genuinely appreciate the value of calm weather and fair skies. This bright blue sky, seen through slits of white clouds, with the warm sun on our backs and a light wind, provides a different *quality* of sailing.

We know this can change but I'm enjoying the energy of the moment.

I normally have to stop and lecture my busy mind. I'm usually so worried about getting to the future that the present is reduced to simply a means of getting "there"—my incessantly planning, thinking and worrying mind tries to tell me how much easier, quicker and safer it would be just to get in a car and drive. Today, at least, I can simply relax and smile at it!

By road map, I would head out of the Five Islands Campground, hit Route 2, turn left and go approximately 15-20 KM and—*Voila*—I'd be in Parrsboro. Even with a road map, I might accidentally turn the wrong way, drive 15 miles and end up having lunch in Economy instead of Parrsboro. Or something catastrophic might happen—I might run into highway construction, be thrust into a lengthy two-mile detour or get lost and have to determine my bearings by the horrible sight of an unmarked dirt road. But, all and all, my worst fear would likely be whether I'd be able to re-fold the road map so it would fit back into the glove box.

In sailing, however, your chart is your lifeline. Land points, rocks, depths, the direction of the wind and harbours are on your 'things to consider list!'. By sailing to Parrsboro, instead of driving, our little journey takes on a personality. When sailing, I've found, I see more of everything and I see it all a bit differently.

Birdwatching, for instance, is not for those in a hurry or driving. You must be still and quiet and scour one section at a time. Doug has taught me to look closely and really *see*.

In the past I'd ask, "What kind of bird is that?"

Then the smart aleck, who's constantly pointing out the inadequacies of his little wife, would respond, "What did it look like?"

Humph! Details! Details! But, try as I might, my descriptions of *big* and *large* wing spans were simply inadequate when I went to check our trusty bird guide. Nowadays, with my amateur ornithology training behind me, I first check out the shape of the bird's beak. Then I try to memorize its coloring, I listen to its call and I observe *how* it flies. Sometimes, now, I recognize birds by their shape and gait. I notice if they walk-and-probe or run-and-peck.

I read in a book somewhere that this is called JIZZ. The term comes from the fighter pilot's acronym, GIS, for "general impression and shape." There is a big wide world of birds out there to discover. I might even one day see what the Maliseet Indians called *Nan-a-mik-tcus*, or, as they call them in Maine, *Rocks in its rump*!

I stare intently at the Five Islands as we sail past them. I feel the slightly warmer breeze coming off the land. Oddly, I still expect to see movement. I feel the beauty and solitude from the day we spent there but this is mixed with the eerie effect the islands had on me as well. I just can't shake the creepy sensation that more goes on out there than meets the eye. "Stop that Eileen!" I silently rationalize, "No ghost worth its ectoplasm would haunt such a deserted secluded place!"

A large gust of wind just flowed through a valley and came out to greet us here in the Minas Basin. The waves encounter the wind and react in random variations. Again my stomach gets a little wheezy over all this unruliness of nature. The unpredictable winds, waves, and back eddies seem higgley-piggley, a chaotic and disorderly system.

I tend to want to deal with nature as I do my garden—clip, dig, and secure it to a trellis.

"A good afternoon!" I cooed. I suddenly feel that my experience is *personal;* not affected by other sources such as a previously viewed landscape from a painting, a photo, or whatever.

It is faint, but I feel a slight pulse of the adventuresome spirit of my great grandparents who ventured from England to homestead in Nebraska, or my other grandparents, Okies from Muskogee, who bootlegged whiskey and wore a belt of two six-shooters.

So, what happened to *my* ingrained genes of adventure and discovery? In the first twenty years of my life, I can identify two culprits: the one-eyed monster—the TV, and TV dinners; both ruled my senses. The next twenty years brought fast food, swimming pools, air conditioning, video games and computers. With all that in the main household, one can hardly remember that there's actually a *world* outside the safe, sophisticated alarm-systemed, perfectly-manicured-dandelion-free-automatic-sprinkler-system of a yard.

Life is a journey with lots of roads. If I continue to travel the same roads, I'll simply get to where I always got. But I'm in charge of the direction and quality of my journey. I can see the map more clearly now and today, at least, I feel presence and excitement. I'm in the driver's seat of my life, there is not another place I'd rather be.

I suck in some fresh sea air and then, with all the confidence of a florescent light just being turned on, I decide to share my feelings and mini-epiphany to my darling husband. He listens intently, trims the sail, checks the chart, looks through the binoculars, leans his back against the coaming surrounding the cockpit. He settles his bare feet on the cockpit cushion, then wiggles his toes.

"Well!" I say.

"Well, what?" The Captain inquires.

I point my eyes to the beautiful skies, as though I'm trying to commune with powers higher than myself. "Well, what do you think of the new *me*? Here, you thought I was beyond redemption!"

There is a long pause.

He sighs, "It's tough to make predictions, but I think we should both just enjoy every moment of this "so-called" epiphany while it lasts. Because I'll bet my last beer that when we start to swerve, careen, tilt and heel over with a wind against tide while we're going by someplace like Black Rock and/or it gets really cold, then you'll

be down below, scribbling in your journal—writing so fast and furious, the fumes from your ink pen will make you light-headed. You'll
be thrown from side to side while whining to me that PJ O'Rourke
is right, *'There is no such thing as inner peace—just nervousness or
death!'*

"Then, when whatever euphoriant you slipped into your tea
this morning has completely worn off, you'll look at your spiritual
road map and decide that maybe there is no promised land while
sailing with me. You'll embed deep ink slashes in your journal,
scratching out *Sailing the Big Flush* and renaming it *Sailing With An
Asshole, Asshole, Asshole!*"

Ahem …

Shadowing Parrsboro, we anchor outside and I notice clouds
that look just like ric-rac. This reminds me of the apron I made in
8th grade home economics class. Doug's last beer wasn't threatened
and our sail was preciously beautiful, two events for which we are
both thankful. The skirts of the sun's robe trails over the basin while
we study our records we've kept of our comings and goings—which
means the tides comings and goings. We put our heads together to
decide when, on the coming tide, we should have enough depth to
tuck ourselves into our cozy spot in the marshes.

A childhood memory of my Great Aunt Florence's music box
playing "Red Sails in the Sunset" chimes in my mind as the sun hits
the sea. The rim of the earth quickly envelopes the glowing ball. We
are a couple of little jiggley jugs, hanging on for dear life, being
thrashed around with the current. In wonderment, I watch the sky
change before me. Almost immediately the temperature drops and I
have to grab a jacket and pull it close around me. The last orange
streak of sunset fades into the indigo night; I contemplate how little
I've always known of the sun. It looks soft and fluffy way up there.
Most of my life I've thought of it as a ball of fire, but fire is the rapid
acquisition of oxygen and there is very little oxygen on the sun (so the
experts tell me, haven't been there lately). They say the energy source
of our sun is the nuclear fusion of hydrogen into helium deep within
its core. I tip my hat to its grandeur and the miracle of it all.

The twilight outlines the birds performing their swerves and
dips. For a few moments I take deep breaths. Awareness of my faith

Sailing into Parrsboro
Shadowing Parrsboro, we anchor outside ... Doug's last beer was not
threatened, and our sail was preciously beautiful, two events which we are
both thankful. The skirts of the sun's robe trail over the basin ...

in the invisible force returns; the force that is always at work and keeps my life flowing. I think that all this flushing of the Fundy, the sunsets, the migrating birds and the winds blowing, will (hopefully) always be here.

It's the storms and the clouds that come and go.

Day 19

Tuesday, September 18, 2001

The bananas and bagels in my skillet are almost perfectly cooked. I am singing my own rendition of "The Birdies Know that the best time to sing is in the mornin'." I turn my fat face to the sky and my lousy voice up higheeee ...

"Eileen, can you coil the anchor rope?"

I stop mid "higheee" and "umph!" I offer an exasperated sigh to the crystal blue sky; I march into the galley, turn off my skillet, place the lid atop my herbal tea and flop onto the V-Berth to do my job. Why is it, one may ask, my husband has chosen this moment of our existence to clean all the anchor line? Timing!

The river mud, on the outgoing tide, has left a rather impressive amount of goo coating our rope and chain. There is just enough water left to relieve ourselves of this gunk before we—as you who have *closely* followed my recorded minutes of the days of our lives here in the Minas Basin will recall—coil the rope back into the fore peak and all that mud comes *inside*, dangerously close to our bed.

I am now fortified with my 409 bottle. My goal is to try and clean the more cleanable parts of our floating palace while Doug mows the lawn. *Just kidding,* I like to check occasionally, to see if you are paying attention. Doug is actually performing surgery on an item some sailors deem as essential for traveling after dark— running lights.

There was merely a toenail clipping of a moon last night. We sat in darkness for a long while, letting our eyes adjust to the moon and the stars before we pulled anchor and started to motor toward the entrance of the Farrells River.

Running lights are most helpful in permitting other boats to see you; they're not usually necessary for lighting a path. So, the fact that somewhere during our journey we'd lost them, didn't seem important last night. We were slowly making our way, happy-happy to have been here before, when we noticed a car, silhouetted on the high abandoned dock, and figured it for a late night star gazer; our eyes focused on the job at hand.

The mystery person in the car suddenly flicked the headlights on bright, spotlighting us as though we were the stars of some surprise show. Then the car started and slowly changed locations, evidently trying to be helpful by shining the car lights at the poor, lonely, slightly daft sailors, sneaking into Parrsboro without any running lights. Again and again the car, hell bent on saving our lives, bewildered and blinded us with its headlights so that we couldn't see jack squat.

We were not entirely surprised that our friend Brian was calling from ashore before we could get the anchor lowered. Excitedly he waved his arms. In one hand he waved a flashlight which was possibly meant to help us, but actually acted as a strobe light over the marsh.

An onslaught of questions spewed from him. "How was our trip? What happened to your running lights? Isn't the Shubenacadie beautiful?"

He wanted answers, in detail, but was simply unable to stop before he thought of new and more exciting questions.

The Captain finally took charge by bellowing out over the water, "We'll tell you all about it tomorrow! We plan on staying over a day or so."

Brian quickly responded, "How about dinner? Ruth and I work tomorrow ... Ruth has a meeting at ... "

So at this point, I interrupted. We already felt that we'd partaken plenty of their generous hospitality. So, in the spirit of conviviality, I suggested, "How about if I make dinner for you guys at your house? Would that be okay?"

Later, I asked my husband as we prepared for nitey nite. "Does that man *ever* sleep? And how on *earth* did he know we'd be pulling in at midnight?"

We both shrug our shoulders in the, *we haven't the faintest idea* gesture.

"Just another one of the many mysteries of the Minas Basin I suppose," the last words from the Captain's mouth before sleep.

Cleaning completed (being domestically-minded is now only a smeared plexiglass memory of my past), I settle confidently into my seat of honor on the cockpit cushion, just as a hen would onto her nest. With pen and pad in hand, I sit firmly upright, feet together, as I flip through the note pad pages, the kind that's 4"x 8" with the spiral on the top.

Woe to anyone who comes close to this pad. It contains all that I hold dear in my life right now—my lists! We have several lists: groceries; bakery; drug store; post office; other on-shore needs (which include firewood, fuel and water); fix-it jobs on board (like the running lights); fix-it jobs for next spring; supplies for next year's cruise; and ideas for next year's cruise.

There's a list for things to do and buy for the Eastport house (this is a very long list), plans for the winter in Pennsylvania, etc. For a "listy" person, like me, it is a joyful moment. I smile brightly as I study the list of priorities for today. I moan with pleasure. The Captain rolls his eyes and shakes his head. He must be a bit too busy with his project; he seems underwhelmed by my list-making capabilities.

Buoyed with my happy moments of pen and pad in-hand caused me, the one normally so "in control" of my emotions, to make a grievous error. Confidentially, just between the reader, my journal, and me, I do have one itsy bitsy, irritating habit (oddly, I can only think of *one* at the moment). This habit tends to try the patience of

my husband when he's involved in a repair job that isn't going particularly well. It is likely his knowledge of my true origins which
makes him question this little quirk of in my vernacular.

To the casual acquaintance, when I say I'm from California,
they picture anything from San Francisco, Hollywood and Sea World,
to beaches with dental floss bikinis. My husband, however, calls a spade
a spade. He knows me for what I was BD (before Doug), pre-coun-
try club, pre-tennis clubs, pre-jewels and world travel. I was a hick
from the east side of Bakersfield. Even more staggering, I was born
in the housing projects of Wainwright Drive in Oildale. We moved
up, when we (which at that point, *we* were a household of four girls
and a mom and dad) moved to east Bakersfield and into our own
home. Of course my dear father had to work three jobs to pay for
our domicile of two bedrooms and one bath. Yes, I confess, I have
on more than one occasion, held my hand high and proclaimed
that this one bathroom to be the tiniest full bath, I have ever in my
entire life seen. That was BD-BG (Before Doug-Before *Guillemot*).

With the music scene in Bakersfield my husband considers it a
privilege to know someone who's taken Buck Owens' children to
Sunday School in his Cousin Herb days and to have known Dwight
Yocum in the early years. My final claim to fame is that my niece
married the dude who grew up in Merle Haggard's house on the
Kern River—the one with the train that ran through the entire house.
In his eyes, these facts are just my real roots.

He's not being mean. Doug and some of his music friends are of
the select few to whom I've actually spoken the words "Hee Haw!"
I can count on one hand those who've been impressed that I was
from Bakersfield.

But, back to the point. When I offer phrases along the lines of,
"Deposit the refuge in the rubbish receptacle," it strikes him as un-
natural and he calls me on it. Today, foolishly and with total lack of
indiscretion, I made a pronouncement, stating, "We need to determine what food items we should purchase."

I know that look. It said, "*Who* do you think you *are?*"

With a rather sharpish tone, he informs me, "I don't *care* to
determine anything! No one I know *purchases food items!* They make
a grocery list and they buy food!"

"Weeeelllll!" I snickered, scooting back on the cockpit cushion closer to the engine. I needed to keep a respectful distance. I stared down at my lists. *Think pure thoughts, think pure thoughts.* I stood straight up to my full 5'2" height and did a sharp inhale and exhale. Then, with a tilt to my head and my chin held high (to emphasize my gentility after being treated so harshly) I slipped a little lead in my boxing gloves. I retaliated with a response that made clear my immaculate breeding—I gave him a nasty blow of … silence!

Down below, I slammed my precious pad shut! That didn't quite do it, so I threw it in the air. Am I righteous or what? How did I ever end up being as good natured as I am? I sat a while, like *The Thinker*—fist clinched, palm under my chin, elbow on my knee.

Suddenly my eyes lit on something that brightened my mood— my shower-bag. This bag is from a full set of Tumi luggage, engraved with my initials, that I use to cart around. I now wonder just why I had my initials engraved? So I wouldn't forget my name? Actually, I'm much more likely to forget my name *now* than in those days—the days prior to sailing off into the wild blue yonder. The days when I wondered where and what is a yonder. The days when I had friends, family and business associates who regarded even my slightest utterances as pearls of wisdom.

With righteous indignation I grabbed my bag. *Humph,* I muttered, *they aren't even the correct initials now.*

Mentally, I check my list of what I need for my slop to town. I spend several minutes rummaging around like an agitated mouse in her hiddy hole. I find my mirror. "Mirror, mirror, in my hand, I don't want to hear a word out of you!"

Ouch! This hurts! My brain screamed. I look like a long-faced battleaxe—at least as much as one can look like a long-faced battleaxe in 4-and-a-half inches of reflection. I've just confirmed a long-standing theory—you have to be young and pretty to scowl and sulk. Positively, the more wrinkles I have, the more I have to smile! There is no getting around it!

Zipped up and ready to go, I allow myself a guilty smirk. I remember a time when my engraved luggage came in handy. I had checked out of my highfalutin' hotel in Athens and they held my luggage for me. Now, I'm not ashamed, of *why* I forgot a suitcase. I can now admit, freely to the world, that I had way, way, too much wine in the Plaka District.

Still momentarily savoring my old world, I forgot I was giving my husband the silent treatment. I placed my arms and chin on the pop top, thought about my wrinkles and smiled. Not very warmly, mind you, but I *smiled.*

I called to the forward deck, "We need to establish what time we should leave to go ashore." He did another eye roll and responded, "In my lifetime, I've never had to *establish* a damn thing. Today you're the determinator. You decide!"

I calmly counted to ten. I silently called him a weasel, then decided he was a worm. No—I struggled to find another noun starting with the letter 'w' when I was rudely interrupted by voices coming from behind me. Hand over my eyes, I squinted to see who could be calling from ashore, from a direction where we are not usually called to from ashore—the Geological Museum.

There they are, a group of ten or more, standing behind the museum, facing the river. I assume this location would be called a viewing area, because there seemed to be a lot of people doing a lot of viewing in our direction. A gentleman speaking to the group, assuming the role of professor, was pointing proudly in our direction. I can make out words, here and there, from his gripping elocution: sailboat … 100 years (how does he know?)… tides … never before … historical … blah, blah, blah!

There are two telescopes. They have people hunkered behind them. Both are pointed at us.

Butt on the quarter birth, head in my arms, nose a half-inch from our little table, I snivel. I can tolerate many things.

1. My beloved, to whom I have pledged my allegiance, has finally flipped his burger over the way I talk. He must be sick of me. (Why shouldn't he be? I'm sick of me!) But I have to face it, my husband is certifiable. Maybe a marriage counselor would say I drove him there, but he's still positively one signature shy of certifiable. (A marriage

counselor my ass! What experience could such a person possibly have in regards to a couple trying to have a relationship in a closet?).

2. I have committed myself to cooking dinner in someone's camp kitchen for which I'll have to pack like an expedition to Malaysia. I must lug all my food and equipment through acres of ooze and mire, which hurts my knee to even think of it ...

And now, I'm ... sniffle, sniffle ... I can't take this! Now! Of all the injustice ...

3. They're watching me through a telescope! I feel like some old fossil ... I'm on the Geological Museum tour!

So I shuffle over to the V-berth. I love having my bed so close by in my hour of need. I put my head on my pillow and curl my little pink toes up.

I'll be all right, I tell myself.

I reconsider.

I may *never* be all right.

Maybe I'll just shoot for *better.*

* * *

According to the laws of probability (I muse), the chances are increasing that, while wading through the muck from point A to point B, I'll fall flat on my face.

When I finally managed to get myself and my gear (enough to cover all possible needs and eventualities involving dinner and my bath) through the goo and up the embankment, it was with an uplifted heart (well, maybe a heart lifted about halfway) that I dragged it all into Brian and Ruth's kitchen.

The Captain shows up a couple of hours later, all smiles and kissy-huggy. He even offers to go to the market for any missing supplies. It's amazing what repaired running lights and the prospect of a good dinner will do for a man. Why, it's right up there with, with ... well you *know* ... or, maybe you don't know. I'm a little shy to have to spell it out for you but—just to keep the record straight— it's right up there with—*beer and boats.*

Contrary to a possible notion on the part of my readers, just because a house has electricity *and* running water, it is not always *easy* for me to cook in someone else's kitchen. I don't necessarily enjoy cooking *all* the time and *every* day. It's just that cooking is my little bit of talent in this spin around the world. Cooking makes me feel *purposeful*.

Purposeful is like a magic ingredient. Purposeful receives high honors in my book.

Although I felt as though I was trudging through insurmountable obstacles when I began considering our meal this morning, it turns out that I *was* able to prepare a decent meal. I have it labeled in my journal as *The Ritual of The Meal,* I served:

1) Bean/barley vegetable soup I already had in my pressure cooker (pressure cookers are big and bulky, but have tight lids).

2) A sun-dried tomato torte made from layers of cream cheese, pesto and diced, marinated sun-dried tomatoes. (I was lucky to have had jars on board) This is chilled in a mold and then inverted onto a plate and spread on toasted baguettes.

3) A colorful vegetable dish of glazed carrots and parsnips, cooked in apple juice, butter, honey, fresh lemon juice, fresh mint, fresh grated nutmeg and fresh grated black pepper.

4) A salad of mixed greens tossed with a marinated shallot vinaigrette and topped with warm goat cheese (the last I had on board) and thyme croutons.

As lovely as Ruth and Brian's house is, even they recognize the inadequacies of their camp kitchen. My brain almost short-circuited when I found *no* cutting board. (Happy me, though, to have brought my smallest one from the boat!) There was a microwave that barely heated, the smallest toaster oven ever sold (no oven) and a two-burner electric unit of which one burner refused to cooperate.

I thanked the Mighty Glooscap that the bakery had a few chocolate macaroon cookies left for our dessert.

When we finished our meal, I even resisted the urge to yell, "Stop that!" When Brian jumped up from the table and began to *stack* the dishes. This is something you *never* do on a boat—stack dishes, that is, when you clear the table. If you stack the dishes then the *bottoms,* as well as the tops, must be washed.

I mentally zipped my lips and gazed thankfully at the sink with its abundant hot running water. Ruth had to run off to her meeting, but not without thanking me profusely. Then she solicited Brian's help in the clean-up. I packed my two large boat bags with the pressure cooker, my knives, my cutting board, my lemon zester, my olive oil, my large sauce pan, miscellaneous jars of this and that, the extra vegetables, pepper grinder, salt grinder, nutmeg and grater, soup ladle, etc., etc.

My two knights in shining armor took on the arduous task of transporting it all (along with the other supplies we had purchased today) back to the boat. I opened the front door for them and they staggered through, arms full, shoulders rounded from the weight.

I merely shrugged and looked repentant. Frazzled and with my knee now swelled to unprecedented size, I limped over to the kitchen sink full of dishes.

Day 20

Wednesday, September 19, 2001

Doug pops open the front hatch above our heads, raises himself halfway out of our bed (men can do these things without being arrested) and proclaims to the world, "Just another beautiful day in paradise!"

I'm sure I agreed, but the sun was so bright and my eyes weren't yet open. Nevertheless, lying still, I felt the paradise—clean fresh air, nice breeze and the peace.

We have a strong NW wind blowing today, but we've chosen to ignore this. We're not at all ready to head out on our merry way. The winds here, at this time of year at least, have proved to be mainly westerly, which is not conducive to sailing out of the Minas Basin. Again, life decides for you; just as it was when we sailed the Shube. It appears to be easier to get in than to get out.

I have the water boiling for our morning tea and the pressure cooker is right alongside, with water heating. I search and find my nice, clean, freshly-washed and dried stretch jeans as I think through the plans for our lunch—chick peas from the pressure cooker with roasted red peppers, two cloves of garlic and jalapenos. Later, when they are really soft, I'll whip them into a hummus with a little tahini paste, fresh lemon juice, olive oil, ground black pepper and paprika. I'll toast some pita triangles with olive oil in my skillet and top them with a light coating of ground sea salt.

Meanwhile, I struggle into my jeans. I can't get them buttoned. Seems that I'm a few peas short of a casserole to be thinking of lunch when I don't fit into my jeans!

My husband walks through the companionway door just as my jeans have stretched enough to fasten. Only when I'm in one of those rare moods of insecurity would I ever consult him on such matters.

"Do you think my thighs are swelling?"

He stood there weighing his options.

Reluctantly, I press on, "Now that I'm going through 'the change,' even if I cut back 100%, I would still take in 50% more calories than I need!" Without taking a breath I went on, "It's good I don't wear white pants (they would be dirty in three minutes anyway) ... all our new friends would be afraid I'd bend over and show slides of our trip!"

I know I'm dating myself. No one shows *slides* anymore. But it's one of Erma Bombeck's jokes that I always related to. "I seem to have a lot of fat that doesn't fit anymore ..."

He stops me, lifts me and my tight stretch jeans off the V-berth, pulls me over by the galley (where we can both stand up straight) and hugs me tight. I bury my nose in his clean, crisp denim shirt and sniff.

"You're the shit Eileen! You're *perfect*—just the way you are. You're my little sweetie!"

Life itself suddenly seems entirely worth living. I've known my husband to possess several lovable qualities. If I were to make a list (and I probably will someday), I think his hugs would be number one. We were in hormone heaven. He was whispering something about doing the humpty in the V-berth, when, suddenly, we heard voices coming from the direction of the museum. A man's loud voice was pointing out to anyone who might listening ...

We took our tea out to the forward deck and decided to ignore the museum tour and lounge in the sun. Stretched out, hand in hand, we sipped our tea. I slid my hat down over my eyes and focused on my inward journey.

These slight twinges and fleeting moments of peace help sustain the thought that I may *not* be just a meaningless fragment in an infinite universe—briefly suspended between birth and death—allowed a few short-lived pleasures followed by pain and ultimate annihilation.

My husband points overhead. Looking squint-eyed into the bright sun, on center stage is a longed-winged fish hawk hovering over a section of the river where there is still water. His sharp spiny projections on his talons are bent, ready to get a firm grip on its slippery prey. Doug went for the binoculars. The blue sky still frames the osprey's performance.

I think about our society and how we are not always so far from nature. I've noticed that some ospreys do not seem to be bothered by traffic and urban sprawl. The male selects a nesting site, just as he would in the wild. Then the search commences with an aerial display for the ladies, a slow sexy undulating flight, high in the sky. Once an understanding is struck between a male osprey of good property and his discriminating partner, nest building begins.

The air is refreshingly cool and crisp and the sky a pure blue. This day has all the earmarks of an alluringly perfect 20th day of September. Just over the embankment, beyond the apartments, I can just glimpse the edges of our friends' home. It frames the open door surrounding Ruth's garden, now going to seed.

This is when it hits me—like a religious conviction! How much better off I'd be if I had pooped at 5 a.m.! At 5 a.m. I was trying not to trip over my flat feet while putting the legs on the boat. It was dark and calm; we had water. However, it didn't happen.

It is now 10 a.m. The tourists at the Geological Museum may have me under observation with their telescopes.

I give a couple of meaningful groans as I grab the poop bucket. I either have to put the canvas curtain up around the pop top, or go through the lowering the pop top and put up the canvas door or go back by the V–Berth and shut the curtain. Urgency is now curtailing my options. My calculations tell me that there's no time for the first two options. This is not my idea of toilet utopia. The impediment involved in this procedure almost keeps one from doing his or her business.

Between our gear, the wall of the V-berth, and the woodstove, it's hard to get your butt and feet in proper alignment. And today I also have the joy of a stiff knee. I have to elevate and twist it to one side. It is moments like these that transform my leg from an asset to an encumbrance. I stifle a laugh and a cry—I normally try to suppress actual screams. What would my public think, hearing screams come from behind a closed curtain?

I have tried, most of my life, to behave the way my mother taught me. Still, I'm fogged to remember what a proper lady does with her poop bucket when the tide is out and the boat is on the Geological Museum's tour. I stop for a moment, as I exit my tiny area, and begin to analyze the situation. Is *analyzing* what I really want to do? Standing with a poop bucket in my hand? One must have stronger arms than I to safely hold one's poop bucket at arm's distance.

I read once, in some spiritual healing book, that if you complain, it's because you want someone to feel responsible and do something about your situation.

Well, duh! Of *course* I do!

I let out a slightly complaining grunt and whine. My husband says, "Poor Fluffy!" (Fluffy was an old, pampered, bitchy, house cat he had when he was a kid on the Bedminster farm, in Bucks County, PA).

Mentally, I went for his throat. Then my mind yelled *AIYEEAAH!* and I gave him a karate chop.

The literal execution of either of these notions, however, was moot because: 1) I had a poop bucket in my hand; and 2) A local in an unfortunate hat was now waving to me from ashore.

With my *free* arm, I waved a cheery *heelloooo*. He waved another cheery wave.

I wondered if he was some newspaper reporter seeking a human interest photo for a Halifax tabloid, if there was such a thing. I smiled a cold smile that said butter positively wouldn't melt in my mouth.

With complete steadiness of movement and Budda-like composure, I handed my bucket out to the cockpit. I had numerous thoughts running through my head—and in all of them revenge figured largely. Suddenly I had this perverse impulse to ... my husband gave me that "Bond-style" lift to the eyebrow. Manfully, he assured me, "One drop on me and you're in the mud!"

Suddenly, I was Mt. Vesuvius and about to erupt.

I eyed the bucket with a look akin to the same nervous discomfort that one would eye a ticking bomb.

There was silence.

Our eyes locked for an icy five-second stare. I wanted to squirm but I stood perfectly motionless; only my mouth kept opening and closing like a goldfish. My left hand sought my throat in flustered affirmation.

He smiled. Then his smile deserted his lips and crept upward, locking itself to a set of raised eyebrows. He cocked his head and I did the same, tilting mine to match. For a brief moment my world tottered; then reason gripped me.

I'm such a *Nim Cum Poop*. I cannot possibly give in to temper and impulse.

I just cannot get in a poop fight with my mate, a man I've sworn to love and cherish, while I'm on the Museum Tour! The ice in my heart melted in puddles around my feet. A glint of triumph filled the Captain's laughing eyes.

He took the bucket, handling as if it contained radioactive material.

I turned quickly, before he could see the guilty smile on my lips.

* * *

You practically have to be a master jigsaw puzzler to fit everything you need on a boat, especially one this size. I eyed the provisions we so heartily acquired yesterday and decided I'd better knuckle down and get to work. My project for this morning is to clean out the refrigerator, so to speak.

Underneath the cockpit sole is a storage area which holds a variety of lesser-seen items. Two of these are large Rubbermaid containers with lids that fit nicely.

Most of you out there in the normal world do not contend with sawdust when fridge duty calls. Here, aboard ship, we fight a constant battle against mildew. So, while these containers do keep the moisture *out,* they also keep it *in.* Sawdust absorbs the moisture and does a great job of keeping our vegetables, particularly root veggies, dry and free of mildew.

In these bins I can store about 10 lbs. of potatoes, 5 lbs. of onions, 5 lbs. of carrots, 3 lbs. of parsnips, garlic, ginger, red and green cabbage for about a month. I went on to organize all our other "food items." I managed to finish this task but, when completed, you might say I lacked sparkle.

The Captain was busy with his never-ending list of "fix-it" tasks. Just what these are, exactly, I can't really say. My mind tends to wander when he discusses fixing centerboards, toe rails, scuppers, grommets, stove pipes and things like bilge pumps.

When I finished, I sat down to enjoy a moment of solitude, under the big wide sky, and write in my journal. No one seems to be telescoping or lecturing at the moment. I love my journal. It helps me savor the passing parade. I think everyone should keep a journal while traveling. A journal permits you to preserve more than just a flirty recall of what on earth you did with the last 24 hours that was graciously bestowed upon you by the powers of the Universe.

I heard a loud ringing *Kee-a-ree Kee-a-ree* (middle note lower) of a loon before he dove for his lunch. Their out-of-balanced bodies on land are good for a laugh. Their feet are strategically placed back on their bodies, which makes them awkward on land, but they work well for them in the water. They can propel as deep as 200 feet below the surface to fetch shellfish when they want a new entree to supplement their regular menu of aquatic insects.

Brian gives the international "Hooty Hoot" call from the banks of the marshes. We both wave and try to respond, but he immediately launches into his dialogue, telling us precisely what time it is and that we must not be morning people because he came by earlier and we weren't around.

I don't claim to understand why anyone cares what we're doing and when we do it. We don't even try to relay, by yelling to Brian ashore, that the Captain was up half the night tending the boat.

The anchor wasn't cooperating in finding just the right place to lay its little head. Doug changed the location three times, much as you would pamper a child with colic.

Then, at 5 a.m., we did the leg drill and they (they, the legs, that is) were, if I may use the hackneyed expression, one big pain in the ass. It seems that they couldn't find a comfortable position either.

With all this going on, I might be lying down, but anyone can tell by looking at me that I didn't get my prescribed amount of beauty sleep.

My husband seems very anxious to get to shore and talk to our visitor. And who can blame him? That's what I say. I'm stuck here with the poop bucket.

I watch the two of them. Brian switching his weight from one foot to the other, swaying forward, then backward. There's a whole bunch of tongue waggin' going on there, a scene full of animation to be sure. But the real show is in the marshes and the banks around them. Large seed pods of lupine and dense, three-inch clusters of the pleasantly aromatic yarrow, are bending in the breeze. The salt marsh cord grass, often called eelgrass, makes a verdant show with its four-foot long, limp, tape-like leaves. It's one of the very few flowering plants adapted to ocean water.

I've searched all the marshes on our journeys and nearly always find the northern pitcher plant, my very favorite. It has a beautiful long stock with a purplish-red, umbrella-shaped nodding bloom at the top, which collects water. Insects are lured by the leaf color and then become trapped inside by hairs. They eventually drown and the plant absorbs the nutrients as the insects decompose.

We had just devoured our long-awaited lunch, when we heard Brian's voice from ashore, "I have your wood ready!"

It seems that, when the two men were ashore earlier today, they were not just conversing cosily or engaging in worthless but animated conversation. Doug had made a date to meet Brian, for tea and scones, (*no, no ... not really just one of my funny little jokes*).

They were actually plotting my heating source for the remainder of the trip. They made arrangements to provide firewood the exact size and amount for our tiny stove.

This man is no slacker! I've had employees that I paid a lot of money, who proved to be less diligent and efficient than this fellow. Our friend and benefactor checked the supply of firewood at his family's cabin and found many small pieces he could easily cut. His act of kindness saved us hours of searching and cutting to replenish our wood supply.

On board, you might think about splitting some kindling to start a fire, but you really want to avoid the commotion of cutting wood in our ... our ... how should I describe our living quarters? Crowded? Jam-packed? Crammed? No, I want a smoother word, one that sounds positive, without sharp edges. Wait, I think I have it ... compact! Our rather compact quarters.

My heart skipped with excitement. "We'll be with you in four ticks of the dollar store clock!" I called to Brian. Truly thankful, now, that he takes a strong interest in our everyday activities, I grab my dream-come-true-Baffins (and my bath bag ... just in case ... you never know, the stars may be in alignment) and climb down the stern to cross the sticky muckhole to shore.

I made it again! I feel like raising my hands and running a victory lap.

Smiling from dimple to dimple, Doug and I peer down into our box of wood. "What a bonanza!" The Captain yelps. We transfer our loot to our canvas boat bag and stash it in some bushes until the tide comes in. At which time, our little ferry boat can float it back over to the *Guillemot*.

Mr. Fix-it slops back aboard through the mud and goo. The Captain plans on entertaining himself with the centerboard. This is a handy little pivoting board that can be lowered and used like a keel to keep our little boat from slipping to leeward. At the moment, the centerboard is stuck in an upright position, diagnosed with a bad case of constipation from Shube mud, rendering it useless.

I have other plans, though what they are at the moment, I haven't decided. They definitely include an afternoon ashore. I have no intention of going back until my gondolier rows me back, singing romantic songs in the moonlight.

"Toodleoo!" I called to my husband and I'm off in a flash in Brian's little buzz of a car.

My spirits were shaken, momentarily, by a small pang of guilt when I remembered the poop bucket still sitting in the cockpit. However, when I turned back, I saw that the river was beginning to flood. Relief and joy reset my mood. *Ahh, 'parting is such sweet sorrow.'*

I pulled my mirror out of the back pack to check what condition my condition was in, I was not sure where I was going, but I might come face-to-face with one of my fans. I managed a four-and-a-half-inch smile.

* * *

Brian Wheaton's wild hair is blowing about in the wind and his eyes are bright with affection as he takes me back 50 years to the time when his family owned and operated the Ottawa House. You may (or may not) recall that this house was originally the site of a trading post. Later it was used as a summer home by the illustrious former Prime Minister of Canada, Sir Charles Tupper (and no, to the best of my knowledge, he had nothing to do with Tupperware). Sir Charles was later known as the father of the Canadian Confederation in the late 18th century. The house now stands as a government-owned museum, honoring early shipbuilding and lumbering. My special deluxe tour isn't about Prime Ministers and shipbuilding, however. Brian paints a picture of a bustling guesthouse.

The Ottawa Guesthouse was usually filled with vacationers who rented rooms by the week, the month and sometimes the entire summer. Brian shares a vision of screened-in porches with Chesterfield sofas, lively conversations, socializing, food, card and board games. Room by room he describes the decor and the style of clothing popular at the time.

When we step outside, Brian sniffs the air as though he can still smell the grilled food coming from individual barbeques on each upper deck. I look up to see most of the decks still in place, overlooking the beaches and Partridge Island. Walking beside the storyteller, I can feel the cool breezes, hear the laughter, and smell the cigars. I feel very much a part of this bygone era and its graceful old world elegance.

I could have gone on, enjoying the memories, but my host suddenly jumped in his car. There followed the erupting roar of a small engine and I took this to be my cue that the tour continued.

We joggle along, hitting an occasional rut or two. The gravel road out of the Ottawa House is certainly not up to U.S. standards for tourist attractions. Oddly I rather like it. The drive is certainly more authentic than the current all-inclusive resort getaways. I hardly notice the jolt which turns us right onto yet another gravel/dirt driveway. There before us is a rustic log cabin. It has a loving, yet carefree appearance. To the right is a cliff with a footpath leading down to the beach. Peering down I can see that, at this point in the flooding tide, that the beach wraps around to join the Ottawa House and Partridge Island. Whoo! The views here are even more gorgeous than the Ottawa House because of the elevation and angle.

I am momentarily wonderstruck.

Then it dawns on me that this must be his family's cabin where our bounty of wood was procured from its neatly stacked woodpile. Brian's father, Donald Edward Wheaton (now deceased only three weeks), and his mother, Grace, purchased this property in a year unknown exactly, for $125. Some 22 years ago, the family started building the log cabin as a summer home for his parents. Brian described his Father's maneuvers in getting the logs in place. Using techniques he learned during his stevedore days down at the dock, he used a block and tackle, hung over the large tree which stands behind us. My guide proudly points to the logs, which are thick at one end and smaller at the other, noting how they fit together perfectly.

It is a sweet modest cabin, but chock full of signs of many family gatherings. I took interest in a framed picture on a shelf. Looking closely, I couldn't tell if was is a black and white photo with color highlights or a painting.

"Yepp," Brian said, using the standard Mariner term, "that's the Newville Lodge at Newville Lake. It's just outside town." He disappeared inside himself for a moment; then his eyes danced as he repeated, "Yepp." Spoken in a near whisper and on an intake of breath. "Yepp, we lived there for many years. I can take you out and show you. The lodge is gone but it's a real pretty drive!"

It took a fair amount of persuasion, but I managed an immediate, "Hey, I'm game!"

This day whispered of promise. I'm not walking long distances, carrying large, heavy loads while clambering over rocks and mucking through mud. Momentarily, I recall Brian's preoccupation with his pastime sport. Would there be a risk of hurtling to my death? *No, of course not! Silly me!*

Here is a rare opportunity to spend time with a man who grew up here. He left but repeatedly returns to love and live in the home of his youth.

Outside we paused, facing the water, the beaches and the Minas Basin. Together we paid our respects to the passing of a generation of Wheatons. It was a sad time for Brian and I was aware of the profound change this will make in his family life. I gave reverence to the miraculous redesign caused by the powerful flush of the tides below. I nodded my head in acknowledgment of the fact that change is eternal, perpetual, immortal.

He spoke, his voice deep, but soft as warm flannel, "This property will always be in the family."

What a comforting statement. It takes tons of work, time and real devotion to a place to call it home. Tears flood my eyes. If I were to indulge in some heavy-duty wish fulfillment, it would be that, especially at my age, I could say the same.

We moved on and, in short order, found ourselves at the Parrsboro Rock and Mineral Shop and Museum, home of the world's smallest dinosaur footprint! They aren't just whistling Dixie, either. That dinosaur footprint is tiny! It looks just like a sandpiper stepped in some mud. The museum houses fossilized trees, ferns, stems, shells and other prehistoric footprints of amphibians, dinosaurs and reptiles.

My own personal "wow" moment was over a large amethyst geode which must have been a leftover from the Mighty Glooscap period.

Behaving like an inquisitive reporter, I quizzed my guide to learn more of his family and their way of life here. Brian, as you know, is the loquacious type, so it wasn't hard to drag it out of him. I listened intently to the history of Donald Wheaton and family. His father joined the St. John Fusiliers in 1939 and went on to be part of the Normandy Beach invasion. Sometime during the war he met his sweetheart, Grace. She was from England but he convinced her to marry him and make her home here, in Parsboro, after the war.

Donald wore many hats in order to earn enough money to provide for his growing family. Being a honest, hardworking stevedore and a grower and picker of blueberries were important jobs for his income. His real love, however, was being outdoors, hunting and fishing, card playing and dancing. All these led to the family business at Newville Lodge.

Donald and his sons built little cabins, close to the lake, which were rented to hunters and vacationing families. He and the boys also served as fishing guides and hunting scouts for their tenants. The lodge provided a hearty breakfast each morning and served as a general social gathering place. There was a dance practically every weekend and his father even erected the first drive-in theater. Folks would come from all around for entertainment. I could almost hear the music coming from the trees. I tapped my foot as his father's face I'd seen in a photo danced in my mind.

Heading back toward town, Brian pointed to a hill where, high up, we saw the Smith family homestead. Brian spent many happy times with the family there. One night, he awoke to find that the main house had burned to the ground.

Driving slowly, he pointed down the hill where the Newville General Store once stood. His head bowed and then quickly popped back up in a large grin, "George the Indian, use ta entertain us kids with trick ice-skating on the small pond in the rear."

He pointed to the remains of the Halfway River School House. A young Brian gathered there, with 35-40 kids of every age, for his time with the books.

As you know by now, these things matter to me, so I calculated that Brian, who is 56, attended school there 45 years ago. I couldn't help comparing his childhood to that of my own in California. It was Brian's job to go in early in order to make the fire in the basement. He smiled and then laughed, when he remembered how he once got an axe stuck on his tongue after a dare from an older schoolmate.

For a long while we drove in silence, lost in our thoughts. Every now and again, I'd glance at his crazy hair and notice a far-off look on his contented face. He has the look of a man who's delved deeply into the past and remembers it fondly.

I was beguiled by the portrait he painted—one of a family and community to whom the land is more important than politics and economics. These are the people for whom the land is home.

* * *

The discovery that this is the only place on earth to find traces of animal life covering the late Triassic (230 MYA—that's *Million Years Ago*) and the early Jurassic periods (180 MYA), must not be very "recent" (meaning in the last twenty years) because I read about this in my old *Dreamers and Doers* guide. On his way to do other errands, Brian deposited me at the Fundy Geological Museum. I figured it was a window of opportunity to get a quick education on what they believe happened in this mysterious place.

Just how much can you learn about 470 million years in an hour? Listen up, 'cause I'm going to have to talk fasssst!

Well, you see, just over a billion years ago there was *Pangaea*, a time when all the continents were one solid landmass. Nova Scotia was a desert with valleys next to Africa ... or somewhere (I'm mentally challenged in this type of museum). I think the eastern seaboard, from New England to Canada (which would include Eastport) originated in Morocco. Then there was this mega big ocean, *Panthalassan,* surrounding it all. Get the picture?

Anyway, 300 MYA there were lots of dinosaurs of all sizes (obviously).

Now, if you don't mind, I'll skip 100 MYA to 200 MYA—otherwise this book will not be easy reading for the masses. So ... at this point in time, some government agency filed an official report finding, "Some *unexplained* turmoil within the earth's mantle ..." This "catastrophe" (although not for everyone as lots of new waterfront property was developed) resulted in the big dance of the land.

Some substantial cliffs of basalt and sandstone were exposed and the "unexplained turmoil" extinguished 43% of all land animals and much of the marine life. Now, we all know, by the time this book is published, all this info might be repudiated, but this is the scuttlebutt at the moment.

Supposedly this has happened more than once and may happen still again! Some scientists think Nova Scotia could be like a rucked carpet and become a new set of Appalachian Mountains. In our computer-oriented and don't-have-time-to-read-a-book generation, most people can't be bothered to worry about the power of the Bay of Fundy's changing and carving, or, for that matter, that India is plowing into Asia and pushing up the Himalayas by a millimeter or so, a year.

The weightiness of dinosaurs, 400-200 MYA, continents colliding/splitting and Nova Scotia heading to be a new set of mountains can have a chilling effect. Of course, so can watching the evening news.

My head does a little spin around as though it were caught in one of those back eddies caused by the dancing tides. I needed some fresh air.

So, with the greatest reluctance, I exited through the back door.

I found myself standing alongside several people already out in the viewing area.

I had to see what *I* could see, of what *they* could see, when I couldn't tell what they were seeing—if you get my drift.

And there she sat, in all her glory—the *Guillemot.* Doug is at the stern, gesticulating wildly, explaining some tidbit of our recent history to someone in a small skiff beside him. Well, this is innocent enough, I thought. Everyone seems to be talking about the sailboat, but none were gossiping about the toilet habits of its inhabitants.

I turned to go back inside, satisfied. My route was blocked, however, by a group on their way out. Their distinguished guide (or professor, or whatever he was), put his finger on his round chin and began with a molasses-paced speech. He moved into geology lingo—Paleozoic, Mesozoic, and Cenozoic (yawn, yawn). Then he dropped some bits about "BP" (whatever that meant) which he kept repeating. I listened for awhile but my eyes kept going to his nose. It was a trumpet of a nose. Men's noses become more important when they lose their hair.

Suddenly he covered his cavernous nostrils and, with great ceremony, sounded it into an immense handkerchief. When he came up for air he looked around, a bit puzzled, then cleared his throat and began the next sentence with "Eeh Hum."

I finally realized BP must mean 'Before The Present'—as in carbon dating—but that was about all I'd gotten out of this portly man so far. One lady, wearing something resembling neanderthal jewelry, kept staring skyward, perhaps offering a silent prayer for an end to this enlightenment.

I decided that my mad-cap geological adventure ride was nearing its end. Just as I was thinking, "Enough *therefores* and *whereas's* ..." the lofty speaker paused, abruptly, and gave a sweeping gesture—as if he were giving an Oscar-winning speech—and directed the groups' attention toward the sailboat in the river.

I went back inside. There was an area of the museum I had not yet toured; my eyeballs came to rest on a large white door. I entered and found myself inside an enormous, clean room. In a trance-like state, I was seated. My eyes followed the white tiles to the beautiful blue trim. Inside this room I had absolute solitude and privacy.

I found myself starting to dose off. I jerked the ole' onion and asked myself, aloud, "How long have I been here?" Then, in a mildly euphoric state, I answered, "It doesn't matter! No one knows I'm here. No one awaits me outside this *land of heart's desire!*"

I felt like a lawyer when I assured myself that it was, "my inalienable *right* to stay as long as I wished" and also to feel free to use "an ample supply of their paper!"

My head was still swaying slightly from the movement of the boat. I closed my eyes and flushed.

I primly adjusted my hat and sunglasses outside the double glass doors. Confident that my bean was crammed to the bursting point and I'd enjoyed the Geological Museum to its fullest extent, I was now ready for a limb-stretching walk.

I stop atop the bridge which leads to town, to view the water world in which I currently reside. It's still startling to see the scene change with each hour of the tide. My thoughts swerved back to the lavatory in the museum ... no, I don't mean *lavatory*. I mean *laboratory*. See where my mind is? Always in the toilet ...

The *laboratory* is a room where geologists work on a variety of discoveries from this area. You know—fossilized footprints and dinosaur bones and the like. Glass walls are provided where visitors can observe their work. Now, some might describe their activities as exciting as watching paint dry, but I found it intriguing. Now, staring down at the full-to-the brim river (previously full of mud) I suddenly have a strong premonition.

Follow me closely here ... millions of years from now, there will be a discovery that will bring real and would-be geologists out in droves. They will all hover around fossils left by my size-five Baffins. Using all their high-tech equipment, they'll discover that I was an ever-so-slightly overweight, 50-year-old, red-headed female in menopause, previously residing in California. I had born children, had my tonsils out when I was 14, and carried heavy loads with a bum knee. In scientific think tanks, they'll analyze the knowledge derived by studying the remains of our civilization. They will theorize, hypothesize, surmise and speculate.

But in the end, they'll still be scratching their heads, wondering ... as I am today ... what the hell was she doing there in all that mud?

There is a bench up ahead—a nice pleasant bench, no graffiti, no syringes. I stopped to rest the stiffening knee. Next to me is a huge rugosa rose bush, with its dark red autumn stems and bright red and orange rose hips. Sitting quietly, I savor the deeper melody of autumn. The sun glows stubbornly overhead. I close my eyes, floating along, resting on my oars.

Well, I'll be darned! My circuitous spiritual path has finally brought me several seconds of inner peace! Some swami-gushyi-gami would likely tell me, *Blessed are those who advance toward the spiritual path without the selfish motive of seeking inner peace, for they shall find it.*

Ha! I say. *Ha! Ha!* For some reason, I'm feeling a few drops of inner peace, even with my selfish, unblessed motives!

I was pulled from my silent revery by a passing cloud of *homo sapiens.* They walk right by me, unaware that they could confirm a sighting of a strange creature from mud-world. All are completely engrossed in the task of eating ice cream before the warm sun melts their scoops off the cones.

Suddenly, I'm really sick of health food.

I set my course. No need for a GPS, here. Years of evolutionised instincts directed me. I make a beeline to the ice cream stand. Wild with anticipation, I can only blush and stammer my order. I glance at my reflection in the glass between the signs of cone prices and topping flavors. What I see is this ... person ... I don't think I recognize her. She's an unfamiliar woman. I can't decide if she looks like an escaped lunatic or someone happily possessed. That woman disappears when the teenage girl opens the sliding glass window to hand me my cone.

There's a bench, not far away, where I sit down, comfortable in the certainty that I'll be able to give this treat my full attention. Uummm! I long to stop the clock and remain suspended in time with this fantastic taste in my mouth. My second is over quickly and I have to lick fast not to miss a drop. I give a sly shake to my head, thinking that there are certain activities about my day the Captain need not be told.

The ice cream will be my little secret or he'll know why I have thunder thighs like an old Buick. I certainly am not going to mention my little episode in the museum's large, clean, white room (or the *necessarium* as the Latins called it). He swears I have kidneys the size of lima beans. He's always having to wait while I use someone's WC. He tells me, "If I kept track of everything, like you do, I'd know just how many hours of my life I've wasted waiting outside some Ladies Room."

I saw my Gynecologist for a yearly checkup a few months back. The nurses gave a "bladder survey" to all patients past a certain age (I hate that!). If you had the correct medical insurance, they would supply the latest drug treatment. I could, in all honesty, answer *NO*, to all but one of the questions on the survey the title of which was, *Is An Overactive Bladder Part of Your Life?*

The exception was, *When you enter a restaurant or a public building, do your eyes divert to locate the nearest restroom?*

My husband must realize that the average person spends a total of about 3 years using the toilet. The average person visits the toilet 2, 500 times per year, which means about 6-8 times per day. It is a documented statistic that women take three times longer to use the toilet than men—and that's if there's no line.

This can mean, in my law of averages book, that the average woman spends nine years of her life using the toilet. Men should show a tiny bit of compassion for this weaker-bladder sex (a problem which is sometimes exacerbated following pregnancies).

Hrumpf!

After mentally detailing these facts, I shot a withering glance of indignation at the first man who walked by.

I wiped away a blot of drippies from my chin and then off my chest. I looked up to see a car, stopped on the road directly in front of me. It was Brian, who leaned over to roll down the passenger window. I expected him to yell out, "Hey! Hey! Hey! Fat Albert!" Instead, he sweetly inquired if I'd like a ride back to the boat. I declined and gave another lick to save a drop.

"No thanks. I'll walk back. I can use the exercise," I said and, with a faint nervous laugh, I added, "You rest, you rust. Move it or loose it!"

Nodding his head in an understanding manner, he drove away.

Issuing a big sigh, I say, to no one in particular, *I'm Busted!*

✳ ✳ ✳

The thought of Cow's big smile and hearty laugh warms the cockles of my heart (and those cockles are always in need of a little warming). However, I declined my husband's invitation to join him in a walk up to his house. Doug had heard that our friend Cow was down with a bad back. So, with optimism induced by a good dinner, he decided to pay a visit. He thought a few tunes and a beer might speed along Cow's rehabilitation.

I, however, felt no need of a long walk to Cow's. After enjoying the guilty pleasures at the ice cream shop, stiff knee or no stiff knee, I decided I needed more exercise than just pushing my luck, stretching the truth, jumping to conclusions and carrying a grudge. So I took a long walk, all over town and through the market one more time, back to Brian and Ruth's, and then back to the boat.

I can hardly believe it is barely 7 P.M. and I'm (I hesitate to say this very loud) *alone!* AAHH … I am ready for some alone time. It's like I'm being nourished without calories. I'll use these golden moments to celebrate the trees. I see many Northern Oak and Sugar Maples changing to their "fall o' the year" (as they say around here) autumn colors. I'd love to stay here long enough to see the Norway Maples turn, then dropping their leaves like musical notes. In

Eastport, we have two large maple trees. The Sugar Maple, closest
to the road, is always the first to turn bright autumn colors this time
each year. The Norway Maple barely turns and falls by the time we
leave for Pennsylvania around the end of October.

We leave, then, to be home for Doug's Nanny Winner's eve of
All Saints' Day birthday (she'll be 90 this year). She knows the magic
secret of these trees, the cliffs, and the marshes; they all grow old
gracefully.

Tonight, in this stillness, I tingle with the sensation of the marsh
grasses and the trees changing before my eyes—all a very fleeting
process. Tonight I float on their moments.

The clock had barely struck 5 P.M. when I started preparing
our farewell dinner at Brian and Ruth's. Brian won my heart, by
saying, "We can all go out for dinner, unless, of course, we want
something good to eat."

He exaggerates a bit, but it's hard for Doug and me to enjoy
food in a normal restaurant. It's either fried fish or too expensive.

I brought out all the leftovers from last night and, having an-
ticipated the possibility of one more meal with our friends, I had
asked the Captain to transport some hummus, pita chips and provisions for another salad from our boat fridge. Yesterday I found one
of my favorite cheeses at the market, Rosenborg Danish Blue Cheese.
Today, while on refrigerator cleaning duty, I found I needed to use
some red cabbage (not green, thank God) and a red onion. Then,
presto—visions of a special salad popped in my noggin. Shredded
red cabbage, slivers of red onion, raisins, apple, local cucumbers,
tomatoes, spinach and parsley topped with a blue cheese dressing of
olive oil, sour cream, red wine vinegar and fresh chives from Ruth's
garden. Add some salt and pepper and we'll enjoy the lovely chunks
of that dreamy cheese. Shockingly, I really wasn't very hungry. So,
playing the role of a martyr, I sacrificed most of my portions to
those who hadn't had a double decker a couple of hours earlier.

Ruth arrived just in time for dinner and then rushed off to a
hair appointment. Tomorrow she works, so tonight it was good-bye
again to my new friend. I now feel a warm connection to this little
village called Parrsboro. I've seen it through the eyes of a fifth generation Wheaton of Nova Scotia.

Almost asleep, I listen to paddles hitting the water. The ferry nears and the stillness of the night is broken. I hear the musical ding of the guitar being set down in the cockpit. My Captain comes through the companionway. I keep my eyes closed and listen. He shuffles around finding his toothbrush and tooth paste. My mind wonders to my journal. I've spent the last couple of hours reading over the events of the last three weeks, ending today, with the drama of the poop bucket.

My husband climbs in and snuggles close.

"Cow says to tell ya, 'You Rock. You're Brilliant!'" he says.

I giggle, "I'll rest better tonight knowing this."

Pause.

"Doug?"

"Yes ..."

"Will, we ..."

"Yes, Eileen?" he answers, with this *What now* tone to his voice.

"Well, I was just wondering ..."

"Wondering what, Eileen ..." patience in every syllable.

"We will get through our lives, won't we?"

Day 21

Thursday, September 20, 2001

I oozily ooze through the ooziest of the ooziness to make my last trek ashore through the Parsboro mud. The ebbing tide has left a line like a bathtub ring around the shore. Our friends are at their respective jobs, but gave their final welcome by leaving the door unlocked for tub and phone duties. After my last delightful dip, I take my last walk through Ruth's garden. I stop and sit, to bask in the sunshine and say my good byes to the pretty little world we've found here and its pleasant memories. Things and people enter your life and then they leave. Just as in nature, when one bud leaves another grows.

The couscous, onion, carrots and hot peppers I'm cooking give off aromas that make the Captain shake his head and smile wildly while rubbing his tummy to accompany his yumm, yumm, umm, yumm, yumm, song. It's good to see him move so quickly and happily, his old strength back after a great night's rest. He prepares for our departure with excited confidence. We now have running lights and a centerboard, if we happen to need them.

It is a lovely afternoon, replete with blue sky, beaming sun, buzzing insects and what not. An afternoon that seems to call one to be out in the open with God's air playing in one's face and something cool in a glass at one's side. I am dreaming of that special somethin' somethin' that I'd like to be drinking out of that glass.

Right in the middle of my day-dreaming, I spot a canoe moving smoothly in our direction.

He has that ageless fisherman look, healthy, buff and weathered. He drops his line to see if the striped bass have paid us a visit. The by-gone arose in my soul and the weight of centuries rested on my head. Why, he could be from hundreds of years ago when most early settlers could feel the oneness of the water and the sky and of all creations.

This relaxed outdoors man knows his painting and scrapping will be waiting for him. He is not haunted by the undone. He notices his dog is waiting ashore. He paddles back, but no-go, she won't get in. When he resumes his place along side the *Guillemot,* his old dog Biggs jumps in and swims to him. Despite her aching arthritis, she climbs in the canoe, not one to miss a *Bon Voyage* party.

We float, our company floats, and we all speak in soft reverent tones, suitable for the harmony of the moment. Our easy conversation uncorks a variety of subjects from fiddleheads and cattails, to marsh hawks, with long pauses of reflection in between.

"Yep!" with an intake of breath, he says, "cattails were one of the most important plants for North American Indians and sometimes colonists from Europe as well. You can eat almost all of it, You harvest the inner leaves in the spring—they call 'em Cossack asparagus. You can eat 'em raw or boil 'em—the flower spike tastes something like sweet corn. You can boil 'em, steam 'em, or fry 'em in butter. Could be one o' most popular of the wild foods. Then you got your root [rhizomes]. They're often ground as cattail flour but you can boil 'em, like a small potato."

"But." I ask, "doesn't that kill the plant? Then you have to re-plant your crop."

I've hardly ever grown a vegetable in my life, but we'd like to have more than just a herb garden someday. We've been reading up on sustainable agriculture, grown, of course, organically.

"Nah, it doesn't kill the plant," he assures us. "You collect the bulb that's connected to somethin' like a rope in the maze of plants. Yep, it's a real smorgasbord. You can even use the pollen! In pancakes and muffins, for instance, where you'd use 2 cups flour, you can use 1 cup pollen and 1 cup flour. In the old days, they dried the leaves for baskets and chair seats. An' all those white fluffy cattail seeds, the ones we've all seen, they use ta' stuff their pillows and mattresses with 'em. What makes 'em even better is that they'll grow in places and climates where most other foods won't grow—wet places, ditches, ponds and (he nods to the area around us) marshes."

He stops to consider all this, check his line, and give Biggs a comforting pat. "I've heard that it yields more flour per acre than wheat or oats."

We all agree that there's a way to feed the masses.

The dollar store clock and the change of the tide seem to be in synchronization. As it loudly ticked 2 P.M., the flow of things changed to give us our ride out of the Farrells River. Doug hoists the sails and I pull anchor, the umbilical cord that binds us to land. We have the top of the tide and we all know it waits for no man's conversation.

We drift away, pulled by a super-human force, along with the water which is being called back out to open sea. We ride along with at least 114 billion tons of sea water, thundering out of the Bay of Fundy. Talk about the ultimate power trip ...

Our friend paddles to keep up and then suddenly answers the question I asked fifteen minutes ago. "Yes," he says, "they do, indeed, see some marsh hawks hunting around here. They're sometimes called North American Harriers."

We barely have a breath of wind so we are suddenly caught in a back eddy. We all watch the swish of the water and bubbles. Then we wave and say our "so longs!" right when the wind catches our sails.

Out of the harbour and past the lighthouse, which stands guard for Parrsboro, we turn to starboard, toward Spencer's Island. Without the lighthouse as a focal point, you'd never know it to be the same scene. Two eagles sweep out from a group of trees and circle the lighthouse, then pass overhead. Fanning their ivory tails, they exchanging shrill peeps, odd sounds that contrast starkly with their size and powerfulness.

I tell myself, "Oh man!" I do a little jerky shiver almost every time I remember the "encounter," as I call it, I had several years back.

* * *

It happened in Eastport on an atypical day in May. The day was unusual for two reasons. It was dry and sunny *and* it was the day of my "encounter"—of the up-close and personal kind.

I was feeling a little peaked and out-of-sorts, so I left the boat yard and rode my bike home. I had been helping the Captain with the most unpleasant of jobs—sanding the bottom of the boat (no wonder I was out-of-sorts—this job was toxic enough to fumigate a cockroach).

When I arrived home, I left the front door open to allow the breeze to flow through the house. I was in dire need of fresh air after hosting all those boat particles up my nostrils. We don't have a screen door (screen doors are still on the long list for Eastport) but that was okay, because there aren't many bugs around. Besides, we find there's something fun and liberating about living in a town where it's safe enough to leave your doors wide open.

Upstairs, I scrubbed most of the blue-bottom paint off my face and hands before I flopped on the bed to rest. I was dreaming of a boat floating in the bay, all its paint and varnish shining and complete, when I was startled out of my nap.

I heard loud commotion downstairs. The racket sounded as though a drunken person had fallen through the front door and wasn't having much luck finding his balance (and knowing some of our friends, this was not entirely impossible).

I lay there and listened to more uproar but still no voices.

I reasoned to myself, *if this is a burglar, he's extremely clumsy.*

In any case, I decided that I was not one to take something like this lying down (*am I?*) I tiptoed to the bedroom door to listen. I tried to think logically—if this were someone I knew, then by now he would have shouted, "Anybody home?" Announcing his presence, even if he (or she) was in a drunken stupor.

I flinched again when there came ominous sounds of crashing, pounding and dishes breaking.

What could they be doing and why?

Did I want to alert whomever (or whatever) was down there that I was *alone* and vulnerable? Next came a heavy, powerful thud against what sounded like the large window in the living room. My heart jumped up to where my tonsils, had I still owned them, would have been.

This was followed by more tapping and rapping on what I guessed was still the front window. The only telephone was downstairs, so there was no 911 in my future.

Curiosity was now winning over my fearfulness. I crept over and grabbed my athletic shoes (I'd left my dirty work shoes at the front door). At this moment, I wished our old house didn't hold so much charm in the form of creaky, old floors.

I moved to the top of the stairs. Dead silence ensued, broken only by the squeaky, *crack-click-clack* of me trying craftily to sneak up on the "noise maker." In fact, the tomblike silence suddenly suggested a sickening notion that *they* were now listening for *me!*

The strategist in me devised a plan. If it attacked me, I'd throw my shoes and aim for the jugular (or something like that), then run back to the bedroom, put a chair against the door (no lock), and scream bloody murder out the window. Someone in this tiny town would recognize it as a plea for help (not wild sex) and rescue me.

Hey, I'm not quite the fool people take me for ...

So my wobbly legs took me, *creaking* and *clacking*, slowly down the stairs. Half-way down I leaned over for a peek into the room where the telephone and two hutches, which contain all my good crystal and china, reside. I braced for the worst.

Nothing. No one here and no sign of disturbance.

I held my breath and two more steps *(creak, clack)* brought the large window in the living room into view. Shocked, I saw ... *nothing. Nil. Nada, Zilch.*

I almost fell down the rest of the stairs in surprise and relief when ... from the back of the house and out of my view ... in flew this huge bird making a thunderous noise ... followed by a *Keeerbooom!* ... as he slammed into the window.

My jaw fell and I tried to scream but my tongue got tangled with my vocal cords.

The huge hawk perched on the 7-inch windowsill, a bit dazed. I wanted to run away, never to return. Let him have the house, the antique china, the inlaid armoire ...

He appeared to be still dazed so this appeared to be my chance to escape. But as I ventured a step forward he heard me ... he spread his wings and scratched the wood with his large talons. He turned his head slowly in my direction.

Oh m'God!

He was hissing, now, in alarmingly escalating tones while raising one foot and then the other, making sure I saw his razor sharp talons.

You've got to be friggin' kidding me.

I quivered like an aspen at his rebuking eye. He flapped his 47" wing span in the 70" opening of the window (I knew, I'd just made curtains). He lifted himself up again and pounded into the glass, becoming even more dazed ... and crazed.

I took another two steps ... the opening to the kitchen seemed very far away. He turned his large, sharp beak my direction and produced an even louder, more convincing, hissing scream.

If there hadn't been a banister to hold me up, I would have collapsed.

My unexpected guest was only two-and-half feet from the wide open front door, from whence he came. But, like most birds caught in a building, he couldn't get his bearings to locate the exit. He turned his large, disk-shaped head away from me for just a few seconds. This was my chance to run for it and your damn tootin' I did.

I flew down the last four steps, into the kitchen, and out the back door. Then, using all my quick intelligence and resources (and you know, by now, how limited that can be) I jumped on my bike and scrambled out of the yard. As I looked over my shoulder, I saw him at the window, looking like a jailer in his own prison.

It's strange what curious visions you'll retain later, in a panicked situation. I recall, vividly, that the sunlight was caught in the limbs of a large maple tree, causing a beautiful, dappled effect on our grass. This had a momentary calming effect.

I made it to the boat yard PDQ. When Doug saw me he stopped sanding the decks of the *Guillemot,* pulled down his mask, furrowed his brow and made an astute observation, "You look whiter than a fish belly. What's wrong?"

Elmer, our neighbor across the street who was home for lunch, had seen me run out of the house and race away on my bicycle. Then he heard unusual thudding and pounding coming from our neck of the woods on Stevens Avenue. When we returned to the scene he handed Doug a pair of welding gloves.

The Marsh Hawk was only half-conscious when he was removed from my living room to the front lawn. He couldn't fly, so there he lay on his back, wings extended and trance-like from his latest blow against the window. Doug gave him a few minutes to recover after which he picked him up and boosted him into the air. The hawk took a few slow, awkward dips and then, suddenly, he was airborne.

Just as he neared the tops of the telephone poles, three crows came out of nowhere and proceeded to run him out of town.

We all escaped unscathed except for a few precious, antique items. I bemoaned the tragic loss of almost all my mother's dishes. I'd proudly displayed them on the window sill, tucked behind the sofa, thinking how safe they would be. My husband gathered all the pieces to cheer me, hoping against hope that he might glue them back together.

A few days later, our friend, David Moses, a birch bark canoe builder from the Passamaquoddy Indian Reservation, came by for a visit; just to see what's what.

Doug was (unsuccessfully) trying to glue the plates back to-gether—a task rendered almost impossible as the remains were in about as many pieces as the 81 years they were old. David's eyes got bigger and bigger as we recounted the story. He nodded respectfully and shook his head at all the right moments.

"The elders of my tribe would consider this a mysterious sign, an *omen* of some sort," he said.

"Omens can be good or evil, can't they?" I asked, hopefully.

Actually, I wasn't feeling good about this pronouncement. Moses, had an expression on his face which could be mistaken for the pain from a toothache.

"Well ... yes," he said doubtfully, "but I can go ask my spiritual leaders in order to know for sure," he offered.

I told him not to bother. I don't ever want to know.

The *National Geographic Field Guide to the Birds of North America* tells me the following about my uninvited guest. He was an adult male, greyish above, and mostly white below with variable chestnut spotting. He had black wing tips and black tips on his secondaries. His general length was about 32" and spanned, wing tip to wing tip, about 48". Harriers perch low and fly close to the ground with wings upraised, as they search for birds, mice, frogs and other prey. They seldom soar high except during migration and in an exuberant, acrobatic courtship display. Adult males migrate later in fall and earlier in spring than females and immature birds.

* * *

The sailing is quiet and smooth. Half an hour after leaving the mouth of the river, we pass by the old Wheaton homestead. Up the beach the Ottawa House shines bright white, almost blinding in the sunlight. There sits Brian on a rock; no explanation for his presence is needed.

He picks up the conversation right where he last left off. "Yep, fiddleheads are a tasty treat."

Always the cook, I call out to him, "How do people in these parts prepare them?"

"Oh, well. Some saute, some like to put a little vinegar on them, some like a little butter on 'em. If you put butter on them they taste like butter, if you but them vinegar, they taste like vinegar!"

We round Partridge Island and as we sail on we can just see, in the distance, his wild hair and his elbows on his knees. He is a "swallow-life-in-big-thirsty-gulps" kind of person, but he savors every last drop. He's the picture of absolute contentment, sitting there on the beach. He recognizes the value of taking these few hours off work to canoe, fish, talk, sit on the beach and see his friends sail away.

I believe we tend not to regret what we *did* in life. Rather, we tend to regret what we *didn't* do.

We wave our last goodbyes and our stay in Parrsboro disappears along with the rocky beach.

The day is sailing magic. The air moves over us in warm, gentle breezes through beautiful stretches of sunshine. The strong tide gives us a cruising speed of seven knots with hardly a touch to the tiller. I can just sit here, close my eyes, and swear I'm in my pool in California, floating along on a raft with a Margarita in the drink holder. Speaking of which—no Margarita handy—but we do have some beer.

Positioned with my sunglasses, beer and paperback, I start to dose. I've found I've read the same paragraph nine times. After finishing *Poisonwood Bible* (which I enjoyed cover to cover) my new book is not worthy of my attention. I put it down a week ago and hadn't touched it since. Well, now I can say, I gave it one more try.

I throw it down for the last time … Shucks, now what do I have to read? Sip, sip. I think about this for a while. When I get up to search my side of the quarter berth shelf, I see a paper slip from my rejected novel. It's the scribbled note from Ruth she gave me ten days ago, when she feared she'd never me or this boat again. We were heading for the Shubenacadie River and she'd tucked this in my care package. It lists some names and addresses in case we had an emergency. I'd forgotten all about it but it's likely if I'd needed them, it would have buried along with everything else we owned in the Shooby Taylor mud.

Well, well, well, I sip my beer Sherlock Holmes style. I read the note one more time to myself.

I grin and give a satisfyingly cocky nod to my Captain. "Auh huh! Mystery solved! Now I know!" I picked up the list and waved it at my husband, giving it a few flips with my thumb and middle finger. "Check this out …" and I began to read:

Number 1. Ruth and Brian, phone number and address.
Number 2. Sandra Hendren, her phone number and her address in Turo.

and … full of self importance, I read on

Number 3. Richard Lewis, phone number and address in (I pause for emphasis) Five Islands! And, written next to his name (drumrolls here) "Old Salt."
I folded the note with a flourish.
"Now, that is cleared up!"

The Captain sighs and stands to adjust the sails. He has his shirt sleeves rolled up but you can still see the large, frayed hole near his elbow. Once he owns an article of clothing to his liking, he wears it until it is not even worth the rag box.

Doug gives me the long-suffering look, and remarks, "Yeah, clear as ditch water!"

I wag my head slowly and endeavor to explain to Mr. Thick Skull. "The *mystery* of how Brian knew we planned to arrive in Parrsboro at midnight!"

"OOHH!" Doug replied. "*That* mystery! He said a friend from the coast guard came by and told him."

"Yes. Rick, the fisherman who talked to us both times through Five Islands is the same guy from the note!" I continued, "Richard Lewis, aka 'Old Salt, ' is a volunteer coast guard and one and the same as Ruth's good friend! He drove over to Parrsboro to let them know we were on our way!"

I tucked the noted back into my book and slammed it shut, "Case solved Watson!" I am a master of deductive reasoning and I'm not going to let the Captain's eye rolls keep me from being impressed with myself!

We see houses perched atop high cliffs and rock faces where continents collided eons ago. Doug sings, "Baby, everything is allright, uptight, out-of-sight . . ." Then, suddenly he stops to tell me, "I love air. Suck it in. Exhale, I can't believe we are actually breathing!" He takes several big deep breaths. "I love life! Life only comes each day once a year."

Inspired by his respect for the miracle of life, I noted, "Did you know the average person breathes 28, 000 times a day, inhaling between three and five quarts of air with each breath?"

No, he didn't. But I'm momentarily given due respect for remembering something from one of my long lists of statistics that's actually worth knowing.

This is followed by a lot more singing, breathing and laughing. Generally speaking, we were loving our "day" away, while, overhead, little fluffy clouds passed serenely over the Poseidon blue sky.

I felt a little tingle of adrenaline in my veins, just as I did that first day, two weeks ago, when we entered the Minas Basin (deep base tones, here) as we pass Cape Blomidon and Cape Split. This time, however, we're hugging the immense sea cliffs. Blomidon Park, according to *Dreamers and Doers,* is supposed to have five miles of trails leading to a beautiful view of the Minas Basin.

I think about someone up there, right now, viewing the Minas Basin, while we are here, "in" the Minas Basin, just like specks of dust caught in the infinity of constant change, viewing the magnificence of the jagged, craggy cliffs that were formed 200 MYA when lava bubbled out of a rift in the earth.

The Captain suddenly becomes alert. He reacts like a calm, peaceful cat might upon hearing unusual sounds. He starts scanning the waters and now I hear it too. A noise, similar to a motor, is approaching us. We both do a 360-turn, looking all around, but there's nothing but the *Guillemot* as far as we can see.

This is a bit disconcerting. Where in heaven's name can it (the noise), be coming from? I clear my throat like I have a log stuck in my creek, and manage to say, "Wha ... what do you think it is?"

Perhaps I do have a tendency to be a bit melodramatic but now I think I can see the hairs on the back of my Captain's neck stand straight up.

This is not a good sign.

Watchful, his eyes keeping the waters around us under surveillance, the noise changed pitch—first to a roar, then to a *thundering* roar and finally to an even *louder* thundering roar.

I wanted to whimper. However, I'm a pretty keen observer. It strikes me that the Captain doesn't need Fluffy right at this moment.

What on earth is this uncertain energy force that seems to coming for us? I feel like I'm on the deck of the Enterprise—First Mate's log, Stardate 2001 ... *Heading towards us at warp-seven speed* ... is ... *what?* I don't think we're in range of any Klingon missiles.

As we approached Cape Split, the noise turned to a positively *deafening* roar. The Captain gave me a furtive look which, I freely admit, scared the bejeegers out of me. I gasped (not one of my more attractive expressions) and let out a screech (the Captain never screeches) that would have broken windows if ours weren't plexiglass.

This was followed by the gushiest relief I've felt in a long time (or at least a week). The rumbling was not an earthquake about to devour us and our boat, dragging us to the center of the earth

It was merely the result of the rush of about a billion gallons of water through the rocks of the split.

Get it? Cape Split?

We rounded the split towards Scott's Bay and I yelled "Yee Haw!" The Captain looked at me in disbelief.

"Ah heck," I said sheepishly, "It's just the Bakersfield coming out in me."

A long crescent beach comes into view, the promontory that is part of the phenomena which causes the world famous tides in the Minas Basin. Now we need ear plugs. The sound has become *fortissimo!* There, before us, is a rip about a mile long. All around us are terrific up swells—a gigantic version of Reversing Falls in Cobscook Bay.

I'm not milking the scene to say we passed all this in one piece by the skin of our teeth ... I was quaking in my mud boots.

We swished and swirled past the ominous sights and the split faded into the face. The setting sun illuminated the ledge while cathedral-like shafts of dusty light wafted down.

We sail some distance without finding it necessary to speak. The swift rushing current is giving that live, persistent call to the listener. The patterns in the water are like tartans of the Scot's.

We were living the time on a different level than usual, where *thoughts* serve best because they were thoughts we had in common. Silently, we veered toward Greyville for our last night in the Minas Basin.

This evening, when the sun sank, it was as though it were drawing a brush across the sea's surface, streaking and blurring it to ultramarine violet smudged with an ember glow of raw sienna, cadmium orange, then chianti! Now, the constellations are flung, glittering from horizon to horizon. We may be seeing the full 6, 000 stars supposedly visible to the naked eye.

With the new moon we have "higher" high and "lower" low tides. Slowly, this strange world of living on liquid, has become familiar to me and often, now, this familiarity has become precious.

It makes me rethink life and value what remains of it. Yesterday, at the pharmacy newsstand, I stood for a long while reading some of the headlines and magazine articles. Misty-eyed, I came face to face with the people involved in the world situation on September 11th. Is it a coincidence it was 9/11—as in 911?

What will become of all this hatred? Is the Taliban really responsible for all this? Who is responsible for the Taliban? Why did the US government train, feed and pay all the salaries of the Taliban until 1997? How will our leaders and country respond to this tragedy? Another war? Nothing will ever change (for the better) through aggression—the root cause of famine, starvation and cruelty. I think the way to stop war is to stop hating the enemy.

If we do go into these countries, which happen to have a lot of fossil fuels, what are our true intentions? Greed? Revenge? Helping the innocent victims and their families? Control? Helping the suppressed? Does it help the suppressed, to bomb what little they have left? Is it a conflict over religion? Will our young people be used as cannon fodder again? What will history say is the root cause of all this? There have been wars fought over, salt, gold and nutmeg!

Is the only reason history has to repeat itself is that no one learned or heard it the first time? Historians say you can do anything you want to those who don't know their history. How many people will be killed or mutilated before we call it over? Is it ever over? How about if we merely think of the economics of it? Who will pay for it? Perhaps what the world needs is an agreement not to have any more wars until the old ones are paid for?

But who am I? What do I know? The more I learn in life, the more I realize how little I know. The only thing I seem to know for sure is what you all know by now, from reading this book, I'm just a 50-year-old, shallow-thinking, pampered, menopausal woman from California who is trying desperately (perhaps a hopeless challenge) to get her butt firmly centered, as to not slip off her spiritual pedestal.

All these questions, with few answers, keep running through my mind. I am trying to sort out my feelings and the reasons why I need to try to talk to the world instead of running from it. Tonight seems pivotal—a time to go back to the headlines of terrorism and

six lanes of traffic and concrete dividers. I search my brain, and all
journals and books I have with me, for something ... some form of
consolation. Answers? Peace? Insight?

I find three quotes—three of many that I've written in my journal—to which I refer, now, from time to time. Tonight, during my
questioning, these three hit me right in my emotional gut.

> *The people of one nation must consider the people of other
> nations to be like brothers and sisters who deserve progress for
> their homelands... but more dangerous than guns and bombs are
> hatred, lack of compassion and lack of respect for the rights of
> others. As long as hatred dwells in the human mind real peace is
> impossible*
> *—The Dalai Lama*

> *Why, of course people don't want war. Why should some poor slob
> on a farm want to risk his life in a war when the best he can get
> out of it is to come back to his farm in one piece? Naturally the
> common people don't want war: neither in Russia, nor in En-
> gland, nor for that matter in Germany. That is understood. But
> after all, it is the leaders of a country who determine the policy,
> and it is always a simple matter to drag the people along, whether
> it is a democracy, or a fascist dictatorship, or a parliament, or a
> communist dictatorship. Voice or no voice, the people can always
> be brought to the bidding of the leaders. That is easy. All you have
> to do is tell them they are being attacked, and denounce the
> pacifists for lack of patriotism and exposing the country to danger.
> It works the same in any country.*
> *—Herman Goering, At the Nuremburg Trials*

> *I am convinced that nothing will happen to me, for I know the
> greatness of the task for which providence has chosen me*
> *—Adolf Hitler, 1932*

We quietly rock at anchor outside Port Greyville. I read that
there is an "Age of Sail Heritage Center" and a cairn at the waterfront commemorating the famous mystery ship, *The Mary Celeste.*

All this does not entice a row-in, tonight or in the morning. We want, for a brief while, to stay on our floating "island"—to see the sky without the distraction of any city lights.

The waves are licking the boat. A breeze blows against our canvas door as I burrow down into my sleeping bag like a caterpillar in a cocoon. The darkness of the new moon tonight brought my thoughts to an enchanted faraway land—The world of Borrowed Black—he borrowed the moon in a Labrador Fantasy written by Ellen Bryan Obed— and he wouldn't give it back ...

> *One night Borrowed Black went out with his sack to borrow the*
> *moon . . .*
> *the moon broke into pieces–a billion and four*
> *So he buried them deep off the Labrador*
> *Borrowed Black greedily grinned with pleasure for he had just*
> *Borrowed a magnificent treasure . . .*

Day 22

Friday, September 21, 2001

The sun was just above the sea and struck straight into the scratched window of the V-berth. I only allow myself one itsy bitsy moan as I turn over and lift my head. I see my husband standing with his hands folded over his belly, staring down at the espresso pot, upper lip folded over the top. It is his early-morning-before-you've-had-coffee-stare. Before I knew him better, I would have said it was the-early morning-before-you've-had-coffee-*blank*-stare. Now I know different.

My husband's thoughts, while staring at the espresso pot could be headed in all sorts directions—sending creative feelers to a new song, an old song, or how to fix or build something. His thoughts could also just be willing the coffee to hurry, because he has to be close at hand when the pot starts to hiss and the water whooshes its pressurized way up to the top half of the pot.

Today, I realize he's standing so close because he's afraid that the unstable boat will knock his little pot off of its little metal toothpick. The burner is way too big for the little espresso pot, so a large metal toothpick (Its original use? I have no idea.) is needed to balance the tiny pot. It emits a series of loud gurgles and then is ready! I get a whiff of the aroma and, for me, this is better than a cup of coffee.

There is a strange phenomenon about the wind which, unless you're a sailor, you might not know. The wind usually changes when the tide changes. Last night the wind whipped up—a stiff "sing in the shrouds," gusty fall wind. We had only Spencer's Island and Little Cove to protect us. We were not tucked up in some marshes or tied to a dock.

In order to describe what it did to us, I'll give you a little science experiment. Place a light-weight toy boat in a bathtub full of water, anchored to a string and a rock. Put your portable fan on high, blowing straight at the boat, and then stir the tub water with the handle of your back scrubber—get it goin' good. You get the picture?

Now multiply this activity by a likely frenzy factor that the anchor could, with all this action, slip at any moment. That's what *went on with us,* all last night.

Maybe the weather came because it is the autumnal equinox—was that last night? In any case, whenever this occurs, the sun crosses the equator and this event usually brings the first freeze of the season to uplands Maine. Also, cool air over the continent meets the warmer air from the gulf stream, which often brings the season's first nor'easter. *Whatever* happened, it was not one of those safe and sound nights which, for me, is not completely unusual. Thank goodness (whoever goodness is) that most of my life I've felt safe (but seldom have I been thought of as sound). I must say, I probably rested a hell of a lot more than Doug. I have a strong, capable husband there, next to me. But in conditions like last night, the Captain never really relaxes—that could mean mistakes.

So why is it that he looks so much more refreshed than I do? I scan my mental catalogue of reasons. He's younger? Darker complexion? What a nuisance my complexion is. I'm confident that real Amazon/adventure-type women have darker complexions. My magnolia white skin has turned to dry, chafed, and potentially cancer-ridden skin. It is really not fair that the freckles of my youth have been replaced by wrinkles. Is it because I'm going through the curse and he's not? Suddenly, I feel the need of HRT. Why did I foolishly tell my doctor, no hormone replacement treatment for me? Conclusive studies show any change in personality involves bio-chemical changes in the brain. With all that tossing and pitching, to and fro business, I feel like I've had a slight disarrangement of my brain. I cannot say this may be totally bad—it was probably needed, but this disarrangement has me stuck in the basement level of my mood elevator.

Forcing myself to keep the upper lip as stiff as possible, I joined the festivities of setting sail. I was barely hanging on, physically and mentally. I didn't care to document what we ate—what time it was—which direction the wind blew—or, the direction in which we were sailing.

"Who let grumpy out to play?" he asked, and the Captain was right. I wasn't doing anything to help his mood and lack of sleep.

I hear a whisper inside berating me, but I gave in anyway, on the grounds of psychological comfort. "I'm going down below and do what I do in moments of being tired, emotional, and confused (we shake our heads in unison and I finish my sentence in harmony with my husband) ... put my keester back in bed."

An hour recharge-nap helped to calm the kicking, crying baby in me, changing my dark thoughts into a sunnier mood—it was the little emotional recharge I needed for risk-taking. I step out into the cockpit just in time to see the last of Cape Split in the morning light. It is still a beautiful, ominous sight. Although I see it differently now, I have to admire the Minas Basin for what it has taught even someone like me in 16 short (or long, depending on which one) days. Knowledge does help erase fear.

I turn to see Cape Chignecto, West Advocate Bay, and Cape D'or (Golden Cape) disappear in the distance. The Captain heads out along the Fundy coast towards Digby. Coming out of the Basin, the current changes to only about three to four knots. Ahh, lucky me—I recline in a happy daze and look toward the coast of New Brunswick across the bay. There seems to be no limit to my vision.

I peruse the charts. Noon just slid upon us and I wonder about tonight's destination. Halls Harbour? Harbourville, maybe? I look down the coast. Margaretsville? It's a hard call. A safe, quiet harbour is top on my list—out of the thrust and throws of this crazy bay.

Speaking of lists, I do happen to have another list brewing in the worry-pot of my head—a tired state produces a worried mind. My husband just told me, "Quit worrying, sweetie, you're always worrying."

Yeah, I finally have that one thing down pat. Negativity seems high on my psychic pollutant list today, so I indulged myself.

1. Crucial, as usual, is our timing—it isn't like we're just trying to avoid rush hour traffic or waiting for three o'clock check-in. We have to have enough water to get our floating abode into the harbour.

2. The tide is completely out now (bad), but coming back in (good), but against us (bad).

3. We do have some fair winds now (good), but that can change any second, especially with the change of the tide (bad).

4. The wind is always fickle (bad).

5. We rely on the inherent power of the wind to propel us toward our goal (good/bad).

6. We don't know when any of these harbours will have enough water (bad).

7. This cruising guide is dated 1994. Out here, open to the Fundy, any storm could change any of the harbours—so we don't know which are safe and which aren't (bad).

8. I look at the chart and just say, *It's a crap shoot!* (bad). I've never been any good at craps.

All things considered, I felt I was half-way maintaining.

Confound the man. He looks at me as though he's checking the pressure valve on a cooker—steam seems to be leaking out of my ears.

I smile and act as cool as an oyster on a half shell. Then I pick up my trusty *Dreamers and Doers.*

Whenever, wherever, if ever, we find a place to lay our little heads quietly, it will be in the area that the book calls the "Evangeline

Trail." I find a column soliciting our membership in *The Order of the Good Time.* The tension is cut and we both laugh heartily over the name. The history of the order goes something like this.

* * *

The four "big guys" who laid the foundations of Canada were Monts, Poutrincourt, Lescarbot and, of course, the explorer and historian Samuel de Champlain. All were in Port Royal, Nova Scotia on November 14, 1606. The story goes that they were slightly depressed (good gads, what's up with that?)—they were only facing their third harsh winter in their new world of unpredictable natives, harsh weather, scurvy and boredom!

De Champlain, "Mr. Good-time" himself, took positive action. Each day a different member of the group (about fifteen at the time) was appointed Grand Master. He wore this fancy gold collar with a bunch of gold medallions encircling the neck (a drawing is shown). A very large, colorful medal on a chain is showcased here and we both agree that, for a group living in the boondocks, their taste ran on the ostentatious side.

The major responsibility of the Grand Master was to create a menu with such delectables as moose meat, beaver tail, fresh salmon, roasted caribou or breast of goose and, I assume, cattails. They didn't have a golf course or a football field, so preparing the meal became a competitive contest with each doing his utmost to surpass the efforts of his predecessor.

The first party or, as they called it, "meeting" (tax deductible that way) commenced. Poutrincourt in all his glory, offered a toast. "We meet tonight to witness an event that will, I pray, go ringing down the years–as marking the sure founding of a league–which under God and France shall ever serve–as a beacon to our goal. Let each one vow that he will strive to play a worthy part."

* * *

Today, (I guess you can, today—at least 20 years ago, when this was printed, you could) ladies and gentlemen, you can stand where they once stood and receive a personalized certificate to adorn your office or home (or boat). You don't get to eat or get drunk, but you can get your membership if you commit to pledge honor to:

1. Have a good time
2. Visit Nova Scotia for at least three days
3. Remember Nova Scotia pleasantly
4. Speak kindly
5. Promise to come back again soon!

"I can just see you as a Hostess Extraordinare with a big gold necklace and brightly colored medallions as you cook aboard in your hooded sweatshirt!" said the Captain.

I nodded in agreement, "It's just the accent my wardrobe needs."

Hold on to your hat! The wind just whipped us around and then settled back down like a sleeping baby—the kind of wind that lets out a big "Waa Waa" and then quickly goes back to sleep. It seems we're doomed to have one of those days. To make matters worse, we just flew past Hall's Harbour! The old guide book threw out a few choice words like picturesque, favorite for bird watchers, an open air restaurant, colorful!

"That was my pick for the night!" I pointed, sounding like a pitiful little child.

With the voice of a patient school teacher, the Captain explains, "We need to get as far as possible while the weather and the wind hold. We've had good luck so far, but we're heading toward the end of September. The weather can turn and make it really hard to get home."

I know, I know. It's just that this wind keeps stopping and going, like a car racing from one light to the next. Then it suddenly slams on the brakes and everything slides forward—wham. My nerves are on the edge and they need to be talked down before I teeter over.

We have a long lull in the wind (good), but this gets us nowhere (bad), then we actually start losing ground. The current takes control (bad), we try to start the motor but, after enough tries to warrant a trip to the chiropractor, it's a no-go (bad). Suddenly the wind gusts through a valley and about knocks us into next week (good/bad).

I try humming and cleaning—my own personal methods for warding off crying. I envision Harbourville. I check the time—would we have enough water to get in? The guidebook calls it delightful—restaurants and a gift shop! Not that I would patronize any of these, but the thought of them comforts me.

I wave, as we sail by. Now, that's pushin' it!

I made encouraging sounds, shaking my clinched jaws, and mumbling, "The Captain knows best. The Captain knows best."

Blessed is a wife who knows her own limits. I leaned into the quarter-berth and reached half-heartedly for a beer.

He flinched as though I'd struck him. I'm too exhausted to think that his little jokes—which insinuates that *all* beer, is *his* beer—are the least bit humorous. I feel like I've been quite the trooper today. I don't even look to see what, if anything, is in Margaretsville.

I just ask the energy of the universe to get us there and to have enough water and daylight to get in. I imagine anchoring outside, in the waves of the Fundy, waiting for the right tide (bad) and then pulling anchor and trying to get settled into a strange harbour at night (bad). What if there isn't room in the harbour or dock (bad).

I know I have shown the ability to turn simple things into deep tragedies and large melodramas but, for the record, just as I'm being tossed around like dice hanging from the rear view mirror of a car with no shocks, while racing over potholes, what happens? Again, I have to pay the debt we women are doomed to pay for eternity … all added penance for the original sin of taking one of Adam's ribs. After only one beer, I have to pump my bilge.

Edging my way back to get my necessary supplies, while holding onto objects like an alpine rock climber, I fell back on the edge of the table, which delivered an excruciating and forceful kick to the right side of my hip. With a measure of class, I kick the table (back) with great vigor. Then, to add to the intolerable burdens of pain and full bladder, I cannot find the precious little adapter for my "Lady John." Through all the jerking and tossing of the tumultuous day, it had pitched about and was finally found lodged in a crevice where the Captain, who is picky about stowing everything properly, would consider inappropriate.

By the time I'd performed all the necessary maneuvers for this project, I was about to throw a hissy fit—I'd had it, up to the gills. My face displayed a carefully-engineered resentful scowl as I enacted an elaborate display of dumping my container overboard.

Sour-tempered, I then begin sharing the tale of woe concerning my peeing expedition.

"Really?" said the Captain, with interest.

I delivered a blow-by-blow, detail-by-detail account of my horrendous experience while he listened with appropriate pity and concern, making sympathetic, "Tsk, Tsk!" sounds. At the conclusion, he paused to consider my misery while, at the same time, trying to keep control of the boat thrashing around. Then he offered his condolences.

"I would like to take this opportunity to apologize for your life. Want some money? Here, let me give you some money!" he said, reaching into his pocket and pulling out a crinkled dollar bill.

At that moment, this little sardonic show was an unfortunate interruption to my peace of mind. He'd touched some exposed nerves—I was trying to buy some *sympathy* but it appeared that no one was selling any.

"Damn it!" I began ... *No*, I thought, *"Damn it" just didn't go far enough.*

"I'm tell'n you," I said ...

"Of course you're tell'n me!" the Captain snapped.

Now I was really infuriated.

"I'm sick and tired of being sick and tired!" I said. "I've had twenty-two days of peeing in this weird-looking red beer mug, Captain *Momus* (the Greek God of mockery and faultfinding) ... I've tolerated all your jokes about peeing over board ... it's so *simple* for *you* ... you just whip it out and smile ...and in your old sailor whiskey voice you say, *'I just need to dreen the ole' pickle, gawfaw, ha ha.'*"

I continued in this vein, bitterly resentful while ranting and raving, cooly certain that I was enumerating all the marks of his low moral character. I stood and tried the "arms akimbo" position which almost sent me flying, head-long, into the pop top, but failed to halt my passionate flow of words.

"And the absolute *worst* is the other charming little saying you use while you're peeing overboard which wasn't even funny 100 years ago when some ole' codger thought of it. '*Awh, ooh, that water is cold! And deep too!*'"

I was ready, now, to battle like a tigress. "I've had it!" I shouted, my arms held high to emphasis my words—then quickly dropped back down in order to keep from falling overboard.

"I want a *normal* life!" I moaned and, with a measure of class, I pounded my fists theatrically on the cockpit cushion. "I want to be a normal tourist who wears a sweatshirt that reads, *I'd rather be at the dock with a drink on the rocks, than in the drink on a boat that rocks.*"

The Captain's smile fades and, eyebrows raised, he says, "I'm gonna miss you Eileen."

I continue...unfazed. Now, even to myself, I sound like a hellfire preacher,

"I want a bed, sheets, a toilet, vanity, porcelain tea cups, watercress sandwiches—without the crust—a hot shower with fluffy towels ..."

He holds his hand up, as conductor would to stop his orchestra.

But I want to go *on* ... I had more ... but ... through divine intervention, I actually halt. I feel like a tuba player with my cheeks puffed full of air.

My husband shakes his head at me, his eyes questioning ... *Out of what blue did you launch this list?* He then calmly remarks, "Twenty-two days? What would your friend, Fay, say to twenty-two days?"

Ouch! Stunned, I feel my mouth open feebly and my vocal cords twitching. I managed to say, "Well ... she ... I don't ... she didn't ..." But, the words die away on my lips. I just glare at him with eyes like a rabbit hypnotized by headlights. There was a seismic shift of power. There have been hundreds of times on this trip when I jumped for joy that the ole' cap-i-tan, God love 'em, was right. This, however, was not one of them.

Fay Angus is my good friend in California. She has written several books, has made a career of motivational speaking, and is respected by one and all. This stemmed from her experiences of being a British subject living in Shanghai during WWII. As a teenager,

she and her mother were thrown into a Japanese internment camp
where they remained for some two-and-a-half years. She tells of
being given a cup of water a day for drinking and cleansing. Nutri-
tional needs were met by the maggots in their soup. Most of us have
read enough books and seen plenty of movies to understand the
deprivation, loss, and humilities suffered during those years.

I climb down off my soap box. I sulk around for a bit. I feel as if
I should be made to stand in the corner. Fortunately, for me and my
marriage, those moments of going berserk (and not ever wanting to
see my husband in this world or the next) are short-lived. Those
thoughts which warn me that (whatever signs we were born under)
our birth dates must be wrong for each other are, thankfully, tran-
sient.

I guess he has me straightened out on this one. I mumble a bit
more about his irritating tendency to be correct. I must have patience! This is not a trait that comes to me easily—but as I look into
those glassy, green-brown speckled eyes, made watery by the wind,
it's worth learning patience.

* * *

A family—which had come together from as far away as
Toronto—and our perfect spot for the night just happens to be
waiting for us at the Margaretsville dock when we pull in (see—all
that worrying for nothing). The family energetically tells us of all
the scenic spots they've found for their family group photo—the
lighthouse up the trail, the dock, the cliffs—but they all agree that
their favorite is the little fish shack. They direct our attention up the
hill.

Doug and I both crack a laugh—it's a funny one all right. I
guess you might call it an old "sea shanty." It was pieced together
from driftwood off the beach and bits and pieces from a lot of leftover building projects—cedar shingles, mismatched windows and
benches, all weathered and worn full of charm. The only thing missing is the old man from the sea standing next to the large sturgeon
drying outside one of the doors.

The smells of dry Nova Scotia ground, curling its toes greets us,
as we set off for a long walk. We figure we have a good hour-and-a-
half of daylight left and we're anxious to take advantage of it in this

postage-stamp-size of a town. The sun sets and the wildflowers, along the roads, breathe a sigh of relief from the warm sun. The thermic breezes and the smell of rain make it feel very tropical. The streets are empty, the architecture is reminiscent of Chula Vista, California, in the 1950's and 60's. Margaretsville is a harmonious little community and it's nice to see that developments, with gates and rock pillars embedded with brass name plates, haven't taken over.

It all has the appearance of a coastal town put to bed for the winter. I feel almost charitable in my opinion that it is a sweet little village. The only commerce I see is a closed-for-the-season ice cream stand. I predict it will be a glorious, pleasant, uneventful evening, with a great night's rest while tied to the town dock. The only movement seems to be the cars of the reunion family making a their quick exit. We head back down toward the *Guillemot* by way of the little lighthouse trail and laugh loudly as we quicken our steps down the steep hill to the dock. We wave our hands in a delightful, carefree manner while singing "Shimmy, Shimmy, Coco Puffs."

Suddenly Doug, who's ahead of me, stops, giving me the halt sign. He points and asks, "What's this? Life forms at the fish shack!"

A fellow with a sunburned face, an engaging smile, and a shock of white hair, turns around to greet us. Beside him, intent upon eating their fish supper, are two seagulls and a cat. The benefactor of the birds and cat wore an expression of contentment—the whiling-away-at-the-town-dock-with-his-fishing-gear, old-man-of-the-sea geezer look.

Doug pipes in with a question which brings joy to the eyes of most anyone hanging around a dock with fishing gear. "Been catch'n any 'round here?"

The old-man-of-the-sea's smile is wide and warm. Something in his movements makes me curious. I wonder if this white-haired man lives here, in this little shack? Nice location, but shabby place to live—poor old man must freeze in the winter. My eyes suddenly flood with tears of compassion for this lonely guy. He's probably overjoyed to have someone to talk to, he's so animated talking to Doug about his mackerel catch.

We'd have to be really hungry to eat nothing but mackerel—not the first of our chosen delicacies from the sea.

So, we make acquaintance with John Fox, whose eyes glowed with devotion as he introduced Ruckus, the town cat and Pete and Repeat, the seagulls.

With our names come our whereabouts and origins—mysterious creatures from the Bay of Fundy who are currently attached to the sailboat. He examines us with deep suspicion and his cheeks go pallid. We try to look as though we pass all the criteria for normalcy.

Under what circumstances does one care what a deprived, derelict-looking, local guy thinks? Well, this appeared to be one of them—perhaps because he was now studying us with a look that might be reflecting pity.

I smile a smile which I hoped would convey the notion, to the puzzled man, that my life really was almost all right. His pallid cheeks flushed again."How about coming in for a beer?" he asked, motioning to the door of the shack.

Doug whispered quietly in my ear, as we headed for the door, "Here we go again …"

Ruckus led the way past the sturgeon, as though he owned the place, through the door of the shanty. I glanced around at all the memorabilia scattered over the wooden walls. In a corner sat a very old phonograph surrounded by a large collection of vinyl. Ruckus settled in for some major paw cleaning and a post-dinner nap.

"Nice digs!" I comment, truthfully. John Fox gave a quick, appraising look around and his chest swelled visibly. Nodding his head several times, he smiled a closed-mouth smile with his bottom lip sticking out. Then he bent over to reach into the ice-chest-with-no-ice.

"Yep, I get a big kick out of this old fishing shack," He said and pulled out two beers and popped the tops. I felt a sudden burst of happiness and hope. We took the beers like they were keys to the kingdom. The White Fox (as I now call him) tops off his styrofoam cup with some Crown Royal and we lift our beers for a ceremonial toast to the moment. I eye the Crown Royal bottle, thankful he didn't offer it up instead of the beers. We hate the stuff but, I think to myself, that's a pricey bottle for a forlorn ole' codger.

The White Fox chose a LP from his large collection and started the turntable spinning. This was just the ticket to begin the gaiety. We listen, tap our feet and sway our hips and shoulders. Our host laughed a hearty one when we felt obliged to do a little jig to music sounding a lot like a rockin' 40's dance band. It was Robert Plant and the Honey Dippers, I'd never heard of them but it turns out that the Captain and the White Fox had something besides fishing in common. They both knew that Robert Plant is one and the same as Led Zeppelin.

We continued to sip our beers, read album covers and get the scoop about life in Margaretsville.

I no longer have to worry about the White Fox freezing to death as a castoff from society in this little shamble. It turns out that Mr. Fox lives with Mrs. Fox, up the hill by the little lighthouse. Yes, in fact, he *does* own the fishing shack and spends much of his summer fishing off the pier. Last year he had a knee replacement, which put a hold on his lobster fishing days.

From the conversation, I gathered that his lobster fishing was more of a hobby he loved than an occupation. His summer here in Margaretsville closes at the end of September. Then, he tells us, he moves to Middleton.

"Middleton?" I ask.

"About 12 miles from here, in the Annapolis Valley," John explains, continuing the telling of his life, "We stay there through January and then we pack up and rent a condo in southern Spain for three months. We find it a whole bunch cheaper than Florida. My wife likes it because she can take short trips all over Europe from there."

I tell him that would sound like my cuppa tea, that's for sure.

John's eyes light up again when we touch on the subject of fishing. He fishes off the dock for mackerel. His excitement is infectious and Doug vowed that if we stayed long enough he'd like to join him. Now, I wondered, what happened to being anxious to get home?

I glance over to Ruckus, comfortably sprawled on a cushion in his cat nirvana world. I always wonder, *Do town cats enjoy their jobs of being at the mercy of those favoring them enough to feed them?* I dare say this one doesn't seem to be in any hurry to change careers mid-stream. The mother in me is suddenly concerned for his welfare in the winter. Just then, the White Fox goes over and gives him an affectionate stroke. I feel better now, reassured that he likely has this covered.

John pointed to his bucket and smiled at his catch for the day. Eager to share, he asked if we would like to have some fresh mackerel for our supper? I chew my lip and wait for the Captain to get us out of this one. We don't want to offend, but we hate to take the fish if we don't intend to eat them. We are none to keen on having an oily, strong fish smell on board, if you know what I mean?

Doug finally explained, "We normally don't eat mackerel—it's too oily."

The fisherman stepped back dejectedly, his face full of shock and amazement. He then explained the trick for preparing mackerel—you must filet them straightaway and then place them in a cool spot. *Never ever* leave the guts in once they are caught. Eat them fresh, if you can. Roll them in a bit of flour and fry them in a little butter. He continued to shake his head in astonishment. "I can't believe you've never had it this way!" He gave us a look that suggested he had possibly misjudged us. His hands were shaking, his eyes rolling, as he claims, "It's the best!"

Okay, all right, already–we are convinced–we agree to try it.

Doug used to be every bit the fisherman and he still partakes occasionally. This meant that he knew what questions to ask in order to get back into the good graces of our new friend.

"How many did you catch today?" He asked.

The landlord of the fish shack tilted his white head and looked up to see if the answer was written on the timbers of the roof. He turned his knitted brow down and looked at Ruckus, who has resumed the licking-his-paws routine.

"Well, Ruckus got two. Pete and Repeat each had one. I gave you four and, if I count the three more I was after, that would make twelve!" he grinned, flashing a bona fide happy, happy smile.

Second beer in hand, we head out the door, fresh mackerel in the bucket gripped tightly in my husband's hand. I'm questioning his addition of the fish catch in my head, when Doug asks about the sturgeon hanging to dry.

"Oh!" Again the fisherman is a ball of fire. "I caught that by accident in my herring net." The healthy-looking, seventy-some-year-old went on to explain how this could happen.

Doug listened intently, but didn't quite follow the story, so he asked, "What does a herring net look like?"

John gave my husband a look that said he surely believed this man must be from another planet (see, I'm not alone on this). Speaking slowly—elbows bent, hands moving up and down pointedly—he spoke, separating his syllables as though he's using the pronunciation key from a dictionary.

"Yoo Meen Too Tel Mee Th-at Yoo Hav Nev-er Seen Ay Herring Net?"

Doug was bitterly ashamed to say he hadn't. The White Fox's face registered deep concern, then his head slumped into his shoulders. He dropped his hands as though the situation was hopeless.

At this point I had the strongish urge to make a run for it with the fish. With every word about fish, my appetite increased. Now, I discovered I was starving and it occurred to me that The White Fox might just change his mind ... decide we aren't worthy or something. However, I changed the subject and asked, "What's in the adjacent building?"

All three sets of eyes settled on a structure about the size of a small garage. The fisherman's hope seemed to be renewed. He smiled and his eyes twinkled brightly, "You'll never guess!"

He walked over and unlocked the door. He managed to keep a straight face but I could see it was costing him dearly. John motioned us over and with pride, pomp and circumstance he swung open the door.

We were purely gaw gaw. No, I never would have guessed, even given another beer and a month to think it over!

"Holy cripes, what is it?" I had no idea at the time, but there sat a 1958 Messerschmitt! In shiny mint condition! The three-wheeled car was hysterical! It was so unexpected that we couldn't stop laughing and soon I was holding my sides. "I never dreamed that *this* was inside when you raised that door!"

On a sudden impulse, all three of us clinked beer cans and styro cup and took a swig. John was still shaking his head and whipping tears from his eyes when he said, "You can get in if you want" Doug jumped in the driver's seat and this started another roar of laughter. He looked like an oversized sardine in an undersized can. Still laughing soundly, we finally closed the door, my capacity for amazement exhausted. We finally set off for our long overdue supper when John called to us, "How long do you plan on staying?"

"Depends on the weather," the Captain replied.

The funny fellow took another sip from his styrofoam cup, and nodded, "I'll probably see ya tomorrow, then. It's supposed to rain!"

Later, back on the boat, we smacked our lips and grinned as we decided who would get the last bite of fish. We shake our heads in disbelief! Over and over in the past we tried to make fresh mackerel tasty, to no avail. Now we know the secret! We weren't finished chewing when a group of wondering eyes appeared, as though by arrangement, so we donned the caps of dockside lecturers.

The first two fellows started into the where, the whens and whys. The guy with the red plaid flannel shirt reared back on his heels in astonishment. The other guy (in the *blue* plaid flannel shirt) hiked up his trouser leg, propped his foot on the dock, and stroked his chin reflectively.

The next group held a comfortingly stout woman in her late sixties. She started into a mild tirade about the sailboat that came before us. "Now, you probably know all about them don't you!" I felt like a slow student disappointing my head mistress when I admitted I knew nothing about them. A man stepped from behind her and started in with the tides, the currents and our "legs." He kept mentioning the sailors who came before us, as well, and each time he did so he looked as if he were biting into something unpleasant.

Next came a character who acted as though he were an FBI agent, writing our names down as soon as he heard them. Doug smiled at all of them with devastating charm. After the fourth amused crowd (and conversation and after conversation about the sailboat which came and went to where no man or imbalanced wife had ventured to go before), my energy finally faded. I mean, we are *people* people, but really ... I was tired of smiling when I didn't feel like it.

I know that the physical workout of the muscles around my mouth increases positive enzymes in my brain chemistry ... but at that point I really didn't care. I just felt like crawling into my book and pulling the pages up over my head. Reading is my way of forgetting my world and entering someone else's. I was out of humor from the long day and the previous night. I escaped down below to clean up our dishes and fish skillet. After a bit I stopped and listened ... ahh, silence on the dock. I do believe our visitors are gone for the night.

✳ ✳ ✳

Doug and I are quietly writing our journal/log entries. I let out a big disgusted sigh. Recounting an intense situation always seems to deintensify the experience—sometimes I feel that I should embroider the story slightly. But, hey, I'm not writing *fiction* here. This account is not trying to be an on-the-water version of, As *the World Turns*.

Our eyes are drooping and my pen falls from my hand. Then we hear a soft voice from outside, "Hello, and welcome!"

I give an eye roll to my husband and ask, "Who could that be? It's almost 10 o'clock!"

Doug puts his chin down to his chest, "You're the sleuth. You tell me." I did another eyeball roll and then stuck my head out the zipped canvas door. I reported back, "There is a man attached to the dock railing." This is the Captain's cue.

Doug greets a sweet-looking man who appeared to be in his mid-thirties. I listened from inside. After a repeat of the soft, "Hello and welcome," this amiable fellow asked the Captain if we'd like to sleep ashore. This is about the 70th time during our trip that someone has asked this, reflecting an unexpected kindness. I admit it sounds pretty good sometimes (like, where were you last night?) but we always have to tend the boat. Doug is going through the best of his docent routine and I catch a few words here and there. My ears perk up when I hear the nicest words ever spoken in the human language. (I believe hearing becomes keener when the question of sanity is concerned.)

"I have a little cottage no one is staying in," he explained, "and you're welcome to stay, cook and shower!"

Get out! A little cottage? No one staying? *Cook and shower?* The Captain thanked him and embarked on his "we think we may leave tomorrow . . ." Three weeks aboard this boat has trained me as a tactful interrogator. I exploded out of the companionway with joy, gave a high-strung toy poodle bark. The nice guy stepped back, slightly startled, his eyes shining in the overhead dock light. I tried not to sound desperate and crazy-as-a-bed-bug. I lifted my chin leaned forward, eager to obtain all the pertinent information.

"To make things simpler," he continued, "I could just take you up there now. I'll show you where it is and where the key is located. Then, if you want to use it, you'll know everything." He smiled sweetly and nodded, just as though he played a part in the natural order of things.

My husband could not miss my maniacal look. "You just hang here with the boat," said the Captain, "I'll go up and check it out."

My heart leaped, while lickety-split, Doug walked off with Jerald, our new best friend of 15 minutes.

They had no more than disappeared into the darkness, when I began to think fearful thoughts. What if I acted too strange? What if he gets a closer look at Doug (he's heading towards the scruffy phase)? What if *reason* sets in, and Jerald changes his mind?

Nahh, he would never sink so low, I reassure myself. But, what if the place is a dump and we don't even want to step inside? I figure I'll just splash disinfectants in great enough quantities to risk a shower.

I discovered, to my intense annoyance, that I'm letting these precious moments of quiet and solitude slip away. Finally, confident our last visitors have come and gone, I sat out in full view of the world with my magazine. I certainly have no intention of not enjoying this time to the max. Surrounded by my first glimpses of evening stars, I'm transported to Centaurus A.

At 11 o'clock we end our conversation with our new patron. Before leaving us dockside, he stood up straight and spoke, God-like (well maybe God-like with a little g). He made three things good and clear: 1) The cottage is ours to use at our leisure, with a bottle of wine tucked into the frig just for us; 2) Tomorrow it is suppose to rain; and 3) If we stick around, he'll be happy to take us on a drive around the countryside.

Wow, oh wowzy. Nice! Very Nice!

By this time we are worn to a frazzle. Doug reads a few lines of Shakespeare aloud, but the yawny-stretchy routine has commenced. Our bellies are full, our leg is on, and we think we have until about 5 A.M. before there's a major production with the dock lines.

In repose, I open the front hatch to the big dark sky filled and overflowing with bright stars. I tell my husband about Centaurus A. It's a fantastic jumble of young blue star clusters, gigantic glowing gas clouds, with imposing dark dust lanes surrounding the central region of the active galaxy (geez, dust even in space). Centaurus A is apparently the result of a collision of two galaxies. The leftover debris is being steadily consumed by the black hole. For an active galaxy, Centarus A is close to Earth—a mere 10 million light years away. We lie there trying to absorb the mystery of it all.

"I wish I knew what it all means or even just my part of the mystery," said my husband, lying there, eyes closed. There is a long pause. I think, well he's asleep now, oops, now his mouth opens to resume speech. "I just can't believe that there are over 100 billion galaxies that they know of—each what do they call it? Galaxian Island Universe? Each with a billion stars!" Slowly coming back to life, he continues, "The mystery would suck if we solved it. There are infinite mysteries, mysteries we don't even know exist yet–like the mystery of lightning. Now we make our own lightning. We have opened up other mysteries of what we can do with that power. You can consider us all nothing in the Universe or you can see us as all miracles fulfilling the mysteries of our lives. We should just do the best with what we know, regard each day as a mystery, one that we cannot entirely fathom, biologically or aesthetically. We should pursue life the way one reads a great mystery novel. We should receive absolute pleasure from the suspense and excitement of uncovering clues."

Propped up on my elbow I look down at him. His eyes are closed. Sleeping? Maybe thinking thoughts that span the Universe? I can't tell.

I hear the soft waves lapping on the beach out past the dock at water's edge—the flopping of the Genoa lulls. I digest his words. I smile to myself. He can be so wise, but he plays the part of the dumb schmuck/stupid bumpkin so well.

Day 23

Saturday, September 22, 2001

The gin began to send warm tendrils into my system, which indicated an enormous shift in attitude. I have to tell ya, I needed a healing drink. I needed fortification against my Captain's cold, disapproving gaze. I confess, I'm numb as a hake. A confession like this is normally reserved for moments when I race around tearing labels off cushions and pillows. Then I move onto the labels on the fruit—there is not enough of either on board (I already checked). *Under Penalty of Law This Tag is Not to be Removed except by the Customer.* Tags like these are reserved for times like these. Sadly, only one lousy float pillow and one bed pillow still had them attached.

Before my sip of inner peace poison, I whimpered quietly (but sincerely) in the quarter berth. Sitting wet and cold, looking as droopy and woebegone as a molting chicken, I did something much worse than leaving the clip off the chip bag (which is pretty bad, on a boat, because they get stale almost immediately). My drink today helps keep reality at bay. The reality is that I have many faults and few redeeming points. I might as well get it off my chest ... as it happens it has not been an encouraging morning.

The Captain started his dance with the dock lines and settling the leg around 4 A.M.. There were many in and outs through the companionway door—retying, climbing here, stomping there, and so forth. The commotion continued until around 7 A.M. I did my best to sleep through most of it, checking the loud ticker periodically. The first sprinkles dabbled the cabin windows around 6:30. By the time the Captain was satisfied that the boat was level and the dock lines and leg lines weren't going to snap, he was wet, out of steam, and tumbled into the V-berth for a nap.

All morning I sat quietly so my husband could sleep. If I crawl back in the V-berth, I'll wake him. So . . .I had tea; I glanced at magazines, but the food and recipes made me want to lick the page. I tried reading, writing and stretching—my normal caught-in-a-tight-spot routine. Rain tends to cause dispositions to droop anyway, but I really needed to either go back to sleep or get outside.

There is vinyl door attached to the outside of our canvas screen door. It's job is to keep the wind, rain and cold out of our lodgeing. Doug had left the vinyl door tied up, to let the fresh air in because the rain and breezes were warm.

Just as I stepped outside, the real wrath of heaven began hovering over us and the wind stepped it up a notch. The pitter-patter of rain increased and soon became a steady, merciless, dreadful downpour. If this is heaven's idea of a fitting retribution for one of my innumerable little sins, it looked to me like heaven was overdoing it. Finally, I decided that I'd better get the plastic door untied so the rain won't get in.

Keep in mind that total ignorance of ropes, knots, old boats and vinyl/canvas door flaps is universal in the world where I come from. The ties are old (like everything on this boat) and broken. The Captain fastens them using this very special knot which has no particular name—it just works. Today it held extremely well. After repeated tries, I simply could *not* loosen the tie in order to get the flap closed.

Now I am cold and my brain is slippery. I go inside. Repeatedly, I stick my head and arms out to fiddle with the damn thing. Normally, I'd call my trusty-good-to-have-around-at-times-like-these husband. Eventually, he would figure it out. Life would go on—just not as cold and damp as if he hadn't been able to get it down.

Today, however, I'm not going to wake him. I will tough it out. It is cold, now, but the rain isn't getting in. I settle in the cramped quarter berth, wrapped in a thin blanket, to shiver and write. I will *not* complain. I will *not* try to start a fire (way too noisy). This rain will stop eventually—it always has before. I'll fix another cup of tea, layer another jacket, and think sweet thoughts. I was being so sweet, actually, that you could have pressed me onto a cookie sheet and made heart-shaped sugar cookies.

I told my journal this heartwarming, sacrificial tale. It looked even better in print. I read it over another couple of times. Why, I may just submit this to *Reader's Digest* for their edition of "Best 100 Most Inspiring Stories."

✳ ✳ ✳

And still she slept an azure-lidded sleep/ in blanched linen, smooth and lavender'd ... only in John Keats' world.

I opened my eyes in a moment of panicky confusion. In quite an alarming manner, the Captain sprang from his refuge as though the boat were about to hit a ledge.

"Eileen!" He chided, "What's with the *curtain?* Why didn't you *shut* it? Now *everything* is wet!"

His statement lacked that indefinable something which we know as charm. He reached out to the crazy knot and, in eight-seconds flat, untied it and let the curtain down.

I emitted a gurgle, not unlike a sick moose, and gave him a doubtful look. My voice was puny and refused to cooperate. I tried to explain, "The wind must've changed ... the rain wasn't coming in ... the knot wouldn't . . ."

I swallowed a huge lump in my throat and tried again. "I wanted to let you sleep. I guess I fell asleep myself ..." Tears stung my eyelids. My explanation faded in the hustle and bustle.

Now, when he said *everything* was wet, he meant the floor, the cockpit cushions, the berth cushions, the canvas, the charts, the table and his log and books. Now, looking tired and pinched, he set about wiping it all down with a towel. Then he moved swiftly back to the wood stove to fire her up and get her going—the only salvation in our miserable miserableness.

Then, with all this accomplished, the Captain, weary and worn, climbed back into the bed with a groan.

Most of us appreciate the feeling of being snug, warm and cozy. Precious few of us ever comprehend our complete reliance on these feelings for relief and mental well-being while living on a cramped boat. Frankly, cold, wet, mildewed and irritated does not equate to sublime time.

The bitter injustice of it all is that it now appears to be *my* fault.

I find myself suddenly drowning in an uncontrollable ocean of self-pity. It floods my very essence. It's almost as though I'd been injected with it.

Really, I should just lash myself to the metal mast and wait to be struck by lightening.

The Captain, however, is utterly unaware of my musings and simply believes that his first mate is as free from sense as a frog from feathers.

At this point there's nothing left to do but to pour myself a Madras. It is my solemn passion and one which I try to keep secret.

This year, there will surely be reports of a red-feathered, red-beaked, round-bellied perching female lush amongst the migratory birds.

I grab my journal. Today, in my entries, I shall make wise decisions. Discernment does not fail me. I'm always right. And ... I'm gonna write whatever I want and stick punctuation marks where they have never gone before!!!!????/// Why, , , ?/ Because I can;;;–I say, apostrophe and exclamation point to you!!! Captain!!!! As the level in my glass moves steadily down, I begin to overcome my closet trauma. My self-doubt seems to evaporate! Haw, haw, haw! In my journal I *am not a thicko*!??? My journal writing and this delectable drug of understanding perform like a shaman ... using drums to drive away despair from my fragile soul. My dark mood has turned to sunshine.

I grin my gin grin.

The warm wood stove, the Madras, my journal, a peaceful nap–
all serve as the mental equivalent of a day at the spa.

* * *

We are both awake now. We're warm and working on sorting out
the dampness on board when John Fox calls to us from the dock.

I stick my head out and he tells me, "Lovely weather!"

I laugh, "Yeah, if you're a duck!"

The White Fox wants to know if we want a ride into town. Very
thoughtful of him, but I related our plans with Jerald for the afternoon.

We give each other a hug and the Captain admits, "I'm having
an off-day—too much space between my molecules." We laugh about
our meeting with John, Ruckus and Pete and Repeat yesterday. Then
we hear yet another voice from the dock. A woman's voice.

We both peek out the door. There, standing in a real, torrential
downpour is ...?

My husband went out to greet our visitor and returned soaked,
but triumphant. His face revealed a "Christmas morning" smile and
in his hands was a large foil-wrapped package.

"Her name is Sherry," he explained. "She lives up the road and
it's hot from her oven!" His grin broadened and he announced, triumphantly, "Blueberry Buckle Cake!"

He rubbed his hands and hooted, "I live a charmed life!" I looked
at the steam coming from the treasure set before us.

"Just wait a cotton pickin' minute here," I interjected, "I want
to live a *charmed* life, too!"

By the time we'd wolfed down all the cake, our teeth and tongues
were stained blueberry blue.

The woodstove was doing its job extremely well. In order to dry
everything, the Captain has it cranked up high enough to heat a
three-story building. Suddenly, Kismet taps me on the shoulder ...
it's time ... I simply cannot wait five more minutes. I have to use
the facilities—now! I can't very well push my husband outdoors
into the downpour, so my only private space is behind the curtain.

This does not put a smile on my face.

Behind the curtain is the 2-foot-by-2-foot space filled with jackets, shoes, the wall of the V-berth and the wood stove. In my hour of

need, the only place to put my bucket is, literally, four inches from the wood stove. You can burn your butt if you make the wrong *move*! It doesn't take long, with the curtain closed, to heat my little space and the V-berth to about 115 degrees. The only possible ventilation is the front hatch but it is still raining cats and dogs and there's a sharp whipping wind. Were I to open it, even for a moment, everything would be soaked (bed and clothes) in about two minutes.

So there you have it. I am forced into my own private sauna. I am dripping with sweat, trying to concentrate on the business at hand. There is courteous silence in the cabin. The only sound is a hissing from the steam created when my drops of sweat hit the wood stove.

Time passes.

While I'm in my situation room, I can hear the Captain's movements. He is filling the little coffee pot with water. I hear the drawer under the stove opening for the coffee and spoon. The tiny aluminum espresso maker makes two espresso cups, so you can imagine its miniature size. As I mentioned before, the 3-inch diameter bottom won't balance on the burner without falling into the flame. So Mr-Fix-It devised a method of balancing this teeny-weenie coffeepot on a 4-inch metal toothpick-looking-thing-a-ma-jig. I hear him wordlessly pursue his coffee-making duty. Soon, however, I hear uncharacteristic noises. There is more shuffling, items being lifted, then put back down, and more drawers opening and closing. A pan's lid is knocked off, resulting in a substantial crash followed by more rumble, rumble and search, search.

All the while, I listen to the coffee-making ordeal with my eyes closed, concentrating on my purpose.

Minutes later, I open my eyes. Through rivulets of sweat, I watch a scribbled note pass under the curtain door. This was quickly followed by an ink pen. I wiped my eyes so I could see to read.

Do you know where the metal tool is for the coffee pot?

I tried to visualize where I had last seen the 4-inch metal toothpick which is vital to his coffee making. I gave up coffee for menopause—not a good exchange, but needed, so I knew I hadn't used it. A metal toothpick, of all things ... I shake my head in wonder at some of the peculiar devices he comes up with to fix things.

To really grasp this approach I have to divulge a secret about the Captain. He has many, but today I'll just say that this man, outside my curtain, receives *fulfillment* in life by fixing things or correcting problems by using devices that were never designed for the problem at hand. One of the favorite tools of his trade are his vise grips.

For six long years. I've cradled in my memory bank countless conversations from Mr. DIY (Do It Yourselfer) about his vise grips! "If I were stranded anywhere with only one tool, I would want it to be a pair of vise grips!" He could write a guidebook called *The Importance of Living with Vise Grips*. He fervidly tells anyone he thinks needs counseling on the subject, "A man in control of his life—drunk, sober, asleep or awake—always knows where his vise grips are." He gives them as gifts for birthdays and graduations. He restrings his guitar with vise grips. I drove the cow car for four years with only vise grips to roll down the windows. He cleans and polishes these little jewels of the trade and then stores them in every glove box, tool chest and utility shelf. I find them under his pillow and in his underwear drawer. I'm telling you, if they had tits I'd be jealous.

I look down at the scribbled note and ink pen. This digression of mine on his tools had seriously delayed my progress. I'm not a great multitasker and now I feel like I may pass out in a room which is definitely not a good place to pass out … I haven't done *anything* with the blasted thing!

All of a sudden my brain bursts its seams. I wipe the profusion of sweat from my eyes with my sleeve, I perch the paper on my bare knee. I scribble

It's a small vise grip's chance in hell, that I know where your metal pick is!

I slip the note and pen back under the curtain door.

After a desert of time, I finally exit, dizzy, my face the color of boiled shrimp. My husband sits in silent repose, happily reading, while his coffee pot brews—balanced precariously atop a pair of vise grips.

He stands and hikes his sweats up high, tight around his crotch. He looks every bit like a dreeb.

"Ooh La La!" I say.

He laughs, "It's to keep the bottom of my sweats from getting wet. I'm going out to check conditions."

* * *

"Rain or no rain, if we want to take showers before our trip into town, we need to pack up and get moving!" The sweetest husband in the whole world is absolutely right. Look at the time!

I peek out the zipper door—not bad now. It had almost stopped raining. With no further encouragement needed I am up the steep ladder at warp speed. I fling my backpack over the side. Splash! I'm thankful for its rubberized bottom. Then I hoist my bod onto the dock. Success!

I don't feel a drop! The afternoon sun illuminates the cliffs to the northeast—two beautiful waterfalls glisten as they plunge off the cliffs into the coming tide. The warmth of the sun and the shock of these two fantastic waterfalls (which were not there yesterday) brought tears to my baby blues.

I followed my husband up the hill. I sniff. Everything smells fresh and clean. I peer ahead and wonder which one of these paths will lead to the promised land of hot water and the waiting, special-just-for-us, cottage. We made a few round and abouts and then, suddenly, a jolt of worry shot through my veins. What if he'd forgotten the way? There are a bunch of winding roads up here ... it was dark last night ... But, naahh—he knows death is permanent.

From the outside it appeared small and tidy. Doug fished the key from its hiding spot and opened the door to reveal a very unpretentious entry of a pieced-together abode from the 60's.

I practice all the patience I have left in me today, by not pushing past my slow husband so I can get to the shower first.

Down the hall to the right is a bedroom with bunk beds. To the left is a small bathroom. Shocking even myself, I walk on. My curiosity propels me to see the rest of the house. To the right is another, neat-as-a-pin small bedroom. To the left, as we move through the hallway, was a kitchen—not huge, but when you've been on a boat, you know, it looked very impressive. Ahead, a dining room and to its left a living room which opened out to what was likely, at one time, a screened-in porch. It is now a sunroom with a wall of windows.

Ooh Awh! All are comfortable rooms done in a casual style. Nothing in the cottage has the sense that it was bought to go with anything else, but it all fits perfectly together. I take a long deep breath. Everything is spic and span, very clean and everything smells of fresh paint!

I walk now, in slow motion, savoring the beauty. I amble toward the sliding glass door which leads to the deck. I would have, quite literally (if mine weren't still so stiff), fallen on my knees in gratitude. I rendered thanks as the unexpected red carpet treatment was rolled out in my direction.

The deck was awash with sunshine, blues and whites quilted the sky. The flavor of rain was on my tongue. The artwork God provided was framed only by the limitation of my eyesight. There were giant cliffs adorned by rushing waterfalls cascading to the sea below, wildflowers were saluting some of their last days, while all around them windswept grasses change the palette to the colors of autumn.

I was left breathless with admiration. I staggered back to the plastic chair to keep from falling. Quietly taking in the panoramic view, I was shivering, my eyes stung, emotions flooded my senses. My chest swelled and heaved. This gift was so unexpected—the cottage, the deck, the artwork. I don't even know where my husband is—still inside I guess. I'm so overwhelmed that I don't even care if he jumped in the shower first! I am so shocked I cannot speak.

The impact of this experience suddenly transported me to another time and place—Florence, Italy.

I ask the reader to indulge me for moment—there is no hard and fast rule for the way my mind works. That day was filled with torrential downpours as well. I had splashed into the Galleria dell'Accademia, as wet as one can be and not float. I rearranged myself and extracted, from a dry spot, the long list of places I wanted to visit that day. I checked the time and decided I'd better get a move on. The spacious Tribuna lay just ahead of me, surprisingly empty. I moved forward when, suddenly, I was literally stopped in my sloshy tracks, my mouth agape. I was awestricken. The magnificence of *David* was overwhelming. I had seen pictures all my life but I was truly taken back by the effect this sculpture had on me. After that experience, nothing else on my list seemed very important.

Today, I take a restorative drink of sunshine. I fill my lungs with squeaky clean ocean air and with *"victorious resistance to the vital desire to do this and that or the other"* (Cabel), I give reverence to the knowledge that five-hundred years ago Michelangelo and the Bay of Fundy worked simultaneously, sculpting their works of art.

With a shower and my half-hour of ecstasy on Jerald's deck, I walked back to the *Guillemot* feeling like a million bucks after taxes. I was all gussied up, I was ready—take me to London and present me to the court. Our chauffeur arrived. He smiled at us as if we were the two people he had always wanted to meet. We jumped in with Jerald for our big trip to Middleton.

Middleton proclaims itself to be the town that makes the most of time. It has a museum of antique clocks, watches and North America's first water-run town clock. Wow, aren't we in luck! This lovely, nice town has a big market *and* a liquor store. So much to do, so much to entertain us on our diversion from water-world. Then I remember—I'm not going back to the *Guillemot*. I have my own special place waiting for me on Jerald's deck for the sunset.

I nudge Doug, to confirm two things: 1) if he thinks Jerald looks like a younger version of Dustin Hoffman, and 2) if he wants to make it back in time for the sunset.

He nods my way and silently communicates: *Why, you're right, to number 1 and, as to number 2, of course he does.* In fact, his eyes glaze over in anticipation.

As our friend, the Dustin-look-a-like, helps bring our load of goodies to the *Guillemot* dockside, he promises yet another field trip tomorrow, if we stick around. He's eager to show us the beautiful Annapolis Valley.

Walking to his car, he calls back to us, "Give me a call to let me know when you decide on your schedule." My mind quickly does a mental search for the closest pay phone in this teeny weeny town, just as Jerald adds, before jumping in his car, "The phone number is next to the telephone in the cottage."

AAHH! Silly me, I'd forgotten that our very own private cottage has a phone too!

Panting and winded from racing up the hill, we opened the door to our Shangri-la. Doug heads directly to the shower he never took earlier in the day. He wasn't that desperate for cleanup duty, seeing that there was no "mud-ectomy" required. I used this opportunity to savor moments of having the deck to myself.

It's never-never land … I never ever want to leave! It's a crowded day for birds. I stand alone under a cloud of wings and the clamor of their cries. They are my only audience. I dance around like Goldie Hawn on *Laugh-In*, singing, "Sock-it-to-me, Sock-it-to-me!" Then I move on to, "It's your thing, do what you want ta do! I can't tell ya who to sock-it-to!"

Every house around here seems to be from an era where, were you to walk by, you'd have been able to hear *Laugh-In* ringing from their rabbit-eared TV sets.

With hair slicked back, looking as though he'd just stepped out of a Brylcreem commercial, my husband arrives on the dance floor, and dances his own little dance. Evidently he'd been hearing a song in his head all day long and, not having his guitar with him, the song had been drumming out his ears. I liked the dance. I immediately wanted to join in.

I shot him a brief smile. He stopped and we both realized that the sun was over the yardarm. We popped a beer.

We closed our eyes in quiet ecstasy. Then opened them to watch the glinting immensity of the sea. His head starts to move, his feet shuffle into his dance.

"Can you see the music I'm hearing?" he asked.

Yes, actually, I could—with every grunt and move, it was clear. It was a cross between Freddie King *Boogie Funk* and a slow version of Stevie Ray Vaughan's *Say What?* "Boom, boom, uga, uga, chuga, chuga, click, click, do-wacka wacka!" With every roll of his arms, sway of his hips, and shuffle of his feet, I can hear his music. I slide right in step. We are groov'n. Clearly it was music we really got into.

"When we gets goin', we really gets goin'!" my dance partner remarked.

The fragrance of the evening is dizzing (or maybe it's the beer). The sun sinks into the sea, fire red. We are infused with energy. Doug began to talk to me suggestively. I get a bit discombobulated. We dance the hootchy-kootchy to music that only the two of us can hear.

"I'm in hog heaven!"

This is me, talking to Jerald on the telephone. "Watching the sun set from your deck takes my breath away!" I panted.

Of course it could be all the dancing, but I didn't mention this factor (he barely knows us).

"I just may never leave!" I cried. He thought I was joking.

"Great!" he replied enthusiastically, "Stay for a week!"

"Oh, right I'm really sure!" I'm in a *weakened* state; he should not be tempting me.

"Why not?" he questioned. "You don't have to be anyplace in a hurry do you?"

I looked in the tiny mirror in the hallway and a wistful gleam passed across my face. I went into happy-world.

I knew that Doug would put the presidential veto on this idea pretty quick. We can't stay. We have to get the *Guillemot* home before we really get some weather.

There is good stuff in Jerald—no artificial code of hospitality here. If I were Catholic, I'd nominate him for Sainthood. He has known us for less than 24 hours and he is offering his adorable cottage (that I have dreamed of all my life), complete with deck, for free! Come to think of it, he's probably offering it because he has *only* known us for 24 hours. (This will be our little secret, readers.) Give this entire sweet town enough time and they may be cutting our dock lines or sawing our leg off as we sleep.

Before I ring off, I give him a, "Let's go!" on tomorrow's tour.

I join my co-mate, out on the deck. We sit, quiet-like, after I tell him of Jerald's offer. I have my eyes glued to the silhouettes in the twilight of the cliffs and the sea.

"Well, if you really want to stay, I can tak 'er home alone and then drive back to get you."

Awh, he's talking rot! *Absolute* drivel! Pure mashed potatoes! I could never let him go alone!

Could I?

Suddenly the Captain in him takes charge, He jumps up. He moves quickly into the kitchen to check the time. "We'd better get down to the dock!"

I waver. I start to say, "I'll join ya in awhile … tomorrow … next week … next year …"

But duty calls. I am his first mate, after all, and he may need me.

I do some more rationalizing. We are tied to the dock, so the regular leg drill will not be necessary. He should be able to go it alone. Still, he may need me. He's my shepherd. I'm his little lamb. We herd together.

This cottage has made my real estate yearnings resurface, double-strength. All the way down to the boat I mentally rub my hands in a mincing way. I feel greedy and unprincipled when I can't stop my deviant mind from calculating ... *How on earth can I get Jerald to sell me that cottage?* With a profit, of course! I wouldn't think of swindling the kind fellow. Jerald is an A number-one guy. I mean him no real harm. I am mindful that he is probably one of the sweetest, most cheerful of men which, I admit to myself, is essential to my scheming (God will forgive me). If I play my cards right, I may be able to persuade him to sign it over as an extreme act of hospitality. He'd give someone the shirt off his back. And, if that weren't enough, he'd give 'em his pants. He would always think of donating to those less fortunate than he. Well, *I'm* less fortunate than he. He has the cottage—I don't!

I shake my head in the pro-Eileen syndrome. My husband looks at me and frowns. He forever seems to know my thoughts when I'm on a "buying a house" binge.

"What?" I ask, innocently.

He gives me that maniacal smile I've learned to dread. He looks at me as though I were a black-minded woman of no virtue.

"Don't give that look, Buster Brown," I shot back, "I'm *well aware* of the warped nature of your soul! If there were a case of Boddingtons (too-expensive-for-us-beer) in that house, you would be plotting, too!" Just this merest mention of his favorite brought a small, expectant smile to his face.

Meanwhile, my mind continues to plan ... and, if all *that* didn't work ... squatter's rights ... I'd simply chain myself to the deck.

A very dark part of the road forces me to focus my attention on not falling prey to some lurking hole or rock, lying in wait to throw my knee out and lay me flat. I slow down, my husband ahead of me. He stops so suddenly that, with my head tucked in looking down, I almost slam into him. His eyes are glued ahead. We could see that a difficult, complex situation had arisen.

With dawning horror, we look at each other.

Doug yells "Oh Shit!" And begins running toward the dock. I see ahead of us, in the lights of the dock, our neglected responsibility.

"Uh-Oh!" Sometimes my most expressive words are not words at all.

I thought about running, too! My brain reacts with lightning speed. It tells me to respond like a Maserati–go fast, and turn a corner on a dime. An observer, however, would hardly categorize my run as being a quite a "run." It was dark. I was carrying my backpack. And, truth be told, I'm built for stability rather than speed. Besides, I have a bum knee.

Still, considering all this, I did pretty well. I was close at his heels.

When I got to the *Guillemot,* Doug had already started down the ladder toward our perilously tilting boat.

I am a mature woman. Sometimes, this helps in my decision making. I knew this to be the precise psychological moment when it was best to say…absolutely nothing! The tide was leaving her fast and the poor girl was heeling over more and more with each and every one of my heaving breaths.

I stood quietly on the dock, as patient as a wading bird. The Captain set about the task of righting her like a Christian with four aces. He began untying the halyards and gathering other dock lines from storage areas. His performance began to resemble a circus performer's balancing act. The Captain moved about gingerly, carefully placing his weight so that he wouldn't increase the pressure on the lines tied to the dock. They were extremely close to snapping from the weight of the *Guillemot* heeling over.

When he enlisted my help (which is generally not a good sign) I just follow his lead. We have lines in our hands. We pull and pull with all our might. I assume we are hoping to keep her from heeling over anymore, beyond the point that we would never be able to straighten her. I don't ask. We continue pulling; the ropes are now ripping my hands.

I fall down on the concrete and jam my knees and legs into the wooden curb railing of the dock. *Hmmm?* I wonder to myself. Am I underdressed or overdressed for this post cocktail pre-dinner party on the dock?

Whatever this is doing to Doug I cannot determine because I'm too involved to notice. I have my eyes closed, my teeth bared. Using every ounce of our combined body weights (finally this has come in handy) and with the rope wrapped around me (by God, I wasn't about to cry "crack" as they say around here), Doug is finally able to get enough leverage to balance her. He manages to cleat her off to the dock, keeping her from going over any further.

I am left on the dock, huffing and puffing. My husband disappears down the ladder.

"What next?" I cry.

"Stay where you are! I have to get more ropes, block and tackle!" he calls back. His comment leaves a lasting impression on my impressionable mind. I see myself lying on the dock, wet and dirty, watching my Captain scrambling below, gathering whatever else is needed for whatever we are going to do.

I watch, silently, as he goes about rigging the lines and blocks from the dock to the *Guillemot*, for reasons I can't begin to explain. Something about gravity, momentum and various other physical laws. The science of the thing is, to Eileen Beaver, simply a closed book.

Now he turns to me, once again, and says, "I have to climb back on board, but this is what you have to do ..." Then he gives me a quick lesson in my part of this confusion.

Peachy, just peachy! Is there a manual for this? In my brief, but spectacular, experiences of sailing, I've never even started to do anything like this. I wish he had time to explain his explanation. Is there no end to the responsibilities loaded upon a woman who foolishly takes up with a sailor man? Apparently not!

With all the assurance of a woman who has no real idea of what she's supposed to do, I stand my post. I watch my master mariner disappear down the ladder once more. Not for the first time, I think that I must surely be *non compos mentis.*

However, when he said "Pull!" I did.

Now, I do have purchase here on the dock. And me, by myself, and my hardly existent biceps pulled the *Guillemot* off her bilge—with less effort than it takes to zip my jeans after a wash and a toss in the dryer.

This is a good thing to be able to do in a pinch. It can have an amazing effect on one's self-confidence! It was a wonderful moment … basking in my adrenaline afterglow, I turn to wave my Queen's wave to all my loyal subjects and I discover that we have no audience for my proud display of strength and groveling.

My senses return. I do believe in miracles.

My man runs up the ladder, smiling the big happy smile of a fellow who's just accomplished something. We collapse, simultaneously, into heaves of laughter. He folds me up in his arms and gives me a big squeeze, still laughing our heads off. Laughter strengthens your lungs. Laughter aids in circulation. Laughter helps digestion. Laughter strengthens the immune system.

While I sit, enjoying the beautiful evening, the skipper puts away, his-come-in-handy supplies. We're remembering, now, the plight of the sailboat that came in here before us, a couple of weeks ago. The gist of their predicament was that they were on a much bigger, heavier boat. The Captain was said to be from Boston and his first mate was a photographer. He was on board to film a documentary on sailing the Bay of Fundy. The method this Boston sailor had in mind to handle the issue of "no water" and a pointy thing down below called a keel, was to make some sort of cradle out of ropes and then tie the boat to the dock.

For whatever reasons—we really don't know why—we can only imagine—this didn't work. (We got this story from everyone here, none of whom have ever really sailed before). This must have been their first harbour out of St. John, New Brunswick, because their floating hotel lay unhappily on its side. The reports are that the skipper wore a scowl of perpetual disillusionment the entire time. After sleeping on the dock a few nights, they turned back around and headed back to the world of deep-water harbours.

We are so happy not to have shown our true colors (mine happened to be black and blue at the moment) to all the people in Margaretsville and the many others who have traveled far and wide to see and greet our little sailboat. Luckily all those folks who have given honor and admiration, more appropriately bestowed on the crew of the *Challenger*, will never know we almost had to spend the night at Jerald's cottage because we were too busy dancing and whoop'n it up on his deck to tend the boat. We will not have to endure the stern serves-you-right-because-of-your-laziness stares. Our new friends will go on believing that the Captain and his swabbie are proper, barnacle-backed sea dogs. We are true hairy-chested sailors all the way!

We spend the remainder of the evening tucked safely on board. Together we share the nosebag of black beans and rice. We greet and chat with all those who come to visit. One of our most esteemed visitors is Gary Lawson. He came by yesterday, then returned today to check our schedule, "Oh, you're spending another day and night? How about dinner at our house tomorrow night?"

To my list for next year's cruise, I add a note to bring a social calender.

Gary is a nice conversationalist, but when he touched on (his version of) the sailboat that came before us, the Captain cut his eyes in my direction. Hey, I can take a hint as well as the next! I just flung my head back, kept my chin pointed to the top of the dock and listened. I only gave a couple contemptuous shakes of my head and few pompous clicks of my tongue.

BD (Before Doug), I thought purchase power involved how high my credit limit was on my American Express. AD (After Doug), the only thing I've maxed out is my patience. We have never even owned a credit card and only recently a MAC card. Tonight, while I was holding tight to that rope, wallowing around in the muck and guck of fish guts on the town dock, I ruefully had a little talk with myself.

"Eileen?" I asked, "What are you doing here? Are you having *fun?*" After I discovered that I'd finally done something right—that I had purchase power enough to straighten our sanctum on the sea without being flung over the side of the dock, landing on the deck or as a splat in the mud. After I was encouraged by the Captain's cheers of, "You rock and you're brilliant!" I answered this question with, "You might as well. It's the same price."

Except for the bad parts, I am having a pretty good time. No one sold me this trip. There were no vouchers, no reservations. I had no *real* expectations–a few hopes–but no concrete expectations. Our big expenditures have been 10 gallons of fuel, the charts, the cruising guide, our provisions and booze. The booze has gone a bit over budget, but I'd set aside funds for emergencies.

There are a few things I've learned in my life of travel. One of them is that, no matter how much you pay, there are *no* guarantees. No matter what hotels, resorts, cruise ships, tour buses, tour guides and package deals you have goin', there is no sure thing. I don't care how pretty the pictures are in the brochures. It is up to you to have a good time.

Now, I'm feelin' pretty haughty tonight—certain experiences can sometimes transform a person. I think I'm ready now for some sorta friggin' *survival* show. This trip has been far more than one of those "deprivation vacations," that they sell in travel magazines, where people pay a bunch of money to be filled with "wonder and gratitude."

Who needs fresh-baked chocolate chip cookies, or a mint on the pillow? Loftily, I tell myself that I'm so glad we are far from the "Let me entertain you type of tourism." The experiences I've had on this journey are the ones that give strength and fiber! My disgruntled moods are merely waves of nausea, like when you first become pregnant. When the nausea passes, then you're excited about being pregnant again.

Let's face it—traveling first class alienates you from the people, place, and country. I've had my share of that kind of tourism and I'm *finished*. Hear that word, readers?

"I'm *finished!*"

I've been to every amusement park in California and many in Florida. No more! All those years of intense planning, of trying to have a spontaneous adventure, are over! I will never again stoop so low that I dance the hula at a wanna-be *luau* or have Don Ho sing to me on stage. Forget all those corny, automated boat rides through the Nile to King Tut's tomb. I will never again be duped into screaming when *Jaws* suddenly rears up alongside me. There will be no more boats floating me through subterranean caves. Gone, too, are singing minstrel Captains who escort me to restaurants or my hotel room. That's that! No more following the crowd or paying to swim with dolphins. I will never again demean myself by dancing, in nothing more than a towel, on stage with a Bobby Darren look-alike singing *Splish splash I was takin' a bath*! I'm swearing off Maori dancing in parades! I will never again play the role of a French perfume heiress at a murder mystery party in France. I'll never again find myself forced to strip for customs officers because I carry all my jewels in an underarm pouch. Above all *else,* no more throwing my underwear at Tom Jones. (Honestly, that was strictly rumor. But if I had it to do over, I would have gotten it out of my system.) The contemptuousness I feel for some of the things I've done, astonishes me. I would need an injection of truth serum to admit to my more humiliating excesses. So much for all that!

Because now, I am officially an Ecotourist! I can turn up my sunburnt, peeling and mosquito-bitten nose at all those folks who typify shallowness. Those who merely lie motionless on flawless beaches so as to not to disturb their perfect tan, legs carefully shaved, with coverups that match their swimsuits. This includes the insipid traveler who flashes her room key and receives a big white fluffy pool towel. I cringe at the thought of swimming through a waterfall to a Grotto Bar for my before-noon piña colada.

These words are not spoken (or written) idly. After we are snuggled in the V-berth, I share with my husband the news that I believe I'm ready for next year. Two months aboard—maybe we can go the Madeline Islands! They are in the Gulf of St. Lawrence and the local language is French. My life seems so stellar tonight, so *par excellence!* Maybe I will practice my French! I love anyone that sounds like Pepe le Pew! It will be so romantic.

Day 24

Sunday, September 23, 2001

I was awakened early morning by my Captain removing himself from our cozy bed to do the leg and the lines. My darling husband said he could do it alone. The routine with the legs and the lines changes for each new place. What you do and how you do it depends on the current, the slope of where we lay, the ground beneath us (rocks or sand), how and where you can tie to the dock—you know the list.

Here at Margaretsville he thinks he knows the ropes by now. Before he leaves, he whispers in my ear, "Just roll over and keep my side warm. OK, my sweetie pie?"

Alrighty now, Wow! He is such an adorable Captain. This cruise really can be fun and romantic. All these years I've tried so hard. I've exfoliated, used expensive eye creams, polished my toenails and exercised my flabby underarms and none of this ever got me as far as having "purchase" power! I can now say, with a confidence I never had before, that he will not be throwing me overboard to the mackerel, or sending me back to the mall that spawned me! A woman with purchase power is enough to warm the heart of any sailor!

He said, (I repeat it over in my head, like a lovesick adolescent)—he said very seductively—"Just roll over and keep my side warm, sweetie pie!" Yahoo! Straits of the Romantic Boom Boom here we come!

Then I heard him call from the deck, "Eileen! Are you on my side? I need you to balance the weight of the boat!"

I keep my groans to myself when we climb the ladder at low-tide. I feel a few twinges in the hinges from last night's dance on the dock pulling the 'G' up to her exalted position. But it's a fine sunny morning for a little walk around the dock, the rocks, and the beach to see what we can see.

Basking in the shallow sunlit water are starfish, sea urchins, mussels, barnacles and sea cucumbers. Sea urchins (called "ose eggs" in parts of the Maritimes) are round spiny animals related to sea cucumbers and a distant relative to starfish. The spines, or prickles, have feelers on them that guide the sea urchins around the bottom of coastal waters searching for algae, their main food source. The delectable flavor of their ovaries and testes make them a prize for Asian countries. Discriminate diners remove the gonads for a dish that is much like caviar. Japan is a big importer of these pincushions. In 1998, they spent $3.5 million in Nova Scotia alone, for this delicacy. It just shows you can develop a market for just about anything. One fellow in the Maritimes makes dog snacks from dogfish.

Sometimes, in the little pools of water left by the ebb of the tide, you can see small (4-6 inches) rock eel. Sculpins are another fish likely to be seen around the dock. I hear they are called "double uglies" by the kids of the Maritimers, and for good reason. This scavenger fish has a large head and mouth, with lots of spines near the head and on the top part of its body. They are easy to catch because they feast on discarded fish entrails which are tossed back in the water after cleaning. Although plentiful, sculpins do not make for very good eating. They say when times are really hard, or if you're down on your luck, you can always fix up some sculpin stew.

While we waited on the dock for own private tour guide, Jerald, Doug's powerful, energetic voice rings out over the cords of his guitar. *"Goin' to the fair down to Perry, Goin' to the fair down to Perry ... Perry's so close to my home ..."*
He continues to strum and sing with such verve that two dogs, nearby, howl in unison.

I'm sitting, not far away, in high spirits, enjoying the sun and the now-slowing waterfalls. In general, I've spent the morning forgiving myself for my perfect existence. My boat bag, pouched full with our picnic lunch, is nestled between my legs. We have an entire day ahead of us for seeing the Annapolis Valley.

Driving along with Jerald, the very names in the Annapolis Valley make me want to stop at every produce vendor to rake in every type of apple, berry and the very last of the tomato harvest—Garlands Crossing, Avonport, Aylesford, Berwick, Oaklane, Curry's Corner, Windsor and Bridgewater. Road names like Aberdeen, Cornwallis, Oakdone, Alders Hot and Canaan, beckon us. As we come down off the mountains which separate the Bay Of Fundy from the valley, we see Canada's first "bread basket." This fertile valley has been farmed for over 300 years. The orchards and rolling farmlands are some of the best in the world for apple growing. There are many small towns, tiny villages and winding rivers. The entire valley extends from Digby to Windsor, an area about 100 miles long and 5-to-15 miles wide. It is sheltered from heavy winds and from the "Fundy Fog" by the North and South Mountains.

For the time being, I force myself to keep my seatbelt buckled—we will make all our stops for fresh produce on the way home. Passing Kingston and Berwick we head straight for Kentville. The agriculture research center here has a walking trail where you can observe Chestnut, Walnut, Cherry, Mountain Ash and Alder trees getting ready for the winter. Along the trail they protect many special species of ferns.

The best part of Kingston is the very large community of pumpkin people poking their heads around every corner. I want to stop and get to know them. Their stuffed clothes are so cute, showcasing the very latest in Fall Pumpkin Fashion Wear. Their funny shaped punkin' heads are all whimsically painted, each one expressing its own little character. I want to shake their hands, get my picture with them …now, now … we'll have none of that, Eileen! I'm not some cornball tourist anymore; but if I sneak a few shots, no one has to see them.

Jerald's small economy car that he borrowed for the trip (he only has a pickup) turned north toward the Blomidon lookout. The Minas Basin looks so calm and distant from this vista. It is already a magic land in my mind but today, as the nuclear fusion of hydrogen glares down, it appears almost like a mirage. In a dreamlike state, I wandered off the path to be alone with the bright red berries of the highbush-cranberry and the gentle red of the wild rose hips. The neighboring Sumac is beginning to drop its leaves to showcase the clusters of reddish-purple berries. The feeling that "right now is wonderful" spread over me as I gazed quietly at the beautiful composition in color of the rolling farmlands and orchards.

Back on the Evangeline Trail we came across Wolfville, a university town with big stately trees and historic homes. In my list book, tucked in my boat bag, I noted that we should make an effort to come back and see the Atlantic Theatre Festival which is held in a 500-seat theatre.

Brumn! Brumn! We make our approach to Grand Pré, the home to Nova Scotia's oldest operating winery. The leaves are more than slightly limp with the suspicion of autumn as we pass through areas of large vineyards, where the late harvest wine grapes are still on the vine.

At the Grand Pré National Historic site, Jerald halts our taxi. There we find a large stone church which stands as a memorial to the Acadians who were forcefully exiled by the British. In the mid-1700s, the 10, 000 Acadians living in Nova Scotia wished to live peacefully and refused to pledge allegiance to either France or England when the two went to war. Eight-thousand were forced to leave their homes and farms. They were sent to many different areas, including New Orleans and the Caribbean, splitting families apart during the Deportation of 1755. This church is built on a site of one of the original Acadian Villages.

Inside we find many paintings depicting their way of life including the dykes which they built in the tidal marshes to let the land dry out. After about three years, the land would be sweet enough to cultivate. Other paintings show the hardships and sadness of leaving their homes and the deportation. Longfellow's epic poem, written in 1847, recreates the saga. A statue of Evangeline, the fictional heroine of their *Grand D'erangement*, represents the indomitable spirit of the Acadians.

The church grounds lure me when I step back outside to soak up some cheerful sunshine. I am instantly enchanted by the beautiful ponds and formal gardens. I spend a good long while spellbound under an ancient French Willow, one of the most beautiful trees I've ever, in my long life, seen. These magnificent trees, with their massive trunks, loom in many areas of the grounds.

Passing the Acadian Village watering well, we sauntered over to the picnic grounds, nestled by farmland cultivated for winter wheat. The picnic bench we selected gave us shade and seclusion. The guys are listening to some birds having an argument in a nearby tree while I place our picnic on the table. We all agree that, from the looks of this spread, you'd have thought I'd been expecting famine conditions! I admit I do have a tendency to pile it on, especially when our guest happens to be our tour guide and the young man of sterling character who owns my cottage.

Everything was precut and ready for sandwich making. I had sliced the sunflower seed rye boule, from yesterday's shopping spree, ready to be topped with tomatoes, onions, pickles, sprouts, million dollar relish, Eastport's Raye's Mustard (sweet and spicy, the Captain's fav) and sharp cheddar cheese. To accompany this tiny sandwich, which barely fits in one's mouth, I had fried some whole-wheat tortilla chips and tossed up some black bean salsa out of leftovers from last night's dinner.

I found out yesterday that, although our tour guide is rather slight of build, he has quite the penchant for sweets. So I brought an ample supply of the extra large, melt-in-your-mouth, peanut butter cookies, purchased yesterday at the local bakery.

With all the exuberance of an overstuffed pig, and ready for a nap, I locked myself into the seat belt (thank goodness it stretches). We continued our tour, meandering through the back roads of this quiet paradise. All about us are hay bales. Not so out-of-the-ordinary you may say, but these hay bales have turned into bats, moons and pumpkins. The bales are stacked and arranged so that the art of the funny painted faces greets you as you drive through the countryside. Feeling very large and round myself, I was surprised that my two male companions just didn't paint a face on me and roll me out the door.

The pumpkin people and the hay bale art brought about a cozy setting for all the bulging produce stands. The stands were loaded with apples, pears, cherry plums, raspberries, gourds, squash and, naturally, pumpkins. They also had shelves lined with locally made pies, breads, scones, blueberry jelly, fudge and cookies. All around us were families on their Sunday outing, gathering produce and preparing for the Canadian Thanksgiving, which is usually around October 10th. We stopped at a couple of stands at the end of the owner's driveways. All were equipped with the "honor system" cash box for making payment.

I bought fresh raspberries and fudge for a mid-afternoon snack, making sure we all didn't fade away before our tour concluded. We uttered moans of pleasure while munching on the tasty raspberries. I can just imagine being around here for strawberry season. They say Nova Scotians eat more strawberries per capita than any other place in the world.

Jerald turns our little car toward the Bay of Fundy coast to take a peak at Annapolis Royal and Port Royal. Large graceful homes, tree-lined streets and a 10-acre historic garden are just a few of its highlights. There are many more, such as 150 "heritage" buildings, including Canada's oldest wooden house, dating to 1708. Virginia creeper, already showing off its orange-red leaves of fall, adorns several of the old buildings.

Just outside Annapolis Royal resides the Tidal Power Project. The first and only one of its kind in North America, it generates hydroelectric power from the force of the Fundy tides. Up the Annapolis River, near the plant, all the fishing boats are anchored bow and stern because of the force of the water.

Along this river there is a custom some still follow. It originated in one of the oldest churches in Acadia, built in 1679. The church sits on the Island of La Valcour, but the burial grounds were across the river, which necessitated the tradition of holding all funerals at low tide.

This trip through this lush valley made me more than a little homesick for the San Joaquin Valley of California. I lived most of my life in the largest producing agricultural valley in the world and I took for granted having all that wonderful produce at my fingertips. We had everything from kiwis to pistachios. In the yard where I grew up, we had grapevines, plum, peach, loquat and orange trees. I have yet to taste better oranges than the ones from those trees.

We were ready to make the loop back to the boat. We headed east towards Bridgetown, then Middleton and on up to Margaretsville. Today we enjoyed hints of the color masterpiece that will hit, likely in October. I have lived on the East Coast long enough now to visualize this landscape when the birch, beech, poplar, elm and witch-hazel turn yellow. The bright red of the red oak, mountain ash, the blueberry barrens and the huckleberry will mix with the big show conducted by the maples. The magnificent maples turn yellow, red, orange or purple depending on the sunlight conditions.

The Museum of Natural History tells me why, in some years, the dazzling palette of fall foliage changes. The leaves of summer are green because of the chlorophyll they contain. They use sunlight, water and carbon dioxide in the making of food. Throughout the growing season they have been setting seeds and making food for winter storage. In autumn the days become shorter, nights become cooler and longer, the food processing in the leaves shuts down. The chlorophyll content in the leaves decreases and the green gives way to the yellow and orange pigments already present in the leaves.

Purple and red shades are a result of chemical changes by sunlight acting on sap that is trapped in the leaves. The intensity of the color depends on the amount of sunlight the leaves receive. Sunny days and cool nights, which is what we have here, will release a more dramatic display and variety of color. We may miss it here, but we'll catch the showy array in Maine and then (lucky us) because of the later climate change in the south, we usually enjoy a second big splash at home in Pennsylvania.

Satisfied in knowing we've seen as much as humanly possible for one day, and have gotten the lay of the land, so to speak, we are content to turn our direction back to our world of the Bay of Fundy–

where the signs along the road are likely to offer fresh dulse (a seaweed), clams, lobster, and periwinkles—instead of apples and raspberries.

In some areas of the Atlantic Provinces oysters are prevalent. There use to be an old adage which recommended that diners eat oysters only in months containing an 'r.' This folk wisdom, however, has gone by the wayside with the advent of modern cold storage. When the great mania of oysters exploded, the Atlantic Canadian fisherman would chop holes in the ice, scoop the oysters from the seabed, take them ashore, and cook them over the coals of a fire. They supplemented their tasty meal with water, crumbs of bread and a little pepper or nutmeg. The islanders could be seen with their pails of oysters between their knees, gossiping, shucking and slurping.

Our arrival back in Margaretsville brought a sense of tranquility–a sharp contrast to the hustle and bustle of a beautiful Sunday afternoon in the valley. Jerald recalled his youth, when he rode many a flatulent school bus home from the valley. They would bemoan leaving the sunny skies of the Annapolis valley for the Fundy Fog of Margaretsville. Today, almost all the seaside's summer people are back to jobs, tall buildings and big cities. We are among the fortunate, to be able to enjoy these last full days of Indian summer. I am encouraged to see that rural Nova Scotia is as quaint and beautiful as I had hoped—as close to a Norman Rockwell scene as I will probably get in the 21st century. We had a perfect day putting faces to the places that had been mere printed words on a map.

To thank Jerald for his mythical portions of hospitality, I sent him home with half the apples. He firmly maintained that gravensteens are the best. Into his open arms I piled raspberries, fudge and squash. We exchange our, "talk to ya latters and we'll let you know about our schedule," good byes.

The two of us, left at the dock, are light-headed with excitement over storing and sampling our loot! Later, when the moment arises, as it does for everyone, that I swear off eating another morsel for the rest of the day and possibly the *rest* of my ever lovin' days, we hear a call from our "balcony parlor door"—also called a dock.

I looked up to see Gary and Pat Lawson's jovial faces, haloed by wispy clouds.

"Hey," they inquire, "is 6:30 good for dinner?"

They nod. I look down at the loud ticker—4:30. Well, I'm sure I can muster up a little appetite, purely to be sociable, of course.

With a broad, anticipatory smile on her face, Pat asks innocently, "Do you like wine?"

Wearing my perma-grin, I answer, "Sure! It's my favorite food!"

Gary and Pat, bearers of glad tidings, then left for their cottage up the road, but not before extending two, now common, courtesies—a ride and a shower! I turn to give my Captain a big hug.

"Hee Hee! Hee Hee!" I giggle and then, in my very best Jesse Burner imitation, I say, "Now, *that's* what I'm talkin' about!"

Tucked away in a corner, when Doug bought the house in Eastport, was a odd book. It was written by an old Chinese philosopher, not hundreds of years ago, but in 1937. The book, *The Importance of Living*, by Lin Yutang, gives advice on practically all areas of life. Doug and I often read from this and get a big kick out of the era and cultural heritage influence of his advice. This is what Lin Yutang wrote about friends.

> *For enjoying flowers, one must secure big-hearted friends.*
> *For going to singsong houses to have a look at singsong girls, one must secure temperate friends.*
> *For going up a high mountain, one must secure romantic friends.*
> *For boating, one must secure friends with an expansive nature.*
> *For anticipating snow, one must secure beautiful friends.*
> *For a wine party, one must secure friends with flavor and charm.*

Can you believe it? Gary and Pat thought those friends would be us! They, like most of modern society, have probably never read any of Lin's advice, but a woman on a sailboat, writing in her journal, can foster her illusions. Lin Yutang, goes on, in the same verse, to expound on the importance of proper surroundings for your little wine party. A little cottage overlooking the bay, as they described their place, sounds more than adequate.

I will need to watch myself in the future. I have to remember to not bring my *shower bag* to dinner parties. Anyone—at least anyone in my BD life—would feel a bit strange to meet people, and then repeatedly, moments later, find yourself in their shower. If this continues, I'll soon expect all engraved invitations to read, *You Are Invited For: Shower, Cocktails and Dinner.*

I remain in a state of innocence; a result of having only my four-and-a-half-inch mirror. This evening, I dress for a "wine party." I pull out my only nice blouse. It is one of those gypsy-looking, wrinkly, gauzy numbers, in a nice shade of blue. It didn't start out being a gypsy-looking wrinkly job, but it is now. *Ironed* is not a word normally associated with my husband's wardrobe, and not mine anymore, as well. Without close inspection, and in candle-light, while posing under a mantle of respectability—a lost cause if there ever was one at this point—it might pass.

Now, more decisions! Geez ... should I wash my hair? I did just yesterday, but I never know if, and when, we will leave. Or, for that matter, when my next shower might be. Plus—I check my four-and-a-half-incher—there may be a remote chance of fish guts stuck here and there.

On the other hand, the downside of this routine is (this is a short list):

1. The hair-slicked-back-just-stepped-out-of-the-swimming-pool look, displayed so well by Bo Derek, is transmogrified into a drowned-rat-look on me.

2. I have to sit through the first half of the lovely wine/ dinner/get-to-know-you party with wet hair. This is the half where everyone has not had quite enough to drink not to notice.

Finally, the current conditions being what they are, I opt for the wash-the-hair routine and pack my shampoo. Our hosts don't seem high-brow enough to care.

After the "Cheerio Ho's and Chin Chin's" were happily executed, we liberally partook of their hospitality. We discovered that our host and hostess (of exceptional social caliber) are newly-weds of about six months. Gary, 58, and Pat, about 50 years old, have left their high-tech jobs in Toronto to dedicate the rest of their lives to having fun. We obligingly join in.

We try like the dickens! We really do! We have experimented with all sorts of tactics for when the variety of people we welcome into our lives show their generosity by wanting to feed us, not knowing that we don't eat meat.

We decided long ago, however, that it's best not to mention this when the invitation is extended. If they ask, we tell them. If not, then we try to avoid the subject. Why? Because most people hear our announcement and react in some version of, "Eeeccckkk! We have vegetarians in our midst!" We just don't want to cause any extra effort or expense. If they happen to serve fish, we eat it. If not, then we almost always can find plenty to eat.

Tonight, holy smokes, I can hardly stop myself from shouting, "Don't you value your furniture? This is why I hate armchairs—one more bite and my husband will need to use the pry bar and he hates when this happens. Look at these hips for cryin' out loud!"

Their bathroom has only a small medicine cabinet mirror but, even in that, I could tell I wasn't about to waste away!

Pat and Gary look just a bit forlorn at the "no meat" announcement, but we both assure them that even if we hadn't eaten enough today for a small army, her hors d'oeuvres of veggies, dip, chips, salsa and cheese and crackers along with the dinner of rice, salad, bread ... and, finally, her famous killer apple pie ...topped with wine and after-dinner brandy was ...read my lips, "Plenty!"

Even if we had wanted to eat the pork chops they had on the grill, it would have been physically impossible.

We headed for the door around midnight. At some point during the evening things got a bit hazy for me. Gary, the kind soul, was ready to drag us, or rather *drive* us back to the dock. During our good byes and thanks-a-lot exchanges, they recited, in unison, "We'll see ya tomorrow. You have to stay one more day!"

I laughed and kinda slurred, "Yep. Tomorrow is another Chardonnay!"

Then I leaned against my husband who, thankfully, was there to catch me, and murmured, "One more day? I don't ever want to leave!"

Day 25

Monday, September 24, 2001

I love being tied to the dock!

What kind of sentence is that? I'm not being kinky, though, like in some florid romance novel. What I mean is, I love the *Guillemot* being tied to the dock. One of the stellar points of our little sojourn here in Margaretsville world (I keep trying to call it *Margaritaville*) is that we have figured out what the tide does in this spot. That means we have something more valuable than … than … *beer?* No. No. More valuable than hot blueberry buckle cake during a torrential downpour? No, not that either—but it's up there.

What we have here is "previous knowledge." The Captain can now read the tide level and know what adjustments will be needed for where we are at this exact spot. He can adjust the leg, the dock lines and, generally, fiddle with whatever needs to be fiddled with. And he can do this without a major production and—most importantly—without little ole' me.

Fantastic!

I can have the pleasure of sitting in the sun, eating my berries and apples, with no concern over alarms and schedules. This is a situation for which I am particularly thankful, after our previous evening's whiffled drunk episode when we almost tipped the boat.

These docks, I discovered last night, were not made for wine drinkers. Once safely on board, I resolved to never eat or drink again. My eating resolution dissolved at 11 A.M. when my queasy stomach screamed for food. On the plus side however, often, when I go on a spree and drink untold quantities of wine, it will put the 'H' in headache. Curiously, I was spared this affliction today.

Up on the dock I can hear Doug talking to who-knows-who, about who-knows-what. I'm tucked down here and have the place all to myself. I could take a nap, read, write, clean (I crossed that one off the list quickly), do my business (you all know, by now, that my body only reacts at the most inopportune moments).

I know ... I'll play day-at-the-spa. If I try giving myself a facial when darling Doug is in residence, he's inclined to view such frivolities with a jaundiced eye. He shakes his head, raises his shoulders and shudders, "If I looked like you, you would wonder what kind of person you were living with!" I am much better off to try and sneak in 15 minutes alone.

I check my spa list, put the goop on my face and neck, lie down, raise my feet, and let the blood flow to my head. I manicure and polish the fingernails and toenails, shave my legs, and end it with the-all-over-the-body-lotion bit.

After I was scrubbed and polished I was ready to meet the world. I climbed the ladder and was greeted by what appeared to be a town meeting. For a coastal village which, three days ago, appeared to be put to bed, there are *tons* of people milling about.

I find my husband, half-hidden in the crowd. He motions me over and points to a fellow next to him. He gives him a few jovial pats on the back, treating him as though he'd just found a long-lost friend. The Captain proceeded to explain.

"Guess where you've seen this fellow before?" he asks.

Before I can venture a quick guess, he pipes up with another one.

"And I bet you can't guess what he does for a living!"

I look at the nice fellow for a long moment. I recall a TV game show of my youth, *What's My Line*. "Nope, sorry," I reply. "No bells are dinging. Spare me the question-and-answer portion of the show and skip to the end."

Bob, as it turns out, is none other than the helicopter pilot we saw several times in the Minas Basin and up the Shube. His job is not to fly over unsuspecting sailboat Captains performing private personal hygiene activities in the cockpit, then file a report to higher authorities. He is paid by a government research group to mark deer and moose with a tag of somesort. Which can be followed by a GPS, which allows scientists to monitor their health, habits, distances traveled, and related activities. So far they have tagged about 500 animals. The moose are netted and tranquilized. The deer are only netted and then tagged.

This GPS thing is something else! The government will soon lodge one (a tag or whatever they will call it) into each and everyone of us at birth (for homeland security reasons, I'm sure), to monitor our habits and activities.

Doug worked for a helicopter company for several years, so I leave them to their helicopter talk.

I strolled over to sit on the stoop of the White Fox's fish shack and gaze at the strange sight of the sturgeon. I read in a book at "my" cottage (aka Jerald's) that the Atlantic Sturgeon is a survivor from millions of years ago. They live to be 125-150 years old (if they don't get caught in a herring net). The Annapolis Royal Sturgeon, which I assume this to be, does not have a skeleton like conventional fish; it is equipped, instead, with heavy plates and a thick hide.

Scattered on the dock were a hodge-podge of characters. I watched them parade by and, when I'm noticed, I offer salutations. What a show of conversation and fun this is! Not a single person has a cell phone plastered to his ear, yapping to "sell, trade or cut the deal." No one carries a brief case or a laptop and there is not one obnoxious car alarm to be heard—demanding attention, but serving no real purpose.

Who, I began to wonder, could the gentleman at the far end of the dock be? He certainly appeared to be a fellow worth a careful inspection. His appearance conjured up a vision usually associated with patterns of wallpaper in a French Hotel. His cow dung cap sat upon a head of white hair which flowed, uninterrupted, to his long white beard. Occasionally this fellow, dressed like a French artist of a hundred years ago, would tap his walking stick and address (which I can't hear) the spitfire of a tiny terrier which is leading him around at the end of a leash.

Then John Fox distracted me from my thoughts. He leaned against the door of the fish shack, placing one leg in front of the other, holding his fishing gear and poised for action. I gave him the lowdown of the past few days. He wagged his head and gave big hearty chuckles.

John called his friend, Scotty, over for a quick introduction. He was courteously friendly but clearly had no time for chit-chat and was quick to move on, fishing gear in hand, in the direction of today's best rock for casting a line. John touched my arm and confided, "Best fisherman to wet a line! He caught 90 yesterday. Feeds his family through the winter!"

Then he straightened up and gathered the rest of his gear. This, apparently, was the signal to Ruckus, a fine figure of a town cat, to lead the way to the end of the dock. I believe I detected a slight reprimand from Ruckus and I heard John chuckling as they walked away, "So, you think I've been wasting valuable fishing time, do ya Ruckus? Postponing your prescheduled lunch hour?"

The group on the dock has grown even larger and I now see Gary Lawson has arrived. Doug, the center of attention, is regaling the crowd with a story, the telling of which required exaggerated gesticulations. He was rewarded with wild cries of laughter from his audience. I sat, arms crossed over my tucked knees. Their laughter was contagious. I giggled, too, I don't need to know what was being said. It does my heart good to see a group of grown men seem so happy. An old school marm wouldn't be able to rub smiles from those faces.

Hey, hey, I thought to myself, as Pat Lawson drove up. I strolled over to her SUV and she gave me a chirpy hello. Why, after last night's food and drink debauchery, does she appear so much perkier than I do?

"Dinner was a triumph!" I announced, "Although I was, in sailor's terms, three-sheets to the wind!" We both laughed. I shrugged my shoulders and waved my hands,

"Wine not! I felt it my duty, in the name of nautical research, to see just how whiffled one could get and still find one's boat and climb back on board." We convulsed once more.

Suddenly she stopped, remembering she had business at hand. "What's happening with you today?" she asked.

I told her she was lookin' at it. I gave her a heads-up on our departure schedule for tomorrow. My attention was drawn behind me, where a voice with a strong French accent called, "Boo Boo! Boo Boo!"

We both giggled and decided that "Boo Boo," pronounced in the manner that only the French can pull off, was surely a perfect title for this little poochie. I asked Pat about the proud owner. Pat couldn't remember his name but confirmed that he was, in fact, an artist. The picturesque French-speaking chap evidently spent 30 years in the Arctic and, subsequently, made a career out of his paintings of the Indians who live there.

"But, more importantly," she said, "would you like to take a run to Guy Frenchy for some shopping? We can pick up some ..."

I didn't hear what she said next, however. My mind was awhirl; my voice quivered with excitement. I assured her I would only be a moment. I tried to appear nonchalant as I made an effort to remember how normal people walk. I carefully lowered myself to my home in the mud. I ran a brush halfway through the tangles in my hair and grabbed my savings.

Climbing rung (in middle English, pronounced *rong*) after rung up the ladder, I was shocked at my adrenaline rush and the strong energy running through my sore legs. I asked myself, "How can climbing these rungs seem so *right?*" My mind reeled and spurted my well-used catch phrase philosophies: *A woman who says money can't buy happiness, doesn't know where to shop. Money cures melancholy. Girls just want to have funds. There is only one more shopping day left till tomorrow. I don't need companionship, I need currency!*

I sprang to the dock like Santa to his sleigh. I was confident of one thing: Doug will not want to go shopping! He believes most department stores and malls produce radioactivity and should be avoided.

Nevertheless, I'm cautious. Care must be my watchword. I waved to him, indicating that I was leaving. I pointed to Pat's car.

His voice thundered, "Where ya goin'?"

In a much too-soft call, I replied, "Shopping."

He looked at me, blankly. Then, with one hand raised hopefully to his ear, he waited for another response. When I didn't repeat myself, he started walking toward me—large strides.

Damn! I was hoping he'd give up and just wave good bye. Now, he's getting too close. I placed my hands over my mouth, funneled them, and shouted "Shopping."

He gave me his exaggerated-skeptical look—the one you might give a rehabilitated drug user about to go for a fix. I ignored this.

"You want to go?" I asked.

He shook his head no. Aahh, what a drag.

I leaped into her SUV and breathlessly ordered. "Put the peddle to the metal and don't stop at the cattle crossings."

Faster than a speeding bullet, we burned rubber out of Margaritaville. With tires screeching and dirt flying we pulled into the unpaved parking lot (which should have tipped me off) of Guy Frenchy. I climbed out of the car and stood beside it, stretching my arm and neck muscles, like a baseball player stepping up to bat. I concentrated on the doors ahead of me when my smile dropped.

"Recycled Clothing? It's a *thrift* store," I whine to myself; not some cute French boutique. I felt forlorn. I stuck my hands in my pockets like a disappointed school kid. My hand instinctively fondled my money.

Then, a sudden realization struck me. I'm really not the shopping professional I use to be, before God took all my money to live with him in heaven!

So… I took the challenge and charged ahead.

Although only a thrift store, merely stepping through the door gave me a soothing feeling. I emitted an audible "AAHH!" as though I'd just climbed into a hot bath. Slowly, but happily, I walked from one bin of clothing to the next, lightly touching certain garments.

My seventh-sense ability—which has long been dormant—now made my eyes flicker and begin to glow like uranium. A voice inside told me, "Now *this* … this is your area of expertise."

I began to case the joint. Many years of proper training helps me see *the one!* It's on the far side of one of the bins which is piled high with clothes.

There! I see the object of my *desire*. But ... there are always buts ... Jack Palance's twin sister is hovering over it. Her hands and eyes are inspecting a tank top which wouldn't fit around her neck, or mine either, for that matter. Printed across the front, in decorative letters, are the words, "Genuine Imported Killer Bees, June 1985."

I plot. I remember I'm in "Kind Canada" where the rules are different. I slip in beside her and smile sweetly. I must divert her attention.

"Surely," I coo, "that tank top will be a collector's item!"

Ha! Ha! Ho! Ho!

My professionally-trained eye, however, ascertains that the long-sleeved, tailored shirt is just *my* size. My shopping strategy, which has always proved successful in the past, is *never* to act excited about something unless I have it firmly clutched in my fist.

It works! Oh, am I good or what?

She steps aside, tank top in hand. Immediately, I transform into a lizard catching a fly—my lightning quick movement snatches it up! The twin never knew what happened. She happily sways her ample hips toward the checkout counter.

I am pleased with myself and the world, I set my course to tack upwind, through the tables, all the while whistling.

Sailing, Sailing, all me life is sailing
Sailing and bailing all me friggen' life—
Sailing and bailing and pukin' over the railing ...

I eased into the dock and then, dramatically, shut the dressing room door behind me. I turned around, triumphantly clutching my prize.

At this precise moment, I almost did puke.

"Oohh, yuck, yuck, yuck!" and with one final "Yuck!" I groaned and slapped my hand up against the side of my head. Here I am in all my glory, face to face with ... *a full-length mirror*. If I could have reached the naked bright light bulb above me, I would have knocked it out with my bare hands. Earlier in this trip, I silently moaned over not being able to style my hair and apply a modicum of makeup while holding my four-and-one-half-inch mirror. Next year, I had promised myself, I'd have a big mirror.

Yep. *This* is the first full-length mirror in a month. And the problem isn't just one thing—it is the whole ghastly picture. The fashion police are at my door and they have a warrant. My once-white shoes, as you must know by now, are "Shooby Taylor" brown— old and grungy-looking. The rest of my ensemble consisted of well-used attire, all prior thrift-store purchases. The Liz Wear stretch blue jeans serve me well my in the acrobatics of getting on and off the boat, rollin' around on oily docks, etc. But whoever originally purchased them (about 20 years ago) certainly never expected to still be wearing them—with the knees and butt now white from wear and permanently accented with poufs where the elastic went bye-bye.

I know the retro look is in, but somehow I missed the mark. My body shape is currently unpopular. These jeans aren't fashionable enough to look this bad. I might as well be wearing stirrup pants. The royal blue t-shirt (which I thought brought out the blue in my eyes) does match the line of royal blue in the cotton over-shirt. Having no choice, I study myself. The only place that isn't wrinkled is where the t-shirt stretches across my boobs.

And my hair ... oh, my hair. I had tried to show the mop who was boss, but now it simply stands up for it's right to do what it wants. Some women look good in a natural state of dishevelment. I say again, *some*.

Why else would Calvin Kline say, *"The best thing is to look natural, but it takes a lot of makeup to look natural."*

No joke. I've been in complete denial. *This* is not a pretty picture. Right now, I don't look anywhere near what someone in her right mind would ever want to look like. My fashion sense is outraged!

It was destiny that did this to me—but destiny knows nothing of fair play. I have hitched myself up with a man ten years younger. This man sets trends with his unshaven-Bohemian look, his frayed jeans and rope belt. Everyone thinks, "Isn't he just the livin' end?" How cute he looks in his stained t-shirts and shorts with boat paint

smeared all over them. He is proudly allergic to neckties and suits.
When it comes to clothing, he's so thrifty he makes a penny holler.

But, it is not me! Compounding the long odds that, even 20
years ago, I might have been able to pull off *Bedraggled Chic,* now
I'm *50* for heaven's sake! Today, especially, I'm feeling the distinct
need to *apologize* for that! I don't look like an eco-tourist—I look
like an eco-terrorist!

Those who know Eileen best, will tell you—BD or AD—that I
need the sophisticated look or, minimally, an expensive, well-cared-
for line of outfitter wear to be given the respect I deserve—or, should
I say, I need. I've crossed a threshold in my life all right. I use to
think only love could break a heart—then I discovered it was trying
on a swimsuit. Now I know that all it takes is a full length mirror.
I've gone from best-dressed to most-stressed.

I take a deep breath. I dig my nails in my palms. Give it up
Eileen. You're a woman who needs a yacht club. You need to be
wearing polo shirts in pretty nautical colors, white shoes that aren't
stained, and a sweater tied loosely over your shoulders. You should
be joining the other yachtsmen and yachtswomen, playing cards
around a fireplace, sipping tea.

This isn't a dressing room it's a depressing room. I have to calm
myself, before I go into cardiac arrest. I need my *Heal Your Body
From A to Z* book. Where is it when I need it? At home, in Eastport,
on the shelf. It would probably suggest new thought patterns like
...let me think ... *I am at peace everywhere and I have the power and
strength to handle everything in my life.*

I have no book and I'm not at peace with these clothes. As God
is my witness, (with a clutched fist over my heart and chin lifted to
the bright bulb) next year, fiscally crippled or not, I will have a new
wardrobe for our cruise!

I grab the Talbots shirt which, only five minutes ago, was *the
one!* I tear off my old flannel one and don the symbol of my new
life—fresh, bright, colorful, *clean,* and only slightly wrinkled. The
bold vertical stripes of bright royal blue, deep red, mustard yellow,
emerald green, aqua and white gave me a slight headache. If it were
any brighter in here, with these stripes and the bare bulb, I'd need
sun screen.

I take one last look. Maybe, if I have the confidence of Ms. Piggy, I'll survive in this Barbie Doll world. I screw up my courage and walk out the door. None too soon, I should add, for the mirror was at the point of cracking.

I headed straight for the checkout counter, without ever looking back. The caption of this picture would read, "She made yet another *wise* shopping decision." The blouse is not quite like the $300 Max Mara blouse I once purchased in a sweet boutique in Perugia—my money is much more expensive now. So, for $3 (three dollars Canadian at that), it will go a long way toward overcoming my era of the great depression.

My new friend was already outdoors. At the sight of me she slips on her chic Toronto sunglasses. Flashing her perfect white teeth in a piano-key smile, she exclaims, "Wow! That's bright!"

We both almost split a gut as we show off our purchases. I threw my plastic bag, stuffed with my old shirt, in the back seat and brushed off my palms in a gesture of "job well done." As we sped out of the gravel parking lot, I gave Pat a blow-by-blow description of the close call I had in the depressing room.

Suddenly, at that opportune moment, I remembered one of the positive thought patterns from my *A to Z* book. I tried it out on Pat.

I am at the center of life and I approve of myself and all I see.
I am perfectly happy to be me.
I have the strength and knowledge to handle everything in life!

She eyed me keenly over the top of her sunglasses. In response, she calmly says, "Riiiight! So ... next stop is the liquor store?"

We continued to buzz around the countryside, laughing and gossiping. As it turns out, she and Gary have big plans for some privacy (I'd go for that). They just purchased a house with 50 acres in the country. Their little cottage in Margaretsville is only about 15 minutes away, so it will serve for a summer guesthouse.

We stopped for a tour of the new house which is, actually, in great condition but in need of some redecorating. Pat wants my expert opinion? Can you beat that! I try not to drool over her large, beautiful kitchen and three normal bathrooms. We were in one of those baths, discussing tile and wallpaper, when I looked in the mirror. I'm immediately struck by what a trusting soul she is to ask advice of someone that looks like me.

Back at the dock, I jumped out of the SUV and waved my goodbyes. I tell her, "Check-ya latter." I turned and there was Doug. Naturally, I do a little spin-around, to show off.

"This," I explain, "is my new ecotourist wear!"

He assumes something of a dazed look and then pretends to not recognize me.

"Niiice!" he says, with that air of smart-aleck'em which is so unbecoming.

I shot him a steamy glance.

"And here I thought." he continued, "that you'd gone and gotten yourself a job with the flag crew."

"Huh! Huh!" Yes. I did. I said *huh, huh.*

"Well," I snorted, "don't you have a way of turning blue skies to gray!" Then I smiled that plastered smile I've worked so hard to perfect and turned toward my refuge I call home.

"Hey, where you goin'?"

I confronted his beaming visage which immediately blossomed into a full blown crack-up.

"I'm abused," I said, stating the obvious. "I'm going to find a telephone and call a hot line."

How *could* he? How could he be so utterly bereft of any fundamental decency? I'd give him a piece of my mind, if I had any to spare. The tediousness of his little joke has sloshed out what few drops of dignity I had left in my cup. I've been caught all day in my over-emotional platitudes.

What does he know of the *trauma* I've just been through? He's some sorta handsome Farley Mowat. Our friend, MacNaughton, has shaken his head in bafflement many times when dealing with the Captain and once summed up his character thusly, "He's a man who requires no dignity."

I head down the ladder, counting—one rung, two rungs, three rungs. There are 22 rungs. Counting to ten might have done it, but it never hurts to have a few in storage (to be put to good use on some other day when I'm pushed to the limit). My resolve never to drink again dissolves immediately. Consequently, for medicinal purposes (I'm suffering from a bad case of being easily humiliated), I tell the only friend I have in the whole wide world—my imaginary bartender—to hand me a cocktail and stand back!

I reached a pleasurable level of zonin', alone in the cockpit. The "zone" is a state of mind where you don't think—you just *do*. I spent a long while doing nothing and I was glad to have gotten that out of my system. Then I had a conference with the nucleus of neutrons still in charge of my brain. We decided that a walk might be a more healthful way of blowing off some steam. Swelled knee or no swelled knee, I needed some exercise.

I reached the top of the ladder and I surveyed the dock side. Good. The Captain is a safe distance away, amusing himself and others—playing, singing, and fishing with the pros. It's hard to be incognito when you are part of the flag crew, but I manage to slip off unseen.

I headed up the coastline toward Gary and Pat's cottage. Pat graciously offered up their yard and garden bench for my outdoor pleasure. She advised they would be off shopping all afternoon for the new house.

I walked vigorously, the warm sun shown brightly on the bold stripes of my Talbots shirt. By the time I flopped myself down on the garden bench, I had worked up a proper sweat.

From the bench I looked in the direction of the dock and saw an apron stage of rocks and fisherman silhouetted in the afternoon sun.

Surveying the beach below, from high atop the ledge, I am reminded that the tide giveth and the tide taketh away. Last night Gary voiced his concern over the eroding cliffs behind their house. This shoreline has been created over thousands and thousands of years but, just in the last 10 years, Gary has seen 20 feet of his land washed away. He's placed signs asking others not to climb or explore on his bluffs but, alas, unless you see it day to day, year to year, you don't understand how just a few people climbing around only makes the problem a lot worse.

All around Eastport we have strong tides, but the shoreline is rockbound and has a very different rate of erosion. Rockbound shores can vary a tremendous amount as well, however. There's one beach where we often sail in the Cobscook Bay. There, the rocks which line the shore, chip away daily. You can touch the massive rocks and they crumble into shards which now cover the entire beach. As the 18-25 feet of tides come and go, the shards make beautiful designs in an ever-changing work of art.

There are all types of erosion in this Universe. Wind erosion has been discovered on Mars. The Martian winds are very fast but, because the Martian atmosphere is so thin, a person standing on Mars would not get blown over.

I listened to the *bzt bzt bzt* of the birds soaring above me. I glanced up from my writing to see a notched tail before it went plunging over the side of the cliff. I wait and soon several others are following suit. The little bank swallows are stopping in Margaretsville, just as we are, for a fall visit. These little guys likely have flown all the way from Labrador en route to South America. I laid my head back on the bench, my face to the sun. I could very easily take a little nap. I ponder the past few days. This sleepy little hamlet of Margaretsville turned into one of those places with nothing to do and not enough time in which to do it.

Back on board, I elevated my leg. While basking in the last of the afternoon warmth, Doug returned and appeared to be quite moved by his fishing experience. His guitar slung over his shoulder, his face reflected deep satisfaction.

"Must have been a great day fishing? I saw quite a few being reeled in," I comment.

Jubilant, he flashed an elated grin. "Oh I caught a couple. They caught a bunch. But it isn't the fish I'm after. It's the fishing! I loved being out there with those guys. I shared in their quality of life and listened to their easy, funny conversations. They're so unconcerned with the rest of the world. It makes me realize, even more, that I don't want to be out "there ..."

At this, he swept his arm in a gesture indicating a world far away from here.

"... rushing around, more intent on producing results than enjoying the experience of being alive at this moment."

I rested my back against the cushion and put another pillow

under my leg. I listened, absorbed in his easy-going enthusiasm and the tranquility of the afternoon. A slow smile of utter contentment spread over his face.

"That Ruckus has a sweet deal goin' for himself.!" he explains, "He lounges lazily on a rock close by John's bucket. He snoozes away, as though he'd just had lunch. Then the White Fox catches one! Ruckuses' keen ears and nose start to twitch. In nothing flat, he suddenly takes great interest in John and his bucket. John tells me, without turning his head from the water, that he revels in the game and holds out for the fun of the chase. Ruckus will wait for the just right moment, when John's back is turned. Then he reaches into the bucket and slips one out. The White Fox is Mr. Softy so, before long, he gives in. Since Ruckus has minded his manners, he dangles his tasty treat. Ruckus snatches it and chomps in down, tail first.

A few minutes later, I turned to check on the Mr. Well-Fed but he has resumed his pose of nirvana."

He whistles, "It's been quite a day!"

My husband pulls me close for a real squeezie-type hug and then places a kiss a top my head. Suddenly, as if an alarm had gone off on the depth sounder, he gave a startled jerk. "I just remembered, my catch of the day isn't getting any fresher!"

My personal fisherman began to prepare dinner. Myself? I'm allowed the pleasure of a few quiet minutes just to drop my line in the deep water of the present. "Doing" is fine just as long as it is balanced with taking time to *be*.

"Hey, we're invited up to John Gilley's house tonight!"

I searched my mental list of *who's who* here in Margaritaville. "I don't remember that name." I tell my chef.

"Remember the canoe builder up the hill? I told you that I heard about him?" he said, helpfully.

Now why would *I* want to remember there was a boat builder up the road?

"Well," continued the Captain, "he and his wife have been gone all weekend. They just got home Sunday night."

The bits and pieces of the story which Doug provided during dinner preparation went something like this.

Bright and early this morning, John Gilley, the canoe builder, was blurry-eyed from a late night and long trip. He was trying to get his coffee going and looked out his kitchen window where the shock of seeing a very strange sight almost cost him his coffee pot. There, of course, was the *Guillemot,* sitting on our leg, tied to the dock. So today, during fishing hours, he came down to the dock for the town meeting. Doug played a few tunes and, like most boat fanatics/musicians, they quickly became friends.

Doug, who'd already heard of his canoe-building shop and his unique designs, was happy to meet him. "He invited us up to see his shop. He told me to bring my guitar because they're having band practice tonight!"

I felt generally let down in the knowledge that this was to be my last shower and sunset at "Jerald's" cottage. Doug has no interest in plotting against such a fine fellow as Jerald—no interest in forcing him to sell or sign over the property. I still say we are letting the opportunity of a lifetime slip through our fingers. We left a note of thanks and a standing welcome in Eastport. As I walked away, the woman inside me was fighting the urge to scream and kick.

Down the hill we went in search of Gilley's Canoe shop. The band was there tuning their instruments. I knew, within 15 minutes, that I was firmly pinned as a victim of music-world. Tuning, tuning, and more tuning. The group's friendship goes so far back, they go in reverse.

The drummer, Thore, is slam dunking and ready to roll. Rich sits at attention behind the keyboard, waiting to set the world on fire. John plays the horn and to the left is Roger, with an acoustic guitar.

John's wife came downstairs for a quick hello; then disappeared, not to return again. I figured she had something better to do than talk to me. I glared at my reflection in the glass bookcase … it could have something to do with this striped shirt. She doesn't know that I'm reflecting my own personal style. She probably thought I was here to sell popcorn and peanuts.

We are in the ground level of John Gilley's home. It looks to be an old shop for a book store, pharmacy or gifts of some sort. The entire length of one side of the house holds a massive bookcase filled with all the miscellanea one might collect: books, artwork, music and artifacts of many varieties. I focus my attention on this collection so the gang won't notice that, for me, I'm always on the outskirts of the music. It's not easy to have a good time by yourself when you're me, especially me without my glasses. I should just start introducing myself as Mrs. Weakling-No-Talent. I can't even carry a tune in a bucket with a lid on it. Besides, my bucket with a lid is reserved for other purposes these days.

On the other hand, it doesn't matter much to me this evening. I am really tired. With the relentless pace of life around here, I feel the distinct urge to curl up in comfy repose to read and write. As a rule, I would have tried to stay and unite our two societies in some interconnected cosmic way. Tonight, however, I really don't give a hill of beans. Just give it up, Eileen, I say to myself. So I tell my husband to stay and play music till the cows come home; I'm heading down to the boat.

Now, if this were a fictional story, I would embellish the narrative at this point. I'd relate how they cried for me to stay and entertain them, whereupon I explained, dramatically (and theatrically), that it defies the will of God for me to sing or play an instrument. I have tried, God knows—all those years in elementary and middle school. I played the clarinet. I sang in the school choir. Those were the days when you couldn't kick a sweet little girl out, especially when she was trying so hard. Later in life, I decided that if I ever "play" another instrument, it will be the timpani—so big and round. So powerful that I could just stand there and every once in a while the conductor would look my way and I'd give the world some very impressive *Boom, Boom, Booms*. As for my singing, it still deadens the will to live for those within earshot.

We all know why they say hindsight is 20-20. So let's just say, in retrospect, that I should have stayed. I should have found some way to entertain myself—tap danced on the table, tried transcendental meditation or just curled up like a vagrant, snoring just outside their front door. But *que sera sera!* I said "Good night everyone!" and Doug shut the door behind us.

"I'll walk you back and tuck you in. It's a little chilly and you may want a fire in the woodstove," he said.

Doug can make a fire out of salt, water and sand so I let him do
the honors. I *can* get it started but it takes too long and I probably
would have needed pages from my journal to get it going. Truthfully, it wasn't that cold, but when you're alone on a boat, it's cozier
to have it warm. I hung my towel up, as I normally did, next to the
stove; it was still very wet from my shower at Jerald's. The Captain
gave me a goodnight kiss, checked the stove, the dock lines and the
leg. It was close to 10 P.M. when Doug left to tromp back up the
hill to musicland at John's.

We planned an early morning departure at the top of the tide.
Just the thought of this made me even more tired. I tried to stay
awake and enjoy the fire, to read and write, but it was "Good night
Margaritaville." I felt as though I could sleep like the dead.

Perhaps that simile is slightly too apt for this occasion. What
awakened me, about 45 minutes later, I'll never know for sure. Do
I believe in a grand prearrangement of events? Yes indeed, when it
suits me. Was I roused because of the chance that I finally discovered and submitted to the authority of my true center where God
makes his presence and purpose for me known? Well, I have no
other explanation but that the boss—God himself—awakened me.

Here's what happened that night.

* * *

My eyes are doing their best to open … I can't think. I don't
know what is wrong, but I hope to find out soon. Where am I? It
occurs to me, suddenly, that I am gasping for air. Breathe, Eileen, I
command. This is something you know how to do without a set of
instructions! But somehow I cannot. All I can do is cough, choke,
and then follow up with some heartfelt gasping. I try to lift my head
but … it feels so heavy. It's as though it's cemented to the pillow.
Everything in view is a stinging fog. Finally … logic prevails. I deduce that fresh air would be good … but where? And how? I keep
my eyes closed because of the stinging. I try to visualize where this
nightmare is happening … I'm on a boat … the V-berth … the
front hatch! Groping and flailing, I use my arms to prop my head
up and off the pillow. Painfully, I'm able to push the front hatch
open—only to have it slam shut again. With my second try, I use
my weakened body as a lever and throw open the hatch with enough

force to make it to stay. The cold clean air is an immediate panacea for my coughing and choking. However, I realize that I'm now gasping out of a hole that is flooding oxygen back into the smoke-filled boat.

Quickly, I deduce that a gust of wind from under the companionway flap (you know—the infamous vinyl flap?) which covers the screen door, must have caught the towel and billowed it over to the stovepipe. The stovepipe, heating at its prime, must have made the wet towel smolder—hence all the smoke (and stinging fog). Now, the few seconds of fresh air from the hatch are enough to cause the towel to burst into flames. These flames are now darting a foot from my pillow. I take a big lung full of fresh air and bolt out of bed past the flaming towel. Blinded by the night and the smoke, I grope about for a knife in the galley. I turn back to the flames and unclip the towel. Now, on the end of the five-and-a-half-inch blade of the four-and-and-half-inch handle of my knife, I carry the burning towel.

However, obstacles stood between my burning towel and the out-of-doors. I must dodge the eating table, the quarter berth cushions, the vinyl cockpit cushions (which line the floor), the zipped-shut canvas screen door *and* the canvas-flap vinyl door. I made it through in a lot less time than it takes to describe.

The fresh air, that once again permitted me to breathe, again fed the flames to new heights. I hurled the towel with all my strength—my chief goal in life, at that particular moment, was to get the burning towel as far away as I could from the boat, the dock and me. A partial accomplishment was my reward. Half the blazing towel however, fell from the knife to the cockpit floor. I jabbed and flipped the fallen half from the cockpit in order to get the remainder of the towel to join its predecessor. I stood there, panting an asthmatic wheeze, staring at the fragments of towel burning in the mud.

Finally. I began to suck hard for fresh clean air. I counted to ten, because my thyroid, pituitary and adrenal glands had began to pump like three diesels. Still breathing deep, I look around and then down at myself. Luckily, when I sleep on the boat, especially at a dock, I normally don't dress nude. Not really having time to throw on my bathrobe and slippers (even if I had them aboard) I am standing here in nothing but my bra and scanties. I'll bet I look really hot in this outfit!

After some considerable shivers and shakes, I go back in the cabin to make sure everything smoldering had ended up in the mud. I grab a jacket and burst back through the door.

"EE Yuck! Pewuuee, holy dyin'!" I've had more than my dose of charcoal air. I lower my tush onto the cold damp cockpit to calm myself. Woo WEE! There is a blessing for survivors of roller coaster rides and smoke inhalation … you're alive! I thanked all the eternal sources for that! Why take any chances when the appeasement of the heavenly powers is concerned?

I try hard to compose myself, but every nerve in my body has been wrenched from its moorings and tied in knots. I wonder how a Zen Buddhist would handle this close of a glimpse of the hereafter? I tried my bellow breath from yoga. I tried the 'Om' thing. I couldn't concentrate—is it *ah/mmm/silence* or *oh/ah/mmm/silence*? The only Buddhist thing I can come up with, is a joke,

How did the Zen Buddhist order his hot dog from the street vendor?

"Make me one with everything."

Alternating between laughing helplessly, wanting to scream, and whipping the tears from my eyes, I suddenly realized that I could have burned Doug's pride and joy—the *Guillemot*—right down to its bare strip-plank underwear. Indeed, *that* might have been a fate worse than death. I curled my legs up inside Doug's large down jacket. I felt a strong wind of happiness blow around me—maybe it was just the "being alive" part.

Waiting outside while the cabin cleared of smoke, my brain starts to work again. One certainty looms large—I was not prepared for this. Where are the fire extinguishers? We have two, but for the life of me I couldn't say for sure where. Life jackets? What if I had needed to abandon ship? Should I have grabbed one? They were stuffed in the front of the quarter-berth. Ahh, but no water! What if I had to climb onto the dock? What if … what if … the dock had started on fire? Dear God, what a mess all this could have been. The dreariness of it chilled my spirits. I felt as though I needed some sedation.

Peering up into the vast blackness of the late September skies, I see the Great Square of Pegasus with its Andromeda trail. In the distance of the quiet evening, I hear the call—*oo-ah-hoo, oo-ah-hoo* (middle note higher)—of a loon. I sometimes think this nighttime call sounds like more of a mournful yodel. Tonight it resembles a wild maniacal laugh, almost as though the caller had watched the recent episode unravel.

The urge did pass, thankfully, to race up the hill and find my Captain—to fall into his arms, blubbering. I waited. I was still in the dry-mouth, heart-pounding state, but I gave my soul over to patience and meditation.

It was more than 45 minutes before I detected voices. One of them was Captain Doug. I raced back to the V-berth in hopes of impersonating a sleeping saint.

Down the ladder they climbed! Oh great—of all the times for some young boat fanatics to come on board. I can tell they're excited to come down and see the ole' girl (the *Guillemot,* that is).

I lie quietly, listening. Their voices all have that ring of impassioned boat connoisseurs.

I keep waiting for one of them to sniff and ask if we had char-grilled boat for supper. Doug is being "quite the Captain" (maritime for entertaining). He stepped inside for a few beers stowed aft in the cockpit bilge. This was followed by a few *pop-pop. fizz-fizzes* and the skipper announces, "And on the 8th day God created beer!"

Finally, one by one, I hear his company depart. I've eavesdropped enough to know they have to work early in the morning, so off they went to their respective villages.

I crawled out of my hidey hole and cautiously came face to face with my husband. Doug, who was sitting in the cockpit sipping the last of his beer, looked up at me. I tried to speak but felt as though my mouth was shot full of Novocaine.

"Something's the matter ... what's wrong? I can spot that look a mile off on a foggy day," he said.

Abruptly, my eyes overflowed with tears. He hugged me tight. I needed to stop shaking long enough to give him an explanation. I told him the story in between sniff sniffs and nose blowing. Slowing, he rocked his head from side to side. He took a long breath and let it out slowly through his nose. Together we made a closer examination. Turns out that we two ole' gals have weathered the near-disaster pretty well.

Later, we lay in the V-berth looking up through the open hatch watching the flicker of creatures flying between the light from the pier and our boat. Every breath I inhale carries the stale aroma of the blackened towel. I wondered silently, if I will ever again sleep in our boat with a light heart? I clutched my husband's arm so tightly that he finally admitted he could no longer move his fingers.

"My poor little sweetie was almost distinguished," he murmured.

"It's extinguished," I corrected, absently.

He always gets those two words mixed up.

He pulled me close, rubbed my tense shoulders, gave me three tight squeezes and then tousled my hair.

"You're just my little Pooh Bear!"

How sweet! After all these years, he still thinks I'm cute, sweet and fuzzy. The frightful night has brought back old affections. I cooed a little, snuggled closer, then whispered, "Ahh, you're little Pooh Bear?"

"Yeah . . .you seem to be always dealin' with a half-a-honey pot."

Day 26

Tuesday September 25, 2001

The skies are overcast, threatening rain, and there is not a breath of wind. Still, at 7:30 A.M. we let loose the dock lines and start motoring out to take the going tide. Perhaps we were acting on a broad general principle—we'd been here long enough. It was now time to go.

Tacked to the door of The White Fox's fish shack is a note for all of Margaretsville. In it we shared our heartfelt thanks for their warm hospitality. As we rounded the end of the dock we looked up to see John Gilley, coffee cup in hand. We waved our last hearty boat-wave at him and soon John, and the little village, disappeared in the distance.

Our schedule was to spend one more night here in Nova Scotia. Then we'll make our big crossing over to New Brunswick, tucking into Dipper Harbour. This is all very, very, tentative. Any respectable sailor who sets upon such a distance should have a fair wind and the prospect of potentially agreeable weather.

Tonight, however, is as far as I can look. We have a few options as we head down the coast toward Digby. The Captain and I agree that anywhere is preferable to Tain'tville. Tain'tville is that lonely, rough, unprotected and in-full-current anchorage where we *never* want to spend the night. Tain'tville is not Margaretsville … and it tain't Port George, tain't Port Lorne, tain't St. Croix Cove, tain't Hampton, tain't Phinney's Cove, tain't Youngs Cove or Parkers Cove.

We do seem to have the knack of serendipitous sailing. One never knows what discoveries may cross one's path. Few people travel these days by taking time to really gain a local experience and an intimacy with a place. Initially, some places often appear unremarkable and anonymous. I never would have thought last Friday evening, when we pulled into Margaretsville, that I would never want to leave. Or that I might die there or would almost burn down the dock!

This morning I forced myself out of bed and I took my emotional temperature. I thought of my life—the drama, the comedy and the tragedy of it all. Aside from feeling wretched, as though I'd smoked a pack of cigarettes, I was excited about life, and what other twists and turns lay ahead. I remembered the words of Joseph Campbell, "*Whatever your fate is, whatever the hell happens, you say to yourself, this is what I need—any disaster you can survive acts as an improvement in your character and your stature.*"

After brushing my teeth, I checked my four-and-one-half-inch image. I couldn't tell if my character or stature was improved, but I did tell myself, Lord only knows why, that was what I needed!

All travel changes a person. Why, just look at me after only 30 days! I give a nod to Mark Twain, one of the greatest philosophers of all time. At the conclusion of his travel book, *Innocents Abroad* (1869), Twain wrote, "*Travel is fatal to prejudice, bigotry, and narrow-mindedness and many of our people need it sorely on these accounts. Broad, wholesome, charitable views of men and things cannot be acquired by vegetating in one little corner of the earth all one's lifetime.*"

Some travel is merely a trip, just chalking up trophy visits. This has been a journey. I am a woman who has skipped along a well-worn path down the road of normal tourism. Now, I have been led astray, finding my way on a less-traveled route.

We all know this trip has not exactly been convenient at times. But I cannot deny the effect that the experiences have had on me. Contrasts in travel, as well as life, are good for us. Or, perhaps, contrasts are what travelers need. Contrasts provide a way of grasping lives which are different from our own.

Some people don't travel because they don't like airplanes and airports; after 9/11, lots of people feel this way. For myself, I'll ignore what happened. I love to travel, I always have. In fact, a major difference concerning my attitude about flying comes directly from this trip. The next time I jump on a plane, I won't be stressed trying to find my pillow and getting my magazines and movie in order. I'll be patient and smile while waiting for my drinks and dinner (or a reasonable facsimile). I'll admire the variety of ways the flight attendant can say, "Baked pasta or beef tips?"

When it's my turn and I say, "Baked pasta, please!"

When she replies, "Oops, I just served the last one," I'll continue to smile. She'll offer comfort, in her sweet southern drawl, "How about some peanuts?" I'll keep smiling. I'll rationalize that peanuts and crackers are the only identifiable food products offered on this flight anyway. Then I'll just pull out my apple or banana I always carry when flying (since the trip when the flight attendants burned all the meals).

So what—I'll say to myself—shit happens!

Everyone should be able to endure something distasteful or uncomfortable for 2 to 36 hours or how else would babies be born? I will not moan and groan when the fellow in front of me reclines his seat so far that it lodges my dinner tray into my boobs. I'll remain calm when the 250 pound salesman next to me (sitting in my requested aisle seat), is snoring and I have to pee. When the baby behind me hasn't stopped crying since takeoff, there'll be no problemo! What does it matter?

Soon, I mean very soon in the big scope of things—say, only 4 hours and 15 minutes—I'll be able to stand, stretch my legs, drag my too-heavy-carry-on off that plane and I can head straight for the nearest bar. All this now seems like a piece of cake, a walk in the park, an absolute no-brainer when compared to the last 26 days, sailing this dinky cruise ship in 54 feet of tides.

The next time you're standing on the sixth floor of a hotel and look down to the ground, remember that the tide changes here that amount every 6 hours. Think of my *galley*, when you rent that condo in Florida and there's no dishwasher—of all the injustices in life! Remember me, when you are in Europe and there is hardly ever ice in your glass. Keep in mind my travels on the Shube when you step out of your taxi into a mud puddle.

I'm gonna share with you what I have learned from this journey. The secret ingredient needed for all travel —set down your wine glass, mute your TV and listen. *LIGHTEN UP!* Enjoy the moment. Don't take yourself so seriously. Look at me. I can't become disconsolate over almost exfoliating (I mean asphyxiating) myself or my gin-grin won't last till the next liquor store.

Today's sail is a version of the tide glide. Most of the morning we just drifted along. It's most enjoyable, while contemplating the mystery of the winds' disappearance, I was able to fix cinnamon toast and slice cantaloupe *while under sail.* Moans of delight resound over the water from the Captain. We savor the flavors and memories of our bounty from the Annapolis Valley tour.

Suddenly, Mr. Wind rejoins us with big shove, redistributing half my breakfast all over the cockpit sole.

The tide changes and the wind decides to be our friend. By late afternoon, the GPS tells us that what we see ahead is Parker's Cove. We stare at the shore, check the binoculars, and check the chart. According to the cruising guide, this doesn't fit the description of Parker's Cove. It appears that this cove has had a recent face-lift. The Captain and his ever-ready first mate have a little conference. We decide to drop anchor, get the sails down, and then motor in.

The wind is against the tide, so out here, we're waving around like a frantic flag. I jump up on the cockpit seat to go forward to drop anchor. The skipper feels we are going to *jibe* (that's the thing that happens when the boom goes *Wham!* and pivots, abruptly, from one side of the boat to the other. If you happen to be in its path, the boom will wack you up the side of the head and drop you into the drink).

I am built, however, just right in some ways (makes you laugh doesn't it?). Oddly enough, here on the boat, it's true. I can stand straight up inside the cabin with the pop-top down or in the cockpit without the boom hitting me. Nonetheless, the sudden change in my elevation due to moving forward, puts me in the line of danger.

The Captain yells the standard warning, "JIBE!"

Whew! I managed to squat ever so quickly to duck the boom. Luckily, I was also able to position my knee so that everything cooperated in the movement. I bounced back up, unscathed, and moved on once more, heading for anchor duty.

Wind change! I'm on the move now and we're about to jibe again. Doug, being the quick, efficient Captain that he is, realizes this, but doesn't have time for warnings. So he simply pushes me down, squashing me as though I were a bag of trash he was trying to reduce by half. What strength this man has!

While this was much preferable to being hit by the boom, my knee wasn't ready for this maneuver and he slammed all my weight down on my bent knee.

Eeeyyyaaaiiiaaahhhooo!

Did I let out an eye-popping yelp? I'm surprised they didn't hear my scream in New Brunswick. Curse it! Waves of pain shot through my knee without mercy.

The irony of it all was that my knee had almost healed.

The poor, sympathetic Captain attended to the dropping of the anchor. I went soggy with relief. I lounged back, propping my leg up.

After about three-and-a-half months, The pain eventually subsided.

Once inside the harbour, we see that this is an all new breakwater. This is somethin' else. It's big enough, for two lanes of traffic to make a full loop—and loop they did! It was like Saturday night on the cruise strip.

As we were tying our lines to the dock, the first of our mingle-mangle-well-wishing-forewarners peered down on us.

His look is one you'd give to the unfortunate. "How's she goin'?" he asks.

Doug gives him the happy-to-be-here smile. "Really good," he beams. "How's it goin' with you?"

The fellow frowns. He unrolls and rerolls his shirt sleeves. "You know, it grounds out here!"

"Yeah," replies the Captain, "we thought it might."

Now the fellow places one hand behind his head, pushes his cap forward and scratches his hair line. Finally, he added, "Not much *wind* earlier today." He removed his cap and reseated it firmly.

"No," Doug concurred, "but we had enough. Say, nice harbour!"

The guy brightened considerably. "Brand *new* this year. Big storm last year! So, how much water do you draw?"

The Captain tells him and continues to put the boat to bed.

The feller's mouth twitches a bit. Then, in a tone that hopes for, but doesn't really expect, a negative answer, he inquires, casually, "Do you have a keel?"

Dumbly, we nod.

He slides his hands into his back pockets, thinks of more things to talk about—everything from weather to politics. Suddenly he stops in mid-sentence, thrums his fingers on his thighs, and says, tentatively, "Maybe you ought to move?"

Doug breaks down and tells him the secret—we have "legs." Then he gives a brief description of how we use them.

Pursing his lips, he ponders this ridiculous plan, then says, "Awful, awful bad place to lay over here."

Doug assures him we have done this before and does a show-tell with the legs.

At this, the kind soul tries to back his head off his shoulders. Worriedly, he rubs his face of weathered skin (resembling the cover of a Bible).

The Captain attempts to change the topic, asking about *his* boat.

"Yes sirree! Brand new! She's the cream o'tarter! (anything new and beautiful). There's a guest house up the road if you need it."

Doug again reassures him that we aren't operating under misplaced optimism. He wants the nice guy to be able to sleep tonight, so he describes our trip up the Minas Basin and shows him, once again, how our legs work.

I guess if you can't convince 'em, then confuse them.

The poor fisherman shook his head and with a blank nod

abruptly said, "Good evening!" He walked away, slowly shaking his head, probably more confused than convinced.

Next!

Another fisherman (a formidable-looking fellow played by a Lee Marvin type) stopped his truck nearby. He gets out, puts his boot up on the curb and calls over to us, "How ya drive'ner?"

We repeat much of our previous conversation.

He straightens up. In an authoritative voice, he informed us, "Tide goes *out* here."

Doug offered more of his standard explanations but Lee now looked as though he smelled something considerably worse than wet wool.

Dramatically, he strutted over and leaned against his brand-new truck, as if to brace himself for this revelatory delivery.

"But the truth of the matter is—the water *leaves* the harbour …"

Doug smiles patiently and delivers a well-rehearsed version of our last 26 days.

Lee turned to examine the cargo area of his truck and then to the back window of his king cab. Concluding that he didn't have his megaphone with him, he cupped his hands over his mouth. In a deep rich vibrant voice, (if a volcano had a voice, it would sound like this), he shouted, loudly and slowly, as if we had a language barrier, "The T-I-D-E GOOOES OO-UU-TT!" There was a heavy emphasis on the "T." He gestured with an exaggerated *swoop* of his arm, emphasizing that he meant *all of it* … all of it went *out*—that'a way!

He stood there—mouth hanging open like that of a just-landed trout.

I turned my back, stifling a giggle.

Doug cupped his hands over his mouth, eyes shining with amusement, and called back in a clear, penetrating voice.

"Yeeesssss! But we have L-E-G-S!"

Lee Marvin harrumphed indignantly, shrugged, walked to the door of his big red truck (with an impressive selection of bugs smeared across the front bumper), and left us flat.

The Captain held court as the procession continued.

His performance went well. His audience was throughly entertained. He reported times and dates of our trip while I stood nearby
like a stage prompter, correcting him.

No, that was 7 days ago … 35 miles … 20 hours … I believe
that was Five Islands … but it only took 5 days … etc.

Finally, at the height of one story, his hands raised and attention
riveted on the Captain, I cut in. "No, that was in the *Shubenacadie*
…"

Calmly, but firmly, out of the corner of his mouth, he hisses,
"Don't let the *facts* get in the way of a good *story*. I let you have your
reality—why can't you let me have mine?"

Well … if *that's* the way he wants it!

I was sure my face matched the marinara sauce I'd been cooking. My pencil was poised like a school teacher. I want to *tell* him
that … but I stopped myself when I notice that all eyes are upon
me. Suddenly, I dazzle them with my irrepressible grin and I scuttle
down below to work on dinner. Self-righteously, I pat myself on the
back. I hardly ever "forget" what I remember.

I grab my journal to jot down a few superlatives concerning my
Captain. I read over certain sections of notes I've taken on the trip
because I want to be sure of my facts before I distort them in my
book. How to deal with this? Even without factual discrepancies—
mine are in blue and white while *his* reside in his foggy brain—two
people can have a totally different concept of reality. It's just the way
it is—two people, side by side, encountering the same places and
people and natural wonders, sometimes see them differently.

Secretly, I've spent more time this evening cooking dinner than
if I were preparing a Wolfgang Puck recipe. Each time a visitor comes
by to greet us, I give my token, "Hey, howya doin'?" and then dash
down below as if my dinner is burning. Tonight's menu will be
Skillet Eggplant Parmesan. I slice the eggplants about one-third-
inch thick, sprinkle them with salt and let them set for about 30
minutes. I toast them in olive oil in my large skillet (because I have
no broiler). Then I assemble the dish: first a layer of warm sauce
and torn basil leaves, followed by an overlapping layer of eggplant,
mozzarella, more basil, Parmesan and another layer of sauce. Cook
on low, covered.

When dinner is served, I get some rather impressive, "Oh, My ... Oh My, My's" from my husband. Instantly he forgives me for being a court stenographer. Again, we give applause to all the farmers of Annapolis Valley.

Halfway through dinner, Doug sighs and exits through the companionway door to greet a significantly anxious-looking group. They are hovering around talking in low tones, as though they're just outside a hospital sickroom.

Doug tries to explain what we are doing here and all about our legs. They all listen like there will be a trick question on the exam.

There are moments when we sense that explanations are futile and this was surely one of them. We seem further away than just one time zone—we seem to be in the language-barrier zone.

We all have *the smile* down pat now. It says "Friend."

We're stuck in the "talk louder and slower" phase. But we never arrive at the "eyes-wide, nod-of-the-head" look that says, "Eureka! I see, now!"

We continued our dinner with tentative mouthfuls. The next visitor is a jolly sweetie-pie of a man. His tall rubber boots, thick work pants and quilted-shirt, said *real maritimer*. He tries to explain the *tides*, clearly and slowly, as though we're people of very limited intelligence.

He keeps repeating, "You know?" and "You know what I'm sayin'?"

As Doug related bits of our journey, the expressions chasing one another across his face were a treat to watch. He went from blank disbelief to suspiciousness followed by astonishment and, finally, a grin of pure delight.

He was followed by Mr. Bright-multi-colored-plaid-shirt-with-striped-suspenders. More questions. He'd peer down at us squinting, then up to scan the sky, then back to us. All the while he checked the elasticity of his suspenders with a few pops here and there. He said nothing as Doug shared details. Personally, I kept my eyes fixed firmly on the book I was reading. Concealing a yawn, I began to count (it' the way I'm made). At 62, when I was dangerously close to falling asleep, he finally said, "To be honest, it all must be wonderful. But I don't understand a bit of it."

The thrumming of conversation continued. I went below to clean up dinner. Later, I stepped out into the evening air and looked up at the dock. There was a lineup of nine men (I counted) of every age, size and shape. Evidently, a meeting of the lobster fisherman was to commence in a half-hour on the other side of the dock. The lobster crew displayed a collective expression of "what are you idiots up to?"

I whispered to Doug, "I'm starting to feel like F. Lee Bailey!" A year or two after the O. J. Simpson trial, he pulled into Eastport in a big mega yacht. A third of Eastport's finest citizens paraded around, pointing fingers in his direction. He even got his picture in the *Quoddy Tides Newspaper*, wearing a big scowl on his face.

The Captain again took center stage, entertaining the lively lobster crew. During his delivery he received a variety of responses. One said, "Remarkable!" A chum of his muttered darkly, "Jee-ru-salem!" When one started laughing, most of them stopped their hemming and hawing and followed suit. Soon, they were holding their sides, belly chuckling.

Other menfolk gave despairing gestures, mystified, shocked, confused and alarmed. "My-God, you're sum lucky!" One bloke stopped laughing, scratched the hair on his chest through his shirt, and then looked at me darkly. I wondered what they would think if they knew how close I had come, just last night, to being *down the drain and up the spout!*

In an abstract sort of way it was all very entertaining. I could tell Doug was getting a kick out of this motley crew and was doing his best to answer the questions flying at him. To confirm his point, he stopped and asked me, "How many times have we sat on our legs?"

I gave him a naughty lift of my eyebrow. I didn't have to check my journal. I'd already counted and was ready to lend accuracy when it was requested. Every cloud has a silver lining. I cleared my throat and announced, firmly, "Twenty-three!"

Evening brought wild music from great flights of birds. It was as though a whole river of life flowed across the sky. In a great show of choreography, all landed on the far wall of the breakwater where they seem to be just hanging out—feathers flying—hell-bent on getting the last squawk in before dark.

We both swear there are times when these seagulls sound exactly as if they are saying, "Ass-hole (higher then lower) ass-hole." This typically happens when we enter a new harbour, where one squawks, "Ass" (high) then another answers, "hole" (lower).

A strong southwest wind has picked up but, lucky us, we're in the lee of the dock. I'm really tired. My knee throbs and I'm still a little cantankerous and shell-shocked from last night. We wait and wait, thinking that, before long, we can put our leg (or legs) on. Then we'll be set and can go to sleep.

"Jimminy Cricket! Here comes another one!" I mutter to my husband. We see yet another fisherman, sauntering aimlessly by.

"What'cha doin?" he asks.

"Oh, we're doin' nothin' much," the Captain says, smiling.

The feller puts his hands in the pockets of his Cardhart jacket and nods a few times. He looks at the birds, places his foot up on the curb, brushes his pants off a few times, places his had on his back, stretches it and then groans as though he has a kink in it. An expression of extreme anguish crossed his face and I wondered if his hemorrhoids were acting up.

I conclude that he's trying to say something. What? We can both take educated guesses but one can never assume. He may be the dock master, here to tell us we can't stay for the night ... or that it will cost $15 a foot for overnight fees (helping to defer the cost of the new dock). We wait in anticipation.

He holds his hands in front of him and tilts his head up to the lights of the dock, like a speechmaker who's forgotten his opening line. He takes on an apologetic look and I think, *Oh no, he's going to ask for money.*

Finally, he opens his mouth. Grimacing he takes on a look as though someone had just thrust a dead, stinky fish in his direction.

"The water empties out of here," he says, carefully.

Relief!

He took the explanation about our "legs" and recent history very well. Confident now, he went straight into stories of the last five generations of his family who have fished in these here parts.

His great-grandfather use to camp on Isle Haute during the fall and winter months. He'd lobster from there, *rowing* to his many traps.

My mind reeled at the thought of being out on that lonely island in the bitter cold and *rowing* (no less) in these powerful currents. One year, during a freeze-one's-balls-off cold winter, his great-granddad, got a toothache. He wasn't the type to invite sympathy, but the story passed down through the years illustrates the hardships endured by these fishermen.

"The poor ole' bugger had to row all the way to Annapolis Royal to reach the closest dentist!" he said.

We personally know that this is a very long distance, even in a sailboat, in good health and in warm weather—let alone in a rowboat. Holy bejeessuss! I shuddered just imagining all the pain he endured from sucking in that cold air.

Oddly, just a week prior to our stay on Isle Haute, I had an abscessed tooth and terrible pain. What would *I* have done out there that far from a dentist? I felt that a shot in the head would have been the preferable option.

The Captain of the *Broadie's Toy* then told us that, "The lobster fishing will start in two weeks time and continue until it snows."

I asked him "Why 'til it snows?" Rationalizing that it must have something to do with roads, boats, engines, laws or whatever.

"Nope." he answered. "We don't know why ...but the lobsters just leave!" With this, he nodded good evening, gave us a big thumbs up and walked away.

Quiet at last! It has been an exhausting 24 hours. We are worn out, the leg is on.

We say goodnight to Parker's Cove and all its well-meaning people.

Day 27

Wednesday, September 26, 2001

The very words *marine radio* used to imply, before I knew better, that one had the latest, most accurate, forecasts available for the general area. We have not, on the whole, gained a great deal from their speculations for our life on the water up in the Bay of Fundy except for bits of entertainment. We chuckle appreciatively when we listen to their deliveries of statistical predictions. They bring to mind the "Whetherman" in *The Phantom Tollbooth*. These prognosticating voices make me wonder whether any of their forecasts will actually happen.

Who are these people and how do they become marine forecasters? When I listen, the sound makes me muse about the advertisement in their Employment Opportunities.

Wanted: Speaker with level monotone delivery. Ability to drone with complete lack of inflection considered a bonus.

Do they receive special training to learn to repeatedly recite, without sincerity or sound factual scientific exactness, certain words—*Mostly, Partly, Likely, Becoming, Probable, Varying* and a *Chance of*—not once but at least three times per local report? The only time an announcer carries any real conviction comes in the grand climax when Mr Computer-Generated voice (if that's what it is) sounds relieved to share a brief synopsis of his observations of *past* weather.

This morning, just to clear the Captain's conscience that indeed, we have done all we can do to determine if this is the day to make our crossing to New Brunswick (or, more generally speaking, that there might be an outside chance that one time in 30 days, the forecast could possibly be accurate), we tuned in. We listened intently to the French version, which sounds so much more interesting than the English, even if, in fact, we only understand five words out of five hundred. When it all ended, the Captain clicked off the radio and said, "I believe that is French for 'It's a floating crap game.'"

We step out to the cockpit, just past dawn, and take our own reading—the probabilities and chances of our day. We have a partly cloudy sky and fair winds. We exchanged satisfied nods. Truthfully, one can't expect much better than this at the end of September, way up here in what some may call the far north, at this very early hour. We flip our imaginary coin and tell ourselves this might be our chance.

As we prepare to set sail, we enjoy the sounds of the day. We watch all the birds going about their early morning duties. It's amazing to see all these birds flying south. But of course they fly—walking would take too long.

We start the motor and remove the dock lines from the cleats. *Brumn Brumn*, we *putt putt* ourselves from the breakwater at Parker's Cove. Perfect ... wi–n–d, it died.

Humm, should we turn back? Should we continue motoring until the wind picks up again? We drone on some more; we stick our lips out in childish disappointment. We wanted to experience these ceremonial moments of leaving the last dock of Nova Scotia unaccompanied by the rumbling of the blasted motor.

A reprieve came when just the tiniest puff of wind pushed us along; we were able to cut the motor. In slow motion, the harbour and shoreline fall back into a deep quiet. With our hands tucked for warmth, the two of us sat silently, transfixed on watching the event of our departure unfold. My thoughts are completely in tune with my husband's. For over an hour we sat there drifting, the sky filled with clouds, the ever-so-gentle wind allowing us to savor our last impressions of Nova Scotia.

We moved, almost in a trance-like state, when a kind wind caught us and we reset the sails. I wonder if I'll ever manage to recapture this tranquility—the smells and the sounds? I went forward to the deck and I found tears rolling down my cheeks. They are quickly swept away with the wind.

What flotsam and jetsam we were, floating through Nova Scotia. No one knew us. We presented ourselves without any social credentials—just us and our good intentions, escapees from the telephone and the time clock. Two temporarily insane Americans living on liquid.

The warm hospitality (far ahead of me in this category) offered by the Canadians not only included their country, docks and towns but their homes, tubs, lives and friendships. Aside from the physical comfort, they gave me a burst, spiritually and emotionally. I felt imbued with their spirit of generosity. I have changed in the innermost core of my being. All the magnificence and beauty we saw, each and every place we stopped and every person we met, tugs at my heart. My vision blurred over with tears.

When investigating the unknown, the outcomes are unpredictable. You must feel free to leave behind what you regard as "civilization." I once read that the Chinese word for crisis includes the symbol for opportunity. Looking back on my days in the Minas Basin, living on the edge (the edge of agony and ecstasy), I wonder how I will now view crises in my everyday life. I have strong hopes that I will be less fearful because I learned not to be afraid of the shadows. There's an outside chance that I'll be calmer, more flexible. I'd suggest that I may even seek opportunities in uncomfortable situations. On the other hand, will I slump back into my well-worn jacket of scared, insecure, unprepared, incapable and inflexible? The odds are great that it will still fit. I hope not! If I really keep trying … if I keep remembering what Lao Chue wrote several thousand years ago:

> *At birth all people are soft and yielding. At death they are hard and stiff.*
> *All green plants are tender and yielding. At death they are brittle and dry.*
> *When hard and rigid, we consort with death.*
> *When soft and flexible, we affirm greater life.*

My meditative thoughts are broken as I am jerked back to the present. My husband calls to me. He points forward and portside. We both give our full attention to the group of Belted Kingfishers. The male shows off his blue-gray breast band; his female friends have a stylish chestnut bellyband. We watch them hover over the water and dive vertically for prey. The sky seems only a hand-span away.

The wind dies; it is replaced with a leisurely, but steady drizzle. This smacks of a long slow sail of a cold, wet variety. The rain tries to dampen my will to be tender and yielding, young and flexible. Heedless of the rain we sit in the cockpit in our bib and tucker rain gear, quietly solemn, blinking away the rain. The weather seems to match the interior of our souls. We turn occasionally to the Nova Scotia shoreline, barely visible in the distance. Both of us look as though we are deep down in the doleful dumps.

I have a *list*—shock of shocks. Activities that virtually guarantee rain … washing windows, washing your car, planning a picnic. You've just had a perm—and your hair will be a mass of frizzies. I have more: attending an outdoor wedding reception; forgetting your umbrella; applying a coat of fresh paint outdoors; attending the opening day of trout season; putting the hay down (that's the Nebraska farm girl in me); replacing your roof; and, finally, I can now add, making a long-distance crossing on the Bay of Fundy.

As the day wore on, the rain lessened and I succumbed to the enchantment. I served hot tea and cookies. Entertainment for our teatime was a slight bit of sun and five Shearwaters. The Captain sighs, a smile of pleasure crosses his face, "The sun's got its back stays down!" This is a maritime description for when the wind is driving the rain at an angle and you can see the sun's rays through the rain clouds. The rays look like a backstay of a sailboat.

This brilliant backdrop sets the stage for the Shearwaters' sensational flying performance. With great poise they fly high and then down, barely skimming the water. They exit behind the curtains; then they are back on stage, flying up and down. Being very adept divers, they usually follow schools of mackerel and other large fish pursuing smaller ones which are driven to the surface. Today, they just seem to be practicing some techniques for our viewing pleasure. Most of their real meals are forged at night, feasting on delicacies like squid and crustaceans.

Our best friend, Magellan the GPS, tells us we are close to Dipper Harbour. This, ladies and gentlemen, is a very good thing ... because, we can't *see* it! The rain stopped, but the fog joined us during the tea party. We relied on Magellan to take us into Dipper Harbour by motor. It's times like these that we couldn't be happier with our little friend than if it baked cookies.

Our day has been one of varied sailing—cloudy, sunny, rainy, no wind, light wind, strong wind and fog. These "variables" (I sound like the weatherman) rotated all day. We would just finish reefing when we would need a second reef. We'd be flying along when suddenly, as if someone flipped the switch, it became as quiet as a millpond.

Dipper is sitting quiet tonight, the wind is light. The docks are filled with many more fishing boats than 26 days ago. Lucky break, we are able to tie up to a floating dock to keep us stable for a nice secluded evening of buoyant bliss.

Day 28

Thursday, September 27, 2001

I peer out and the scene that meets my eyes in not highly untypical of my mind in the early morning—foggy. Dipper Harbour is *stuffed* with fog. You won't see this first mate down below muttering about poor sailing conditions. I cast my vote for a day of personal hygiene, cooking, cleaning, reading, writing, and long walk. I can bring out my pink weights and practice Tai Chi without entertaining those in the harbour ...

It wasn't long before I decided "something was the matter."

"Yes!" I say, arms raised as though I'm delivering a sermon.

"Yes! Yes! Triple Yes!" It is *foggy!*

I feel my perfect timing in this surely shows I'm getting closer, by almost anyone's standards, to an acceptable level of enlightenment. I breathe in emotionally, momentarily confused by my thoughts. Where does destiny stop and free will start? I shake my head ... has this fog rolled in on my mullet? I had better get a move on, if you know what I mean?

Suddenly, I'm struck by a scary scenario. What if the fog lifts *while I'm out there?* I swat at the negative thought as if it were a pestering fly.

All those Victorian romance novels never address this issue. How did women handle the basic needs of the human body. Just because they had servants to attend them while touring, say, the deserts of Egypt, doesn't mean elegantly-clad women, never had to go number-two in the middle of an excursion to a pyramid. And this, while wearing enough material to make drapes for three large windows. Personally, I am curious. I grab my bucket and head out to commune with nature.

What happens next has been the subject of much discussion. The upshot of the story is that I had given my soul and thought over to patience. I hear my loved one, the one revered above all else, chuckle a satisfied chuckle, and exclaim, "That outta be a good one!"

I turn to the direction of the zipped screen door where my husband displays an ingratiating smile, camera in-hand.

I hissed urgently, "You'll be hearing from my attorney!" I've taken tons of pictures of him as the almighty Captain on this journey. But this *certified public menace*, finally gets out the camera, *not* when I'm in a handsome nautical pose, wind in my hair, firm hand on the tiller and all that!

Of all the cruel cunning. Nostrils aquiver, I shouted three things that I was going to do to him once I was "off" the bucket. What they were I can't remember, but all were undoubtedly in the derogatory vein. The fourth was on the tip of my tongue when the skipper stopped me,

"There's no need to go further, Eileen, I get the picture. Don't sweat it. If you don't have to make a long list, save it for when you do!" With fake indignation, he shoots me a rotten smile, "I was just trying to get a good cover shot for your book!"

I proceed with my humming, sweeping and scrubbing. To settle my temper, I exercised emotional muscles I didn't know I had. Can't blame anyone but yourself. I will pay for the rest of my days for running off with the lounge singer.

Then, lo and behold the weather clears! Suddenly, we not only have a beautiful sun shining, but, to *really* upset my best-laid plans

Dipper Harbour
I hear my loved one, the one revered above all else, chuckle a s
atisfied chuckle, and exclaim, "That outta be a good one!" I turn to the
direction of the zipped screen door where my husband
displays an ingratiating smile, camera in-hand.

for the day, we also have a southwest wind action goin' on. Son-of-a-gun! I keep cleaning. I'm on my hands and one knee, the other stiffly out behind me. I ignore the Captain while he stands above me, arms crossed as though he's Mr. Clean. Without looking up, I inquire, "Wouldn't this be a great day for one of those time-consuming projects like splitting atoms or something?"

Once out in the bay, the wind steadily picks up and starts blowing us willy nilly. "If this keeps up," he tells me, "I'll need to change back to the jib."

Yesterday, when there wasn't a trace of wind—when you could giggle the tiller forcibly, but nothing happened—he changed the jib to the genoa. Wind! I tell ya, it can be such a strange phenomenon. I never gave it much thought 'til I started sailing. You can either have too much or too little—a puff, a breeze, a whole gale. It can be at your back, head wind, tailwind, beam reach, fair wind, close hauled, broad reach. You can be in the lee, heading off, or falling off the wind. You can have calm winds (George Carlin said, "*if they're calm, they're not really winds, are they?*") I often wonder about the who or the what behind the movements of the winds which we feel but never see. Wind deceives you constantly with its direction and velocity. If you want to sail you have to tune your senses to the subtleties of the wind.

Doug struggles to keep her on course; my mind moves southward, where it is hurricane season. I'm very glad not to be anywhere near 100 or 200 MPH winds. One of the books I've been reading about the universe is so wild; it talks about real wind. Until now, when you talk about stars and galaxies I never thought of wind. Well, listen to this.

The Red Spider Planetary Nebula shows a complex structure that can result when a normal star rejects its outer gases and becomes a white dwarf star NGC6537 (nice flowery name). This two-lobed symmetric planetary nebula (say that three times—fast) houses one of the hottest white dwarfs ever observed and is probably part of a binary star system. *Stay with me, now.* They say internal winds emanating from the central stars have been measured in excess of—get this—1, 000 KM *per second!* For those of you not metrically inclined, this is approximately 620 miles per second. I'll break this down even further. To get the full picture, this is, 2, 232, 000 miles per hour! This is all happening around 4, 000 light years away! To refresh your memory, a light year is the distance light travels in one year, which is about 6 trillion miles. A trillion is a million, million. My mind reels with the reality of our universe.

Today, although we are being whipped around, I feel comforted to touch all sides of my little world; to be able to bring out the charts and our cruising guide and read numbers that make sense.

Ah oh! Doug jumps up and hands me the tiller, commanding, "Stay on course!"

OK, I tell myself—check the compass, check where we are from shore, concentrate on the job at hand. Suddenly the wind changes again and decides to try out being a monster. We are rocking and flopping hither and thither in the big waves.

Doug—as you may have guessed—is changing sails. The process of changing sails while underway in these winds, in my opinion is … is … what is the word I'm searching for? Is *ridiculous!* It is a bit of a high wire act. Sails are flying everywhere like a big circus tent. It takes tons of time to complete the whole process and is dangerous, especially with me at the helm. Maintaining control in these waters is a trial for me, even in the best of times. The responsibility of keeping us on course and away from the rocks and ledges is one thing. But to do this with my Captain forward—maneuvering the boat and keeping her steady enough that he doesn't plunge overboard—is another thing altogether.

Bottom line—to do this properly, I need to be a hellava lot better at this than I am.

In the time that could have accommodated the fall of Rome, the rigging and flapping are completed and we are back to our normal jib. He races back to the cockpit and says, "I *said* to keep her on course! Look ahead and behind—watch out for everything!"

Honest to goodness, the Captain normally reserves his reprimands for those times when even *I know* I botched things. This time it beats the hell out of me what I did wrong! I thought I was right on course according to the compass and the shoreline. I didn't hit a rock or a hidden ledge and, thank heavens, he wasn't thrown overboard! My heart sank, "Oh!" I said, white.

I went down below, my eyes swimming, and hid amidst the circus tent genoa, the legs, the dingy mast, miscellaneous sail bags and sail bag covers. This remark really knocked the wind out *my* sails. I will *never*, I mean *never,* said with my hand held high, "I will *never*, get this."

I am not even given an hour to lament over my failure. I am still lying prostrate with grief, deep in the black hole of self-pity, beating myself up over the whole deal, when the wind—the trickster that toys with my emotions—dies. Hardly a breath.

My mind was drifting toward the reward of having auxiliary power through our ever-ready 9.9 Johnson. We haven't used five gallons of gas in 27 days. I, for one, can in all good consciousness, act like the veritable slacker sailor that I am and pretend the motor doesn't bother me and zone out for a while. Well, have I popped my cork? The Captain will have none of that! Lucky me. The Captain has now proclaimed that we need the genoa *back!*

I call out, "Cut the 'we' business! *I* don't *need* the genoa back. You can make parachute pants out of it as far as I'm concerned!"

Seldom is there a functioning democracy on board. The Captain is the dictator. "Eileen! Come and take the tiller!"

"Excuse me, but I haven't figured out what I did wrong last time!" I reply, giving him an "on my knees look."

Strictly for encouragement (because he has no backup support) and to avoid mutiny, he calls to me, "You rock, Eileen!"

"Yeah, only because I'm on the blasted boat."

"We *need* the genoa back," he repeats.

He doesn't explain. I don't complain.

Changing the jib to the genoa (as you might have figured out) is much easier than vice versa, mostly because the wind isn't howling. The Captain can set about accomplishing this task in a calmer fashion. I watch him waltzing around up forward, dealing with the two sails, snatch blocks, jib tracks, genoa tracks, clues, batons, halyards, and shackles. Amongst it all, he smiles a bunch, and talks to me.

"The world is a funny place. You have to ride it out, smile if you can. Still, it's the same in the end—dead and done. Death is the big equalizer. It sets everyone on the same level; it tells us we have a very limited amount of time—we are all gonna die." He lifts and lowers

Sailing to Beaver Harbour
Changing the jib to the genoa is much easier than vice versa, mostly
because the wind isn't howling. . . he smiles
a bunch, and talks to me.

and stuffs the sails. "When you don't face the facts, it becomes easy to postpone the things you want to do."

He burst into song, *"We're all gonna die some day! We're all gonna die some day—if you're gonna kiss my ass, you better kiss it fast—cause we're all gonna die someday!"*

He contemplates this for a while, looks to the sky, then continues, "The moon turned red in January of last year, when we had a total lunar eclipse."

"Why red?" I wonder aloud.

"They think it was because of the different clouds and volcanic dust in the Earth's atmosphere. When I see pictures of the earth from space it makes me realize, Wow! We are spinning and breathing this minute on a fantastic ball. But out in space this ball seems so insignificant. It makes me think there must be some reason for something; otherwise there would be no reason for anything."

More thoughts, more maneuvering. "You know when you think of it ..." He stops.

"Think of what?" I ask.

"Being is worth it!" he tells me.

"Worth what?" Am I missing something?

"Worth *being* alive on old planet earth as a *human being!*"

He finishes his task and gives a large sigh. Then his face changes to his most happy smile. "I'm so glad we aren't at home playing Monotonous!"

I received a small bit of grim satisfaction from the fact that, genoa or no genoa, we ended up having to start the motor to get to Beaver Harbour.

As I fixed skillet lasagna with the leftover marinara sauce from the other night, I quietly watched the tide and the fog roll into the cove. We ate dinner out in the cockpit. The woodstove warmed us from below. The Captain halted in the midst of singing the scale of the foghorn, to point to a jaeger (*yay-ger*) in swift flight. The jaeger was chasing a seagull and, after some sincere harassment, caused the gull to drop his food. The harasser swooped to catch the stolen meal before it hit the water.

We sat a long while watching and listening. We didn't bother to move even though we were spit with rain.

Day 29

Friday, September 28, 2001

"I need a holy water refill," I tell my husband as I slide into the cockpit cushion and slurp my tea, The *Guillemot* floats serenely, tied to a wooden raft which is anchored by a mooring. Fishermen might normally use this raft to store traps and boat containers. We had ourselves a big hearty chuckle yesterday evening when we pulled into Beaver Harbour and proceeded to tie up to this raft which has taken on a new identity—that of a frosted, buoyant lawn. The "turf" growing on the wooden surface is made up of grass, moss, algae and whatever else is composting there. It is white from the gulls that prefer it as their stomping grounds. We confiscated the raft by right of eminent domain from a group of these seagulls, The Captain told them that he was sorry, but it was ours—just for the night. It was doubtful they heard this over their loud, protesting squawks.

We were very happy for the barge. Not only were we stabilized from the roly-poly current, but it removed all speculation about what our anchor may or may not do in this harbour.

The morning temperature continues to climb. Once the Captain deems it warm enough, he removes the canvas side curtains from around the pop-top. After the canvas is tucked away at the foot of the quarter-berth, he goes to the V-berth, lifts the cushions and the door to the storage area beneath. He pulls out one of our large, 5-gallon water containers still half-full of "holy water". Then he refills our gallon-size container we keep on the bilge floor under the stove. This is the water we use for drinking and cooking. This water is as smooth as silk. This water is as free from chemicals as any water we can get our hands on.

In Robbinston, about 15 miles from Eastport, is a church. On the grounds of this church is a free-flowing spring that gushes with this delectable water. Over the years, the different owners of the property (many different church groups) have tried to cap off the spring but to no avail. The spring is so full of this life-giving force that it blows it right off. It is tested regularly by the State of Maine "water-something-or-other," and is said to be the best anywhere around. A few times a season, usually en route to Calais, we take our six five-gallon jugs and stop for a refill of holy water. We also take small water bottles in the car which we refill. Each of us drinks about a quart of the fresh cold-from-the-ground water right then and there. I visualize the White Fox talking about mackerel when I say, arms waving, "Ooohhh! There is nothing like it!"

I make our holy water pancakes. Up on land, in full view, is a very large gray warehouse. The roof is speckled with seagulls of every variety. The roar of their squawks escalates

We happily smack our lips over our pancakes and real Vermont maple syrup. We watch the warehouse and we speculate what their conference could be about? Through observation, we notice that they appear to squawk loudly at each other and then turn in our direction! We watch intently. Yep, it does seem as though we are the topic of much conversation.

"I pass," I say, "I have no idea what is going on. Maybe it's like a Friday morning Rotary Club breakfast?" I rise and move to the galley for KP duty, shaking my head, still wondering and musing over the squawkers. As it happens, a body of theory wasn't long in coming ...

At the top of the ebbing tide we untied and pushed off from the wooden barge. We were not ten feet away, floating serenely, when four gulls take turns pooping on the Captain's head.

Proof, after years of scientific conjecture, that people and nature *can* co-exist to their mutual enjoyment!

Once out into the bay we enjoy a tide glide. We reminisce over the tree-lined craggy coast of yesterday and we relive, in our minds eye, the oohs and awhs over the thunder holes and caves. Today, we pass a layer of rockweed setting solemnly astride a fishing weir, which appears to be still netted and in use. This is a low-tech trap first devised by the American Indians and which once caught thousands of pounds of herring annually. Very few are now in use. These fishing weirs are made of wooden stakes placed in the water almost in the shape of a question mark. The nets are placed to form a channel. They say the herring, swimming in large schools, swim in and can't find their way out. The herring boats come by and suck the fish into their storage tanks.

Between Beaver and Deadman's Harbour lies a rocky shore with a sight unusual for this coastline, a private three-hole golf-course. We are not given long to observe this verdant sight, because *Wocjowsan* (the wind, in Passamaquoddy Indian) gives us a very strong, giant push from behind and we are swished ahead to view a coastline that is striped with all varieties of color.

The loom of land, off in the distance, is one which is deeply familiar to us. Campobello Island is the large Canadian Island that shelters Eastport from the more open waters. Starboard, are the Wolves, an archepelago of five islands set out all alone and uninhabited, except for a few lurking salmon pens.

The tide changes and the clouds clear as we view East Quoddy Head (Head Harbour) Lighthouse to port. The Captain requests his hat, complaining that his noggin is getting burnt. As he arranges his Tilleys hat to sit tightly on his head, he swiftly shifts in a rakish style, off to one side. He smiles conspiratorially, and says, "How about one more night, my sweetie?"

Are you *kidding?* I mean really now—how can any first mate/ little sweetie/wife, resist an offer from a smile and eyes like that? You would have to be a stronger woman than I am.

We ignore our turn toward Eastport and head for L'Etete passage. In the far distance we see the imposing, large white ferry heading toward Grand Manan. Passing in the opposite direction is the Deer Island ferry crossing the L'Etete Passage toward St. George, New Brunswick. Sailing through L'Etete we are caught in the mighty current of the tides and the wind which continually swoops through here. I hold tight like a snapping turtle, compensating for the gyrations of the craft with a hard driven' skipper.

I stare at all the ripples. Now the knowledge that the wind blows and the tide flows to make those swirls and ripples is part of me.

Just on the other side of the passage we are caught again, this time in the doldrums. Now, this is what I'm talkin' about—quiet, smooth, the tide glide. Aahh! Relief, floods my soul; under the bright sun our whole world is the sea. At this moment, in my mind, land points don't exist. The only sounds are the lapping waves of our faithful dinghy and the raucous ducks, their wings striking the water again and again before they lift into the air.

The ocean now sleeps. I feel as though, when the giant is sleeping, we can climb the bean stalk and partake of the treasures it has to offer. I sit and stare down at the water and try to focus on what is passing beneath us, I try to see so much but I realize I see so little. The water stares back at me with a thousand eyes. Eyes as green as jade, Adriatic Sea blue, raging sea gray, reflecting pool crystal—some subtle smoke, others silvery, and seaweed brown. There has been a discovery that, in a single teaspoon of saltwater, there are more than 75 million viruses—those tiny particles composed of gene and protein that exist somewhere between the living and the dead. Scientists estimate that they have surveyed less than a tenth of one percent of the sea floor. The sea floor is about 300 million square kilometers; it could hold millions of yet undiscovered species.

Several moon jellyfish pass as part of the parade, moving through the water in slow, rhythmic pulsations. I peer down at their elegant symmetrical shape, like little parachutes 4 to 8 inches across, nearly all white and slightly transparent except for the four horseshoe-shaped, light-pinkish gonads located in the bell. You can handle these little guys because the stinging cells are not toxic to humans. When you get them close you can see the numerous short tentacles arranged along the edge of the bell. The larger jellyfish, commonly found in the Maine waters, is the lion's mane jellyfish. They use their robust tentacles to subdue their prey, injecting poison like a bee sting. Some humans have a strong reaction to the toxins in their stinging cells, so watch out!

The Captain brings my attention to seven small guillemots, in their winter plumage, floating all in a row. Suddenly, as if the leader commanded, "Ready, set, go!" they all dip, then pop, pop, pop, up they come. They look to each other and smile. Three dive together, then 2, always popping back up. They go through their game once again. They're so cute, just like kids playing in a sprinkler.

A few minutes later, forward to port, we see a loon trying hard to swallow his prize catch, a sculpin. His head swishes around, tugging and gulping. All the while a seagull watches overhead. He flies low and dives suddenly to try and grab the sculpin but the loon is too quick. He plunges deep down, fish still in its mouth, to escape. We wait for the rest of the drama to unfold. The seagull threatens overhead. The loon pops up some fifty feet further to the east, sculpin still dangling from his beak. This same scene is repeated two more times! Finally, upon surfacing the third time, the loon proudly, and well-deservedly, swallows the sucker.

The sun is shining on the water, sparkly-sparkly. We are still adrift. I'm melting into richness. The Captain steps over me, sprawled out over the cockpit cushion.

"Excuse me," he says and repeats, "Excuse me!" Uncharacteristically formal. "I must go expose my private parts. I must visit Aunt Sally."

I started to admonish the man's warped nature of his soul—you promised no more pee jokes, (visiting Aunt Sally, is what the old Mainers use to call the privy) but I can't quite open my mouth. The water and the movement of the boat is as hypnotic as a snake charmer's song, I think to myself ... I wonder if ...

I woke to the fact that someone was speaking to me. The voice was miles away. "Eileen! Eileen! We've got the thrill of the krill goin' on here!" I came out of my trance to see teeming mackerel chasing krill and herring all around us, thousands of them jumping and splashing. Sometimes the disturbances can be so subtle that you can easily miss the indications of a swarm of herring below. Other times, like these, the water boils with the teeming fish. Doug the fisherman grabs his fishing line and drops the hook. The ever-ready Captain has the flour and seasonings mixed and the frying pan ready at hand. In four minutes we have four fish, fresh out of the sunstruck sea!

The wind appears to want to join the party, "Wow! Sweetie, grab the tiller, we're sailing again!" I think, when I'm centered, I become more efficient because under press of sail we caught, cleaned, cooked, consumed and I performed my scullion duties before the dollar store clock had loudly ticked 35 times!

The sun shone so bright on the white pages of my book I was having trouble reading when the Captain solicited my attention. "We need to put our heads together and select a possible destination for tonight." We concentrated on this for awhile. We would love to head to the Mascarene Shore of New Brunswick and pop in on Harry and Martha Bryon. Doug wants to get an autograph for his fan club in Maitland, Paul. But, alas the wind is not cooperating.

"How about Charlene's? Do you think we have enough wind and daylight to sneak into the Bocabec?" Yes, in fact, the Captain believes we do. So, decision made, the Bocabec River just outside St. Andrews By The Sea, is our goal for the night.

For a while, we make good time. Then, once again, the elusive wind escapes the grasps of our sails. Here we sit in the Passamaquoddy Bay, bobbing along like we are waiting for the 3:59 p.m. commuter train to ferry us across the bay. Quietly we bob. I'm getting sleepy again! I'm forcing my eyes to stay open when I see, starboard, a couple of harbour porpoises. They are making their way toward us, swiftly jumping out of the water and down again. They typically come up about three times before they swim quickly away underwater. If you are close enough, quietly walking the waters, like we are now, you can hear their *swoop swoop* as they glide in and out of the sea.

Doug points, "There are more about 10 o'clock port side." It seemed as though a magician waved the magic wand because up pops another dozen or so.

"How about that? Awesome!"

At my "awesome," several more appeared. All started encircling the boat. They were swimming all around us. Then many would disappear under the boat and come up on the other side. We must have looked like a weird new fish in the sea because they apparently called to more of their friends for a peek. Soon oodles of them surrounded the boat!

"Oh m'God they're smiling at us!" I giggled. Up and down they swam; turning to look up at us, then, they'd make a little squeaky noise. Most definitely, we both agreed—they are smiling at us!

"They are so adorable!" Archetypal sounds came from me, as if I were cooing over a baby. "Do they have eyelashes?" I ask my Captain.

"Beats me."

"I have no idea either, but if they do, I'd swear a few are seductively batting them your way!" What a joy! We just watch and talk to them, moving from one side of the boat to the next, front and aft, not wanting to miss any of the show. There are tons of them, far more than we have ever seen at one time. I felt it my duty, as the court stenographer, to try and count them. It is not a stretch to say 150! Way, way, cool—as big-time exciting as you can get.

I take several deep breaths and we hug as we bob along, "It's as if they're saying, Welcome Home!"

After this purely amazing sight, we hardly cared what the wind did with us. But I swear it can behave like a child. When you aren't giving it any attention, it's prone to act up. It first came up as a gentle prod and, suddenly, the wind she does blow! We are soon honkin' over the bay, then up the Bocabec River.

Up the river, as we expected, lay the *Avonturr*. The *Avonturr*, with the home port Tortola printed across the stern, is anchored for the hurricane season. She is a pretty sight with the last of the sun's rays hitting her masts. We believe her to be the only sailing cargo ship still in existence. Towards the end of October, Paul-the-Captain, gathers a willing and able crew to sail down to the Caribbean or over to the Mediterranean, whichever direction he may find work.

While putting the boat to bed, the Captain speculates excitedly, with a cunning finger under the eyeball gesture, "We can call one of our friends and connive a ride to town!" Nodding in affirmation, he continues, "St Andrews is a paradise!"

The plan is becoming clear to me now—it is all about satisfying Doug's eating disorder. He has been feeling, for the last couple of weeks, this elusive, elemental "something" missing from our hallelujah culinary moments on board—pizza. There's this great pizza joint which serves pitchers of beer and has a back deck that overlooks the St. Andrews harbour ...

We quietly row into shore past the *Avonturr*. All is quiet aboard the large steel ship. We look back over our shoulders to see the *Guillemot* gently rocking. We both smile large contented smiles, relieved that we've found a confident anchorage here in the Bobabec River. We row in the direction ashore where we hope to find the meandering trail up to Charlene's cozy cabin.

A mosaic carpet of color and texture wreaths the trail from the dropping leaves of the white ash, mountain ash, white birch, yellow birch and maples. If you know what you're looking for, you can just detect the board and baton of her small snuggery tucked up the hill. All appears very quiet, as we emerge from the trail. There's a silence which is unfamiliar to us, for the only times we've been here were for music nights in the St. Andrews area. Music nights consist of about 20-30 local musicians, gathering for a whole lot'a guitar playin', and fiddle playin' and singin'. All this is accompanied by a concertina, cello or two, a flute, drums, bongos and other miscellaneous percussionists. We all gather for potluck, drinking, singing, dancing and carousing. For these lively events we drive over and sleep in the van in whoever's yard happens to be hosting the party. Some of the most fun can be had the following morning. We stick around, usually a group shows up for breakfast, socializing and possibly a group hike.

Last year we hosted a music night for all our Canadian friends at our house in Eastport. I cooked a big dinner, we had a fire in the Tiki bar and many of our local friends joined in. News travels fast in Eastport, and a group of about 15 hiked the hill from *The Mex*, to join the shindig. One couple from Indiana were amongst the group. They were staying at the Weston House B&B and told Jett, the proprietor, about the party the next day, "Best time we've had on our trip!" When morning arrived, the rip-roaring time over, we found 28 people had spent the night.

We knocked and poked around but concluded that no one was home. Shucks! Conveniently, I had my shower gear along, just in case the opportunity arose. We started to walk back down the trail, when we heard, "Yo!"

Ace, Charlene's son, greeted us from the door, hair still wet from the shower. He knows not where his mother roams, but welcomes us to take a shower. All righty! Out of the shower, I'm feeling groovy! We bid Ace good evening, as we hear the 17-year-old making plans to go to St. John for the Friday night activities. We become our own party-poopers and decide we are not energetic enough to try and call and fang-dangle a ride to and from town.

The sun is very low in the sky, showing us its green-blue glow. The waves come closer and closer upon us. Our footsteps break the crust of sticks and seaweed on the shore. As we climb into the dingy, the evening chill seeps through our layered clothes, autumn fights for a foothold.

We row close to the *Avonturr,* just in time to see Paul, the Captain, stick his head out to say, "Hello!" We offer up beer and soup aboard the *Guillemot.* We can see, even in the twilight, his pale face. He rubs his stomach and tells us, in his Dutch accent, he's feelin' none too good. He has the flu. He waves and says he is going to start the generator for some heat. I shiver when I think of how cold it must be on that steel boat.

September evenings in the woods of New Brunswick can be very chilly, but the absence of mosquitoes, out in search of a blood meal, makes these days and evenings much more enjoyable. Even wading birds are not excluded from the torture of the female's stabbing mouths. The pesky mosquitoes find their bills and eyes and their exposed legs. The mosquito is one species that is not in danger of extinction. Our blood provides the protein to produce a new generation; the females can travel up to 50 miles and suck up to 4 times her own body weight in one meal. This meal, even for a mosquito on her last legs, provides enough nutrition to produce 200 eggs. A female mosquito can lay a batch every two weeks, up to

3 or 4 batches a summer! Don't ask what the males do during all this, because I haven't the faintest idea. Mosquito golf?

Back aboard Doug fires the wood stove and I prepare corn chowder. I made a quick vegetable stock last evening so I can have our chowder ready in about 40 minutes. Our lunch of fish was really filling, but the aroma of this chowder makes us both ravenous, we "umm, umm," in the anticipation of our meal, I sauteed fresh kernels, new potatoes, leeks, yellow bell pepper, onion, the last of my fresh basil and thyme sprigs. Once all is tender, I add my veggie stock and let the flavors mingle. Toward the end I add some powdered milk to make it creamy.

We cozily bask in the warmth of the cabin and the memories of our past month. We talk for hours and take deep breaths of happiness in rhythm with the fire cackling softly. I passed along to my partner how I felt today while lying on the cockpit in the peaceful quiet and warm sun.

"I felt I was melting into richness! I remember reading about this once but I never felt it!"

Our communal thoughts tonight are that we, as a society, do revel in richness almost every day of real life—that richness being far different than what I felt today. The richness of money, gadgets, toys, of satellite TV channels, internet information and dot-com stocks. I feel a deep delirium of the soul when I think of traffic, phones, faxes, taxes, the hustle and bustle. Many times on this journey I didn't know where I was going or why I was in a handbasket, but tonight this makes so much sense to me—our world of little boat, but our big world of vistas, sky and trees. Here, among the solitary sounds of the loons, the only "rushing" is the water; the only traffic signals are the buoys and the luffing of the sails. Out here our needs are basic and there is more fresh air than your tired, polluted lungs can suck in.

We move out to the cockpit. The air is full of evening scents and there is not a person, car, or airplane to disrupt our view of the moon edging its way through the filigree of the trees. The rest of the sky is a black velvet cloak sewn with diamonds.

Before lights out, I read some of my earlier journal entries. Judging from these, I really did always feel I was going to survive this journey. Hey, I remember when I even bought green bananas! I remember the day when I didn't eat the last piece of fudge. It also reminded me of how I felt at the beginning of this journey. I felt that I was pretty much doing this trip for him—you know him, the alien abductee? I'm shocked at the many glimpses of the peaceful harmony I've experienced out here. The same type of feeling which seems to naturally exist within my husband. I needed to be still and calm long enough to feel it. I needed to stop seeking solace and fulfillment someplace other than right here—right now!

The Captain looks up from writing in his log, yawns and stretches his legs across to me in the quarter-berth. He scratches his head as though searching for something, making his dark hair stand straight up and out,

"You know?" he stops.

"Judging from my past, probably not." I reply.

"You know?" he repeats, still rubbing and yawning.

I stop and wait, hoping my strong, completely honest Captain, will finish his yawn talk. "I think …" He yawns and yawns, patting his mouth and shaking his head. This conversation is somewhat like sailing; you have to maneuver with patience and fortitude. "I think the …"

I watch silently, his elbow on the table and fist to his cheek. He closes his eyes, other hand still rubbing his head. OK, I'll wait for one more tack up wind.

"I think the balder I get, the dumber I get! It must be the sun's ultraviolet rays."

Day 30

Saturday, September 29, 2001

Jeepers, creepers, do I have a splitting headache or what? I keep my eyes closed for a minute to try and figure this out. The pain continued. I covered my head with my pillow. I am coming to the conclusion that something, indeed, is splitting, but luckily, not my head.

There is a big 18 inches between my covered head and the wood my ole pal Doug is splitting to start the woodstove. This is the price I pay to have the cabin warm and comfy when I decide to drag my derriere out of bed.

I crawl out the canvas door, toothbrush and cup in hand. The bright clear sunshine is blinding. I sit down in the cockpit, wrapped tight in my triple thermal sweatshirt. I can almost pretend I am basking in the tropical sun because the woodstove is pouring its heart out for me.

The wind is howling through the river channel which makes eating breakfast an exercise in eye-hand coordination. In a channel like this, we really have no way of knowing what the wind is doing out in the bay. We keep looking to the west, checking the feel of the wind and looks of the clouds. The question runs like a refrain through our morning, "Will the wind blow us back to Eastport or simply provide us a day of American Bandstand (rock and roll)?"

All sorts of opportunities present themselves as possible plans for today. Should we row ashore, rustle Charlene out of dreamland, call a large number of friends for potential rides to town which, in all probability, would lead to all types of fun activities? Ultimately, we "ixnayed" all the ideas which came to mind and opted for a fair tide and a sunny day to sail home to Eastport. The tide has changed. We have a full 6 hours of ebb tide going our way. I adjust the depth sounder, push the "on" button, then menu 2 then 5.

"Are we ready to go?" I ask.

"No." the Captain informs me. "I need to change the head sail back to the jib!"

Geez Louise!

It turns out to be not as unpromising a project as other times, when the wind is ranting and raving. We are, after all, still at anchor and he said "I" not we. However, a new responsibility for the first mate suddenly arises in the routine. The trusty woodstove is now hot enough to singe my eyelashes and the Captain needs the genoa sail lowered through the front hatch and safely stowed below in the V-berth where it will be exchanged for the jib.

The jib then has to be taken out of its bag and shoved up through the hatch to the Captain. All without dangerous consequences to me or the sails.

With the smell of the woodstove still pumping out heat to us here in the cockpit and the wind at our backs, we set sail out of the river. There is some rambunctious bird business going on upon the shore and up in the trees. We listen and give silent waves good bye to the Bocabec River and the *Avonturr*. Sailing past her, she displays her massive size next to our little *Guillemot*.

The autumn days up here have a clean, crispness to them and the autumn light is strikingly vivid. This is just one of the many reasons that artists gather in the area. The morning wind, out here on the Passamaquoddy Bay, has been magic. We quietly sailed by

Avonturr Sailing by Eastport, en route to Bocabec River
The Avonturr, *after weathering a hurricane off of Cape Hatteras, flying*
what sails she had left. (Photo Credit: Edward French, The Quoddy Tides)

Hardwood Island, Hospital, and Ministers Island. All silent and beautiful. The sunny skies, the ripples, whirlpools and the back eddies beckon us on. We have lunch and pleasure at the helm. All morning long we laugh and muse. Then we sit in quiet joy with just the companionable noise of the water and our vessel moving through it. We enjoy the constant sense of beauty out here.

I take the tiller, happy to be back in some of our home waters. The Captain moves forward and stands like a ship's figurehead. Looking up, he raises his arms and, as if struck by the sun, he speaks, "It is horrible to be this bored!" His words grabbed me and brought to mind some conversations with a variety of friends before departing on this journey.

They said, "Don't you think you will be bored?" This question, especially the first time it was asked, shocked me. That was one thing that never even crossed my mind. If it had, I would have put it on my list entitled "The Least of my Worries." So, when asked, I answered, with a casual nervous giggle. Then I added, confidently, "I love to read, so I'm seldom bored."

Today, even *thinking* about being bored makes me crack up! I ask myself, "Self, were you ever bored?" While sailing along in our transport of delight, I answer myself.

"Eileen, over the past 30 days you have felt blistered and sunburned; strained, tired, fearful and exhausted; stretched, achy, and stiff-kneed; muddy, frustrated, rocked and rolled; stressed, annoyed, cramped and frayed; hot, cold, wet and frizzy; sad, tearful, and sleep-deprived; peaceful, rested, relaxed and unhurried. You've been full of delight and indignation, joy, rage and self-doubt. You've been awed, amazed, euphoric, ecstatic, thrilled, excited and captivated— overly grateful and appreciative. You've felt spiritual presence, been inspired, occasionally/slightly enlightened, loved, rich, romantic, at peace and changed. But, Eileen Beaver, I can tell you that this is one of the rare times in your life that you can say something with such cosmic certainty, NO! You were not bored!"

Sun is pouring on our backs with all the strength of noon. There is gladness in the air, such brightness in the sun and such beauty in the sea. Doug is down below, searching for something in the bilge under the cockpit. Suddenly he pops up with the buoyancy of a lobster buoy. Using the antics of one who's just struck gold, he holds up our prized bottle of elderflower wine, smiles and says with relish, "Shall we celebrate?"

Joyfully, we prance around the cockpit letting the tiller temporarily do what it wanted. I brought her back on course while my personal wine steward found the wine opener and successfully opened the bottle without bits of cork floating to the bottom. The Captain takes the tiller—he's a better multitasker than I am. I sit, poised for the occasion. I tip my glass to my jolly husband. I feel, at this moment, like the favored wife of the renowned African tribal leader of the Cameroons, *The Fon of Bafut*. I adjust my imaginary, brightly-colored turban. I fondle the jewels and carved bones around my neck and I sip my wine. The dialogue in my head goes like this.

(Delivered in a very seductive, husky, low voice) "Dis mon done have plenty good power. Me like'em too too much. We done have too happy time!"

I watch my #1 husband trim the sails, adjust the cushion behind his back, cross his legs that are stretched across the cockpit. I peer down at his frayed cuffs rolled around his ankles, I watch his dirty toes wriggle.

With a glad eye, I remember the scene at Roger and Connie's beach house at Five Islands; the four of us chugging (I mean *sipping*) this same wine, Nolan, playing with Doug and laughing till tears rolled down his face. I remember the words of Emily, in Wilder's *Our Town*. "Do any human beings ever realize life while they live it?"

Oddly enough, Emily, most of the time this *unfeathered two-legged* (Dryden) Homo sapiens does! I may have mentioned casually, before, that this man is out of step with the rest of the world. It's not so much that he walks to the beat of a different drum, but rather that he carries an orchestra around in his head. But I've found I rather like it.

I look past my cheery scruffy husband and I see the nest of bald eagles on Casco Bay Island. There are dozens of seals sunning on the rocks near Sandy Beach. We watch silently as we glide by. Every few minutes, one of them rolls over, wriggles to a more comfortable position, stretches, raises up as though to take a reading on the weather, hears a sound, turns to check safety conditions. A few jump up quickly, jerk to wide-eyed attention and hit the water with a splash. Others appear uncertain, daring to be the last on the rocks. Several gulls pursue some feast on the island while an immature brown bald eagle, soars overhead.

If we really concentrate, we can see the colony of Great Blue Herons that live on Spruce Island. It will not be long before we are sailing close to the vortex of Ole' Sow, North America's largest whirl-pool. The Captain knows exactly how to sail it. I'm not going to allow my brain even one tiny little thought of a worry that we may be sucked spirally to the center!

Woowoo, woowoo. I look back to find my #1 husband smiling a smile the size of a yardstick at his favored wife! He's giving me that special look ...

If I were writing heartthrob romances for the masses, this would be the highlight of the story—the part you all would be waiting for. This is my story's equivalent of the skies opening, angels singing, eyes glistening, lips lightly parted declaring undying love! This is where my man's infectious charms would over whelm me, no mat-ter how rough the going—the storm clouds may lower and the ho-rizon may grow dark, but I'd know in my heart, that I will follow him to the ends of the earth—or Eastport (same place). This is where the imagery would be especially powerful, the dialogue gripping. There would be some bumps and grinds, hubba hubbas, eyebrow movement up and down. You'd have plenty of provocative talk about cleavages and such; the dialogue would be so mushy the bilge pump would be clogged, your reading glasses would be fogged, because I'm here to tell ya—it doesn't get any better than this. My Captain/husband tips his glass to me and with earnest love and affection, pride and respect, gives me a toast, "To Eileen! You Rock! You're Brilliant!"

Oo-la-la! I'll drink to that! Life does add up! My eyes blink shut and then open wide, much like Howdy Doody. For a bit, I'm driven wild with emotion. This boosted my sensations to where mere words cannot describe, so I pinched my mouth shut concentrating on leav-ing this beautiful moment wordless. I'm positive the wine and the toast, gave me a flush that made me seem younger and more engaging. Could I possibly have him wrapped around my nautical little finger? I felt the hum of satisfaction run through my bones.

You're damn tootin'! I'll be his first mate on next year's cruise! When I think of Prince Edwards Island, the Gulf Stream—warmest waters north of North Carolina—miles of sandy beaches and French bakeries. (Scratch that—I'm on a diet! Right now the only thing I own French-cut is green beans. From this point on, I'm planning my wardrobe for the Isle de la Madeleine's which includes French-cut-you-know-whats!)

Cela va sans dire! I can't let him go alone! I can hardly contain my mildly hysterical giggle.

Thinking objectively, would anyone not agree that it is a foolish first mate who neglects to make full use of the strengths of her Captain? Wouldn't a romantic song played on his guitar make my *oogah oogah* moment even more stupendous?

Yes, he agrees, a song on the guitar is in fact a good idea.

I wait while the getting-the-guitar and the tuning commence. I see the Perry shore, off in the distance and the sweet visions the Perry song conjures up in my mind. The soft squishy part of me sees myself dancin' and twirlin' on the arm of an honest man! My heart goes thump, thump and a strong rush of affection runs through me. I feel a real connection to this place! I feel so extremely happy!

I silently admonish myself, "I must remember my spiritual goals. Happiness is such a shallow place. Now I'm shooting for inner peace and serenity—they come from a deep place." I'm not a woman who demands romantic satisfaction from a bouquet of flowers—not me! I don't need a man to take me to fancy restaurants for candlelight dinners. Phooey on that! I'm a full-fledged-confident-in-my-relationship-middle-aged-woman. I don't go for the superficial romance cards with conventional salutations written by employees sitting in an office cubical. The expectations some women have seem depthless when I have my very own sailor-singer-songwriter-husband ready to perform just for me!

For pause and effect, there is a long pregnant silence. He takes his plastic cup of wine from between his feet and gulps a large swallow. He rolls his eyes heavenward, "Ummmmmyes! Great wine!"

Then he plays a few cords as if he were a classical guitar player, *woo woo*. Enchanted, I utter a soft moan. While awaiting his seductive wile, I smile for about the upteenth time at my co-conspirator of one of the greatest romances of all the ages. Take the word of one who would not deceive you, it doesn't get any better than this ...

I see my hickey on her neck—
I chew another nicorete.
I'm drivin' down to the dollar store—

What? What's up with that, my romantic song is ...

Her eyes rolled back,
her knees gave way?
My fate is slumped over on the passenger side?

I fell for Mr. Teaser-bait-the-hook-becharmer! He has devilry in his eyes. Then he sings like Ray Charles, eyes closed head swaying. He peeks over in my direction every once in awhile, to check my romantic temperature. To set the record straight, I am *not* the inspiration for "Slow Drivin' with My Baby"! This cad ... if I wasn't sailing and drinking wine, I'd throttle ... it is hard not to laugh and cry so I did both. No wonder I'm a wack job!

Call 511 for wack control, get the goons over for backup. "I promise you Captain Beaver, there will be payback time!"

The Captain puts down the binoculars, "The floating docks are still there!" This is happy news because, at some point in the Fall, the city floating docks are hulled along with most all the other sailboats and pleasure crafts. We glide by Deer Island Point, Dog Island, and Todd Head. It is 2 p.m., low tide (20 feet today) it will be a few hours before we have enough water to row in from our mooring in Broad Cove.

Our plan of action is ... we will dock at the breakwater. The Captain will stay with the boat while I walk up to the house, jump in the Egg (our 1987 Toyota van painted egg shell white) and drive down to the dock. The unloading process will be tons easier here, even with the steep ramps of low tide. At Broad Cove we would have to row everything into shore in the dinghy. From there we'd have to cart it all up from the rocky Cony Beach, then up a very steep, narrow path to the Shackford Head parking lot.

Shouldn't I feel relief? Shouldn't I be heaving a great big sigh of relief as we pull up next to the Eastport dock? Shouldn't a woman who may not be the worst sailor in the world—but in the running—who has spent half her adult life wondering what part of her closet she can wear her pearls with, feel emotional release and physical deliverance? Why is it that all I feel is this all-sweeping awareness that the Captain and his first mate are finding it hard to pull in and tie up? Why is it, then, that the sight of the dock and the realization that, in minutes, I will climb over the life lines, walk away from the *Guillemot* and our experience together, makes me want to burst into tears?

With sunglasses hiding my runny eyes, I say goodbye, too emotionally and with 18 too many syllables. I square my shoulders, take a deep breath and walk down the dock. The Captain calls to me, "Careful out there, my sweetie! It looks flat but it's round!" This makes me laugh. I wave back at him—one of those one flop-of-the-hand-and-wrist waves.

At the top of the steep ramp I turn back. My husband is leaning one hand on the pop-top, one hand on his hip; one leg is bent and one bare foot rests on top of the other. His back is to me and he's facing out to sea. I suppress the urge to make this story much more "box office" by running back down the ramp, down the wooden dock, jumping back on the boat, throwing my arms open wide and giving him a big kiss, untying the dock lines, and pushing off.

I don't. I acknowledge to myself that we made it to Ithaca, ending our odyssey.

Once on the tarmac of the breakwater, I walk backward for a few steps keeping the *Guillemot* and the Cherry Island Lighthouse in view. A beautiful picture, if there ever was one. Gratitude rolls over me to have this scene be part of my section on the canvas of life. I feel the pure simple joy of being alive. I'm one of God's magnificent thoughts that originated out of an energy field! Laughing I turn toward Rosie's Hot Dog Stand.

Once past Rosie's, I cross over Water Street to head up Sullivan

Street. I am greeted by a string of white Christmas lights hanging outside the quonset hut which is home to Jim Blankman's world. His 1946 Woody sits in its rightful spot outside his party workshop. Custom skateboards, luges, restoring old woodys, building teardrop trailers, caskets and urns are but a few of the projects to come out of this hive of industry. I see Greg's (Pugh "The Man") 1948 Pontiac parked out back. He's likely to be just home from the golf course and in there drinking beer and working on his latest guitar project. I stop and peek in quietly. Yep, there they are. Johnny Wonderful is sipping wine and holding up a violin he just completed. He's discussing the finish with his fellow woodworkers. I don't dare to make my presence known or Doug would be waiting for hours, I can't get side-tracked! I quicken my pace.

I pass Moose Island Marine where several fishermen are going in and out preparing for urchin and scallop season. I walk on, passing the skeletons of wild flowers sowing seeds. I welcome the shade of the tall trees, which serves as a buttress on each side of the road. I stop at the top, out of breath from the steep hill. I turn around to see the breakwater and several fishermen with their lines dropped over the side. Campobello Island sits peacefully across the bay.

On I trudge, deeper into the unique community of Eastport. This small island is one of the last untouched by the masses in Maine. Route 190 off Route 1 leads nowhere but to delightful little Eastport. Eastport is home to several art galleries—showcasing many of the artists in the area. There is a very active arts center which attracts talented actors, poets and musicians. This eastern most city boasts several cozy little shops, unique architecture, and my personal favorite, the Peavy Library. One aspect we find surprising and unusual about living here, on Moose Island, is that people of all ages and backgrounds intermingle socially. We can enjoy uneventful days living in a place where everyone waves and stops to talk about the weather. When you are in places like Eastport and Nova Scotia, you forget there is a world where there are streets you wouldn't want to walk.

I round the corner off Orange Street where Mugsey, the Persian cat, basks in the sun. Not long ago she was found in the street, face-to-face with a moose. I pass the Catholic church which boasts a banner proclaiming that, "Catholics can always come home!" Two blocks up, off Chapel Street, I turn right. Just a couple of years ago I learned the names of these streets when the street signs were erected. So now I can tell people we live off of Chapel instead of the next block up from City Hall.

I make a right onto Stevens Avenue. Once here, I feel so removed from the water. The salt air has to travel up the hill to this part of the middle end. With countless corrections from my husband, I no longer call it the upper middle end. He insists there are three ends to Eastport—the north end, the south end and the middle end. That's all. I believe there should be a lower and an upper middle end because of the big hill. Nevertheless, it is about a 12-minute-walk up the hill and an 8-minute-walk back down to the breakwater.

I slip through the tall hedges that surround our house. A porch light of turning maple leaves glistens in the fall sunlight. I stand amidst the last blooms of my garden. A showy late blooming clematis and silver lace vine drape the trellis and fence. A few spare lilies are nodding their heads like tired parents waiting to greet their wayward child.

If I were coming in after dark, I would be stomping my feet all the way up the sidewalk. We do this to forewarn any skunks out doing their nocturnal foraging. With their sniffers always close to the ground and their poor eyesight, I might just have an accidental encounter of the very stinky kind. They will run from you if given a chance. One year we had a family living under our garage. In the evenings, while sitting in our little bricked courtyard, we would see mom and her three babies in tow. They would be out for their how-to-find-dinner lessons. One of the little rascals must have been hungry in the day because, while mom slept, we saw him eagerly munching away under the birdfeeder which hung in the tree next to our old iron park bench. This became a routine for him and several days in a row we spotted him out investigating the world on his own. One day I walked out the back kitchen door and an unexpected sight stopped me in my tracks. There stood Doug, barefoot (as he most always is) resting very quietly, hands folded over his belly, laughing as our furry black and white visitor nibbled on his toes.

The large painted Deruta fruit bowl in the center of the kitchen table holds the key to the Egg. I don't bother checking the answering machine. Worry probably called wondering where I've been. Sitting next to the phone is our local telephone book. I laugh each time I receive one in the mail. This year, when I tore into the plastic shrink-wrap which held our new phone book attached to a half inch thick piece of Styrofoam, I noticed the white and yellow pages totaled 54—the very same number of pages for the 90 localities included in the book as there were four years ago.

I walked upstairs to check the bed, toilet and tub. I opened our bedroom window for fresh air, then turned to look at our lonely bed where I have lain for six years listening to the horns from the big ships and the foghorn from Dog Island. From the window in the landing I see gulls that preside over the neighborhood from Glenna's rooftop. Earlier this year, a few smarties learned they could see and hear Glenna coming out to feed them better from our roof top than hers. Doug constructed sticks and twine to keep them from perching on our roof and composting our fairly new shingles with their colorful droppings.

Walking back through the house, I feel slightly disoriented—like one who's been blindfolded and spun around. Surrounded by walls and ceilings, our small modest home, especially our kitchen, seems so spacious to me now, I sigh when I look up and I see two large areas of peeling paint. The upstairs toilet leaked, yet again, earlier this summer. This old house, for 150-years-old, is doing pretty darn well but, like me, is showing her age.

With astonishment, I looked around and for the first time in my life I could say, "All this I can live without!" Well, for 30 days anyway. It feels liberating! If civilization collapsed tomorrow, I would be a little bit self-sufficient! Having toilets, showers and running hot water at my fingertips seems, oddly, too normal. I never thought I would come to understand, let alone agree, with Socrates.

I have lived long enough to learn how much there is I can really do without. He is nearest to God who needs the fewest things.

There is a big difference in needing and enjoying. I still appreciate the beauty of fine things and beautiful homes, I just don't *need* them as much. Simplicity is not self-denial, it is a return to those values that matter most in life.

> *If I am what I have and if I lose what I have who then am I?*
> —Erich Fromm

I feel healing in this area of my soul. I also know full well that healing is an ongoing experience. It doesn't have a period at the end of the sentence. Today, at least, the yardstick has changed by which I measure my personal self-worth and, therefore, my happiness. Things come and go just as the tide comes and goes.

All those flipping through my reminiscences, who knew me BD, are likely shaking your heads in wonder. She must be finally living her hippie days, (growing up in California in the 60's you might wonder how I could have missed them, I guess I was too busy trying to be just like Betty Crocker, which is nutty as a fruitcake, because some marketing genius invented her!) Are you thinking I'm missing some buttons? Or, as they say around here, "She's just haven' a bad spell!" Of all things, chasing after a barefoot singin' sailor! I want to pat your backs and set your mind at ease. I am not going to change my name to Earth or Tofu. I don't really do Tai Chi (although I'd like to, it's on my *Someday List*). I put that in there earlier because I used to think that anyone who searches for enlightenment and is a vegetarian would do such things. You will not see me along the roadside selling crystals and macrame plant holders. I don't subscribe to *Rolling Stone* instead of *House and Garden* and I haven't forsaken my diamonds for mood rings. Our vans are absent of peace signs and Grateful Dead stickers. My skin in only wrinkled not sprinkled with tattoos.

James Baldwin said, "Most of us are about as eager to be changed, as we were to be born, and go through our changes in a similar state of shock."

Through all my changes of seasons, I have come to the conclusion that life is to be experienced—lived! Every stage of life is risky. I don't want to live life with my emergency brakes on or swimming close to the side of the pool, so I can always touch. It may not turn out the way we planned or hoped and it may not be totally enjoyable, but it should always be exciting. Joseph Campbell said, "We must be willing to get rid of the life we've planned, so as to have the life that is waiting for us."

Ever since the infamous day when we were in the Shube and the river rafter boss asked the question, which at the time I thought was almost as funny and as absurdly silly as, "Have you ever sailed a boat before?"

He asked, "Are you here on purpose?" It was ridiculous question but, oddly enough, one that has had a profound effect on me.

"Eileen, are you here on purpose? Am I on purpose?" Over and over, these past few weeks, I've pondered this. Just as when we were in the Shube, I am tired of saying "I don't know?" So now, I'm goin' with, "Yes! I'm on purpose." It's amazing, but I'm here on purpose. I was *there* on purpose. I'd say everything is on purpose. Events that seemed random will show themselves to be parts of a coherent whole. It seems to me that part of being centered, being in perfect balance, you must come to understand that everything is related to everything other thing you learn in life.

In *The Natural*, Glen Close said, *"I believe we have two lives; the life we learn with and the life we live after that."*

I know the Captain waits, so I hasten out the back door, and up the slate path. I turn to see the school bus drop Ethan very conveniently right in front of his house. What a pleasure it is to live where you have neighbors like Ms. Watts (she lives catty-corner), who looks out for your house all winter. She and Brother (her brother, our next door neighbor, whom she calls Brother so we do too) come over for some music and neighborhood socializing and lots of laughter, Ms. Watts proclaims, "Laughter is better than high blood pressure medicine."

David Leroy (Brother) tromps over with a padded cooler slung over his shoulder. No matter what I say or do, he says, "Darlin' I love ya!" His beer cosy tells us "I take my wife everywhere, but she keeps finding her way back!" (His wife Jeanie says it's the other way around!) His slippers have duct tape around them to hold them together.

It such a funny place, Eastport.

I want to stay and talk to my garden, I notice my rosemary plants are ready for a trim. My mind drifts to some veggies grilled with rosemary sticks then brushed with olive oil. Look at that borage, it's goin' nuts! Hurrah! Should we have *frisceui di borraggine,* borage leaves deep fried in butter?

Stop Eileen! You're making yourself hungry and late, besides remember, swimsuits. I force myself to walk toward the Egg which sits next to the now-quiet Tiki bar we made from wood gathered from the beaches.

I sit high above the road in my trusty little Egg. I go *zoom, zoom, sputter* and rumble down Boynton Street past Richard and Sydney's house. I give a little *toot toot* to signify my homecoming. It is then that I see Richard painting some outside trim on their stately old home. Years of hard work has transformed the Hayden House back to the grande dame of our little city. Inside and out it is splendid—even their laundry room seems like the Taj Mahal to me at this point in my life. Their acre lot now boasts glorious gardens. This year's project of a teahouse and pond makes me want to stop and have a cuppa tea. But I'm a good girl, I keep the foot on the gas peddle.

I come to a screeching halt at the end of the steep hill when it dead ends on Water Street. I give another wave and *toot, toot* to Ronnie Hall, the king of rock and roll. He is heading up the road towards north end. I turn left and accelerate past the huge stone customs building, which also houses the Port Authority, the U.S. Coast guard and the post office. This reminds me—I'll need to go collect my month's worth of mail. Often, when arriving back in town, we never have to notify the post office to resume delivery. Usually someone notices we are back and mail starts to appear in our little blue mail box.

Once all the gear is loaded into the Egg, we leave her parked at the breakwater. We untie the boat and set sail around the island to Broad Cove where there is a little dot of a mooring called Guillemot home. We have a coming tide. It carries us past the breakwater, then past the municipal pier where the big tugboats rest when not bringing in a large cargo ship. Attached to the pier is the NOAA tide sensing station. Onward we go—I can just see the cupola of the brick building which houses the Peavy library. The Motel East sits

Eastport
We have a coming tide. It carries us past the breakwater, then past the municipal pier where the big tugboats rest when not bringing in a large cargo ship. Attached to the pier is the NOAA tide sensing station.

quietly, perched on its bed of pink granite. We slowly glide past the site ashore where once stood the first sardine factory in the United States. Eastport looks so charming from the water. I love the rockbound coast and the little city which resides upon it. Many of its homes have been under repair ever since I arrived. Some of the old homes have been completely restored but many still sit lonely or without time and finances.

The overall economy in all of Washington County has been low for years—not enough jobs for people to support families. With low economy and deep water ports, there is the constant threat of big industry coming in to build dangerous, polluting eyesores which can (and will) ruin this garden paradise.

The nutrient-rich waters of these systems of bays create an ecological diversity which makes it one of North America's great natural resources. Unchecked industry in the entire last century managed to pollute thousands and thousands of miles of shoreline on the west and east coasts, the gulf coasts, the great lakes, the Mississippi River, and the Missouri River. I know jobs are needed. But allowing where you live to be ruined is not the answer. I've seen it happen too many times.

While shopping at the market in Middleton, I read a headline dated September 21—just ten days after the twin tower tragedy. In the southern district of Toulouse, France, a deadly blaze raged at the Grande Paroisse AZF factory. It killed 30 people and wounded more than 3, 000. The effects of this nitrate explosion were felt all over the city, to a distance of several miles and *ten times* farther than the so-called security zones. Why can't we preserve one of the last untouched coastlines in the US? What price tag can you put on lives and homes of everyone in a ten-mile radius, most of whom live on islands with a single road on and off? Why can't we preserve the most unique system of bays in the world?

The demographics are changing in this sleepy hollow of a town— more people from large cities are moving in searching for a peaceful existence. Some are retired; some can earn their living from the Internet. Many families have found living close to all the conveniences of larger cities can be very inconvenient. They are willing to sacrifice a lot of what other areas have to offer to gain so much. We have found, in Eastport and the surrounding areas, groups of unique, abnormal people, gathered together in a beautiful place. It is not a Bar Harbour; it is raw beauty.

Such were my thoughts when the wind gave us a swift kick and we fly pass Princes Cove and round Estes Head. Up on the Head we can see a speck of a picnic bench, where we often sit and watch the strong activity of the tide movements in the water below and the seagulls play in the updrafts of the wind above. The empty docks of the easternmost cargo port in the U.S. lay ahead of us. To the south, toward Lubec, is Treats Island, where Benedict Arnold, after the Revolutionary War, traded at an American store. Our final turn takes us into Broad Cove and puts Shackford Head to port.

We see a cormorant sitting on our mooring ball drying his wings—he appears to be applauding our return. He hears and sees our approach and prepares for flight like a competition diver readying for an intricate dive. Poking his head into the wind, wings set as if limbering up, he does a few circles of his head and neck, a couple of rotator cup motions—a peck here, a peck there. Poised for take off, he takes a crap on the mooring and then dives beautifully.

We tuck in the *Guillemot* and climb in the dinghy. We row around the ole' girl and give her a congratulatory pat on her hull, for a job well done. We row in. Every stroke of the oar brings us nearer to shore and the remains of five Civil War ships here in Broad Cove. All were brought here between 1901-1920 to be burned and for Cony Beach and Broad Cove to be their proper burial grounds. Once acquainted with the water levels and the shoreline, we can judge if there is enough water to render the dinghy up to the rocky shore out of the mucky goo and to successfully float around the one skeleton which still protrudes at lower tides. We lift the dinghy and carry her up the steep, rocky, slippery, half-covered-in-seaweed beach, to her resting spot.

Cony Beach shows off her underworld at all levels of tide—sea grass, rockweed olive-green and olive-brown, wrinkled green leaves of sea lettuce with edible, purple-red dulse and bleached sea moss, with slimy and gelatinous cords seven and eight feet long. Up at the wrack line, there are all types of driftwood, wild morning glories and lively red ants strewn in with the lumpy tangles, wisps and matted festoons of ocean vegetation. In the warmth they slowly wither without their nutrients of sea water, sending the smells of ocean and vegetation into the warm air.

Down the beach is a barely distinguishable path which takes us up the steep hill to the Shackford Head State Park parking lot. I visualize the trails up Shackford, now colorful, speckled with fallen leaves. A few days a week, I enjoy getting my exercise by riding my bike out to the trails. I hide my bike in some trees and continue afoot on the different meandering paths.

I'm slightly out of breath when we hit the dirt road. There is a grassed area in the center where rock and bronze monuments stand giving tribute to the civil war ships. Something odd catches our eyes.

"What do you think it is?" I ask my husband.

"Your guess is as good as mine!"

We quicken our pace. In the dimming light of dusk we see a formation which we have only seen pictured in the Audubon Mushroom Field Guide. There, in the grass, is a growing fairy ring. A composition of beautifully colored and shaped mushrooms which, as they age, begin to form a mysterious ring. We walk around it, marveling at the perfect half moon. I look up and out over Broad Cove. The moon shines brightly over the quiescent ocean, in a sharply defined crescent. The shape of the moon is almost exactly the shape of the fairy ring. My words are choked.

"Doug, come and stand where I am!" We stand side by side in silent harmony, as if on sanctified ground. The moon shows almost exactly half of its 2, 160 miles across, moon beams shine over the water from 238, 857 miles away. We let out moans of pleasure. The moon and the fairy ring, at this exact moment, are in perfect alignment. We both stood there, holding on to each other, trying not to stagger backwards at the phenomenal scene.

How long have they been growing there? It takes years for the spores to spread over this large an area and we haven't seen them. It would take just the right climate and moisture, in between the structured mowing of the lawn, for them to be this big, just for us, for this evening, for this moon. A loud squeaky cackling startles us, making us both jump. Adding even more amazement to our beguiling scene, one of the bald eagles, which nests out on Ships Point, soared overhead. We backed away, not wanting to take our eyes from the angle of the moon and fairy ring. Another strange and beautiful mystery of nature.

Doug told me the first month I met him, "Nothing manmade is as awesome as nature!" I'm sure many of you out there are using the blowing-on-your-fingernails, then polishing-them-on-your-vest type gesture, saying, "I already knew that!" Well, maybe. I say a very narrow possible maybe. Somewhere deep down there with my deepest human emotions, so did I. But now, I can nod my head, affirming Luther Burbank's observation, that *"there is no other door to knowledge than the door nature opens; there is no other truth, except the truth we discover from nature."* When I look around me, back at Broad Cove where, minutes earlier, I counted 14 Great Blue Herrons sitting quietly ashore after their evening meal, I'm astonished at what I can see right now, just within my 360-degree vision. It's hard to be bored and astonished at the same time.

I'm thrilled to have to have our walk back home; not to climb in a car to zoom away from all of this. My senses seemed toned like they've never been before. We head out in the direction of Deep Cove Road, past the Washington County Boat School and the Eastport Boat Yard. Once out on the paved road, we turn right towards town. The many trees show off their fall colors, tons of interrupted ferns are bright with yellow and gold. A mile later we pass the Mustard Mill, North America's last stone-ground mustard factory, which has been owned and operated by the Rae family for over a hundred years. Across the road is the IGA, bustling with last minute shoppers.

Unwilling for our day to end, we pass our turn on Brighton Street and cut back behind the Havey Wilson Pharmacy. This short cut takes us up a rock ledge, past an old teak schooner sitting in someone's door yard. We pass Folis Place where we wave to James to tell him of our homecoming. James, a long-time sailor and boat builder will enjoy the tales of our adventure. I spot some bright red peeking from his five gallon buckets of tomatoes growing outside his windows. We climb up the hill to the playing fields adjacent to the elementary school.

Our goal is the "Top of the World"! My husband believes it to be the highest point on Moose Island—if not the highest, then the highest we can get to. For the last six years, I thought everyone called it the top of the world. Until, this last summer ...

Tachiana Alexeeva, our artist friend from Russia, was here visiting. She now lives with Richard, her husband, not far from us in PA. We love her paintings, so we have contrived a deal which has apparently been good for both parties. She and her family can come here and stay in our guest house for a week, in exchange for one of her paintings. This last summer is the second time we have made the exchange. Her family arrived to enjoy Eastport in July. One especially beautiful, sunny day, while the rest of her family fished contentedly off the breakwater, we took her to see the "Top of the World." She was so excited over her newfound knowledge about the island that she wanted to show her family her discovery later that afternoon. We were out on the boat, so no navigational help was available. She tried to locate the trail, but no luck. Realizing she was all turned around, she started asking directions. She inquired of many town people in her soft Russian accent, "Where is the top of the world?" They merely peered at her quizzically. She received several sets of directions. When they ended up 6 miles out of town, past the Passamaquoddy Indian reservation in Perry, she realized that not everyone calls this high bluff the "Top of the World."

We found the path covered with wild blueberry bushes turning their very own shade of red and burnt orange for the fall. If you veer right, a path will take you to Devil's chair. We climb the rock ledge to the left. We both utter a heartfelt, "AAHHH!" Here we are at the "Top of the World"! Our heads swivel to take in the panoramic views. From left to right, first we see Canada's Campobello Island (I can just see Franklin and Eleanor Roosevelt's summer cottage). Next is Friar's Head and Friar's Roads. I visually cross the International Bridge over the Lubec Narrows to Lubec. We see Roger's Island where many a time we have sailed friends over and enjoyed a cookout at the picnic bench and brick fire pit. My eyes move on to Sewards Neck, Shackford Head, and Broad Cove, where the *Guillemot* rests, bobbing and lonely, but in plenty of water! To the far right, Deep Cove frames the pink and orange blazes of the setting sun.

In the foreground is Eastport. The trees and church steeples of this tiny New England town poke out of its surface. There are no billboards rearing up out the ground, or words towering from the sky. There's not a stoplight or a set of golden arches for 35 miles. It is a complete contrast of how I've spent most of my life. You can never underestimate the power of contrasts.

The darkness falls and we hear the church bells informing the community that it is now 6 p.m.. The church bells ring daily at 9 a.m., 12 noon, and 6 p.m.. In between, we all have to figure the time on our own. I know I should move and get down off this ledge, head back home to my fluffy pillow and down comforter before it is pitch dark, but not yet. When one is having an epiphany day, one must ride it out to its fullest. My mind is still sorting through my life.

I feel as though messages from another time and place were brought to me by way of the largest tides in the world—the *big flush of the Bay of Fundy*. Until recently, most of life's lessons I'd learned, or partially absorbed, or once thought I heard someone talking about, didn't end up being life-changing.

While trying to survive this adventurous journey, I was forced to face certain fundamental truths of life. In the past I have lived with a highly-developed state of mind, a habitual waiter—if you're always wanting the "future" (a better job, more money, the kids to be grown, to be appreciated, the perfect house, for my garden to grow, or for enlightenment) then you don't acquire gratitude for and appreciation of the *present* moment. No matter what you have or achieve, it is often never quite good enough. A perfect recipe for dissatisfaction and nonfulfillment is wanting a time, place, a situation, an object, that you haven't got. Consequently, you are not *really* living. You've got to ask yourself, "What are you waiting for?"

My entire future lies ahead of me; all the experiences, joys and sorrows of my past behind me. That's what it took for me to learn the ropes. I found, with the turbulent tides, that if you tried to resist them, you would suffer and be torn, ripped and stifled. They could always cause more pain than if you just went with the flow. The powerful tides come and go just as life's cycles do. Good conditions and bad conditions don't last. All conditions are highly unstable and in constant flux. Flush symbolizes cleansing and change; this journey taught me peaceful acceptance of the ebb and flow of life. I can, with much effort and struggle, resist, but this leads, inevitably, to much wasted energy. Or I can just sit back, bob along and enjoy the view and the ride—and what a ride it can be.

I affirm the words of Mark Twain

Twenty years from now, you will be more disappointed by the things you didn't do than by the ones you did do. So throw off the bowlines. Sail away from the safe harbour. Catch the trade winds in your sails. Explore! Dream! Discover!

I feel like flapping my scrawny wings and testing flight. For the past 8 years, I've found myself precariously perched in the center of a tipping scale–old life versus new life. Today, I have my feet firmly planted on the "Top of the World" and the view from here is … Spectacular!

EPILOGUE

January 17, 2002

My journal still serves to sort out my jumbled mush of feelings. After being back to the rigors of everyday living, life again starts to zap me like electroshock therapy. I begin to feel beat up about politics, the news, jobs, traffic, our children's needs, money, wrinkles and the fact that all my expensive suits from my old life have shoulder pads and are clearly not for the 21st century. I feel weak, as if I've been left out in the desert and I need to be brought in from the sun and given some water. I try to drag my limp tired body with just the strength of my arms and elbows. It is all starting to get to me, I am starting to feel very old.

January 21, 2002

I stomp my feet on the front door step in an attempt to knock the chunks of snow and ice off my boots. I open the door and the snows of pessimism fly in with me. I complain to my husband, "The traffic was terrible. It took me an hour-and-half to get home. That's a lot of time on the 309 with many icy spots and snow drifts. I'm sick of Christmas decorations, I don't care if I ever see another Christmas tree in this life or the next. How I ever got to be a part-time professional Christmas decorator, I'll never know. Working with the public can be very trying. I'm going into voluntary exile. My back hurts, my feet and legs ache. I'm starting to get varicose veins from standing on those concrete floors. I couldn't even count how many times I bent up and down today. I think I'm finished with winters in all this frigid weather, I'm too old for this! Did you hear on the news …"

I slip out of my work clothes. I take a warm shower and don my robe and slippers. By then, my #1 husband has a fire lit and I sit down to drink a restorative cocktail. My quiet-sit-down-legs-curled-up-on-the-sofa project this evening is to sort through and organize a large accordion folder of notes, lists, sayings, poems, and journal pages which I brought from California and have hardly looked through since.

I found two typed pages, dated 21 years ago. I read them through. Tears rushed to my eyes. I felt the warmth of the fire, I looked out the windows to see bows of the tree branches heavily laden with snow, bouncing in the breeze under the moonlight, making shadows over the white serene blanket.

I had a heart full of wonder. This confirms that I'm on the need-to-know-basis with God.

I knew, with moral certainty, when I placed these words in that file, that there would come a day in the far off future—like when I was pushing 51-years-old, that cynicism would start to creep in like arthritis. I somehow knew there would come a day when I would have to say, "Now wait a cotton pickin' minute here! I'm not going to let pessimism rule my life! I'm not ready to be put out to pasture!" With sheer defiance tonight, I pull myself up. I stand straight, not humped over with the burdens of life. I put my hands on my metaphorical hips in an acutely pissed-off position and say to myself, "Listen here, Eileen Wimpy Beaver …"

We are here to drink beer. We are here to kill war. We are here to laugh at the odds and live life so well that death trembles to take us!
—*Bukowski*

No pessimist ever discovered the secrets of the stars, or sailed to an uncharted land, or opened a new haven to the human spirit
—*Helen Keller*

Next, was Samuel Ullman's *Youth* poem 1934—*what profound words*—"Youth is not a time of life—it is a state of mind!"
He tells us that, "It is not a matter of red cheeks, red lips and supple knees ..."
Rather, youth is,

Predominance of Courage over timidity . . the appetite for adventure over a life of ease.

He's right when he said, "Years may wrinkle the skin, but to give up enthusiasm, wrinkles the soul."
And there's more. "You are as young as your faith, as old as your fear, as young as your hope, as old as your despair."
He wants you to make sure your heart receives messages of beauty, hope and grandeur.
Don't allow your wires to be covered with snows of pessimism and the ice of cynicism—then are you grown old indeed!

January 25, 2002
I thankfully have the day off. Number 1 on my To Do List is to make several copies of the quotes. Miracles never cease. Doug's parent's copy machine is operational and produced the pages which are to connect the wires back to the central places in my heart. I will now have a heart of wonder and be undaunted by the challenge of events. I prance around, placing them in strategic locations through-out the house. I'm going to memorize these words and follow them like a low-carb diet. I will be emotionally prepared the next time I look at myself in the full-length mirror of life. The central place in my heart will receive messages of hope, cheer and grandeur and all that!

I pointed an authoritative finger at my copies and smile like some Pollyanna Gladgirl, "These words are my new credo. I am going to act and think positively and embrace the belief that I'm not old!" My husband calmly goes about filling the bird feeders. Then he sits down with his *Lindsey Publications Technical Book Catalogue*. I am charged and he is still reading the catalogue. I'm once again enthralled with life and he tells me, "Eileen, I think I'll get you this book, *I Just Love To Fart Cook Book!*"

I tell him most truthfully, "This is one area of our lives in which a technical book is by no means needed."

Laughing hard now, he goes on, "you get fantastic recipes like Chinese Pickled Cabbage, Swamp Gas Stew á la stink, Vegetarian Grenades, Butt Bustin' Bean Soup, Zucchini Zingers, and Rectal Rocket Fuel, just to name a few, my sweetie!" He looks up from the book, expectantly. I'm not smiling. He ignores this, and continues, "Get this, it is written by Pazzin' Gazz—64 pages, for only $6.95. A bargain!" I realize a young person would likely think this to be funny, so I start to give a lip quiver. "They describe it as tasteless, irreverent and disgusting!"

A young wife would think it clever and vow to get a copy for her husband as a little surprise to share with his other irreverent friends. So, I make a note on my list entitled "Fun and Optimistic Things to Do and Say!" This is a rather short list, but I am challenged to make it one of my more impressive, imaginative lists.

OOOHHH! I quickly add something to my list. This is good. Patting myself on my enthusiastic back, I note that I am going to make Youth Cards and place them alongside my Yoga Deck. I will pull them out one at a time. I will focus and meditate on key words and phrases including: Imagination!; Courage!; Adventure!; Enthusiasm!; Undaunted Spirits!; and Love of Wonder!; Youth is not supple knees!; and Vigor of the Emotions!

Hey! It'll be almost as good as a face-lift.

EPILOGUE II

You aren't thinking clearly if you believed I wouldn't have something else to tell you. A wordy person like myself always has something else to say. I actually have a long list, (now *there's* a surprise) but, as the Captain says, why make a long list when a short one will do. You can all be thankful for small mercies. I actually listened to him and, by and by, I narrowed it down to my three all-time-favorites. These three funny things, which happened over the next two years, helped to melt the snows of pessimism. One was charming, one uncanny and one was payback time.

Charmingly Funny

Thelma and Bob (longtime friends of Bill and Jean, Doug's parents) heard of our trip to Nova Scotia. When we told about the lovely, generous people we met, they smiled at each other knowingly. The Delaneys have been worldwide travelers for many years and have countless exciting adventures to share. One occasion which stands out concerned a story about a driving vacation through Nova Scotia. Their travels through central Nova Scotia came to an abrupt halt when two tires received severe damage. The description of their location was only that was in the middle of nowhere. Every car that passed stopped and offered help. Calls were made to locate the nearest tow truck. The owner of the garage was very busy but dropped everything to drive the very long distance and come to their rescue. Many hours later, the pleasant garage owner had their car towed and tires repaired. The two vacationers were ready to be sent on their merry way.

Bob's hands were a bit sweaty in anticipation of final settlement. A businessman himself, there was no doubt in his mind that all this towing and fixing business, in the height of tourist season, would cost him dearly. Bracing themselves, they checked the amount of cash they had on them, wondering if there was an ATM close by. They had noticed the garage owner had posted a "No Credit Cards Accepted" in his window. When asked what they owed him, the Blue Noser merely smiled contentedly, wiped the grease off his hands and then offered a friendly handshake. "Oh don't worry about it, " he said, "just tell your friends how good they treat ya here in Nova Scotia."

When we were told of their adventure, the words of Doug's song *Perry* came to my mind immediately.

What do you need but honest eyes?
What do you need to feel inside?
What do you need but a honest hand,
on the arms of a honest man?

Uncannily Funny

It was a cold March in Pennsylvania and Minneapolis. Doug and I met Brooke and Adam in Florida to celebrate their engagement. We camped in Bill's backyard. One of those days, when we weren't canoeing or making a beeline over to Boca Grande Beach, we had a leisurely time hanging around the ole' casa. Bill and Becky were at their respective jobs. I fixed lunch. Doug poked around in the stack of books. Brooke and Adam had walked to the store.

"Hey, Eileen, you gotta read this, " he said, holding a small pamphlet-type book of about 64 pages. (They weren't numbered, but you all *know* I counted.) The book was entitled *Bruce and Iona (Kilgore) Ruff—Their Forefathers—Their Descendants*, written by Keith Ruff, Becky's father. Doug looked up amazed, "Holy smokes, can you believe that!" Here's the quote from page 4:

> *A one-time sea captain, John Ruff arrived on these shores from Ireland, probably at Halifax in the late 1700's. Nothing is known of his early days in Nova Scotia until John and his wife, Susannah, arrived in the little town of Five Islands, early in the 1800's. They chose uninhabited Moose Island, just off the mainland, to be their home. Located in the Copequid Bay, where fifty-foot tides and chilling fogs roll in from the Bay of Fundy, Moose Island seemed a perfect match for the notorious dark moods of John Ruff.*
>
> *John and Susannah began clearing land and building a home in this lonely, isolated place. Their first-born was Isaiah, followed by Noah, Arthur, Andrew, Benjamin and Anthony. Driven by a cruel father, the boys worked hard clearing forty-five acres for raising crops and livestock.*
>
> *Life on Moose Island must have been disagreeable, to say the least, because Isaiah and Noah left home as soon as they came of age. A year or two after they left, their father was killed when a tree he was cutting fell and crushed his skull. Two years after his burial, number four son, Benjamin, was saying that John had been killed in cold blood by the two other sons. One of them would stand trial for that alleged crime . . . Meanwhile, according to local folklore, foggy, forbidding Moose Island remains haunted by John Ruff's ghost to this very day. I am not sure about his ghost, but John was my great-great grandfather.*

Could it be that the eerie feelings I experienced that day at Five Islands and thereafter, while sailing by en route to Parrsboro, could be from none other than the ghost of my friend Rebecca Ruff's great, great, great-grandfather? I say, "Case closed Watson!"

Payback Funny

From generation to generation a wealth of superstitions, traditions, legends, popular beliefs, and old wife's tales have been handed down through the Wabanaki, Euro American, New England and Maritime cultures.

One never knows what event or rumor on the tongues of the locals will become permanent folklore around these parts of the Passamaquoddy Bay.

Why, just a short time ago, there was some buzz around the bay about a certain Captain! One account goin' 'round is said to be wicked funny! As the story goes …

* * *

It was one of those prize days of July, warm, clear and full of promise. The *Guillemot* was said to have been seen sailing through L'Etete passage, possibly headed St. Andrews way.

From here, there seems to be some recorded documentation of events, the journal of the Mrs of the Captain. The Captain has been known to scoff with indignation at her reality of the facts, but nonetheless, this is her testimonial.

* * *

The Captain had two first mates aboard for this voyage—his ole' galley slave and swabbie, Eileen, along with his shanghaied son DB.

My Captain made a suggestion (miracles do happen—he has learned to "suggest" not "order" whenever possible so as to prevent a possible mutiny!) "Wouldn't a one-night-stopover on McMasters Island, be fun?"

"Yes, Captain!" the crew obediently agreed, standing feet apart, hands clasped behind our backs.

Gripped with animation, eyes glowing with vision, the Captain offered his plan to his crew; we would pull up on the beach, let the water recede from under the boat, set the legs and enjoy an evening of beach tromping for rocks and sand dollars. Sinbad's son caught the excitement in his father's voice and, eyes alight with tales of old, added, "and buried treasures!"

Myself, an experienced mate/wife, found my thoughts sinking into that deep sticky mud of "old." I judged that anchoring the boat and rowing ashore in the dinghy might be preferable to the dance with the legs. Memories of the Minas Basin and a couple'a dozen nights on the legs didn't sound nearly as intriguing as the Captain portrayed it.

We all know that the Captain of the ship on the high seas, whatever tactics he uses, gets his way. So, not long after the legs were seecured, the drover and his lamblike crew sat at the *Guillemot's* small wooden table, gathering energy for our time ashore. The sounds of the waves hitting the beach echoed in the cabin. Unbeknownst to us, with each lap, more sand rolled out from under the Guillemot's belly. As we ate our snack, we heard unusual groans coming from the deck.

I remember the exact moment when the realization of what was taking place flashed across the Captain's face. Simultaneously, the crew heard a loud POP! followed by a substantial jerk. The two mates sat like ruminants—chewing, silent and wide-eyed. The Captain raced out to the deck just in time to catch the last movement of the sand breaking the ropes tied to the halyards. He called to the crew in a very captain-like voice, "Hold on Maties! We're goin' down with the ship!" I believe that, never in mortal memory, has a ship lain down on her side with such dignity.

The appearance of resigned humor fell from the Captain's face when he looked up to see that we were in full view of the ferry. "Damn! I hope they don't think we need to be rescued and call the Coast Guard."

Common talk, 'bout town, was that the *Guillemot* and its crew were the topic of the day aboard the Canadian St. George/Deer Island ferry. The scuttlebutt plays the scene like this:

The ferrymen, through their binoculars, watched the crew climbing on and off the stern.

"Yepp, (said in a near whisper and on intake of breath) they'll float sometime late tonight! (deep chuckles) Those crazy yachters EH!(pronounced long A) Don't realize there are tides out here EH!!" There was a great deal of head-shaking and tons of laughter while they went humdrumming along through the Letete Passage.

"A lot of those poor son-a-guns ain't even got a chart!"

"EH, they might'in but they can't read it, don't ya know!"

McMasters Island
I believe that, never in mortal memory, has a ship lain
down on her side with such dignity.

A few slaps on the back and more quick peeks through the binoculars, they continued their merriment.

"In *spite* of it (ho, ho) or 'cause of it, they seem to be havin' a
jolly good time! Doesn't that beat all. One of 'em takin' pictures.
Probably Americans. They don' know they'll be sleepin' an maybe
cookin' an' such with 'er layin' ov'r!"

Yes, according to local folklore, for the entertainment value alone,
it was the source of much local gossip!

I will end this memoir with one last reflection.

I remember that Kodachrome moment there on McMasters Island when I felt a surge of aliveness! In that moment, however, I
was not the woman who strives daily toward spiritual realization. I
was not the woman who, at one time, had a long-standing membership in the "Nice Girl Club"! I was a woman who received an unexpectedly intense pleasure in delaying revenge!

> Fairwinds,
> Eileen Beaver

The Guillemot *at rest on its legs.*

Detail of the Guillemot *leg.*

The *Guillemot*

The post-World War II period was a time of rapid development in sailboat design. Most boats were still being built of wood, but new glues, quality plywood, and laminating technologies perfected during the war enabled builders to create boats that were significantly lighter than their predecessors, while still retaining sufficient strength. The new boatbuilding methods also proved to be less reliant upon highly skilled labor, which helped to hold the prices down.

The 1950's saw an upward trend in the wealth of average people, and when families had reached the point where they had acquired a home and a car and some leisure time they were looking for ways to have fun.

In Maine, boat builder Farnham Butler and designer Cyrus Hamlin teamed up to produce a line of boats aimed squarely at this market. The new wealth of the middle class was real, but it was limited, and by necessity buyers were looking for the best cost-to-benefit ratio in a cruising sailboat.

Until Butler and Hamlin, post-war advances in sailboat design were primarily aimed at the racing fleet, where lighter-weight boats were sometimes faster and often cheaper, and were sometimes successful in beating the handicapping rules of the day. Butler and Hamlin were among the first to perceive the advantages the new technology offered to family cruising boats.

Hamlin was primarily a yacht designer, and had developed a practical new method of building boats using glued strip planking over bulkheads. He was open to new ideas in boat design and had a lot of personal experience in cruising.

Butler was mostly a boatbuilder and yachtsman, and had a gift for promotion. He was excited about the new technologies and had a clear vision of new possibilities.

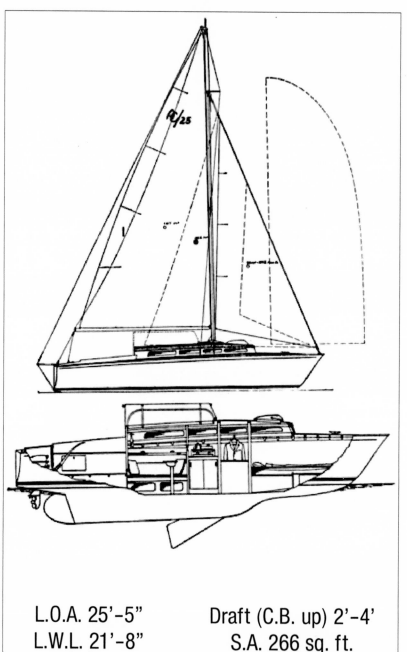

L.O.A. 25'-5"   Draft (C.B. up) 2'-4'
L.W.L. 21'-8"   S.A. 266 sq. ft.
Beam 7'-9'   Disp. 3900 lbs.

The boats they produced were revolutionary, not evolutionary. The construction was completely non-traditional, strong, easy to repair and maintain, and economical. To create more space in the hulls, which were shallower than their heavier predecessors, they adopted reverse sheer, meaning that the curve from bow to stern was convex—higher in the middle than at the ends. Most of the designs feature a large opening in the top of the cabin, covered by canvas on hoops, to provide headroom, light, and ventilation. They so little resembled what had gone before that a lot of people hated them on sight and argued every difference. Farnham rather enjoyed the flap, and with good humor he and Cy named the whole line of boats "Controversys".

Guillemot is an 1956 Amphibi-Con, short for Amphibious Controversy. While earlier Controversy's were of deep draft, the Amphibi-Con was shallow, and specifically designed to be trailerable, hence the amphibious part. At the time it was unusual to trailer such a large and capable cruising boat, but it was among the features that made the Amphibi-Con a hit. Owners could haul and launch the boat and stand the mast up and down themselves, and the boat could be stored at their home, freeing them from boat yard bills and making it convenient to do their own maintenance. It also made it possible to trailer the boat to far-off cruising grounds a working family would never have time to sail to—the "expeditionary" quality that appealed so much to Doug Beaver.

The Amphibi-Con was designed with an outboard auxiliary installed in a well just aft of the cockpit, thus combining the light weight and economy of the outboard with some of the convenience of an inboard engine. Because of the shape of their hulls and their light weight, most of the Controversy line is relatively fast under power, and *Guillemot* is no exception. Doug hardly uses his engine at all any more, but for many owners the Amphibi-Con's sterling performance under power is a major virtue.

An Amphibi-Con will float in only 2'8" of water, and while this shallow draft makes trailering practical it is primarily its impact on cruising that makes it the single feature most former Amphibi-Con owners miss the most. Shoal draft cruising is quite a different thing from deep draft cruising. A shoal draft boat can find shelter in

Sailing, sailing, all me life is sailing . . .

harbours a deep draft boat cannot enter. She can navigate in water shallow enough for her crew to jump out and push, and can get close enough to shore for one to wade ashore. She gains access to large areas of water that are simply inaccessible to deeper boats. Few have exploited this aspect of the design as thoroughly as Doug and Eileen, for it made the whole Minas Basin cruise possible, and many are the shallow, narrow places in Fundy and Passamaquoddy Bay where *Guillemot* is the only sailboat to have made her way in recent memory.

An Amphibi-Con has a remarkable amount of room in it, comparable to that of much larger, heavier, less economical boats. Like the other members of the Controversy line she was designed very much around the dimensions of the human body and the way one must move around in a boat, so the space utilization is both comfortable and efficient. Amphibi-Cons were originally designed with a canvas top over the main cabin and galley, providing standing headroom, light, and ventilation. In *Guillemot*, as in many others, this top has been replaced by a solid pop-top that can stand on legs, with a canvas panel that can complete the enclosure. One of the features that non-owners most object to, this canvas hood or pop top is universally beloved by owners.

Owning an Amphibi-Con is like having a friend who is reliable, easy to get along with, can do a lot of things well, and is nearly devoid of obnoxious habits.One's affection for it grows over time while other boats come to seem worse and worse by comparison.

Doug added one important feature to *Guillemot* that was a virtual necessity for the Minas Basin cruise, namely her legs. Common in Britain and nearly unheard of in this country, legs are just a pair of supports that enable the boat to stand upright when the water goes away. The weight of the boat is taken by the boat's keel, resting on the beach or harbour bottom, so the legs just hold the boat upright. They need not be very large or heavy. Shoal draft makes this a safe and practical arrangement, within limits, and as you will read in this book, cruising with legs is a unique and practical experience.

I am fortunate to have owned an Amphibi-Con in the past, named *Yes*, and I loved her. By my current reckoning, even better is the Amphibi-ette I currently own with my partner Greg Pugh, which is named *Spar Hawk*. Basically a smaller version of the Amphibi-Con, introduced somewhat later, she is in some ways a refinement of the concept. Thus in some ways her virtues are proof of the validity of the "Controversial" ideas brought out in *Guillemot* and her many sisters.

In quite a few years of involvement I've never known a boat to be as universally beloved and as passionately defended by owners past and present, as the Amphibi-Con. Along with Doug and Eileen Beaver, *Guillemot* is a cornerstone of this voyage and its story, for there are few, if any, boats out there as well suited to the requirements of this cruise, and many in which it would have been impossible.

There were about 250 Amphibi-Cons built—a remarkable number for a pre-fiberglass design. Far fewer Amphibi-ettes were built, primarily because the advent of fiberglass effectively ended main stream wooden boat building during her time. However, boats of both types do come up for sale, so anyone who decides they have to have one might be able to find one. Check out www.amphibicon.com for boats which may have become available. There are many boatbuilders who could easily build either boat new, and there is ample justification for doing just that. Plans are available. Unfortunately the cost of building boats has risen faster than the income of the middle class, so a new Amphibi-Con or Amphibi-ette is now out of the question for many of those they were intended to serve. A dedicated amateur could build either boat for a reasonable figure, and it might be that new computer-driven material-cutting technology can take enough of the labor out of building such boats to make a project like this less costly and time consuming.

However you went about it, you could do a lot worse with time and money.

—Daniel MacNaughton

Glossary of Sailing Vernacular
While Sailing The Big Flush

This special edition (lucky for all of you) includes valued tips and notes by a most respected decorator/able-bodied crew member of the *Guillemot*/author of ... (Drum roll, please!)
Sailing The Big Flush!
Before we go any further, so we are all on the same page, I'm going to try and explain, what I mean when ... and just what is a ...

Aboard—on the boat.

Adrift—a boat drifting without control.

Aft—at or toward the stern or behind the boat.

Aground—a boat whose keel is touching the bottom.

Anchor—a heavy object, usually a shaped iron weight with flukes, lowered by cable or chain to the bottom of water to keep a boat from drifting. (*Decorator's tip*: The anchor on the *Guillemot* is rather formidable looking and it adds a subtle use of geometry to her decor.)

Athwartships—across the boat from side to side. (*Crew's note:* I know I'm just in training ... but really, I can't say it without sounding like I have a lisp.)

Backstay—the standing rigging running from the stern to the top of the mast, keeping the mast from falling forward.

Ballast—weight in the keel of a boat that provides stability. (*Crew's note:* I came to think of myself as professional ballast. I didn't really mind, it gave me purpose. Purposefulness ranks high in my book.)

Batten down the hatches or battening down the hatches—to prepare for trouble, a storm, or in our case a tidal bore.

Beam—the width of a boat at its widest point.

Beam reach—(point of sail) sailing in a direction at approximately 90 degrees to the wind.

449

Bearing—the direction from one object to another, expressed in compass degrees.

Beating—a course sailed upwind.

Below—the area of a boat beneath the deck.

Bilge—the lowest part of the boat's interior, where water on board will collect. (*Decorator's Entertaining Tip*: Always have thirst quenchers in your bilge for unexpected climb-aboard company.)

Bitter end—the end of line.

Block—a pulley on a boat.

Bluenoser—a nick-name for Nova Scotians. *Bluenose* was a Canadian schooner from Nova Scotia, a celebrated racing ship and hard-working fishing vessel, launched in 1921. It became a symbol of the province. In January 1946 it collided with a reef off the coast of Haiti and sank.

Boat hook—a pole with a hook on the end used for grabbing hold of a mooring or retrieving something that has fallen overboard.

Boom—the spar extending directly aft from the mast to which the foot of the mainsail is attached.

Boom vang—a block and tackle system which pulls the boom down to assist sail control. (*Crew's note:* Boom vang? I mean really, you're saying to yourself, who's heard of it? (*Decorator's tip:* In some elite coastal social circles, this is a commonly-used term. It's a definite "add to" your nautical vocab. list for clever cocktail conversation.)

Bottom—1. The underside of the boat; 2. The land under the water.

Bow—the forward part of the boat.

Bow line—(BOW-line) a line running from the bow of the boat to the dock or mooring.

Bowline—(BOE-linn) a knot designed to make a loop that will not slip and can be easily untied. (*Crew's note:* learning to tie, use and pronounce all these knots may cause your head to throb and a burning sensation around the temples.)

Bow and stem lines—lines which keep the boat close to the dock, but do not prevent it from surging forward or backward in the wind or waves.

Broach—a sudden instability in the heading of a sailboat when sailing downwind.

Bright work—the varnished wooden areas of the boat. (*Decorator's tip*: Wood suggests strength and stability.) (*Crew's note:* Bright work commands, not suggests, sanding and varnishing twice a season!)

Buoy—a floating navigation marker.

Cabin—the interior of the boat. (*Decorator's tip*: The *Guillemot's* look is that of "shabby chic-authentic nautical." The open floor plan lends itself to a feel of more spaciousness.) (*Crew's note:* This open floor plan can cause "PDS"—Privacy Deprivation Syndrome—and, just like me, this cabin is need of a facelift.)

Can—an odd-numbered, green buoy marking the left side of a channel as you return to port.

Capsize—to tip or turn a boat over. (*Crew's note*: I don't like the sound of this much.)

Captain—1. the commander or master of a ship; 2. the leader of a team or crew. (*Crew's note:* The commander is Captain Doug; his crew—that would be me.)

Centerboard—a pivoting board that can be lowered and used like a keel to keep a boat from slipping to leeward.

Channel—a (usually narrow) path in the water, marked by buoys, in which the water is deep enough to sail.

Chart—a nautical map. A chart shows not only the channels and the buoys, but also the shorelines, the water depth, obstructions, shoals, the positions of wrecks, and characteristics of the bottom. In addition, it indicates the positions of landmarks, lighthouses and much more. (*Decorator's tip*: Accessorize, accessorize! Charts carry the nautical theme throughout!) (*Crew's note:* All this valuable info wasn't necessarily available or applicable for the Minas Basin. She, the crew, and the skipper cursed rather effectively and imaginatively.)

Chop—rough, short, steep waves. (*Decorator's tip*: Interior patterns, in general, should be keep at a minimum to avoid busyness—on a boat, however, it is to avoid dizziness.)

Cleat—a nautical fitting that is used to secure a line; making the line safe and secure. (*Author's note:* in the "Flush" the word cleat is used more often as a verb than a noun. It became a well-used *action* term).

Clew—the lower, aft corner of a sail. The clew of the mainsail is held taut by the outhaul. The jib sheets are attached to the clew of the jib. (*Crew's note:* Having not a clue that this was called a clew until half-way through the journey, seemed to matter not.)

Close-hauled—the point of sail that is closest to the wind.

Coaming—a raised border around the cockpit, which is the lower area in which the steering controls and sail controls are located; helps keep out water. (*Crew's note:* Which provides much needed back support if you're on the boat for long durations.)

Cockpit—the lower area in which the steering controls and sail controls are located. (*Decorator's tip:* Give your meals instant panache! Serve in the cockpit, for elegance *alfresco*.)

Coil—to loop a line neatly so it can be stored.

Companionway—the steps leading from the cockpit or deck to the cabin below.

Compass—the magnetic instrument which indicates the direction in which the boat is headed. (*Decorator's tip:* Every chance we had to inject the "Marine Motif" we took! A compass adds that circular motion needed for flow in every good design. It gives direction, shows knowledge, and achievement.)

Course—the direction in which the boat is steered.

Crew—besides the skipper, anyone on board who helps sail the boat. (*Crew's note:* Loosely speaking that's me).

Current—the horizontal movement of water caused by tides (going out is ebbing and coming in is flooding), wind and other forces. Depending on their direction, these currents can either assist or hinder your progress.

Cunningham—a line running through a grommet about eight inches up from the tack of a mainsail that is used to tighten the luff of the sail. (*Crew's note:* I confess with shame in my heart—I've never heard of this term and would never use it.)

Dead downwind—sailing in a direction straight downwind.

Deck—the mostly flat surface area on top of the boat. (*Decorator's tip*: Seattle Gray by Interlux, a very pale gray, was chosen to cut the glare of the sun. This gives you a warmer feel and instantly says "Welcome Aboard!") (*Crew's note:* Seattle Gray does not blend well with Minas Basin mud!)

Depth sounder—an electronic piece of equipment which registers the depth of the water beneath the boat. (*Crew's note:* And maybe, if you're lucky, you'll have this information in time to react to keep from going aground when you're not ready.)

Dinghy—a small sailboat or rowboat.

Displacement—the weight of a boat; therefore the amount of water it displaces.

Dock—1) the wooden structure where a boat may be tied up; 2) the act of bringing the boat to rest alongside the structure.

Dockline—a line used to secure the boat to the dock.

Down East—is a New England geographical term that is applied in several different ways. In the narrowest sense. "Down East" refers to the coast of the U.S. state of Maine from Penobscot Bay to the Canadian border. At times it is jokingly referred to as any point along the coast, east of the speaker. The origin of the term came from a time when ships sailed from Boston to ports in Maine (which were to the east of Boston), the wind was at their backs, so they were sailing downwind, hence the term "Down East." And it follows that, when they returned to Boston, they were sailing upwind. Many Mainers still speak of going "up to Boston" despite the fact that the city lies approximately 50 miles to the south of Maine's southern border.

Downwind—away from the direction of the wind. (*Crew's Note:* The most beautiful words in the sailing glossary.)

Draft—the depth of a boat's keel from the water's surface. (*Crew's note:* The *Guillemot* is shallow draft and, now that I'm a advanced beginner sailor who's been in my share of shallow water, I can say unequivocally that = Good!)

Ebb—an outgoing tide.

Eddy—a current of water moving against the main current and with a circular motion; a little whirlpool.

Fairwinds—winds blowing at a speed and direction which is pleasing.

Fake—to lay out a line on deck using large loops to keep it from becoming tangled. (*Crew's note:* I would like these words carved in my tombstone "She Faked Fast.")

Fast—secured.

Fender—a rubber bumper used to protect a boat by keeping it from hitting a dock. (*Decorator's tip*: Nothing says drama like large, rubber, phallic-looking objects hanging over the side.)

Fend off—push off.

Fitting—a piece of nautical hardware.

Flood—an incoming tide.

Fore—forward.

Forepeak—a storage area in the bow, below the deck. (*Decorator's tip*: charming idea—some may even think romantic—to have rope and chain "Nautical Bling" coiled right at the foot of your bed. The mud and seaweed left behind from the anchor's rope and chain gives the bedroom an earthy feel.)

Foresail—a jib or a genoa.

Forestay—the standing rigging running from the bow to the mast to which the jib is hanked on.

Forward—toward the bow (the pointy part).

Foul-weather gear—water-resistant clothing. (*Crew's note:* Imagine sailing along, trying to get to a safe place to anchor, "Foul weather" kicks in, i.e. heavy winds, downpour, choppy seas = Bad! You have "foul-weather-gear" = Good! Your professional/conveniently-designed "foul-weather-gear" are bib overalls with no zipper and your Captain has to pee = Bad!)

Full—not luffing.

Furl—to fold or roll up a sail.

Galley—a boat's kitchen. (*Decorator's tip:* The *Guillemot's* kitchen, by the standards to which I had grown accustomed, is not exactly my dream come true. It is, however, nothing short of a miracle what one can do when one is forced into a small, well-designed space.)

Gear—generic term for sailing equipment.

Genoa—or jenny, is a large jib whose clew extends aft of the mast. The large surface area increases the speed of the craft in moderate winds.

Go on the hard (or hit hard)—when the boat hits the ground.

Grommet—a reinforcing metal ring set in a sail.

Guillemot—beside being the name of our 1956 wooden sailboat, it is the common name for several species of seabird in the auk family. The word, of French origin, apparently derives from a form of the name William (Guillaume). The *Guillemot's* name board on the stern has a pigeon guillemot painted on it—black with white spots on the wings and bright red feet. We pronounce it Gil-a-mot.

Gunwale (Gunn-nle)—the edge of the deck where it meets the topsides. (*Author's note:* Some of these terms require a very strong accent, of undetermined origin, to pronounce correctly.)

Gust—a sudden, strong rush of wind.

Halyard—a line used to hoist or lower a sail.

Harbour (or haven)—man-made or natural inlet, a branch of the sea. It is used as a shelter or anchorage for protection from weather and currents. The British spelling of harbour is harbour. All the Canadian harbours are spelled harbours.

Hatch—a large covered opening in the deck.

Haul Anchor—the act of pulling up the anchor.

Head down—to fall off, changing course away from the wind.

Head up—to come up, changing course toward the wind.

Headway—progress made forward.

Heave—to throw.

Heavy weather—strong winds and large waves. (*Crew's note:* Didn't nurture or contribute to my sense of well-being.)

Heel—the lean of a boat caused by the wind.

Heeling over—to lean or tilt to one side.

Helm—the tiller. (*Author's note:* AKA "The Command Center.")

Helmsman—the person responsible for steering the boat.

High side—the windward side of the boat.

High tide—1.) the highest level to which the tide rises (flooding tide);

high water; 2.) the time when the tide is at this level. Typically there are two high and two low tides each day on the east and west coast of the U.S.

Hike—to position crew members out over the windward rail to help balance the boat. (*Crew's note:* I always ask first, *What are my other options?*)

Hiking stick—tiller extension.

Holding ground—the bottom ground in an anchorage used to hold the anchor. (*Crew's note:* Yes, yes, very important information to know! But to make life for the anchor woman even more exciting, this holding ground could be a rock, a log, or ten feet of mud and sand! Seldom, do you ever know.)

Horn cleat—the type we have on the *Guillemot* and the most common on boats and docks.

Hull—the body of the boat, excluding rig and sails.

Hull speed—the theoretical maximum speed of a sailboat determined by the length of its waterline.

In irons—a boat that is head-to-wind, making no forward headway.

Jib—the small forward sail of a boat attached to the forestay.

Jibe—to change direction of a boat by steering the stern through the wind.

"Jibe-ho"—the command given to the crew when starting to jibe.

Jiffy reef—a quick reefing system allowing a section of the mainsail to be tied to the boom.

Keel—the heavy vertical fin beneath a boat that helps keep it upright and prevents it from slipping sideways in the water. (*Crew's note:* The *Guillemot* is a keel-centerboard design. Yes, it has a tendency at times to get in the way. Those *in the know* say that keeping the boat upright and preventing it from slipping sideways makes a very persuasive case for having a keel.)

Knot—one nautical mile per hour.

Land breeze—a wind that blows over land and out to sea.

Lazarette—a storage compartment built into the cockpit or deck. (*Decorator's tip*: It is so very vogue to have a lazarette here and there. The perfect place to store those little necessities and personal items one needs to make your cruise comfy.) (*Crew's note*: Great place to store ropes, fenders and the Captain's old horse bucket which we still use to wash down the decks.)

Leeward—(LEW-erd)—the direction away from the wind (where the wind is blowing to).

Legs—poles used to keep the *Guillemot* standing upright when the water went to wherever it goes every 6 hours and 13 minutes. (*Crew's note*: It is as if she were a 4, 000-pound woman, precariously balanced on one pointy high heel.) (*Author's note*: Personally, it was the first time I've ever been supported by long thin legs.)

Lifeline—plastic coated wire, supported by stanchions, around the outside of the deck to help prevent crew members from falling overboard. (*Crew note*: Believe it or not, some boats don't have these!) (*Decorator's tip*: Speaking from experience, lifelines and very strong sturdy stanchions should be on a girl's "*must have list*.")

Line—a nautical rope.

List—to tilt to one side, as a boat. (*Crew's note*: Not to be confused with "make a list, " which is what the crew likes to do.)

Low side—the leeward side of the boat.

Low tide—1) the lowest level reached by the ebbing tide; 2) the time when the tide is at this level. Typically there are two high and two low tides each day on the east and west coasts of the U.S.

Luff—1) the forward edge of a sail; 2) the fluttering of a sail caused by aiming too close to the wind.

Lull—a decrease in wind speed for a short duration.

Mainmast—the taller of two masts on a boat.

Mainsail—(MAIN-sil) —the sail hoisted on the mast of a sloop or cutter or the sail hoisted on the mainmast of a ketch or yawl.

Mainsheet —the controlling line for the mainsail.

Marine radio—a VHF radio used for a wide variety of purposes, including rescue services and weather broadcasts.

Mast—the large aluminum or wooden pole in the middle of a boat from which the mainsail is set.

Mooring—a permanently anchored ball or buoy to which a boat can be tied.

Nautical mile—or a sea mile is a unit of length equaling one minute of the earth's latitude. A distance of 6, 076 feet or 1.1508 mile. For all you folk in the rest of the world—1, 852 meters, or 1.8520 km.

Nun—a red, even-numbered buoy, marking the right side of a channel as you return to port. Nuns are usually paired with cans.

Offshore wind—wind blowing off (away from) the land. (*Crew's note:* Usually warmer! Yes! Yes! Yes!)

Off the wind—sailing downwind.

On the wind—sailing upwind, close-hauled.

Overpowered—a boat that is heeling too far because it has too much sail up for the amount of wind. (*Crew's note:* This is when my face becomes nuanced and expressive. The Captain, to spare himself the outcry of mutiny, uses our jiffy reefs and saves the day!)

Painter—the line attached to the bow of a dinghy.

PFD—abbreviation for Personal Flotation Device; a lifejacket. (*Decorator's tip*: Think versatile, versatile, versatile, with your accessories! On a boat, the PDF can be used as a pillow, stacked and used as a back cushion while in the quarter-birth, or even save your life! Lifesaver orange is not my fav, on the color chart—my palette prefers raucous or Osage orange, but one learns to compromise.)

Pop-top—cabin top can be raised to provide headroom, ventilation and 360 degree views. Often compared with the Volkswagen camper bus with its pop up roof. (*Decorator's tip*: Now for the showstopper! This pop-top is the *pièce de résistance!* It provides you a breezy, soothing, meditative way to stay in touch with nature. No need for botanical prints here—mission accomplished with a view of a constantly changing array of artwork.)

Port—1) the left side of a boat when facing forward; 2) a harbour; 3) a window in a cabin on a boat.

Port tack—sailing on any point of sail with the wind coming over the port side of the boat.

Prevailing wind—typical or consistent wind conditions.

Puff—an increase in wind speed.

Pull anchor—to release it from the holding ground and haul it up on the deck to a stable position on the bow pulpit so it will not fall back in the water.

Pulpit—a stainless steel or bronze guardrail at the bow and stern of some boats. (*Crew's note:* The *Guillemot's* bronze bow pulpit and I came to have a very intimate relationship by the time this journey came to its end.) (*Decorator's tip*: Don't be afraid to copy! Every boat's decor should include some bronze. There can never be too much bold and beautiful bronze in this world.)

Purchase—1) to move or raise by applying mechanical power; 2) to get a fast hold on so as to do this; 3) any apparatus with which such a hold is applied. (*Crew's note:* The level of my purchase power was brought to platinum on this journey!)

Pushpit—a stainless steel or bronze guardrail at the stern of some boats.

Push-pull principle—the explanation of how sails generate power.

Put the boat to bed—a list of necessary tasks to close the boat.

Quarter—the sides of the boat near the stern.

Quarter birth—a cushioned area where one can sit or recline. When you lie down, your feet extend into the storage area under the seat of the cockpit. (*Decorator's tip:* I re-covered the cushions in the quarter births in an inviting nautical blue canvas. The symmetry of having one on each side of the cabin strengthens the eye. To add comfort and texture to a quarter birth, I give you two words: Fleece Throws! I just fell in love with them! They came in this wondrous leisure blue. It will be our little secret, two for a denari at … Marden's. Fabulous isn't it?)

Rail—the outer edges of the deck.

Range—the alignment of two objects that indicate the middle of a channel.

"Ready about"—the command given to the crew to prepare to tack. (*Crew's note:* Captain Doug just says "tack" or "we're gonna do the tacky thing.")

"Ready to jibe"—the command given the crew to prepare to jibe. (*Crew's note:* Captain Doug, just yells "Jibe!" Usually there is no time for commands or "ready to, ")

459

Reef—to reduce the area of a sail, which can improve the ship's stability and reduce the risk of capsizing, broaching or damaging sails or boat hardware in strong wind. (*Author's note:* The *Guillemot's* main has two jiffy reef points—one for when it's blowing hard and one for when it blows like hell.) (*Crew's note:* This = Good!) (*Author's note again:* I always thought a reef was a great place to snorkel.)

Rig—1.) the design of a boat's mast(s), standing rigging and sail plan; 2.) to prepare a boat to go sailing. (*Crew's note:* the *Guillemot* is a Marconi rigged sloop, the most common modern rig. It is excellent for sailing upwind, to which all I can say is, "Thank goodness for small favors" (whoever goodness is) because me and upwind don't always get along.)

Rigging—the wires and lines used to support and control sails.

Ripples—small waves or undulations, as on the surface of the water, caused by wind blowing over it. Surges of stronger wind stir the water's surface creating a patch that appears slightly darker.

Rode—line and chain attached from the boat to the anchor.

Roller furling—a mechanical system to roll up a headsail (jib) around the headstay.

Rudder—the underwater fin that is controlled by the tiller to deflect water and steer the boat.

Running lights—the lights that a boat traveling at night is required to to display.

Sail cover—the protective cover used to preserve sails when they are not in use.

Sail ties—pieces of line or webbing used to tie the mainsail to the boom when reefing or storing the sail.

Schooner—a two-masted boat whose foremast is shorter than its mainmast.

Scope—the ratio of the amount of anchor rode deployed to the distance from the bow to the bottom.

Scupper—cockpit or deck drain.

Sea breeze—a wind that blows over the sea and onto the land.

Secure—make safe or cleat.

Shackle—a metal fitting at the end of a line used to attach the line to a sail or another fitting.

Sheet—the line which is used to control the sail by easing it out or trimming it in. (*Decorator's tip*: This is not the 1000 count sheet that we are all use to—let me clarify. This is a *rope*. The pure white cotton blend, to contrast with the cerulean sea, is my pick.)

Shoal—shallow water that may be dangerous.

Shroud—standing rigging at the side of the mast.

Singlehanded—sailing alone.

Skipper—the person in charge of the boat.

Sloop—a single-masted sailboat with mainsail and headsail.

Snub—to hold a line under tension by wrapping it on a winch or cleat. (*Crew's Note*: so this is what it was called. I count myself lucky, at this age, to be learning something new!)

Sole—the floor in a cockpit or cabin.

Spar—a pole to used attach a sail on a boat, for example, the mast, the boom, a gaff.

Spring line—a dockline running forward or aft from the boat to the dock to keep the boat from moving forward or aft.

Spotter—designated crew member to spot and point at a person in the water. The spotter should never take his or her eyes off the victim.

Starboard—when looking from the stern toward the bow, the right side of the boat.

Starboard tack—sailing on any point of sail with the wind coming over the starboard side of the boat.

Stay—a wire support for a mast, part of the standing rigging.

Stem—the forward tip of the bow.

Stern—the aft part of the boat. (*Author's note:* this is spelled s-t-e-r-n for some unnameable reason. When I type it on my computer it looks the same as stem.)

Stow—to store properly. (*Decorator's tip:* You might call this s lifestyle, *Stow and Go Living.*)

Swamped—filled with water. (*Crew's note:* Unless my memory is giving way, this = *Bad.*)

Tack—1.) a course on which the wind comes over one side of the boat, i.e., port tack, starboard tack; 2.) to change direction by turning the bow through the wind; 3.) the lower forward corner of a sail. (*Crew's note:* Would it be so hard to think of a new name for the lower part of the sail? "Tack" seems to be already taken.)

Tackle—a sequence of blocks and line that provides a mechanical advantage.

Telltales—pieces of yarn or sailcloth material attached to sails which indicate when the sail is properly trimmed. (*Decorator's tip:* I love, love, love these! Nice touch and an eye-catching focal point!)

Tidal Bore—a tidal bore exists when an incoming mass of water flows into a narrowing channel such as a bay, estuary or river. This funneling process causes the water to flow much quicker than it would were it allowed to spread. The water at the front of the tide tends to slow down because of the narrowing, but the water behind it rushes up at normal speed, so the water increases in height and velocity, resulting in a wall of water which surges up the channel causing rapids with waves from three to sixteen feet. (*Crew's note:* Wouldn't you know, I get myself knee-deep in a problem, which has no USG [Universal support group].)

Tide—the rise and fall of water level due to the gravitational pull of the sun and moon.

Tiller—a long handle, extending into the cockpit, which directly controls the rudder.

Tiller extension—a handle attached to the tiller which allows the helmsman to sit further out to the side.

Toe rail—a short aluminum or wooden rail around the outer edges of the deck. (*Crew's note:* The *Guillemot's* rail is wooden and served many times to keep the first mate from being in the drink)

Toppinglift—a line used to hold the boom up when the mainsail is lowered or stowed.

Topsides—the sides of the boat between the waterline and the deck. (*Decorator's tip:* The whale stripe is painted white and the boot top is painted black which nicely compliments the hull which is painted Petit French gray—serious, while at the same time, colorful.)

Transom—the vertical surface of the stern.

Trim—1.) to pull in on a sheet; 2.) how to sail is set relative to the wind.

Turnbuckle—a mechanical fitting attached to the lower ends of stays, allowing for the standing rigging to be adjusted.

Underway—to be moving under sail or engine.

Unrig—to stow sails and rigging when the boat is not in use.

Upwind—toward the direction of the wind.

VHF radio—very high frequency.

V-berth—a bed at the pointy end of the boat. Your head and shoulders are positioned toward the stern and your feet toward the bow. (*Decorator's note*: Every room should start with an objective. The V-berth is a dreamy touch of grandeur on this small sailing vessel. The nautical blue placed forward in this large space takes on a misty-floaty look. It really brings the boat together. Talk about the classic waterbed!) (*Crew's note:* It is staggering to note the quantity of stuff, gear, necessities—whatever you want to call it—that you can stow in one area and still have room for the crew and her Captain to sleep.)

Vang—see boom vang.

Veer—a slight change of direction, either of the boat or of the wind.

Vessel—any sailboat, powerboat or ship.

Wake—waves caused by a boat moving through the water.

Waterline—the horizontal line on the hull of a boat where the water surface should be.

Winch—a deck-mounted drum with a handle offering mechanical advantage when use to trim sheets. Winches may also be mounted on the mast to assist in raising sails. (*Author's note:* Not to be confused with a wench—a somewhat derogatory or jocular term for a female servant or loose woman.)

Wind against tide—when the wind is blowing against the current (tide), rough water results. The stronger the wind and current the rougher the water.

Windward—toward the wind.

Windward side—the side of a boat or a sail closest to the wind.

Wing-and-wing—sailing downwind with the jib set on the opposite side of the mainsail.

Working sails—the mainsail and standard jib.

Author's note: In one of those moments of extreme clarity, I made the decision not to include in my list all the sailing terms in the sailing vernacular—it would have become encyclopedic! Enough is enough—my splintered personality has to move on with my new life.

These days …

She, the crew, when not sailing and celebrating the beauty of nature, can be found continuing her search for wholeness in her spa/tub, bridging her old and new life by painting her toenails a bright Tunisian coral.

She, the decorator, can be found in decorating rehab.

She, the author, when not sitting with her lap-top open and working on her next book, *Living on Liquid,* exercising (not to get any better, but to keep from falling apart), gardening, or cooking, can be found gazing into her Captain's eyes (when they're not closed in silent exasperation at the length of my latest list).

Music Soundtrack and Audio Book
available from
www.sailingthebigflush.com

Printed in the United States
145157LV00005B/1/P